MW00559946

Integral Psychotherapy

SUNY series in Integral Theory

Sean Esbjörn-Hargens, editor

Integral Psychotherapy

Inside Out/Outside In

R. Elliott Ingersoll
— and —
David M. Zeitler

Published by
State University of New York Press, Albany

© 2010 State University of New York

All rights reserved

Printed in the United States of America

No part of this book may be used or reproduced in any manner whatsoever
without written permission. No part of this book may be stored in a retrieval system
or transmitted in any form or by any means including electronic, electrostatic, magnetic
tape, mechanical, photocopying, recording, or otherwise without the prior permission
in writing of the publisher.

For information, contact State University of New York Press, Albany, NY
www.sunypress.edu

Production by Ryan Morris
Marketing by Anne M. Valentine

Library of Congress Cataloging-in-Publication Data

Ingersoll, R. Elliott, 1962–
    Integral psychotherapy : inside out/outside in / R. Elliott Ingersoll and David M.
Zeitler.
        p. ; cm. — (SUNY series in integral theory)
    Includes bibliographical references and index.
    ISBN 978-1-4384-3351-6 (hardcover : alk. paper)
    ISBN 978-1-4384-3352-3 (pbk. : alk. paper)
    1. Eclectic psychotherapy.   I. Zeitler, David M., 1973–   II. Title.   III. Series:
SUNY series in integral theory.

    [DNLM: 1. Psychotherapy—methods. 2. Spirituality. WM 420 I47i 2010]
    RC489.E24.I525 2010
    616.89'14—dc22   2009052827

10 9 8 7 6 5 4 3 2 1

To five wise women who have been central to my own Integral Life Practice. First and foremost my wife Jenn for her love, patience, and support. She takes on the world so I can retreat from it to write and always welcomes me back when the books are done. Next to Susan Wilcox and Dr. Jaclyn Miller, two healers who walked me through my own shadow so many times. Also to Lisa Shiu—my awesome trainer who worked me so hard in the gym that sitting at the computer for 8 hours seemed like a good idea. Finally to Heidi Longauer who helped me hear the music again and sing my own tune (even when nobody else sang along).

—EI

For Rich, David, Bert, and Keith, for all the learning and the laughter . . . especially the laughter.

—DZ

Contents

List of Illustrations

Tables

Figures

Prologue

R. Elliott Ingersoll

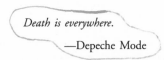

Death is everywhere.

—Depeche Mode

In many ways Integral Psychotherapy heralds the death of psychotherapy; a death like all others that yields new life. Statements like that are not well received by psychotherapists and academics (I know this because I am a psychotherapist and an academic). I am reminded of the scorned "madman" in Nietzsche's parable who runs about proclaiming the death of God (running about proclaiming anything makes psychotherapists and academics nervous). When I say that psychotherapy (as those of us trained in the late 20th century learned it) is dead, my colleagues roll their eyes and mutter, "here we go again." In response all I can say is: "Well, here we go again."

In all fairness, my more literate colleagues have seen their share of "death." Nietzsche proclaimed the death of God.[1] Alexander Kojeve proclaimed the death of man[2] and Michel Foucault noted that the death of God was a "doubly murderous gesture which by putting an end to the absolute, at the same time murdered man himself."[3] It gets better. Roland Barthes proclaimed the death of the author concluding that the intentions and biographical background of an author are unimportant in interpreting a text.[4] Queer theory proclaimed the death of the subject in the context of the HIV/AIDS epidemic because the individual subject as an agentic focus in studies of sexually transmitted diseases scapegoated gays.

All this "death" is old news for those familiar with postmodern philosophy but postmodernism failed to grasp the mythic image of a garden where new life sprouts from rotting (or in this case deconstructed) remains. As both gods and vegetables die and are resurrected, fresh sprouts push through discarded frameworks for psychotherapy. These sprouts include efforts to integrate psychotherapy theories[5] and missives that explain away psychotherapy by explaining away the existence of the mind.[6] If anything can be said of postmodernists generally it is that they were lousy gardeners—they didn't even suspect that new sprouts would appear (I'll refrain from the temptation to announce the death of post-modernism). The result in psychotherapy was a dismissal of the postmodern-ists, a marginal existence for constructivists and a disinterest in the sprouts. A majority of psychotherapists have retreated into parochial theories focused on quantitative exploration and a disturbingly fanatical fascination with biological psychiatry[7] that Freud, were he alive today, would call "science envy."

This "fascination" with "brain sans mind," led to psychologists' campaign for psychotropic medication prescribing privileges (which is succeeding in many U.S. states and territories). There is an old joke that psychiatrists studied medi-cine but don't practice it and practice psychology but never studied it. A similar joke may soon be apt for the psychologists running around with prescription pads. Just as Kant summarized the modern era by noting that modernity was typified by people feeling embarrassed to be found on their knees praying, in our post-postmodern era many psychotherapists seem embarrassed to admit that they do "talk therapy" even though we know talk therapy is as effective as ever.[8] Therapists can usually assuage the embarrassment noting that they are "up to date" about the latest breakthroughs in psychotropic medication or gene expression[9] and by taking continuing education courses in medical colleges.

From an Integral perspective what is it about psychotherapy that is "dead?" Part of the difficulty answering this is that human beings never agreed on what psychotherapy is, or for that matter, what the psyche is that is the subject of such therapy. This may surprise the lay reader and I summarize that issue known as the "mind–brain problem" later in the book. These questions aside, my conclusion is that what is *dead* in psychotherapy is the *way* we have tried to map the psyche, the perspective we use to do it and the "version" of ourselves that is doing the mapping.

If the obituaries listed here are accurate, what is the growing edge in the post-postmodern[10] world for understanding the individual, the mind, and the complex relationship referred to as psychotherapy? I maintain in this book that Integral Psychotherapy is this growing edge and that the application of Integral Theory to psychotherapy revitalizes it and gives therapists a way out of deconstruction, theoretical parochialism, and further retreat into explaining away the psyche as a side effect of the brain. Ken Wilber's pioneering insights presented here as Integral Psychotherapy, provide therapists a way to embrace and move beyond the individual, embrace and move beyond the context of two subjects in dialogue, and embrace and move beyond any biogenic variables that may play dominant roles in the manifestation of psychological suffering. These are just some of the ways Integral Psychotherapy heralds the death of psychotherapy: a death like all others that yields new life.

Normally, a prologue would stop at the last sentence but there is more. Integral, as David and I explain in these pages, is not just about recognizing what is dead and what is resurrecting but it is about the ground of all that—the ground of the rotting remains, the ground of the fresh sprouts and the realization that all is well and as it should be—bizarre as that may sound staring at the rubble of discarded theories and the enormous psychological suffering in humanity. The final chapter on psychotherapy and spirituality will explore more in-depth the most radical ideas that Integral Theory brings to psychotherapy—ideas that not only make sense of how the field has evolved, but ideas that bring you face to face with your truest face, your purest mind, the very basis of the mysterious psyche that we explore in these pages.

Finally, I want to emphasize to the reader the context in which I do psychotherapy. I am a licensed psychologist and clinical counselor in the state of Ohio. I am obligated to follow all the legal and ethical codes that apply to activities carried out under those licenses. Clients who choose to work with me are placing their lives, or some part of their lives, in my hands. This is something I am very mindful of. In that context it is not only unwise but also selfish to offer treatment based on speculation or one's preference for a theory with no research supporting it. For that reason, David and I have worked very hard in writing about Integral Psychotherapy to illustrate how it relates to the mainstream literature in psychology and psychotherapy. Unfortunately, too often speculation is uncritically applied where it is not appropriate. You can see this for yourself in all the money changing hands around speculative constructs like the Enneagram, Spiral Dynamics, or less rigorous applications of emotional intelligence. It is frighteningly easy for a therapist to take his or her own wishful thinking and dress it up as a valid or reliable construct. Being mindful of this dynamic in myself, I have tried to include as many references to the peer-reviewed literature as I could to make points throughout the book. I have not just studied Integral Theory but have spent the better part of my life studying and practicing psychology.

As a result, this book has a lot of endnotes but I think that is the best format because endnotes don't have to interrupt the flow of reading unless the reader is trying to follow the scholarly "trail of breadcrumbs." Some of these may seem minute and obscure but I feel one flaw in some of the Integral literature is that authors have not left a clear trail of scholarly endnotes so it is hard to investigate their conclusions. I believe that an approach to Integral Psychotherapy that uses scholarly literature as a context is responsible and likely to help the field grow in healthy ways by fueling research and encouraging readers to think for themselves. Anything less is potentially unethical and dangerous for clients.

The title of this book (suggested by our dear friend and colleague Dr. Andre Marquis), *Integral Psychotherapy: Inside Out/Outside In* is in one sense playing with words because "insides" and "outsides" are part of the integral model. In another sense it is meant literally. Psychotherapy always includes the subjective experience of the therapist and client. One of the most demanding aspects of Integral Psychotherapy is how the therapist maintains his or her health—physically, psychologically, emotionally, and spiritually. This is addressed by Integral Life Practice (ILP) and interested readers should consult the book on that topic.[11] ILP turns up repeatedly in this work as well. As a clinician in private practice I have used an ILP for years to take care of myself. I work with a loosely affiliated group of professionals that includes psychotherapists, physical trainers, yoga teachers, massage-therapists, and financial advisors. We refer clients to each others' services when the need is there but not as a matter of habit.

It is my hope that you will experience this book, in a manner of speaking, inside and out. There is plenty of mental stimulation for cognitive work as well as questions and exercises here and there for the interested reader to engage in emotional exploration. I hope this book helps readers who are not therapists but may be searching for one. Knowing who you connect with is an important component of "shopping" for a therapist. This book offers some guidance in that area. Finally it is important to me to be clear about spirituality. David and I make no ontologically certain claims in this book. I have found in my own experience (and consonant with many of Ken Wilber's writings) that there are riches in any healthy spiritual path. I cannot tell another person what path to pursue but I can support the wisdom of choosing pursuit. Here again I see this as an ethical imperative. Western society is filled with what I call "for-profit prophets" those who are all too eager to make claims of a spiritual nature and sell their wisdom (witness the 2012 craze sweeping the New Age market). My own experiences of what I call spiritual are right where I'm sitting now. Anything or anyone claiming to be spiritual that isn't relevant to where you are sitting now seems to me a fraud. There is no substitute for experience and where spirit is concerned, the universe (and wherever you happen to be sitting right now) is oozing with potential experiences.

Finally a word about humor. As lead author there are times throughout this book I share my sense of humor, which has been described as ranging from perverse to odd. I can't honestly write even a scholarly book without some humor. I prefer being sincere rather than serious as the latter conjures up images of someone who thinks they will cogitate better if their brow is furrowed and their back painfully hunched over. I use a great deal of humor in my work as a professor and psychotherapist and it would be disingenuous to delete it here as I'm writing about that work. Humor, like seasoning, is an acquired taste though and I leave it to the reader to decide if my choice to include it was wisdom or folly.

Finally, there is one important housekeeping item regarding how we have authored this book. Each chapter in this book was primarily authored by either

David or myself. Although we agree on many issues related to Integral Psychotherapy, for grammatical ease we each speak in the first-person singular ("I") in the chapters we have written. Thus, whoever's name is on the chapter you are reading, that is the person addressing you (the "I" in that chapter). This does not mean that we disagree on the content but it was our strategy to use the first-person singular to increase the readability. Here endeth the prologue.

1

Introduction

R. Elliott Ingersoll

A work of art is never finished, only abandoned.

—Paul Valery

Do you ever feel like something is wrong? That's the feeling a lot of people share in psychotherapy sessions. For some it is a subtle unease like the "splinter in your mind" referred to by philosophers and movie characters like Morpheus in *The Matrix*. For others it is a sense of anxiety or despair that they numb with alcohol, consumerism, or *Sex and the City* reruns. For still others it is an inexplicable sense of guilt or embarrassment about being alive. As sages have instructed us for millennia, psychological pain does not have to cause suffering but let's face it—without a concerted effort to shift one's psychological state or stage of development—suffering happens.

Psychological pain can birth suffering so great that people turn to medication or hospital treatment. Others try self-medicating with everything from nicotine to heroin. Still others end their lives by their own hand. Of course, nobody comes to psychotherapy because everything feels right with their life. Even therapists can be plagued with a nagging sense that something is wrong. I certainly number myself among those who can't shake the suspicion that, where life is concerned, some mistake has been made. We engage in psychotherapy to explore this sense of something being "wrong." If there was a mistake made we want to know who made it and how to address it (as well as whether insurance will pay to fix it).

Most suffering arises from what we psychologically identify with and psychotherapy helps us make our identifications objects of awareness. What we identify as "I" can be found at the root of much suffering. Some of us define "I" in a way that makes demands on others ("I'm the boss here"). Others of us identify "I" in a way that is based on a transitory circumstance ("I'm the toughest or most beautiful one in the room"). Still others mistake temporary pain for a sign that they aren't even worth existing ("I suck," "I'm a fat pig," "I'm a loser"). From the perspective of psychotherapy (and most spiritual practices), all of these are mistaken identities. They are more like stories that we tell ourselves—stories that may be hurtful or even lies. However you regard them (stories, lies, or both) the stories we tell ourselves evolve and psychotherapy may be thought of as someone sharing their story with a hope of rewriting the ending. If we use psychotherapy to change the stories we tell ourselves it can decrease our suffering.

There are three ways we explore the self in this book that are related to how we identify what is "I." First there is what you call "I" at any stage of your development (the topic of Chapter 3). This "I" is what is differentiated from the rest of the world; what for all intents and purposes feels like a "real self" at any particular stage ("I am this, not that; I am married, not single"). Second, there is a possibility at every stage that you may disown a part of yourself leaving a false or at least incomplete "I." This disowned part of self that is related to what we call "shadow" in Chapter 3 is frequently made up of aspects of ourselves that we pretend are either not there or belong to someone else because they are related to our weaknesses ("because I am married I never get attracted to people other than my spouse"). Finally, there is something that is the ground of the awareness that allows any identification of "I" to take place and in Chapter 8 we discuss that as the true self (who is it who is aware of a self that identifies as married?).

Our psychological experiences; real selves, disowned selves, maybe a true self are artistically crafted in the larger context of an ever-evolving "work in progress" called life. If life is a work in progress perhaps mistakes (suffering, false selves) are part of a design or a part of evolution. But whose design; whose evolution? Some clients feel there is an intelligent design to the universe, whereas others will only go as far as an intentional design. Whether or not the design is *well* intentioned, mean as hell, or indifferent is another issue that may relate to psychological pain.[1] Psychotherapy is one way we explore the universe, our place in it, and increase our awareness about what is really going on. In the best of all situations, psychotherapy can shift your focus from what seems wrong to what is going on and there a richer life begins for those willing to take the journey.

If there is such a thing as spirituality,[2] where psychotherapy ends and spiritual realization begins is unclear. One idea we explore in Chapter 8 is that if one can and does transcend (and include) their sense of "I" to identify with the awareness that the sense of "I" arises in, is working with that awareness really psychotherapy? One view is that psychotherapy ends and a deepened spiritual practice begins at the point where you are participating fully in the joys and pains of life without being attached to either. Knowing what you want, feeling a purpose in life, becoming the author (rather than recipient) of your rules for life—these can all be results of psychotherapy that may even lead to spiritual growth. This is a book about a new approach to therapy called Integral Psychotherapy. Integral Psychotherapy is an integrative framework for exploring these questions and understanding how to unlock the richness of your life using Ken Wilber's Integral Model.

This book was initially aimed at the layperson but, as the writing progressed, David and I realized that we couldn't write to a layperson without also addressing psychotherapists. Because there is no introductory text on Integral Psychotherapy proper, my hope is this book will fill that need while also being accessible to the interested layperson. As far as nontherapist readers, it is important to note that psychotherapy is ideally done in person with a trained therapist who can meet you face to face. Despite the proliferation of online psychotherapy, there is still much to be said for an embodied presence with the client that we can never capture beyond a physical distance of more than 10 feet. For the 21st-century client, Integral Psychotherapy offers a broader deeper map of change processes available. That said, many of Integral Psychotherapy's features can be understood and worked with from the printed page for reflection and personal growth. Readers without a background in psychotherapy proper can use this book for self-exploration, as a warm-up for therapy or as an adjunct to therapy. This chapter is divided into seven parts as follows:

- What is Psychotherapy?: This section introduces an Integral description of psychotherapy

- Rules, Tools, and Development: This section introduces the idea of tools that you use to navigate life and the rules you work from and how both change over the course of your life in what we call you center of gravity.

- Expanding Integral Psychotherapy and Introducing Integral Theory: This part elaborates on the description of Integral Psychotherapy while giving a quick tour of the Integral Model. This section also explains why psychotherapy done in an Integral way can be a work of "Kosmic" proportions

- Getting Started—Breaking Taboos: This part of the chapter describes how psychotherapy requires a willingness to break the taboos against changing the story you tell yourself.

- A Primer on the Integral Attitude: This section describes the Integral attitude we use in therapy and you can use to learn to trust yourself. The conundrum presented is that if you can't trust yourself you really can't do anything.

- A Closer Look at the Quadrants and Related Treatment Issues: This section elaborates on each quadrant or perspective as it relates to psychotherapy.

- The Integral Heuristic and *DSM*: This section discusses the implications of Integral Theory for improving *DSM* and as a framework within which to understand some of the changes that will be part of *DSM*-V in 2013.

What is Psychotherapy?

I'll "cut to the chase" here—I do not find the question "What is psychotherapy?" very useful however it is important that I address it in a book on the topic. We know that psychotherapy is a relationship in which a therapist uses certain techniques and processes to assist in the unfolding of the client's self, the identification of disowned selves and (in some cases) pointing clients toward what seems a more fundamental or "true" self. No insurance company will pay for that, however. We therapists have to be able to explain to insurance companies what it is we do but asking "What is psychotherapy?" gives the illusion that there is a simplistic answer. Some brilliant therapists have tried to answer this question but each one eventually concedes that the question is too general. The best you can do with an overgeneralized question is offer an overgeneralized answer. Ericksonian hypnotherapist Jeffrey Zeig[3] began his answer to the question "What is psychotherapy?" by quoting Mark Twain ("if the only tool you have is a hammer, an awful lot of things will look like nails"). Zeig went on to say that you couldn't answer the question "What is psychotherapy?" without describing a context in which the answer is given. The closest Zeig gets to an answer is defining psychotherapy as

> a change-oriented process that occurs in the context of a contractual, empowering, and empathic professional relationship. Its rationale . . . focuses on the personality of the client, the technique of psychotherapy, or both. The process is idiosyncratic and determined by interaction of the patients' and therapists' preconceived positions. (p. 14)

If you're anything like me you find this answer is a good start but doesn't touch on the details and it is in the details that we unlock the richness of psychotherapy. I am going to offer an integral description of what psychotherapy is and then spend the rest of the book unpacking that description. The initial description is this. ***Psychotherapy is the scientific and artistic process of helping clients make aspects of themselves or their lives objects of awareness,*** *helping them identify with and own these objects and then integrating them through a process of disidentification.*[4] Making difficult or painful aspects of your life objects of awareness, owning them and integrating them is one of the keys to unlocking the wealth of possibilities in your life.

Rules, Tools, and Development

To help clients with the process of psychotherapy, therapists must meet clients where they are developmentally, which is one way of understanding what "rules" the client has for living. In therapy we help clients use these rules to make sense of (translate) the world in as healthy a manner as possible given the "tools" they have in their developmental "toolbox." So here we have two concepts—tools and rules—that we come back to frequently in this book. Your tools and rules are the basis of how you translate (make sense of or "metabolize") reality. You use your tools and rules in the story you tell yourself about who you are and what is going on in your life.

A complete answer to the question "What is psychotherapy?" requires a framework that includes the depth of what it means to be conscious, what it means to be in relationship, and what the *Kosmological*[5] context is for being human and being in relationship. Imagine having treasures buried in your own backyard but never suspecting that they are there. Imagine that digging up even one of these treasures would increase your life satisfaction tenfold. Now imagine someone shows up with a map that not only tells you "hey—there are treasures buried in your yard" but shows you where to dig. Integral Theory provides such an integrative map.[6] I offer a summary of Integral in a moment but first a bit more about tools and rules.

Center of Gravity: Tools and Rules Again

Who are you? How do you experience life? How do you want to "show up" in the world? What are your gifts? What are the rules you have for life? These questions give focus to self-exploration, psychotherapy, and this book. There is an exercise you can do alone or with a partner that consists of asking, "Who are you really?" over and over again (and answering each time with whatever comes to mind). You can do the exercise in a mirror for that matter asking, "Who am I really?" It is simple but powerful. The idea is that you answer the question each time until you begin to exhaust the obvious responses and are driven to closer examination of the "gap" between who you think you are and who you "really" are. For some this "gap" points the way to who you may consciously become.

Your initial answers to the question "Who am I really" depend on what I refer to as your center of gravity.[7] Your center of gravity is an important component of what in Chapter 7 I call your "psychological address." Your center of gravity includes what I call your "developmental toolbox," your worldview, self-sense, and your values[8] and is the underlying force for the rules you make for yourself. You may not think you make the rules but you do—that is an important component of self-knowledge. As is seen in the forthcoming pages, I try to use valid and reliable constructs when describing aspects of our center of gravity but let me complicate this by adding that there may be no such thing. A *center of gravity* is a therapeutic metaphor that may be resourceful for some (but not all) clients. Some Integral writers refer to a center of gravity as if it were as valid as constructs like ego development or cognitive dissonance. It is not and I would no more speak about center of gravity with ontological certainty than I would claim to have seen a pooka[9] at the local tavern.

Like the story you tell yourself, your center of gravity and your rules evolve as you grow. The *content* of consciousness changes as your center of gravity broadens and deepens. Put simply, self-identity is "drawing the line" between what is self and what is other. This "line" then leads to rules we make to defend it and to what we think is "wrong" when our life breaks our rules and rudely crosses that line. Who we think we are, what rules we make and what seems wrong at one stage of our development is frequently not a problem at later stages. Of course our rules are not just those we've made consciously. We spend our early years in families soaking up whatever rules that family has and many of us never question those rules as adults. So rather than rules we've made, these are rules we're embedded in.

As our rules and tools evolve, so does our self-identification. The sliding nature of self-identification is the focus of Chapter 3. Self-identification undulates between stabilization and moving on to a new, broader, deeper identity. In psychotherapy there are times when you have to stabilize where you are and times when you have to move on. We call stabilizing where you are *translation*. Translation is making sense of the world with your existing tools and rules in the healthiest manner possible. In Integral Psychotherapy we would say health is translating accurately from our current center of gravity. This is similar to what Carl Rogers (founder of client-centered therapy) called accurate symbolization. When we accurately symbolize what life presents us with we have the greatest probability of coping with it. If we distort or deny our internal symbols of what life is presenting then we risk psychological illness.[10]

An example of a client that psychotherapy helped with translating is Ann, a devout Christian who came to see me for severe anxiety. Ann's Christian faith reflected traditional values that she was quite happy with. Her anxiety was related to her husband losing his job and becoming verbally abusive. According to her center of gravity, her rules, she had somehow failed in keeping the family healthy through this employment crisis. Although a feminist counselor may have tried to get Ann to change her rules, my sense was her rules were adequate to the task—we just needed to make them objects of awareness and help her discern what the purpose was behind the rules. Discernment was an important "tool" in her toolbox that she learned to use in prayer and in life to refocus on what she really valued. Once she discerned her purpose was to reflect the love of Christ in family life, she was able to modify the level of responsibility she had for her husband's feelings and confront him with *his* responsibility. When she did this they entered couples' counseling with a Christian counselor and were able to work things out. Ann's tools and rules worked fine once she could make the purpose behind them an object of awareness.

Psychotherapy also can help us move to a broader, deeper center of gravity. When the tools and rules we have are not enough to do the job, we are forced into a situation where we can collapse in on ourselves or move forward into the great unknown crafting new tools and rules along the way. When we begin to feel adequate with new tools and rules, we are stabilizing at a new center of gravity, a new story we tell about our life. An example of this was a colleague of mine (Sam) who was denied tenure at the university. Sam was a psychology professor and a licensed psychotherapist. Sam's father was a university professor and Sam's desire to be a professor seemed more geared toward pleasing his father than himself. Sam was very good at the type of narrowly defined study that typifies university departments but he did not like to write academic papers. Even worse, he despised other people critiquing his work. This is a problem in most universities where the phrase "publish or perish" is more than a cliché. Initially, Sam went into a deep depression after he was denied tenure. In therapy he began looking at his tools and rules and realized that his tools were more geared toward working with clients and his rules were more derived from his father than himself. This began a reframing process wherein Sam began to lean on his strength and see clients again. He also reformulated his rules and became entrepreneurial in building a private practice. He began to see himself as an effective and joyous free agent outside the reach of the university and living on his own terms. His center of gravity shifted as he refined his tools and made new rules for this next phase of his journey.

Co-Creating Our Rules: Magic and Effort

I always tell clients that life is a combination of magic and effort (how's that for an invalid construct?). I offer for their consideration that if they put forth some effort life may meet them part way with magic. If, instead of effort, you coast on "autopilot," life coasts with you but there's not much magic. If you coast fearfully, you may "see" more fearful things. If you coast optimistically you may not get very far but the ride is pleasant. This relates in a key way to some psychological studies. Psychologists Lauren Alloy and Lyn Abramson discovered that clients who were moderately to severely depressed were also more

accurate than nondepressed peers in judging how much control they had during an experiment (they were instructed to push a button for a reward but the
conditions varied on how much the reward was really linked to the button).[11]
The more depressed clients were, the more accurate they were in judging how
much control they had pushing the button.

This phenomenon is called *depressive realism* and several studies have
supported the idea that depressed people are more accurate in assessing how
much control they have in experimental and even social situations.[12] So what
does this mean? One interpretation is that those of us who are happy are good
at lying to ourselves—life really sucks but if you face that squarely you get
depressed. This is only one interpretation, however. Another interpretation has
to do with the fact that we co-construct our experience. This is very different
from believing that you create your reality like in "new age" systems like *The
Secret* which, if it were true, would lead to every 2-year-old living in a candy
store. This is more like recognizing that we have choices in how we focus our
attention and how we think about our choices. We can focus attention on
moving away from painful realities ("I never want to be in another abusive
relationship!") but then as a consequence we become focused on what we don't
want ("Hmm . . . that guy looks like a jerk"). We can also focus attention on
moving toward what we *do* want. In this case we are then focused on moving
toward what we want rather than *away* from what we don't want. Going back
to research on depressive realism, people who are optimistic about attaining
a goal are actively co-constructing ways to do that despite evidence that they
may in fact fail. Although they may fail more initially, they are more likely
to see the failures as building blocks they can use to move toward the goal.
This might be referred to as "thinking outside the depressive box" or thinking
from "within a positive box." The latter turns a "failure" into a piece of useful
information. People focused on what they don't want often interpret failure as
evidence that they shouldn't be pursuing the goal in the first place.

Often, depressed people are not engaging life. Being on autopilot keeps
basic functions working but doesn't create anything. Focusing on what you
don't want is to live ever vigilant to disappointment rather than possibility. I
had one client (Sarah) who put it to me quite clearly. She said, "Dr. I, I'm
not going to get my hopes up because I hate being disappointed. If I look at
things realistically, I save myself the pain of disappointment." In working with
Sarah I tried to help her shift her perspective so that she might see how she
was co-constructing failure in the way she was looking at things. Sure, she
protected herself from disappointment but at what cost? *get stuck?*

To co-create we must engage life so somewhere we need a rule that gives us
ourselves permission to do that. Some of the recent research on depressive realism
has suggested that depressed people actually gravitate toward pessimistic biases in
their evaluations, whereas nondepressed people are freer to craft optimistic biases.[13]
We might say that depressed people are responding to one set of rules, whereas

∧ or create

optimistic people are responding to another. And the rules we are working with will determine the tools we employ. In Integral Psychotherapy we always want to help clients move toward what they want. We balance this of course with the legal-ethical context of the society the client lives in and with the need for the client to have at least a conventional ego (conventional meaning they understand and respect the conventions of society. In other words, if clients want to move toward destructive actions that is a different therapeutic approach). We come back to this theme but first an introduction to Integral Theory is in order.

Expanding Integral Psychotherapy and Introducing Integral Theory

At this point I want to take you on a short tour of the Integral Model with emphasis on using the model in psychotherapy. In subsequent chapters I spend more time explaining each aspect of the model but, as Mason said to Dixon, "you've got to draw the line somewhere" so let's begin with this overview. Although Integral is a vast transdisciplinary philosophy, for our purposes we focus on Integral as a way to understand yourself. As you are reading right now, all aspects of your being are embraced in the Integral framework so this really is a book about you. This includes your tools and rules, your surroundings, your body, mind, spirit (if there is such a thing), and the "big ticket" items like (in the immortal words of Douglas Adams) life the universe and everything.[14] Integral Theory uses the word *Kosmos* to describe life, the universe and everything. Kosmos includes the nature or process of all aspects of existence, including your body and psychological states, culture, society, the physical universe, and the force (or forces, gods, goddesses, etc.) underlying it.

"Wait a minute," you might object at this point, "I thought this was a book about psychotherapy, feeling better, functioning better, that sort of thing." I get the tools and rules thing but why get into 'big picture' issues?" This *is* a book about psychotherapy and it is about feeling better and functioning better. It also is different than other books on the topic because the Integral framework embraces everything. This might sound daunting but it needn't be precisely because everything in the Integral framework is an aspect of your being. This goes back to *why* the question "What is psychotherapy?" is inadequate. Unless you first specify the framework through which you are viewing psychotherapy, you really can't give a complete answer. By using a Kosmological view, Integral Psychotherapy provides a richer variety of tools to approach a more complete answer to the question. Equally, by attending to as many different aspects of yourself as possible, you increase the probability of feeling better and functioning better. If something really feels "wrong," you want to have as complete a map of yourself as possible so you can pinpoint where the problem is. The less complete your map, the more likely you'll miss an important aspect of yourself and the more limited your tools and rules will be. As my university students say, the Integral Model helps us "not miss things."

Another reason you want a complete, Kosmic map in psychotherapy is because, in the Integral framework, you are intimately connected with life, the universe and everything—in a way you *are* life the universe and everything. Let me unpack that a bit. For most of us, the sense that our rules have been violated or that something is wrong is rooted in alienation. As you navigate life you constantly make decisions regarding what is self and what is the rest of the world. As noted earlier, your center of gravity and sense of self evolve by making fine distinctions about what is you and what is the rest of the world. In making these distinctions, you are telling a story about who you are and setting up rules for what you want to embrace as "you" and what you want to push away as "other." What we embrace or push away may be actual parts of ourselves, other people, places, or experiences. The more you embrace, the broader and deeper your sense of self becomes. The more you push away the greater your chances of experiencing alienation *and* the greater the chance that what you are pushing away may be an aspect of *you*.[15]

A highpoint in our ability to discern self and other is actually the developmental achievement of what philosopher Richard Tarnas calls "the modern mind."[16] This is a mind that can differentiate itself as subject to behold the rest of the universe as object. In Integral Psychotherapy we call this differentiation the subject–object balance and it is a colossal achievement developmentally. It is *not* the apex of development however because after we differentiate from something we next need to consistently make it an object of awareness and then integrate it. We achieve this integration through disidentification (rather than dissociation). Disidentification is owning something as an aspect of yourself while not being unnecessarily attached to what that means.

By way of example, think of a love affair you were in that didn't work out (this example works best if you were "dumped" in the relationship). At first maybe you made rules like "I never want to see that person again!" You really wanted to differentiate from her or him and regroup as a single person. In the weeks following the break-up you may have even found yourself avoiding places where you might run into your former lover. As time passes, however, if you are getting over the break-up, you find that you can integrate what you learned from the relationship and move on. You can digest it rather than choke on it. Part of this "moving on" includes changing your rules. Maybe now the rule is "we shared a lot together and I can be civil with my former lover." Perhaps when you can do this without feeling like you're breaking down emotionally, it is a sign of successful integration.

One of Sigmund Freud's greatest insights was that we frequently differentiate by psychologically pushing things away from awareness to make them unconscious but, if all goes well, once we've achieved differentiation we can return to those unconscious contents, make them objects of awareness, identify with

projection, → becoming conscious of the un conscious

them or own them, then begin integrating them.[17] The final step of integration is a *disidentifying* from the very things we made objects of awareness and *identified* with. Failed integration is when disidentification becomes dissociation and the things brought into awareness are pushed out of awareness again. This has consequences for more than just our mental health. In the case of your former lover, dissociation might include psychologically pushing into unconsciousness any thoughts or feelings related to the relationship so you don't have to deal with them. In this state if you run into your former lover and your defenses fail, you have an emotional meltdown as the "pushed away" aspects of the relationship come flooding into awareness like ice water into the Titanic.[18]

Now consider the implications of a more Kosmic vision in the example about your failed love affair. If you are *only* an isolated individual in a mechanistic universe the damage is limited to your own psychological suffering. If, however, you are deeply connected to life, the universe, and everything, then differentiation that derails into dissociation sets up a dangerous tear in the fabric of the Kosmos. In his second book *Psyche and Cosmos*, Richard Tarnas alluded to this writing "in the history of Western thought and culture, the community and larger whole from which the heroic self was separated was not simply the local tribal or familial matrix, but rather the entire community of being, the Earth, the cosmos itself . . . we have not understood yet that the discovery of the unconscious means an enormous spiritual task, which must be accomplished if we wish to preserve our civilization." Integral Psychotherapy recognizes this enormous task. Because each of us is connected to life, the universe, and everything the work of psychotherapy can be a work of Kosmic proportions.[19]

In the psychotherapies of the modern era we used to think that a healthy person had simply made the most of what Alan Watts called the "skin-encapsulated ego." Basically, the healthy person reached adulthood with an adequate ego and sallied forth into the marketplace of humanity to function as an isolated entity until death. Postmodern currents then began deconstructing this notion of the skin-encapsulated ego to the point where individuals were seen as nested in biological, psychological, cultural, and social contexts. Although many postmodern thinkers stopped there and gleefully announced the death of the individual, Integral Theory proclaimed the birth of a far more complex individual. This more complex, expanded map of the self included the impact of relationships, shared beliefs, and meaning-making. In addition, we include the revival of the wisdom traditions and decades of studying the relationship between spirituality and psychology.

Experiencing Your Being Through Perspectives

Before reading on do the following exercise in your imagination.

1. *Make an "I" statement that pertains to what you are experiencing at the moment you read this.*

2. *Talk to yourself about a problem in your life supplying dialogue for two points of view (e.g., "I'd like to buy a motorcycle." "No, bad idea—they are dangerous.")*

3. *Reflect on a time when you felt so overcome by emotions it was as if you were possessed.*

The first stop on this quick Integral tour is perspectives. Your being is complex and elegant. Part of the complexity includes the three perspectives represented in the exercise. That each of us shifts between first-, second, and third-person perspectives makes our psychological world stunningly complex. Our first-person perspective refers to the one speaking ("I"), second-person refers to the one spoken to ("you"), and third-person the one spoken about ("him," "her," "it"). In the last exercise, your "I" statement illustrates your first-person perspective. The internal dialogue in Item 2 reflects your capacity to take first- and second-person perspectives within your mind. Finally the reflection on overwhelming emotions should illustrate your ability to take an aspect of yourself and make it "other."

We use these perspectives psychologically everyday as we own parts of our being ("I feel better with a lower body weight"), disown parts of our being ("I'd feel better if I could lose *the* weight"), and dialogue with parts of ourselves ("I want a doughnut." "Doughnuts are fattening and you're trying to lose weight." "Well I worked out today, I'll just have one" "Well, ok, you've earned it"). As Wilber has emphasized, the fact that almost every language known to humankind has first-, second-, and third-person perspectives is elegant.[20] These perspectives would not occur in every language if they weren't part of our psychological reality—our being. As part of our language, these perspectives appear in every psychotherapy session as signs along the road to self-knowledge. Chapter 2 details how these perspectives relate to the quadrants of Integral Theory and the practice of Integral Psychotherapy. Chapter 3 explains what I call the "wiles of the self"—the various ways we can deceive ourselves and how this comes out in our language. In that chapter I describe how psychotherapists listen to first-, second-, and third-person language to understand which part of the self a client owns and which part the client pushes away.

Lines and Levels of Development

Our second stop on the Integral introductory tour is lines and levels of development. In addition to perspectives, psychologists have reason to believe that you embody several lines of development, some of which are more developed than others. A line of development is an aspect of your being that unfolds in a predictable sequence. The various plateaus in the sequence we call stages or levels. This is a thorny issue in academic psychology because it requires enormous rigor to support the hypothesis of a stage theory. That said, there are many stage theories in existence but only a few with rigorous support. Chapter 4 introduces levels and lines of development. One example of a developmental line is our sense of self called "ego." Our self-development occurs dialectically through differentiation and integration.[21] As infants, we learn to differentiate our body from our caregiver's body and establish a physical self. The integration of a physical self takes us to a new level. In the "terrible 2s" we differentiate our emotions from our caregivers' emotions, develop an emotional self and move to yet another level. If things go well, our sense of self develops through stages that encompass more and more of the world. In each differentiation we use cues we get from others around us that introduce dissonance. We resolve the dissonance by redefining who we are and who we are not (the dialectic component).

For most of us, things don't always go smoothly and instead of integrating a differentiated aspect of self (e.g., the emotion of anger) we split it off and pretend it is not part of us, a process of disowning that we call dissociation. When we split off aspects of our self it is as if we have taken out a credit card with a really high interest rate. We get what we need in the short term, but the pain of re-owning what is now foreign to us grows and grows with each day. Eventually, we must hunker down and repay the debt (a debt that we owe ourselves), or we risk permanent emotional bankruptcy. I elaborate on this later but for now suffice it to say; you can't disown parts of yourself forever. The disowning takes psychological (or psychic) energy and sooner or later you're going to want that energy for other things. To reclaim it, you'll then need to make the disowned parts objects of awareness, own them and integrate them. For example, people who disown anger may do all right for a while but often they will find themselves lacking in passion in general and not having enough energy to take on new projects. Integral psychotherapists assist these people to free up the energy they are using to push away the disowned anger, help them make the anger an object of awareness, then own and integrate it. In some ways the therapists help clients retrieve these disowned parts of self somewhat like a shaman retrieves lost souls.[22]

Types or Styles

Our third stop on the Integral introductory tour is types or styles. In addition to perspectives, levels and lines of development, and the wiles of your self-system, you have a *style* of moving through life—what is sometimes called a *type*. You might have taken a "type" test (called a typology) like the Myers-Briggs Type Indicator or the Enneagram. In a less formal sense you may think in terms of masculine and feminine types. These are covered in Chapter 5. Although we don't have what are called valid or reliable tests to help us understand types of personalities, we can learn through dialogue with people what style they like to lead with in certain situations. One client I treated tested out at a very late, postconventional stage of ego development referred to as Magician. This same client though preferred to blend into the background and work more "behind the scenes." In terms of type or style we might say he was more an introvert than extrovert. Another client who tested at the solid conventional level of Diplomat could enjoy leadership positions if those positions required her to assist others in being team players. Although her ultimate concern was the team (in this case her church), her style was more outgoing. When we hear a client's life story we can come to an understanding of the complexity of type through that story.[23] Thinking in terms of styles is more fluid than types and thus my preferred label for this aspect of Integral Theory.

States of Consciousness

The final stop on this introductory tour of Integral Theory is states of consciousness. We all experience different psychological states daily. Everyone has access to waking, dreaming, and deep sleep states. Recall your last dream and the differences between that state of mind and the state of being awake reading this page. You may have suffered from states of depression or anxiety. Perhaps in peak moments you have experienced states of sexual ecstasy or nonordinary states induced from things like fasting, sleep deprivation, or meditation. All these states are part of the human experience and their relevance to psychotherapy is covered in Chapter 6.

That is Integral in a nutshell—perspectives (what I describe later as quadrants), lines, levels, types, and states. In this psychotherapy book, we focus on how the model relates to our tools and rules as well as our wiles and styles. As you become reacquainted with dimensions of yourself through the pages of this book, I hope your focus will broaden and deepen from what is wrong to what is going on and what is actually available to you in living a human life. Awareness is a primary tool but to open to it, you have to be willing to break some taboos and that is our next topic.

Getting Started—Breaking Taboos

> I won't know myself until I find out whether life is serious or not . . . it's dangerous, I know, and it can hurt a lot. That doesn't necessarily mean it's serious.
>
> —Kurt Vonnegut

To know yourself sounds easy but we all have a knack for erecting obstacles to accomplishing easy tasks. If you doubt this, remember that hot dogs still come in packs of 8 while hot dog buns come in packs of 10. Recall in my brief description of Integral Theory I noted that most of us disown aspects of ourselves. Usually the aspects we disown are things that conflict with an ideal image we have of ourselves or what authorities in our lives (like parents) have told us we should be. The combination of idealized images and internalized authorities is what Freud called the "over-I" (mistranslated as *Super Ego*).[24] Part of the conventional game of being human includes this "over-I" and results in us pretending there are parts of ourselves we shouldn't own *or* look into—parts we should in fact dissociate.[25] Because our "over-I" contains introjected[26] authority figures, our process of dissociating can be reinforced by our cultural norms and social structures making it even harder to reclaim or even investigate these dissociated pieces of "I."

I intuited this at about 12 years old in one of my many "trainings" in the world's spiritual paths, all of which are ripe with taboos to experiment with. At age 12, I was being prepared for what is called "confirmation" in the Anglican/Episcopal church. Confirmation is serious business. Where baptism initiates infants into the church, confirmation is when the pubescent (or "barely pubescent") initiate must "decide" for him or her self to make a conscious, lifelong commitment to the faith. Of course no 12-year-old is ready for such a decision but that's part of the fun—asking the bewildered possessor of new intellectual abilities and a budding sexual body to make a life-altering decision they aren't ready or informed enough to make. I recall the priest talking about the decision to accept Christ and how Christ saves us. One boy (whose parents must have been Communists) asked, "If we choose to accept Christ and Christ saves us don't we really save ourselves?" It seemed like a good question to me and I perked up to hear the answer. The priest furrowed his brow and sternly replied, "There are some things we aren't meant to question." That was that.

One woman with whom I worked, who now goes by her Pagan name Brigid, was raised in a household where the adults used religion as an excuse for violent behavior toward the children. Although she genuinely identified as Christian in her formative years, life in her "Christian" family raised more questions than she could answer about a personal God. Growing up she learned how important her family's taboos were by being physically struck each time she questioned them. At one point, her father said she should consider herself lucky because in the "Old Testament" or Torah book of Deuteronomy (Deuteronomy 21: 18-21), disobedient children could be stoned to death (but to be fair, the editors of Deuteronomy did not have access to good day care). As a reminder, Brigid's father kept a large rock as a paperweight on his desk. Brigid had an aunt, uncle, and three older male cousins who sympathized with her plight and supported her by inviting her to spend summers working on their farm. These were like real vacations for Brigid and, although she still had to go back home in August, she felt the support of this extended family. It was her aunt who pointed out that in learning the family taboos, Brigid also learned a great deal of what some might currently call "emotional intelligence."[27] She learned to "read" other people's emotional states and her aunt coached her to use this ability to avoid her father's anger.

Brigid married young to get out of the house in a "respectable" manner (leaving just to get away from adults who had the humanity of rabid ground-hogs was apparently not a "respectable" reason). Her new husband seemed, by most accounts, to be loving and hard-working, virtues her family approved of. Unfortunately, he also had a temper similar to Brigid's father and had physically struck Brigid 3 months into the new marriage. At this point, Brigid contemplated suicide but said, strange as it seemed at the time, she didn't because she would have felt bad leaving such a mess for others to clean up. So, what to do? She was terrified of the thought of a divorce and, although it seemed the only option, she wasn't ready. What she did do amazed even her. The next time her husband beat her, she asked her cousins to do some beating of their own. When her husband was in the hospital recovering from a skull fracture and broken jaw, she served him with divorce papers. Looking back 20 years later she marveled, "I didn't think I had that much vengeance in me. But if I could barely see it in my ex-husband, why would I be able to see it in myself?" As satisfying as this story is for those who hate bullies, it doesn't end there.

In looking into aspects of herself that her family claimed were off limits, in breaking these taboos, Brigid also became aware that when she was happy there was a part of her that was *aware* that she was happy. When angry, there was a part of her that was *aware* that she was angry. When being beaten by her husband or father, there was a part of her that was *aware* of her being frightened. When she served her husband divorce papers, she felt power, revenge, and was aware of a part of her that was *aware* of all these feelings as well. This intrigued her but she quickly forgot about it first because it seemed weird ("taboo") and because she had to make some fast decisions about where to live and how she was going to earn money.

Brigid spent 3 years in what she describes as a "limbo" state. She had some money from her divorce settlement, but it didn't last as long as she thought. She was renting a room in a house, working part time at a café, and dating occasionally with disappointing results. She decided she needed more change. She found a new job (with better pay) at a cleaning company working nights and moved in with a friend who was in need of a roommate to help pay the rent. Her new living arrangement helped Brigid get on her feet financially and had some other unexpected payoffs. Her friend (Robin) was a lesbian and Brigid discovered herself to be happily bisexual. She and Robin had a sexual relationship after 7 months of living together. Robin was also a practicing Wiccan (sometimes colloquially referred to as being a "witch") and she began initiating Brigid into the mysteries of "the craft." What a year! Brigid had broken more taboos than a burlesque show in Amish country. What was telling, considering her upbringing, was that rather than feel crippled with remorse or guilt, Brigid felt a genuine coming home. In her work with Wiccan ritual, she pondered her "Goddess Eye," which was her name for the "witness" to her emotions that she had noted then forgotten in the flurry of starting her new life. Her Wiccan friends felt this was an important porthole to her soul and that practicing awareness of this witness would aid her growth. So during ritual, after casting her circle, visualizing the earth's energies flowing through her, she would just sit and "be" the Goddess Eye. After spending a year-and-a-day practicing Wicca, she committed herself to the craft in a ritual with a small coven of practitioners. While still primarily identifying as Wiccan, Brigid has also studied world religions and concluded that this "Goddess Eye" is a sort of Ariadne's thread to the true self and that following this thread is possibly the biggest taboo of all because it is the path to knowing who we really are. We might say that Brigid had settled into a new center of gravity, a new self-identification that allowed for the possibility that she was more than a "skin-encapsulated ego."

If, as Alan Watts wrote, the biggest taboo is against knowing who we really are,[28] then *not* knowing this is likely a huge source of feeling something is wrong. It makes sense then in psychotherapy to use an approach that aims directly at discovering who we are in as many respects as possible. Because we are complex creatures, it is also important to use an approach to self-knowledge that allows as many self-exploration techniques from as many places as possible. Breaking taboos is no easy task and having taboos about which taboo-breaking techniques are "allowed" and which are "prohibited" cripples you from the start. As becomes evident in the following section, Integral self-exploration honors the most truths from the greatest number of approaches to understanding who you really are. In this sense, it provides a framework that embraces your taboos while also providing tools to move beyond them. If you're ready to break some taboos and look into some things you may have left unexamined, you're ready for a primer on what I call the Integral attitude

A Primer on the Integral Attitude

Science is not enough, religion is not enough, art is not enough, politics and economics are not enough, nor is love, nor is duty, nor is action however disinterested, nor, however sublime, is contemplation. Nothing short of everything will really do.

—Aldous Huxley

For every complex problem there is a simple solution. And it's always wrong.

—H.L. Mencken

The general approach of Integral Theory and Integral Psychotherapy is called AQAL which stands for all quadrants, levels, lines, states, and types. As I noted, each of these elements reflects an aspect of who you are—aspects we explore in this book. A good place to being is with a point that is one of the most important contributions of Integral thinking:

Everybody's right about something (but not equally right about everything).

This statement is at the heart of Integral thinking. Did you ever wonder why there are so many self-help books? So many theories of psychotherapy? So many people who are ready to tell you what is wrong and how to make it right? Because experts are legion in our quasi-free market economy, it takes some discernment to decide who to trust. Do those crystals really align energy or just collect dust? Is my guru enlightened or a "moon-muffin" who is insulated from reality by living off other people's money? Is my therapist a genius or am I just too neurotic to see he is a quack? These are important questions and, as I know from experience, they are difficult to answer.

Just as I am among those aware of a sense that something is wrong, I am among those who have spent a lot of time and money with teachers and therapists that I thought could make things right. I have spent a good bit of my life as a client in analytical, gestalt, cognitive, and transpersonal therapies as well as a seeker in spiritual direction, meditation, yoga, and vision questing. Every one of these experiences has had its blessings and curses (remember that the Latin meaning of "sacred" includes that which is blessed and that which is cursed). The blessings come as insights into how I am co-creating my life. The curses almost always come in the temptation with each success that I have found the "one true path." Just as there is no shortage of psychotherapists, there is no shortage of what writer Eric Hoffer called "true believers."[29] The true believers are those who, out of ignorance or the prospect of personal gain, are evange-lists for their own "one true path." The primary goal of the true believers is to swell the ranks of believers regardless of truth or experience (which is at odds with every other healing endeavor where the goal is to give the "patient" what they need and then send them away back into the world). Although many of Brigid's acquaintances insisted that Wicca was the *only* "old-time religion" and that considering others would diminish the power of her "Goddess Eye," Brigid had no evidence that this was the case because her Goddess Eye developed while she was a battered, Christian woman. Similarly, there are true believers in the ranks of psychotherapists and the buyer must beware. Although it is common to specialize in one approach to therapy, it is not common or recommended to pretend that that one approach will fit all clients.

This is where Integral may be viewed as heresy by many "true believers" and where the Integral attitude begins (and for the record Integralists can also trip into the mistaken identity of a "true believer"). Approaching something (especially self-exploration) Integrally is to look for the gifts and the truths offered in each experience, each framework and each encounter. In this book, David and I draw on many approaches to psychotherapy and spiritual growth assuming that they are all right about something (and certainly not everything). Because everyone is right about something, aspects of every experience can potentially be taken in, digested, and the truth metabolized. Because everyone is not equally right about everything, experiential "waste" can be excreted—"chew the meat and spit out the bone" as one of my students says.[30]

Trust and the Integral Attitude

Trust me.

—Indiana Jones

This leads to another important part of the Integral attitude and a premise of this book (and psychotherapy). This premise harkens back to the question my 12-year-old classmate asked in confirmation training. *You have to trust yourself to take the journey.* There is a paradox here. Many of us, sensing something is wrong, seek out therapists, gurus, psychotropic medication, and so on, to guide us, to help us, to lead us to the right decisions. I have always felt it ironic that clients who had made progress working with me or with a particular treatment would make statements like "you really kept me going through that crisis" or "Prozac saved my life." When people share such statements with me I am likely to respond "I'm wondering if *you* played a part in keeping yourself going by engaging in therapy with me?" "I wonder if it wasn't *you* who saved your life by taking Prozac when you felt you needed it." These are slightly different perspectives on the same issue and, as I share later in the chapter, taking perspectives is an important experience in Integral Psychotherapy.[31]

But to try on different perspectives, you have to have some degree of trust in yourself. Years ago when Fritz Perls was developing Gestalt psychotherapy, he emphasized trust in the organism, in oneself, as an important component of treatment. Without that he claimed the patient would chain himself to an endless succession of therapists rather than standing on his own two feet. Similarly, Alan Watts made the same point about the spiritual journey. Like the boy in my confirmation class, Watts noted that if we can't trust ourselves we are in a terrible mess. It is ourselves who ultimately decide the truth or falsity of any doctrine by deciding whether we can trust our experience. If we decide we can't trust our experience can we trust ourselves to make the decision about whether or not we can trust our experience? You see the problem. In Christianity, if Jesus only saves those who accept him then you have to trust yourself to make the choice to accept him. If a guru can really lead a person from darkness to light then you have to trust yourself to become a disciple of

the guru. If you think a given psychotherapist can help you dispel your sense
that something is wrong, you have to trust your choice to go see that therapist.
How we trust ourselves also has a sliding nature to it and, as our developmental
altitude broadens and deepens, the way we experience trust in ourselves (and
others) also changes.

The issue of self-trust requires at least a few screening tools to discern
healthy groups from unhealthy groups; healthy spiritual teachers from unhealthy
spiritual teachers; and good therapists from "quacks." In research done on
cults and cult dynamics, there are four common dynamics that characterize a
group, leader or healer as unhealthy. In unhealthy groups or cults proper, the
dynamics are as follow:

1. Emphasis on compliance with the group

2. Emphasis on dependence on a leader with no checks or
   balances

3. Stifling dissent with threats of banishment or ending the
   relationship

4. Devaluing all outsiders[32]

Each of these four dynamics is directly related to decreasing trust in
yourself and giving your own power away. Now, of course, the paradox is that
in giving your power away whether to a self-proclaimed representative of Jesus,
a guru, or a cult leader, you are the one making the choice to vest the recipient
of your subjugation with the power to save you. There is no way out. At some
level you have to trust yourself. It is making this trust an object of awareness,
identifying with it and refining it like any ability that is important.

Starting to Trust Yourself: Three Steps

So you may be asking, "*Okay, how can I learn to trust myself?* This is an excellent question and should be one of the processes in any psychotherapeutic or
spiritual work. Ken Wilber has offered a succinct outline for three steps you can
take (and that we practice with in this book) to trust yourself.[33] The first step
is to decide what you want to find out and then engage in practices designed
to address that area. This has been called the *instrumental injunction*. The name
comes from scientific method where instruments are used to carry out experiments. As Wilber noted, this can be thought of as the "do this" injunction.
Simply put, it is the instructions for how to go about finding something out. If
you want to find out whether your sense of something being wrong is related to
your psychological functioning, you select a therapist and begin psychotherapy.
If you want to find out whether it is possible to have an experience of God,

Goddess, or the "force" of life, you select a spiritual practice, find a teacher, and begin. If you want to find out why hot dogs come in packages of 8 and hotdog buns come in packages of 10 you find an expert on American wieners and begin your research.

The second step is called *direct apprehension* and is the experience that you have as a result of trying the injunction (Step 1). In the example of psychotherapy, most studies indicate that after 8 to 10 sessions, 50% of clients experience significant relief from the symptoms that brought them to the therapists. After 6 months, several researchers concluded that about 75% of clients improve significantly.[34] So if you entered therapy with the hope of understanding why you don't feel quite right, within 6 months chances are you'll feel you are making progress. If you sincerely committed yourself to a spiritual practice, you hopefully found a teacher or spiritual director who could guide you and help you understand your experience with the practice. Based on this relationship, after 12 months you should be able to discern if there is something in the practice for you that might lead you toward an experience of "ultimate reality." You may have even had such an experience (what we discuss later as a temporary state) and decided there is indeed some God, Goddess, or force of life at work. Finally, if you consulted an expert on hot dogs, you have probably given up eating meat but are hopefully closer to understanding the weirdness of the packaging issue.

The last step is *communal confirmation*. This consists of checking your results with others who have mastered the injunction you have been working with to see if you did it properly. In the case of psychotherapy, your therapist may work with a group of therapists who provide supervision to each other, discuss the latest treatment approaches and how to use them with clients. In the case of a spiritual teacher or director, that person is usually linked to a tradition or lineage that contains practitioners who can evaluate how the experiences you feel are related to your spiritual practice. And in the case of hot dogs, we have numerous executives who you can get Michael Moore to interview about the history of their industry.

The step of communal confirmation is critical because, although it is important to trust ourselves, it also requires that we learn the many ways we can deceive ourselves (what I call in Chapter 3 the "wiles of the self"). That's the real challenge. Let's face it, if you're anything like me, it would be far more comfortable to continue deceiving yourself and pretending someone else has all the answers. In the late 1990s, I left a university faculty position and spent 7 years as an administrator. This move changed my relationship to a lot of the faculty who had once considered me, if not a friend, at least a harmless acquaintance. After I was put in control of the budget one of them came up to me and said "you know you can be a real pain in the ass" to which I responded "I know but I'm very good at hiding that from myself so please don't ruin it." In this book, I refer to what is called *shadow work* in Integral Theory. It is a concise way to explore your shadow aspects or in my words, the things you're really good at hiding from yourself. Next I take you on a tour of this and the other three perspectives of Integral Theory, as well as discuss relevant treatment issues and how the quadrants personally impact mental health professionals.

A Closer Look at the Quadrants and Related Treatment Issues

The most well-known symbol of the Integral Model is a pair of intersecting lines forming four quadrants, as shown in Fig. 1.1.

There are many ways to explain this, but let's get you a little more involved first. Imagine the quadrant diagram flat on the floor then imagine yourself sitting down right on the point where the two lines intersect. As you sit at this Integral crossroads imagine that you are uniquely positioned to see all aspects of your being. You can see them flowing from/through your body and mind like colored ribbons of life force. In one sense this is what is happening all the time and the quadrants is a model to capture it. Now let's elaborate. In Fig. 1.2 we see the four quadrants of the Integral Model labeled.

In Fig. 1.2, I have simply added some labels to the crossroads. These labels act as compass points for different aspects of your being. Now let's explore these quadrants, these aspects of your being.

Welcome to the Matrix: The Upper-Left Quadrant

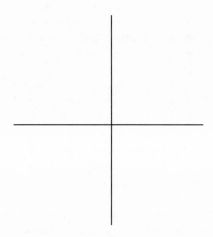

Figure 1.1. The intersecting lines of the Integral Model.

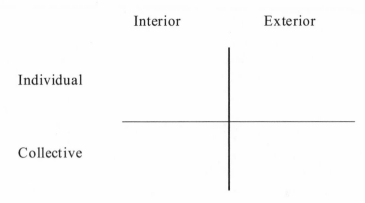

Figure 1.2. The four quadrants of Integral Theory.

Now quickly look at the last figure and again imagine you're sitting on the inter-section of the two lines. If this page were flat on the floor the words "interior" and "exterior" would be directly behind you and the lower quadrants in front of you. Ok, now that you're oriented, let's play some Integral "Twister." From where you're sitting on the crossroads twist to your left and place your left hand into the upper-left quadrant. This quadrant represents your subjective, phenom-enological world and is the focus of most psychotherapy. As you contemplate this aspect of your being you contemplate those things you consider "I."

Now in this imaginary game of Integral Twister, you are facing away from the upper-left quadrant. This is my effort to symbolize the reality that much of what is in this quadrant is not an object of our awareness (just like in the Integral Twister game the quadrant is barely an object of visual aware-ness). This quadrant includes your hopes, dreams, sense of self, and values, but also an important element referred to in Integral terms as your shadow.[35] This quadrant contains raw psychological experiences, literal dreams that occur dur-ing sleep as well as peak or spiritual experiences. This is the quadrant of the first-person perspective where everything is ultimately "I" (although you can pretend it isn't and make it "other" turning what is "I" into "you" or "it"). In Gestalt therapy we ask clients "what are you most aware of right now?" Stop reading and answer the question.

Really, try it: "What are you most aware of right now?"

Chances are your awareness centered on thoughts, feelings, physical sensa-tions, or maybe some combination but as you reflected on the question you had a psychological experience that is the hallmark of the upper-left quadrant.

In the movie *The Matrix* the main character is awakened from a computer-generated reality that is wired into his nervous system by machines that have

taken over the world. Upon awakening, he is stunned almost into psychosis
to realize he has been living in a dream world. The world he believed to be
true in every fiber of his being was nothing more than a computer-generated
dreamscape.[36] This is an experience many people have in psychotherapy. Things
they thought were flesh-and-blood real turn out to be ephemeral psychological
interpretations they were co-creating (remember that phrase?). A man who is
dependent on alcohol "hits bottom" and realizes his whole life revolves around
his relationship to drinking. A woman who believed herself to be wholesome
and achievement-focused realizes she has "stabbed in the back" dozens of co-
workers to advance her own career. A teenager whose sister died of cancer 4
years ago realizes she is suicidal because she blames herself for her sister's death.
In many ways, the perspective of the upper-left quadrant can indeed be like
living in a dream world.

Psychologists and other mental health therapists spend most of their time
exploring this quadrant with clients. "How do you feel today?" "Tell me about
your week," "What are you most aware of right now?" are common questions
in psychotherapy sessions and they point to another important characteristic of
this quadrant or perspective: It requires sharing and interpretation. The client's
style or type is also found in this quadrant. Sometimes the client's type or style
is what the source of the problem is (as in Personality Disorders, which we
cover in Chapter 5 on types and styles).

We say that clients suffering from depression are suffering from a depressed
state. The way the client interprets (co-creates) the depression is vitally important
in treatment. Interpreting and co-constructing reality leads to attributions. Even
committed behaviorists relented that attribution was critical to understanding
a client's depression and attribution can vary client to client.[37] For example,
clients who attribute their depression to things outside their control are far more
difficult to treat than those who see some aspects within their control.[38] Even
though a group of 10 clients may describe the same symptoms of depression,
each one will likely have a different story behind it, make different attributions,
and need a unique approach to treatment. Now of course, a person may not
know why he or she is depressed. As Freud noted, people rarely know how
they feel because they push unpleasant feelings out of awareness. Some clients,
because of early traumas, develop negative schemas or maps about the world
that remain largely unconscious. Until these become objects of awareness the
client will likely remain depressed.[39]

OBJECTS OF AWARENESS

This phrase *objects of awareness* is important in Integral Psychotherapy, so let's
review it in more detail. The training of psychotherapists is primarily focused
on making aspects of the client or the client's life objects of awareness. Why

therapists do this (and how) differs from theory to theory but essentially we are doing the same work. An object of awareness is something that we consistently have the ability to be aware of. This does not mean we are aware of it 24 hours a day, but that we *can* be aware of it when we so choose.[40] How that awareness manifests depends on the object. If you have a tendency to push shame out of awareness, part of therapy might include making your feelings of shame an object of awareness. If you suffer from a lack of awareness about how other people experience you, your interpersonal style may be something that becomes an object of awareness in therapy. In this sense, the object of awareness is a psychological experience that "registers" in this upper-left quadrant on the map of your being.

The things that are made objects of awareness are primarily things we identify with the upper-left quadrant even in couples and group therapy. For example, if I am doing couples therapy, I am working closely with the couple and the way each person perceives the other and the relationship. The aim of couples therapy is to help the couple understand themselves (upper-left quadrant) and craft the relationship into a sacred "we" space for both parties (lower-left quadrant). What is made an object of awareness may differ for each member of the couple. Again, let's pause for a short exercise.

"Hotspot" Exercise

Bring to mind a difficult or challenging event from your past—an emotional "hotspot." It doesn't have to be profoundly traumatic but just something that, at the time, was emotionally painful. For the sake of this exercise, let's assume it is a hotspot that you have resolved psychologically. Take a moment and think about the event then write down responses to the following questions:

1. What were your dominant emotions at the time the event occurred?

2. What were your dominant emotions in recollecting the event just now?

Don't forget to write down your responses.

When one of my clients (Robert) did this he recalled being badly beaten up by another boy in fourth grade. The boy had caught Robert off guard, thus he remembered the surprise and then the pain of the first few punches. Robert remembered being dazed, the taste of his own blood, and feeling profound shame when the beating was over. The shame was the dominant emotion immediately after. He came away with the image of himself as weak, an image that persisted until he won a few fights over the next several years. The dominant feelings at the time were fear and shame, but the dominant feeling as he recollected it 35 years later was sadness. The sadness was partially related to the fact that after the fight he had created an inner world that all but guaranteed he'd be looking for fights until he felt he'd won enough to restore his sense of "man-hood." In this sense, Robert had programmed his "matrix" to experience the world in terms of dominance and submission and that had real consequences for how he experienced himself and the world.   ?

In Robert's psychotherapy, this event (sauntered into) his awareness one session as he was working through a conflict he had with a male co-worker. He was confused about its relevance until I walked him through it. It is a variation of what we call a *transference reaction* and was first outlined by Freud in psychoanalysis. A transference reaction is when something from the past has such psychological power over us, we react to all similar events (and our therapists) in the present as if they *were* this event in the past repeating itself. Perhaps more astonishing than the power of the past event is that we recreate it unconsciously in the present.

Robert made the emotional connection that he felt bullied by the co-worker so he tended to respond aggressively to him (naturally exacerbating the existing tension). This was an important insight. He recalls walking out of the session amazed at the complexity of the mind and grateful for my skill. Immediately after that he totally forgot the episode, its relevance to his current life and proceeded to pick a fight that same day with his co-worker. He reported feeling really angry with me on his way home from work and wondered if he shouldn't find a better therapist.

In the next therapy session we started reviewing his memory of the fight between the two 10-year-old boys and his experience of having "forgotten" the whole thing within 24 hours of the session. He got even madder at me for bringing it up—more transference. After the session, he was more than a little embarrassed and wanted to go through it again so as to practice making this an object of awareness. So, we practiced recollecting the fight episode and how it may relate to his problems at work. Recall that when we have made something an object of awareness we can be aware of it when we *choose* to be. But this takes practice. One of the amazing things about our subjective, psychological realities is that we can have powerful insights one minute then act a minute later like the insight never happened.

Upper-Left Practice: Start a "Hotspots" Journal

A "hotspots" journal is a log of emotionally challenging life events that may have shaped the way you are experiencing the world and that, if they are really hotspots, you are likely to "forget." The hotspots can be years old or relatively recent. Each hotspot can be dealt with on three levels. The first is a simple, brief (no more than a paragraph) description of the event, your emotions at the time, and your emotions as you recollect it. The second and third levels are addressed later in the chapter on shadow work.

Getting Real: The Upper-Right Quadrant

Let's return to our game of Integral Twister. Go back to your imaginary position sitting at the intersection of the four quadrants in Fig. 1.2 with your left hand in the upper-left quadrant.

Seated as you are, you are likely staring at the upper-right quadrant. Imagine placing your right hand there. This quadrant captures the "exteriors" of you as an individual. The aspects of your being that arise in this quadrant include all aspects of your body (from brain cells to shoe size), behavior (from subtle facial expressions to kicking the dog), and what some believe to be your energy field, which includes several levels of energy expressed through the gross, subtle, and causal bodies.[41]

The upper-right quadrant is heavily emphasized in disciplines like biological psychiatry. If you watch television you may have noticed commercials for psychotropic medications. Such commercials were illegal until the late 1980s when congressional and senate representatives (who get a great deal of campaign money from pharmaceutical companies) repealed the laws and allowed direct-to-consumer (DTC) advertising (currently the United States and New Zealand are the only countries that allow such advertising). Most of these commercials are for antidepressant drugs that are used for a number of disorders ranging from depression to anxiety to Post-Traumatic Stress.

One sample commercial begins with a young man standing with his head against a wall wearing an anguished expression on his face. The narrator says something like *"Would have, should have, could have . . . is anxiety ruining your life? Well it doesn't have to."* Next the narrator names the medication being sold and makes the claim that it will improve your life. At the end of the commercial we see the same young man rising to applause at what looks like an awards dinner (the narrator chimes in *"your life is waiting"*). We also see the young protagonist of this commercial getting an eerie nod and grin from an older man who we can only assume is an oedipal representation of a company CEO or perhaps a Youngstown, Ohio mafia don. In a microsecond the narrator becomes the fastest-speaking human in the Kosmos and goes through a list of possible side effects including sexual dysfunction, diarrhea, headaches, and your eyeballs dropping out of your head onto the floor. Welcome to the brave new world of DTC advertising.

What you may not be aware of is that such commercials represent a long-standing battle between proponents of psychotropic medications who maintain that mental and emotional disorders like anxiety and depression are the result of a "chemical imbalance" and those who say they are the result of psychological factors like those I outlined in the last section on the upper-left quadrant. Some of the biological psychiatrists even go so far as to say that things like brain chemistry are "more real" than things like transference reactions. I recall a lunch conversation at a medical school with a renowned researcher in pharmacology. After listening to him talk for about 15 minutes on the role of gene expression[42] in depression, I foolishly interjected. I asked him why he hadn't discussed new research on the role of psychological factors like trauma in the way genes express themselves because there is evidence that psychological events (upper-left quadrant) can impact physical events (upper-right quadrant). He responded by asking me if I was saying psychological influences could be *just as* powerful as the genetic map endowed to us by our parents. When I answered "yes" his parting comment was "get real." I'd sort of hoped for a more sophisticated response given his expertise.

The luncheon dialogue was a good example of where academics and practitioners often "choose sides." From an Integral perspective *both sides* have a piece of the truth and the more truths you explore (the more quadrants you consider) the more effective treatment is going to be. Genetic expression and brain chemistry are "real" *as are* psychological events that in turn affect the physical body including the ways genes express. Although the "chemical imbalance" theory of depression is just that, a theory, some clients experience life-giving relief from symptoms of depression by taking medication. In other words, we don't have a baseline for individual brain chemistry to say whether or not it is "balanced,"[43] but we do know that many people are helped when they take medications that effect changes in their brain chemistry. This is different than saying that because a person experienced relief after taking a medication the medication "restored" some mythical balance in their brain chemistry. That would be like saying that people who smoke marijuana feel better when they are stoned because they have corrected a cannabis deficit. What the pot-smoker and user of psychotropic medication have done is intervened chemically (upper-right quadrant) to bring about changes in their psychological state (upper-left quadrant).

We don't know why most psychotropic medications affect changes in mood but we know they can be beneficial for some clients. It would be foolish and cruel to rule out treatment with medication in the case of someone experiencing severe psychological suffering. Medications can provide wonderful relief for some (but not all) clients. From an Integral perspective, in such cases medication creates a chemical "window of opportunity" for clients to feel strong enough to deal with things like psychological trauma. In more extreme cases, medications allow contact with consensual reality. What is done with that contact therapeutically and the choices the client is able to make once contact is established can then be the emphasis of treatment.

We know that the human brain is a complex organ and I hope you won't be too disappointed when I share that we really know very little about it. We are learning more and an Integral approach is able to embrace what we have gleaned from the neurosciences and make a place for it in our map of what it means to be human. One historical problem that arises when you understand the different domains of the upper-left and upper-right quadrants is the "mind–brain problem" and it warrants some explanation before going on to discuss the last two quadrants.

The Mind–Brain Problem

Being aware of the mind–brain issue is one example of being integrally informed. Let's pause for another exercise.

Mind and Brain Exercise

Think of a time that you were suffering psychologically. Write a brief description of your symptoms (e.g., anxiety, depression, panic) and, if you sought treatment, what type of treatment did you seek and how effective was it?

The mind–brain problem addresses whether or not the mind and brain are distinct entities and what their relationship is. Integral psychotherapists value the importance of both but this position is not as common as you would think. Consider the exercise at the beginning of this section. When I do this with groups in workshops, many participant responses emphasize either mind or brain. One woman told me she had done every type of therapy possible over an 8-year period to deal with her depression. It was only with the arrival of Prozac that she got relief. Thus, she concluded, she had something wrong with her brain. Another man shared that he had been on six different antidepressants over a 3-year period and none helped him feel better. It was only after meeting a therapist who addressed his lack of meaning in life that he experienced significant relief. In between these types of responses are people who say they had tried both medication and therapy but were uncertain which one really contributed most to their recovery. Their uncertainty makes sense in that it mirrors the ambiguous results of research on mind and brain.

Currently, knowledge of both the mind and the brain is incomplete. Consider being asked to define "the mind." At first glance, this seems simple enough—"Mind is, well, it's sort of, it feels like, umm . . . look; I know it when I feel it!" Okay, maybe it's not as easy as it first appears. In Integral Psychotherapy the perspective we experience with our minds is reflected in the upper-left quadrant. As hard as it is to admit, to specifically define mind requires a leap of faith in some theory you believe most accurately reflects the reality of what the mind is. Just as an Integral approach embraces what we know about mind and brain, there are hypotheses that focus on one, the other, or both and it is to these hypotheses we now turn.

The Side-Effect Hypothesis of Mind and Brain

The first hypothesis discussed here I call the "side-effect" hypothesis. In science and philosophy it goes by the name *epiphenomenon hypothesis.*[44] This explanation of the relationship between mind and brain borders on what I call a fundamentalist materialist approach to the human mind. The basic idea is that all things, including your mind, derive from other things (namely your brain) that can be objectively observed and measured. In short, this hypothesis states that the mind derives from the brain or is a "side effect" of having a developed brain. This hypothesis was popularized by the 19th-century biologist Thomas Huxley (known as "Darwin's Bulldog" for his fervent support of Darwin's theory of evolution). More recently, neuroscientists like Antonio Damasio[45] and neurophilosophers like Patricia and Paul Churchland[46] have set forth varieties of the theory. Patricia Churchland has even engaged in dialogues with the Dalai Lama about the nature of mind. In one such dialogue, the Dalai Lama suggested that to assert that mind was dependent on brain for its existence was like asserting food was dependent on stomachs for existence.[47] He showed her!

Advocates of the side-effect argument would support it by first noting a brain structure responsible for a particular function (e.g., like the relationship of Wernicke's and Broca's areas to language). Next they would point out that if either Broca's or Wernicke's area is damaged, language is impaired. The reasoning is that one's sense of self (one's mind) is a consequence of brain functioning and if those parts of the brain responsible for the sense of self are damaged, the sense of self would either be impaired or vanish just as language becomes impaired if Broca's or Wernicke's area is damaged.

A frequent example used to explain the side-effect hypothesis is the 19th-century case of Phineas Gage. Gage was a railroad construction worker who had a tamping iron driven through his skull as the result of an explosion. Although he miraculously survived the accident, his personality became so altered that those who knew him say Gage was a different person after the accident. From the fundamentalist materialist perspective, Gage had changed because the areas of his brain responsible for maintenance and expression of personality changed when damaged in the accident.

The pharmaceutical companies who produce the commercials you see about antidepressants constantly allude to this explanation of the relationship between mind and brain with regard to depression and other psychological symptoms. If psychological symptoms like depression or anxiety mean something is wrong with your brain, the first thing you should do is get a pill to correct it. Many people do just this despite the fact that the most conservative treatment protocols for depression recommend both medication and psychotherapy.[48]

THE "TWO-SUBSTANCE" HYPOTHESIS OF MIND AND BRAIN

The "two-substance" hypothesis of mind and brain (also called the dual-substance hypothesis) is dated to the philosopher Rene DesCartes who we introduced in the section on modernity (the two-effects hypothesis predates DesCartes as it exists to some extent in both Hindu and Buddhist philosophy). DesCartes' proposed the existence of a divine being that created two effects. One effect (related to mind) was thinking things (*res cogitans*) and the other effect material things (like bodies and brains) that extend into the material realm (*res extensa*). The thinking things were not thought to exist in time and space and could not be externally observed. The extended beings were believed to exist in time and space and be externally observable. Somehow the thinking things got inside of the material things until such time as the material things died. At that point the thinking things were liberated from the material things in the way the soul is described being liberated from the body at death. As you can imagine, there is a lot of resistance to this theory among biological psychiatrists.

One exception is transpersonal psychiatrist Stanislav Grof, who summarized the two-substance hypothesis stating the relationship of mind and brain is like that of television transmission waves to a television. Grof critiqued the side-effect hypothesis noting that if you break the picture tube of a television, the broadcast waves cannot be totally expressed through the damaged television but the waves still exist. Equally, if damage to Broca's or Wernicke's areas of the brain causes difficulties with language, it does not necessarily mean that the mind seeking to express speech has its origin in the brain it is trying to express through. Grof sided with the Dalai Lama basically concluding that consciousness is a basic building block of the universe that may interact or co-arise with brains but is not a side effect of them.[49]

AN INTEGRAL UNDERSTANDING OF MIND AND BRAIN

As stated previously, the Integral understanding of mind and brain is that they are both aspects of your own being that arise together, mind being the interior aspect and brain being the exterior aspect. You can no more have one without the other than you can have a burrito with an empty tortilla. This understanding is not limited to Integal psychotherapists. Nobel prize winner Eric Kandel has done groundbreaking research that links life experience to changes in gene expression. The American Psychiatric Association named Kandel a Distinguished Fellow for his work colloquially labeled "mind meets brain." His conclusion based on decades of research is that mind and brain can and do inform each other.[50]

Let's review the "two-substance" hypothesis in the context of what we know about depression. Until a year or two ago, well-educated psychiatrists could still be heard discussing depression as the result of a chemical imbalance in the brain. Correct the imbalance and the depression should remit. But it doesn't happen for up to 50% of the people who take antidepressants. In fact, in a meta-analysis of all the antidepressant trials in the FDA's database, it was discovered that the antidepressants were no better than placebo in more than 50% of the trials.[51]

Through decades of brain research we have learned that one of many effects from antidepressants is an increase in a brain cell nutrient and growth factor called brain-derived neurotrophic factor (*BDNF*—sometimes referred to in the plural brain-derived neurotrophic factors). This result only became observable once we had technologies sophisticated enough to peer inside neurons and track changes related to taking medication. What we have also discovered, however, is that this same change—increase in brain cell nutrients—is correlated with physical exercise.[52] Other brain changes thought to result only from medication also have been seen to result from interpersonal psychotherapy.[53] Both these findings suggest that what we do with our minds (whether intend to exercise or make things objects of awareness in psychotherapy) is much related to what arises in our physical brains.

Given that researchers with the academic clout of Eric Kandel are articulating an Integral understanding of mind and brain, why are so many educated therapists still taking outdated sides in this debate on mind and brain? Part of the answer comes from understanding the lower two quadrants in our four-quadrant diagram.

All Together Now: The Lower-Left Quadrant

Let's return to the game of Integral Twister. Recall your position at the intersection of the two lines in Fig. 1.2 facing the lower quadrants. You've got an imaginary left hand in the upper-left quadrant and right hand in the upper-right quadrant.

Now imagine rocking up on your knees, glancing over your left shoulder, gazing into the lower-left quadrant and sliding an imaginary foot into it. Where we can say that the upper-left is the domain of the subjective aspects of your being, the lower-left quadrant is the intersubjective domain. Simply put, this aspect of your being reflects what Integral psychotherapists refer to as "we" space—the space where two or more people share things like understandings, beliefs, and values. Gazing into this quadrant you see things like your sense of community, the shared understandings in your family of origin, your current relationships as well as the beliefs and values you share with other people including shared beliefs about race, ethnicity, and other aspects of culture. You might even see how language itself can liberate or constrain your understanding of life (while Eskimos don't really have 200 words or phrases for snow, most of us have at least three for the phenomenon of a plumber's pants riding too low when he bends over).[54]

In Integral Psychotherapy, the lower-left quadrant is also where we represent the therapeutic relationship between client and therapist. When therapy is "working," you should have a sense that your therapist not only understands your life cognitively but can actually "feel into" your suffering, joys, hopes, dreams, and yes; your failures. Psychotherapist Stephen Schoen once said that the therapeutic relationship was a "sacred ground" and that the magic of one human being so fully engaging and understanding another is a high-point of human experience.[55] Although sharing life through the intersubjective magic of this quadrant is one source of human joy, it is also a source of suffering. Clients who have lived in abusive homes and relationships know all too well how being vulnerable in relationship can result in others abusing your trust. This is the profane aspect of our intersubjective being and one of the risks associated with intimacy and shared understanding. Going back to our example of depression, there are whole schools of thought developed about the interpersonal nature of depression and how interpersonal situations can make one vulnerable to feelings of depression as well as be the cure for depression.[56] Additionally, the research on cognitive therapy now shows that irrational beliefs linked to depression usually are fueled by unconscious negative maps or schemas of life that are related to early experiences of abandonment or neglect.[57] Even more astonishing, it now seems that the schemas we create are related to the ways that our brains function—it seems that we can impact the level of brain cell nutrients available in our central nervous systems with the types of thoughts we regularly engage in.[58]

Now let's return to our question posed earlier: Why do so many educated therapists still take outdated sides in this debate on mind and brain? It seems that many times the shared beliefs of professional groups override the individual therapist and that same therapist finds it increasingly difficult to voice legitimate concerns because of the pressure to conform. This has to do in great part with the impact of shared beliefs on the individual. The psychoanalyst Erich Fromm wrote that a powerful influence on the development of our personalities is the beliefs of groups we want acceptance from. For Fromm, we are constantly balancing the tension between who we feel we are or want to be (upper-left quadrant) and the beliefs of groups we want acceptance from (lower-left quadrant).[59] One of the most intense periods of this balancing act is in adolescence when peer groups become the primary object of reference for developing teens; however this balancing act continues throughout our lives. For an example one need look no further than the academic and professional groups that make up the mental health and related professions.

The most common types of training for psychotherapists are psychiatry (which is a specialization in medicine), psychology, counseling, and social work (there also are marriage and family therapists and chemical dependency specialists and in some states these specialties are subsumed into the licenses of the latter four disciplines, whereas in other states they hold their own licenses). With the exception of the medical training in psychiatry, each of these professions draws from the same psychological knowledge base, has a similar scope of practice, but uses different training models. Counselor training is said to produce "educator/

practitioners," the majority of psychology training produces "scientist-practitio-ners," and social work uses an ecological model that looks more at sociocultural contexts. In an ideal circumstance, psychiatry uses a biopsychosocial approach[60] that asserts that biology, psychology, and social context cannot be reduced to one another. That being said, most psychiatric training is not the ideal and focuses more on biology than psychology or social context.

In competing for status and third-party insurance reimbursement, each nonmedical psychotherapy profession (social work, counseling, psychology) claims to be different from the others despite the knowledge base and scope of practice being essentially the same. In some counselor training programs, students are forbidden from taking courses in the psychology department because psychologists are viewed as competitors and (in the minds of the more bizarre faculty) the enemy. The attachment to the partial truths of their training models keeps many of these professions "at loggerheads" rather then viewing themselves as complementary.[61]

It is interesting that the claims of success for these training models are not supported by research. For example, the Boulder Model in psychology supposedly trains psychologists to be scientist-practitioners. Studies spanning a decade have concluded that the majority of psychologists end up being either scientists or practitioners even though they were supposed to be both.[62] What happened? One answer is that the climate of academia and the economic marketplace of psycho-therapy make it easier to focus on science in both research and practice.

Competition between mental health professionals rests to a great degree on the extent to which each profession is perceived as a "hard science." The phrase "hard science" is a complimentary term in academia and usually refers to one of the natural sciences (physics, chemistry, biology) characterized by scientific method and research with quantifiable data. The phrase "soft science" is a derogatory term that refers to something that really should have been relegated to the philosophy department or the trash heap depending on who you talk to (William James was said by some of his contemporaries to be a "fuzzy-headed philosopher," not a "scientist").[63] Thus, to be considered a hard scientist is a disciplinary aspiration in academia and many professional associations of psychotherapists. This fuels a dynamic (said to be akin to professional penis envy)[64] where disciplines work to be perceived as, if not a hard science, at least as relying on quantifiable, objective measures, measures that serve well as tools in quadrants like the upper-right but not so well in quadrants like the upper-left.

This dynamic dates back to Freud as Freud himself was a member of the Helmholtz Society. The society was named after German physician and physicist Hermann von Helmholtz and dedicated to applying the laws of Newtonian physics in other disciplines. Helmholtz's student Wilhelm Wundt is held out by most psychologists as the founder of experimental psychology even though the mystic Gustav Fechner has an equal claim to the title (mystics are, well, embarrassing in disciplines trying to look scientific).[65] In the late 19th and early 20th centuries, as psychology was growing as a discipline in the United States, many academicians were embarrassed by pioneers like William James who were trying to develop methods to explore the mind (upper-left quadrant). Such embarrassment won the day resulting in the ascendancy of Behaviorism as the dominant school of psychology for most of the 20th century.

The current manifestation of professional penis envy is the rush to accept all the theories of biological psychiatry that state or imply all psychological symptoms are manifestations of brain malfunction (upper-right quadrant). In the current climate, psychotherapy professionals seeking legitimacy from their peers and competitors will emphasize the role of the brain in psychological suffering as being more "real" than the role of the mind. As many professionals know, the yearning to be accepted by those holding the most political clout has resulted in all mental health professionals using the diagnostic manual of psychiatry (the American Psychiatric Association's *Diagnostic and Statistical Manual of Mental Disorders*—colloquially labeled *DSM*). Wellness-oriented subdisciplines like Counseling Psychology that began by differentiating from the pathology-oriented Clinical Psychology have ended up right back in the hall knocking at the door of the pathology-based training models they sought to distinguish themselves from.[66] Again, third-party insurance reimbursement that also relies on the *DSM* was a main driver. The *DSM* is not the only diagnostic manual in existence. There also are psychodynamic and family dynamic diagnostic manuals, however, because these are not afforded the legitimacy of the *DSM* they are rarely used in training or practice.[67] We return to the *DSM* at the end of this chapter.

Here we have an excellent example of how each quadrant can impact the others and how emphasizing one at the expense of the others will guarantee problems. In seeking the acceptance of the leaders in a profession like psychology, many psychologists defer to the leaders' shared belief that psychology will be more politically powerful (taken more *seriously* by people with power) if it focuses on the upper-right quadrant like its cousin discipline biological psychiatry. Wilber referred to partial pursuit of truth through either the right and left quadrants as the right-hand and left-hand paths to truth. The right-hand path (biological psychiatry) emphasizes the objective, measurable aspects of the individual and group, whereas the left-hand path emphasizes the subjective, phenomenological aspects that require disclosure and interpretation.

The power of Integral Psychotherapy is that it recognizes the importance of both paths rather than emphasizing one over the other. Because all the quadrants are aspects of your own being they arise together and impact one another. Because they impact one another (changes in brain chemistry can provide temporary changes in states of mind) it is tempting to try to *reduce* one to the other (states of mind *are nothing more than* brain states). This is what we call a *category error*; trying to collapse all or most of the quadrants into one or two others. A common manifestation in Western society (including Western approaches to mental health) is trying to collapse the left-hand quadrants into the right-hand quadrants. Where the right-hand quadrants represent objective perspectives, the left-hand quadrants represent perspectives that are subjective and require interpretation. Even though some psychotherapists like to present themselves as "scientists" who only use "objectively validated treatments," this view itself is a belief that is frequently proselytized in the professional associations to which the therapist belongs.

Professional associations for psychotherapists can be thought of as akin to families that impart values. The leaders in the professions are the parents and the newer members take the role of children receiving the values of their elders (if not their betters!). Just as Freud said our over-I (Super Ego) is a combination of our ideal self-image and the rules of authorities, so the conscience of a professional association offers members the seed of what an ideal therapist is and the values and beliefs that will bring that seed to blossom. Now let's return to how the shared values of the lower-left quadrant can impact clients.

Values as Shared Beliefs

Values also are an important component of the lower-left quadrant. I have found that a good indicator of a client's values is their behavior. Here the upper-right quadrant reveals much about one's affiliations in the lower-left. One part of many clients' shadows (the things we hide from ourselves) is their true values. Consider the case of Jack. He came to see me because of his failure to hold a job for more than a year. Educated in computer-automated manufacturing (CAM), he was talented and knew the industry but drifted from position to position without much commitment. He was able to secure new CAM positions because of his talent but his career drifting was catching up with him as two companies did not hire him because of the short length of time he had spent in previous positions.

One way to understand a client's values is to find out who his heroes are or, at least, who are the people he admires. Jack, a political conservative, had a list of heroes, including General Douglass MacArthur, Nixon advisor Patrick Buchanan, William Buckley, and an uncle of his who was killed in the Korean War. When I asked him what these men had in common Jack replied "Loyalty. MacArthur was loyal to the country, Buchanan to Nixon, Buckley to conservatism, and my uncle to the platoon he commanded." As we discussed loyalty, it was clear that Jack's intersubjective experience growing up included a lot of family emphasis on the values of loyalty. With this said I wondered aloud how loyalty figured into his work life. "That's easy," Jack replied, "not one of those bastards who hired me ever showed me any loyalty—they'd just let me quit after a few months!" Now we were getting somewhere. In subsequent discussion it was clear that Jack expected counteroffers when he threatened to quit a job, even if he had only been at the job 3 months. Because this was too soon for most employers, they simply let him leave.

Although Jack knew the values his family expected of him, there was a huge gap between those and what he really valued. Because one of the values Jack did hold was that family values were important, he gave them lip service but interpreted them radically differently than anyone else in his family. Jack also had a maverick, mercenary streak that he kept safely tucked away in his shadow. Like many of his heroes, he really preferred to go his own way regardless of what those in charge wanted. This of course led to some tense interactions in the workplace as well as in his personal relationships. For Jack, making those "shadow values" an object of awareness was the first step in the therapeutic journey that included experiencing the positive side of his mercenary streak when he went into business for himself.

The "We" of Psychotherapy

I want to end this section with a more detailed discussion of the import of the lower-left quadrant in the actual psychotherapy relationship. Recall Stephen Schoen's sense of the "sacred we" of psychotherapy that he believed characterizes the relationship and calls into action healing factors. What are these healing factors? Some psychotherapists like Carl Rogers felt it was appropriate to include among them a nonpossessive love between the client and therapist. This love is expressed as compassion for the client and an acceptance of the client that Rogers called unconditional positive regard.[68]

If you watch demonstrations by expert therapists from diverse theoretical backgrounds, this nonpossessive love is a dominant variable. The late psychiatrist Scott Peck described love as "the will to extend one's self for the purpose of nurturing one's own or another's spiritual growth."[69] It is in the heart of the "we" space of psychotherapy that we encounter the other as self. If the relationship is developing in a healthy manner (e.g., outside the boundaries of intimacy reserved for friends and lovers) the client and therapist experience an awe-inspiring connection with one another. Carl Rogers included this in what he called the "greenhouse effect" of psychotherapy. In this effect, his core conditions for therapy, which include nonpossessive love, act as a greenhouse for the wilted being of the client who is nourished by a force that is, for lack of a better term, spiritual.

Intersubjectivity Exercise

Describe your most sacred "we" space. In a paragraph or two describe the space (who you share it with, where it occurs) and the impact of this sacred "we" space on you. Do you get as much of it as you'd like? If not, how might you increase it?

So how much "we" space do you have in your life? Relationship is one of the prime movers of humanity. We do things for love relationships, work relationships, our relationships with God—you name a motivation in human life and there is likely a relationship involved. One of the challenges of the 21st century is maintaining relationships in a fast-paced world. In Integral Psychotherapy, we use Integral Life Practice (ILP) for self-care. I discuss this later in the book but suffice it to say that ILP has multiple modules including how we deal with relationship.

The Lower-Right Quadrant

One final round of Integral Twister: Going back to your imaginary position on the intersection of the lines in the figure, look toward your right shoulder into the lower-right quadrant and slide your remaining foot into it.

Gazing into this quadrant, you might see aspects of your being that are related to social wholes or the exteriors of the collective. What are social wholes? Well, they include material, economic, and social aspects of groups you are part of. The physical group of your family, social institutions you are part of (e.g., the educational or economic institutions), and the material means of social exchange like money or sex (or both in the case of Las Vegas).

In recent decades, psychotherapists have begun to pay more attention to the social whole that clients are embedded in. Psychologist James Garbarino works with young felons who live in what he calls "toxic environments." A toxic environment is one where a person is chronically exposed to "social poisoning," which renders the individual a "psychological asthmatic," unable to function psychologically due the sheer weight of social poisons he or she has soaked up.[70] In the Integral approach the quadrants all arise together and what happens in one quadrant goes with what is happening in others.

For example, one client, Jerome, was raised by a single mother who was addicted to various illicit drugs. She would trade sex for drugs with an endless string of "boyfriends" who were dealers. Her drug dependence left Jerome neglected although he managed to survive his first 10 years in this situation. At age 10 Jerome witnessed the murder of his mother by a man who had come to rob her of her drugs. When he was 15, Jerome shot and killed another 15-year-old boy. As Garbarino points out, crimes like Jerome's are horrible tragedies but they cannot be divorced from Jerome's 15-year immersion in a toxic environment. This idea or hypothesis has been clearly supported in task force publications by the American Psychological Association.[71]

Similarly, you cannot fully understand yourself without understanding your role in and your access to the media of social exchange. Access to the media of social exchange (money, positions of power, educational institutions) is a predictor of achievement. Take money for an example. Although money may not buy happiness, it certainly buys things that can increase comfort and decrease stress. Psychologist and stand-upphilosopher Robert Anton Wilson refers to money as biosurvival tickets.[72] These are the tickets we exchange for things that facilitate our survival. Although money is a symbol, it is a powerful one. Most of us, if threatened with job loss, respond with signs of physical stress as if our very life were being threatened. Here again is an example of how the quadrants arise together. If money is a psychologically accepted symbol of wealth needed to survive (upper-left) based on the shared beliefs about money in your culture (lower-left), then if business is conducted in a manner that threatens your job (lower-right), you suffer anger and anxiety from stimulation of your parasympathetic nervous system (upper-right).

In an interview with Warren Bennis, Wilber noted that the way we do business in the lower-right quadrant is one of the primary determinants of the average mode of consciousness in the upper-left quadrant.[73] Simply put, this means that the social structures we are embedded in play a large role in the developmental center of gravity of our society. Because this center of gravity attracts members of a society, we get a lot of support up to it but experience a gravitational pull backward when we try to exceed it. This is particularly important where human growth is concerned. In two books examining the role of psychedelics and their relationship to society, Daniel Pinchbeck makes a convincing case that the reason for prohibition of psychedelics is not their inherent danger but the threat they pose to the power brokers in a society whose center of gravity is based on excessive consumerism.[74] If addiction can be thought of as unhealthy attachment, then consumerism feeds on such attachment driving purchases regardless of their necessity. If a psychologically stable person takes psychedelics, one of the more common experiences is self-knowledge that has been associated with decreased addictions of many types.[75] Pinchbeck notes that if a majority of people had access to compounds that might allow them to be happier without things like consumer culture, this could shift the center of gravity away from consumerism to a more self-aware economic model.

The main point here is one that I echo with every new client: The biggest risk in psychotherapy is that you may change and the changes you experience may not be welcomed by other people in your life, culture, or society. In some senses, psychotherapy is a subversive activity. The implication of this is far more staggering than your individual sense of well-being. An important point about the quadrant model I just summarized is that *these aspects of your being arise simultaneously and impact one another.* Psychological suffering is an all-quadrant affair. Change anything in one of the quadrants and you change the self-system nested in those quadrants. I have already hinted at the implications of this. The way we do business (lower-right) can impact our psychological (upper-left) and physical (upper-right) health. The need for affiliation and acceptance by groups (lower-left) powerfully shapes the way we act (upper-right) and feel (upper-left).

The structure of our physiology (upper-right) determines artifacts of society (lower-left) as well as the way we make meaning as individuals (upper-left) and groups (lower-left). We could go on with examples but I want to bring it back to psychotherapy.

In Integral Psychotherapy, because we address all aspects of your being, we leave open-ended the impact of a good therapeutic relationship combined with a commitment to growth, to truth, to that which is real. There are always true and false prophets (for-profit prophets) with us proclaiming everything from messages of impeding doom (the hype around the year 2012) to a need for self-transformation for the good of the whole (the Christian message of how God's love can transform the world). Some prophetic cries seem baseless and even silly (harmonic convergence), whereas others seem to deserve our attention (depletion of energy resources and shift of the magnetic poles). Author Daniel Pinchbeck recently wrote that the current *intensifying global crisis is the material expression of a psycho-spiritual process, forcing our transition to a new and more intensified state of awareness.*[76] For Pinchbeck, the global crisis can be attenuated by making the forces at work in ourselves objects of awareness and channeling them. Whether or not you agree that there is a global crisis, my point is that Integral Psychotherapy holds promise for reconnecting the individual with not only themselves but with the whole world, the whole Kosmos because that Kosmos as reflected in the quadrants is really a part of self.[77]

The Integral Heuristic and *DSM*

In this final section, I address the relationship between Integral Psychotherapy and the way psychological suffering is currently diagnosed. From a heuristic viewpoint we might ask, "Is the Integral approach to psychotherapy totally different from all systems that have come before?" In some ways the answer is "yes" and we explore those in the upcoming chapters. In another important way the answer is "no" and we can see this through direct comparison to the current nosology of psychiatric disorders, the *DSM*-IV-TR (Fourth Edition, Text Revised). The history of the *DSM* shows the evolution of a diagnostic scheme from the *DSM*-I and *DSM*-II, which were heavily based in upper-left quadrant subjective psychodynamic and psychobiologic models, to the *DSM*-II,I which was a radical shift to what is called the five-axis diagnosis.

The five-axis diagnosis, which is still the central feature of *DSM*-IV-TR, includes the following components:

> Axis I: This axis is for the primary mental/emotional disorders, as
>   well as what is called the principle or primary diagnosis, for
>   which a person seeks treatment.

Axis II: This axis is for ego-syntonic symptom clusters[78] like personality disorders or mental retardation. Also, defensive styles are described on this axis.

Axis III: This axis is for physician-confirmed allopathic or organic diseases (meaning diseases/problems originating with some pathophysiologic variable like high blood pressure or diabetes).

Axis IV: On this axis, the clinician lists variables in psychosocial functioning that may be contributing to the symptom cluster being treated. Examples include family dysfunction and socioeconomic issues.

Axis V: This is called the Global Assessment of Functioning (GAF) and is a 100-point scale on which the client's current functioning is assessed. The manual gives guidance on point ranges for everything from normal functioning to severe pathology.

Reviewing these axes we can see that Axes I and II reflect variables in the upper-left quadrant, Axis III reflects variables that would show up in the upper-right quadrant, Axis IV reflects variables that would show up in the lower-right and lower-left quadrants, and Axis V offers a quasi-developmental scale wherein the clinician can show the course of symptoms over time.

The five-axis system is the work primarily of Robert Spitzer who headed the *DSM*-III task force. It was in part inspired by the biopsychosocial model discussed earlier.[79] He reflected that the *DSM* was making psychiatry a laughing stock of sorts in medical schools because so much of the early systems were not grounded in science. The *DSM* is called a diagnostic and statistical manual because the symptom clusters, beginning in *DSM*-III and continuing to present, are the result of statistical exploration of results from field trials for symptom clusters. The symptoms reported by clinicians as clustering together are the ones that make the final listing in the manual. This is called *categorical psychiatry* because the statistical analysis of symptoms results in clusters that form categories of mental/emotional disorders.

There are benefits to the categorical approach. It gives clinicians a common vocabulary with which to work across the different mental health professions and it provides an empirical basis for the creation of dependent measures to assess symptoms severity. Critics of the categorical approach note that most human behavior/symptoms occur on various continua and the categorical approach does not allow this reality to be reflected.[80] Using continua is referred to as a dimensional approach to diagnosis. Also, one tragedy of insurance-driven treatment is that, despite the almost integral flavor of the five axes taken together, the axis emphasized on insurance forms is Axis I because no other axes are considered reimbursable for treatment rendered.

Another drawback to the categorical model is that it has in part supported the delusion that psychopathology is, rather than an all-quadrant affair, in many cases a one-quadrant affair—namely the upper-right quadrant. Biological psychiatry and pharmaceutical companies have spent decades and millions of dollars in search of underlying biological causes to mental and emotional disorders. The recent task force on the upcoming *DSM*-V (due out around 2013) has refuted this emphatically stating "the field of psychiatry has thus far failed to identify a single neurobiological phenotypic marker or gene that is useful in making a diagnosis of a major psychiatric disorder or for predicting response to psychopharmacological treatment . . . current classification in psychiatry therefore resembles the medicine of 50 to 100 years ago, before the underlying pathophysiology of many disease processes was understood.[81]

Therefore, we are standing at the edge of a critical juncture in how psychopathology and thus psychotherapy are conceived. I believe this juncture is marked by the rise of a mainstream Integral understanding that will greatly enhance the effectiveness of therapy. It is in part toward this understanding that this book is addressed. At this point, *DSM*-V appears to be moving closer to an Integral approach as that approach has been outlined here in this first heuristic understanding of how to use the model in psychotherapy. *DSM*-V task forces are examining how to understand mind–brain interactions,[82] as well as the impact of relational processes on the mind of the individual.[83] Additionally, the *DSM*-V task force on chemical dependence is re-examining the benefit of dimensional versus categorical diagnostic criteria, the role of typologies in chemical dependence, and the developmental considerations for different types of drug dependence.[84] It appears that a hole has been punched through the Kosmic horizon where psychotherapy is concerned. We need only follow through to usher in a new vision for treatment.

I hope this chapter has offered a user-friendly introduction to some Integral concepts that will be further unpacked in subsequent chapters. Now you've been introduced to the model, had some time to reflect on what psychotherapy is, considered the mind–brain problem, gotten a more detailed tour through the quadrants, and considered how Integral Theory may related to *DSM*. The rest of the book is really an elaboration of the concepts addressed in this chapter.

Chapter 2: Perspectives and Psychotherapy: This chapter discusses four main uses of perspectives (and quadrants) in Integral Psychotherapy

Chapter 3: The Integral Self-System and Ego Development in Psychotherapy

Chapter 4: Lines and Levels of Development: The Reality of Altitude

2

Perspectives and Psychotherapy

R. Elliott Ingersoll

U nderstanding perspectives is one of the most important aspects of Integral Theory as well as Integral Psychotherapy. Integral offers a unique
understanding of perspectives not to be confused with earlier philosophical
approaches to perspectivism that, however admirable for their time, are more
general than what is summarized here.[1] As noted in Chapter 1, the question
"What is psychotherapy?" is too general to be useful. Similar to questions like
"What is education?" or "What is enlightenment?" we have to spell out some
specifics before trying to describe what psychotherapy is or how to do it. In
the spirit of General Semantics,[2] we also try to avoid any *is* of identity because
psychotherapy seems to manifest as a process, a relationship, and in many cases
a learned way of experiencing and co-creating the self.[3] Because clients and
therapists have differential access to perspectives based on different altitudes in
different developmental lines (Chapter 3) we will learn to discern what I call
the *psychological address* (Chapter 7) of the client, the therapist, and even the
therapeutic "we" (referred to as the therapeutic alliance). Determining these
things enhances our ability to describe "what" psychotherapy "is."

To create a framework for this notion of psychological address requires
understanding both perspectives and developmental altitude. In Chapter 1
I gave an overall sketch of the elements in the Integral or AQAL model and
detailed the quadrants more specifically. In this chapter, I summarize four primary understandings of how to use perspectives in Integral Psychotherapy that
have been outlined by Wilber in numerous seminars and publications. It is
these four primary understandings of perspectives that structure the four parts
of this chapter. The chapter parts are as follows:

- Perspectives as Indicators of Cognitive Development: I examine
  both how perspective-taking abilities evolve and how therapists
  can work with them.

- Perspectives as Reflections of the Four Integral Quadrants (and
  thus reflections of aspects of your being: I further elaborate on

the quadrants introduced in Chapter 1 and their relationship to perspectives and perspective-taking.

- Perspectives Expressed in Language as a Reflection of Psychodynamics: I explore how therapists listen to the way clients use first-, second-, and third-person language which give therapists clues about what aspects of self clients are pushing out of awareness.

- Perspectives as a Way for Client and Therapist to Balance Across the Quadrants: This is one of the hallmarks of Integral Psychotherapy that I refer to as the "1-2-3" of psychotherapy.

Perspectives as Indicators of Cognitive Development

Cognitive development is an important determinant of psychological address and is partially understood as the number of perspectives a person can take. As Wilber has noted, cognitive development is characterized by what you are aware of. Ego development is, of all the things you are aware of, what do you identify with? Thus, cognitive development is *necessary but not sufficient* for development in the ego and other self-related lines (which are the basis of Chapter 3 on altitude). You cannot identify with something that you are unaware of. Getting back to perspectives as an indicator of cognitive development, we can see that a person's ability to grow psychologically is greatly enhanced by his or her ability to take perspectives. Following is a summary of four perspectives, how they unfold developmentally, and how they come into play in psychotherapy.

The First- and Second-Person Perspectives

The first-person perspective emerges in us as children when we are beginning to use language to gratify our needs. This perspective evolves the rest of our lives (excepting things like organic brain damage). Its initial emergence corresponds with what Piaget called preoperational thinking where children begin to use language to represent objects but are incapable of taking the perspective of another (what we refer to as the second-person perspective later). At about ages 2 or 3, children begin consistently asserting their emerging sense of self (and emerging first-person perspective) with words like "no!" and "mine!" The first-person perspective reflects a sense of self (however primitive) separated from the rest of the world. The child is cognitively aware of this difference between self and the world and thus can begin to identify with it (ego).

Recall from Chapter 1 that the Latin root of *sacred* means something that is both blessed and cursed. Development also can be thought of as a sacred impulse. The blessing of an emerging first-person perspective is the seed of ego and the beginnings of mastery over the world you've just differentiated from. The curse is that when you differentiate from the world, you also can feel threatened by that world that you now perceive as "not you" or "other." Thus, the average 2- or 3-year-old begins to suffer from nightmares now that he or she has a separate sense of self that can feel threatened. As noted, the first-person perspective continues to develop throughout our lives and is basically what we think, feel, experience, or believe at a given time and how we make sense of all these things.

When the first-person perspective emerges it is the only perspective a small child can take. Numerous studies have demonstrated the difference between the ability of 2- to 3-year-olds and 5-year-olds to take perspectives. The 2- and 3-year-olds by-and-large are limited to a first-person perspective. The ability to take a second-person perspective begins *emerging* in these early years but is not *consistently adequate* until around age 5. This pattern from initial emergence of a level to adequacy at the level we call healthy translation in Integral Psychotherapy. The second-person perspective is the ability to psychologically open one's mind to what another person thinks and similarly to feel into what they may be thinking or experiencing based on the circumstances. The earliest emergence of a second-person perspective seems to be at about 2 years and is when the child understands that what he or she sees in a room may be different from what a caregiver sees.[4] The second-person perspective helps you understand that another may see and experience things differently from you and to accept feedback from that other.

A blessing of the second-person perspective is this ability to begin feeling into the perspective of others; a curse is that you become more aware of the suffering of others. What we understand about this process is that the second-person perspective is essential for empathy[5] and when people are mistreated, it retards the emergence of this critical ability.[6] Taking a second-person perspective also is necessary for things like prejudice reduction and living in a pluralistic society.[7] These all can be blessings, however, they also imply more responsibility, more restraint, more willingness to delay acting on first impulses.

As noted, the second-person perspective emerges over a period of time.[8] Barbara Abrahams[9] dissertation at Stanford University demonstrates the differential emergence of a second-person perspective in 3-year-old children. These children clearly understood what another person physically *saw* from a perspective different from theirs but could not infer what that other person may have *thought* from that different perspective. In the same study, 5-year-olds could both understand the difference in what was *seen* and begin understanding differences in what the other person was *thinking*. Mastering the second-person perspective is correlated with Piaget's level of concrete operational thinking typified by an ability to learn from personal experience and perform operations with concrete objects but not consistently in the abstract (e.g., a child can form a larger group of blocks from smaller groups of similar blocks in the preschool but could perform the operation intrapsychically). Clinically, teaching the skills of taking a second-person perspective are being used with sex offenders,[10] in employee–customer relations,[11] and in couples/family therapy.[12]

The Third-Person Perspective

Susanne Cook-Greuter writes, "a conceptual watershed is crossed when one can take the third-person perspective."[13] This "watershed" is accompanied by a greater ability to introspect, a desire to further individuate by differentiating from family and develop a sense of individual personhood. Cook-Greuter notes that from a third-person perspective, self and others are experienced as separate people who are unique.

In psychotherapy an example of third-person perspective is more easily understood by describing a situation. Assume a therapist is working with a husband–wife couple. The therapist has a third-person perspective, meaning that based on the clinical work with the couple she has a sense of what the husband thinks of his wife and his role in the relationship, as well as what the wife thinks of her husband and her role in the relationship. The therapist is then in a unique position to help both members of the couple make objects of awareness those things related to the relationship that they are not aware of *or* are pushing out of awareness.

With formal operational thinking, the third-person perspective evolves to include a clearer separation of self and other, subject and object. At this level of refinement, the third-person perspective includes understandings of self and others both forward and backward in time hence, you can recall your past self, fantasize about your future self, and link it all to your present self. These same operations can be conducted with others whose perspectives you are taking. This fluidity in time is a resourceful use of the third-person perspective for any mental health practitioner. Going back to our earlier example of a therapist counseling a couple, the ability of the therapist to feel into or empathize with both the husband and wife is greatly enhanced when the therapist understands how both came to be who they are and how who they are may affect their futures individually and as a couple. For example, there is some evidence that maltreatment can disrupt perspective-taking ability[14] so if the wife's primary complaint about the husband is that he doesn't care what she thinks, the therapist may consider that the husband's *style* of interacting is related to his upbringing. Should this prove an important variable in how the husband sees the world, the therapist will suggest as much to the wife and help both wife and husband make an object of awareness of how his history shows up in the relationship. A third-person perspective also is important for the therapist to step outside of the therapy relationship and reflect on it. This is exercised by making case notes, consulting with colleagues, and in supervision. A blessing of the third-person perspective is the ability to objectify things for the purpose of better understanding them. A curse is retreating into this objectification to avoid really dealing with things.

The Fourth-Person Perspective

The fourth-person perspective is rooted in late-formal operational and post-formal operational thinking referred to by Wilber as *vision logic*. In vision logic or post-formal operational thinking you do not simply explore hypotheses and form conclusions from one perspective but from as many perspectives as possible. In this sense there is a systems-like quality to vision logic that is directly related to the ability to take a fourth-person perspective. Again, let's return to our example of the couples counseling situation. The ability to take a fourth-person perspective would be helpful to the person who is supervising the therapist who is counseling the couple in the example. In this example, a fourth-person perspective means that the supervisor (the "fourth person") can hold all three perspectives of the therapist, the wife, and the husband simultaneously. From this fourth-person perspective the supervisor can feel into what the therapist thinks of what both the husband and wife think of themselves and each other. The supervisor can use the fourth-person perspective to help the therapist refine his or her third-person perspective of the therapeutic relationship.

Although this may seem like mental gymnastics, it really isn't for the supervisor. If the supervisor has adequate mastery of the fourth-person perspective it helps him or her consider all the perspectives held by the clients and the therapists without feeling a need to privilege one over another. Indeed, by holding all perspectives simultaneously, the supervisor is better able to help the therapist make objects of awareness things that (if left out of awareness) might inhibit effective therapy for the couple.

Let's assume that the supervisor and the therapist have worked well together over a period of years. The supervisor has helped the therapist work through some countertransference related to growing up in a household where the father was an alcoholic. In the therapist's case, her father was verbally abusive and she lived with a great deal of fear growing up. The therapist worked through much of this over a period of years in her own therapy but when she works with clients who suffered maltreatment as children, it brings back some of her own memories of growing up in an alcoholic household. Now this process of recollection in the context of similar situations is perfectly normal and should not interfere with therapy as long as the therapist keeps the recollection of her childhood an object of awareness and owns it (rather than dissociating it or pushing it out of awareness). Keeping her own childhood an object of awareness and owning it[15] allows her to use the experiences of her own life to empathically understand where people like the husband in our hypothetical couple are coming from. Problems (countertransference) can emerge if the therapist begins to respond to the emotions without making this part of her past an object of awareness or by not owning it.[16] The supervisor, knowing the therapist's background, helps her keep that background an object of awareness, process whether she really owns it or not while discerning the impact and relation it has to the husband of the couple in treatment. The supervisor gives this feedback to the therapist to better help the therapist serve the couple. All of this is much easier for a supervisor who can use the fourth-person perspective.

The fourth-person perspective can expand to a sense of self as embedded in history and multiple cultural contexts. The embeddedness in history may take the form of experiencing yourself in the context of your parents' past and your children's future. Many times people ready for the emergence of this refined fourth-person perspective experience it when they marry and have children as the latter activities bring generational realities clearly into focus. This refinement of the fourth-person perspective is an elaboration of the fluidity with regard to time that emerges in the elaborated third-person perspective. It could be thought of as a hint of later expansions beyond a fourth-person perspective where one experiences the self even more fluidly as an evolutionary agent united with humanity in the great drama of the sacred developmental impulse (perhaps experienced as the play of Sprit).

Fifth-, Sixth-, Seventh . . . nth-Person Perspectives

If you have been following along with this discussion of perspectives you can see that perspective-taking can easily be a lifelong practice. We could expand our examples to include fifth-, sixth, seventh-person perspectives, and so on. Each expansion of perspectives is an expansion of the individual's ability to add new perspectives in an intrapsychic system, hold them equally, AND make judgments based on the ability to see things from multiple views. Just because a person can see things from multiple perspectives does not in any way mean that they hold all those perspectives as equally true or equally valuable in all situations. That would be relativism, which is particularly dysfunctional in psychotherapy (I return to this point in the next chapter on developmental understandings of client and therapist).

The Brain and Perspective Taking

Just to remind you that all phenomena are all-quadrant affairs, it is important to touch on what we are learning about the neural correlates of perspective-taking abilities. As noted in Chapter 1, the Integral approach to the mind–brain problem is to view phenomena in the mind and brain as arising together. The brain-scanning technologies of the late-20th century have greatly expanded our understanding of the neural correlates for psychological activities and perspective taking is no exception. In a recent study of empathy, psychologist Claus Lamm and his colleagues[17] used a technology called event-related functional magnetic resonance imaging (fMRI). While subjects viewed videos of people experiencing pain during a medical treatment, the researchers instructed them to imagine the situation of the patient in the video or to imagine themselves in that situation. The results indicated that experiencing empathic concern via perspective taking caused the subjects to use their brains differently. Another study conducted by Ruby Perrine and Jean Decety at *Universite de Liege* used positron-emission tomography (PET) scans to investigate differences in brain functioning when subjects are taking a first- versus a third-person perspective. As the researchers suspected, different parts of the brain are involved when taking first- versus third-person perspectives.[18]

Again, this is not to conclude that the brain centers involved in both studies "cause" the perspective-taking abilities under investigation. The perspective-taking abilities had an impact on how the brain was functioning just as the brain centers involved facilitated the tasks the subjects were engaged in. While fundamentalist materialists may jump to the conclusion that brain *causes* mind, that is not necessarily the case. At this point in our understanding, we need to entertain what psychiatrist Roger Walsh calls "causal indifference," which reflects an acceptance (rare in our society) that "subjectively identical experiences can be produced by multiple causes."[19]

How Understanding Perspectives as Indicators of Cognitive Development Helps the Integral Psychotherapist

Many training models in the mental health professions claim to emphasize development but it has not been my experience that such claims are honored by inclusion of what we know about perspective taking (summarized in the last section). Indeed, many master's-level training programs require only one survey course in human development and many doctoral-level programs settle for two courses. As noted in Chapter 1, developmental gems are woven throughout the Integral (AQAL) framework, including perspectives as indicators of cognitive development. This first understanding of perspectives serves practicing psychotherapists by providing a means of understanding how clients experience life (and thus assisting in the creation of the therapeutic alliance), offering structural psychoeducational interventions to help clients who may be ready but struggling to take a certain perspective, and finally they provide the therapist a vehicle for self-reflection.

Perspectives Regarding How Clients Experience Life

Most of us, over the course of a career or course of a week, serve clients with various developmental potentials. Understanding a client's potential to take perspectives (and comparing that with how much of the potential the client is using) allows you to meet the client where they are (Rule 1 of good therapy) while also helping them translate in the healthiest manner possible based on the developmental tools and rules they have (Rule 2). Many potential disasters can be avoided by perspective taking on the part of the therapist or other staff and realistically assessing the client's capacity in a given situation for the same.

I recall taking one of my clients to the pharmacy to pick up his medication. This client (Frank) suffered from schizophrenia and was taking what is called an atypical antipsychotic olanzapine (Zyprexa). Frank struggled to keep his life organized, often forgot things, and would sometimes lose his medication.[20] This had happened the previous month although Frank had forgotten. When we arrived to pick up the medication, Frank saw that he only had one refill left but believed he should have two (having forgotten he used one with doctor's permission to replace the lost medications). The pharmacy staff (pharmacist and tech assistant) had sheets showing Frank had signed for the medication. Frank did not remember and assumed the signature had to be forged. The staff knew that Frank was being treated for schizophrenia and were wonderfully empathic, understanding that Frank struggled to take a second-person perspective to see their point of view. They promised him they would investigate the possibility of a forgery and this seemed to calm Frank down.

From a third-person perspective, I could see that Frank was factually wrong (especially because I had been with him the prior month when he in fact signed for the medication). I could also see that the pharmacy staff knew Frank was wrong but also understood he suffered from a condition that impaired his ability to take their perspective. Knowing this, they compassionately accommodated him in a way that honored what he was experiencing but also did not alter the facts as they existed.[21]

Now consider what could have happened (and happens everyday really) had the staff working in the pharmacy not had the ability or the inclination to fully consider Frank's inability to take perspectives. What might have happened would be one of the small tragedies that occur daily in the form of an argument, hurt feelings and perhaps worse. Perspective taking facilitates communication and being able to live together in ways that have far-reaching implications. Perspective taking is so important in the mental health professions that most programs screen for the minimum cognitive ability that is necessary (but of course not sufficient) for a therapist-in-training to be able to take at least a third-person perspective.[22]

PERSPECTIVE TAKING AS PSYCHOEDUCATIONAL INTERVENTION

Depending on the type and developmental altitude of the client, perspective-taking exercises can serve as in-session interventions or homework. In Chapter 3, I summarize Jane Loevinger and Susanne Cook-Greuter's work on ego development, which will provide a template for ways to optimize your interactions with clients. For now, however, let's look at another clinical example of how perspective taking can be used in a session.

The client in this example was a 40-year-old woman named Linda. Linda was seeing me in the aftermath of a bitter divorce she initiated after learning that her husband of 15 years had been engaged in several extramarital affairs over the past 5 years of their marriage. Linda held a master's degree in history, seemed to have adequate mastery of formal operational cognition, and the capacity for an elaborated third-person perspective. She was furious and bitter about the break-up of her marriage but did not see herself as the type of person who felt such negative emotions. Among her symptoms was a crippling anxiety that she had never experienced before. After 10 months of work around her failed marriage, she reached a point where she wanted to move on but felt frustrated in her attempt to, in her words, "get outside of this whole thing."

The words "get outside of this whole thing" reminded me of the third-person perspective. Linda had been raised with a lot of traditional ideas about marriage and although she did not agree with most of those, much of her grief work was around the loss of an idealized image of marriage she had held since childhood. It was this image, the expectations she had held closely to her heart, and the marriage itself that she wanted to be able to view in a different perspective. As noted in Chapter 1, all psychotherapy is to some extent helping clients make aspects of their lives and themselves objects of awareness. As seen in Chapter 3, this is a bit more complicated than just taking new perspectives because the person has to emotionally own the thing being made an object of awareness. Without *owning* it, making it an object of awareness increases the risk for *dissociating* it.

Because Linda had done almost a year of work emotionally owning her role in the marriage (positive and negative) she seemed ready to disidentify from it. We discussed the use of a third-person perspective to "step outside of" her relationship and view it from that perspective. To start that process we needed something concrete that could symbolize the emotional distance she was experimenting with so we drew up a basic genogram[23] of herself and her ex-spouse. In basic genograms, females are depicted by circles and males by squares (although any and all creative reworking of basic symbols is used). Likewise, there are symbols for pregnancies, abortions, and miscarriages. We reviewed her parents' marriage and what we knew of her ex-spouse's family.

Because they had no children, once we depicted the divorce on the genogram I asked Linda what she wanted to see next. At the time she was overcome by tears and said separating the symbols for herself and her ex-spouse (the circle and square) seemed final but "not right." We spent the rest of the session processing that and her homework was to decide how to finish the genogram. In the next session she reported that she knew how she wanted to finish the genogram. Beginning at the symbols of her and her ex-spouse she drew a double helix extending down the page and separated the two lines of the double helix. She began drawing the separated lines as solid, then dotted, then as arrows pointing to the now-separated symbols of herself and her ex-spouse. She said this idea came to her as she was waking up 2 days prior to the session. Looking at it she said it was a good way to depict the connection with and influence of someone while also going your separate ways. Although some may interpret this as difficulty in letting go, Linda said it represented how the person she is today was powerfully impacted by the years with her ex-spouse (and, she assumed, vice-versa) and how long it takes to "unwind" that impact.

Linda's next homework assignment was to hang the genogram in her kitchen or somewhere she could look at it everyday and then journal a few lines about her emotional reactions looking at it. The first few days her reactions went from tearful to numb. After 4 days she taped a picture of she and her ex-spouse next to the genogram on the left and a picture of her alone to its right. At this point, she noted her response became more curious. After 2 weeks, the curiosity seemed to hold some excitement mingled with the sadness that she was used to feeling. At this point, she reported feeling more stable, feeling more herself but feeling that in the context of being a single person. From there onward, our sessions became more focused on what she wanted to do next with her life.

Perspectives as a Vehicle for Therapist Self-Reflection

One aspect of ILP is that of perspective taking as a personal growth exercise. Again, in this definition of perspectives we're viewing them as indicators of cognitive development. The Integral Model provides therapists several ways to work with perspectives, including studying and trying on first-, second-, third-, fourth-person perspectives, and so on. Anytime a therapist seeks feedback, he or she is practicing shifting perspectives. From understanding the second-person perspective of the client, a third-person perspective of the therapeutic alliance, or the fourth-person perspective of the supervisor, therapists have multiple opportunities to practice shifting perspectives.

To enhance one's understanding of the second-person perspective of the client, therapists can do shadow work (described in Chapter 3). To enhance the third-person perspective of the therapeutic relationship, therapists can draw modified professional genograms of their relationships with their clients and colleagues, creating symbols to denote the emotional feel of each relationship and look for patterns. Finally, therapists can use peer supervision (ideally in groups) to practice taking a fourth-person perspective on their work.

Reminder: Quadrants and Quadrivium

Before jumping back into the quadrants, I outline two primary ways we use the quadrants in Integral Psychotherapy. In Chapter 1 I outlined two ways to use the quadrants to "plug in" different things you are dealing with. In this section I summarize two ways to use the quadrants overall; these have been outlined by Wilber. The first is understanding the quadrants as four primary perspectives of all sentient beings (as noted in Chapter 1). As Wilber emphasized, a sentient being with a dominant monad will have at least these four aspects of their being or four perspectives that we represent as quadrants.[24] Now quadrivium is using the four quadrants to look at something that may or may not be a sentient being. One example is an earlier book on psychopharmacology wherein my co-author and I examined psychopharmacology from the perspective of the four quadrants.[25] Psychopharmacology is a field, not a sentient being, but it can be viewed through the quadrants in what Wilber calls a quadrivial fashion.

Andre Marquis' book *The Integral Intake*[26] does this with the client in the intake process. As a researcher or a therapist, using the quadrants or perspectives in quadrivial fashion forces you to examine as the object of your research from at least the four primary perspectives. This would seem logical and good practice but it is amazing how many researchers don't do it. They don't do it because the majority of training they receive in higher education is parochial at best and elitist at worst. Rather than being viewed as an ability to specialize and develop expertise in one or two areas that can then be reconnected to the Kosmos, disciplines in most universities are viewed as bastions of separateness. From the fiscal structure of universities developed in 18th-century Germany to the outdated tenure system and editorial agendas of specialized journals there is sadly very little encouragement for cross-disciplinary work.

Perspectives as Reflections of the Four Quadrants of the Integral Model

The second important use of perspectives in Integral Psychotherapy is as reflections of the four quadrants of Integral Theory. The four primary perspectives of Integral Theory are represented by four quadrants. Citing G. Spencer Brown's *Laws of Form*,[27] Wilber noted that as soon as a sentient being arises a perspective arises with it. Although there are potentially many perspectives, Wilber outlined four primary perspectives that are aspects of all individual holons.[28] As noted in Chapter 1, these four perspectives are represented using the four quadrants in Fig. 2.1.

First, a quick review of these quadrants: Recall that the upper-left quadrant represents the subjective, phenomenological experience of an individual. In other words whatever you (whoever is reading this page) are aware of intrapsychically *right now, and now, and now and now*. Moment to moment the perspective of this quadrant represents the stream of consciousness that you experience. This could include a sense of following what I've written, not following me, wishing I'd choked on a doughnut before ever having had a chance to write this, pondering a grocery list, having a sexual fantasy, and so on. I can't really know much about your first-person or upper-left perspective unless you share it with me and we engage in a hermeneutic[29] dialogue. The perspective represented by this quadrant is a main focus of psychotherapy, but of course cannot be considered in isolation from the other perspectives represented by the other three quadrants. The perspective represented by the upper-left quadrant also captures the signifieds[30] of language and these signifieds frequently require interpretation for understanding to be reached between two or more people. Understanding and working with this is critical in psychotherapy and virtually impossible without the ability to take the perspective of the client.

The upper-right quadrant represents the objective perspective of the individual or, all things that could be measured without you ever needing to say anything. This could include your behavior, aspects of your physical functioning (e.g., blood pressure, levels of serotonin in your central nervous system, endocrine functioning, the words you speak, etc.). This perspective also includes the *signifiers*[31] of language. The perspective represented by this quadrant has always been the emphasis of behaviorism and more recently, biological psychiatry.[32]

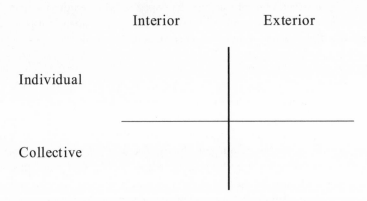

Figure 2.1. The four quadrants of Integral Theory.

The lower-left quadrant represents what we call the *intersubjective* perspective or the intersubjective aspect of your being. Just as the upper-left quadrant represents your personal, subjective, phenomenological experience of life, this quadrant represents the perspective of *shared* subjective experiences of life. Also like the upper-left quadrant, I can't simply measure things like shared beliefs—I must engage in dialogue with those who are part of the group adhering to the shared beliefs. Things like the subjective aspects of social institutions or groups, culture, shared understandings of language (things like the rules of grammar and syntax as well as semantics), and the shared understanding that grows out of relationship (e.g., in psychotherapy) are represented in this quadrant. The perspective of this quadrant has been exhaustively researched by linguists and those interested in constructivism, postmodernism, and multiculturalism.

The lower-right quadrant represents what could be called the *interobjective* perspective. Unlike the intersubjective, the interobjective perspective represents the exterior aspects of collectives or groups—those aspects of groups that can be measured without hermeneutic dialogue. Things captured in this perspective include objective aspects of social institutions or groups, and systems theories that focus on the relation of the elements of units like families or ecosystems.

As noted in Chapter 1, a fascinating thing about these quadrants is that most languages have words to reflect the different quadrant/perspectives. It is these words and their expression in the English language that forms the basis for this section of the chapter and the next. In this section, I also summarize how the four basic perspectives can be further refined by exploring them from their own inside or their own outside. This is explained in detail in *Integral Spirituality* and I restrict my description here to how it applies to Integral Psychotherapy.

Another Dance Around the Quadrants

Let's take another waltz through the quadrants with regard to how we use language to reflect perspectives. In this section I emphasize how language relates to the quadrants or perspectives and summarize two ways to explore each perspective that Wilber refers to as zones or "hori-zones of arising." This latter phrase is in reference to the fact that each zone brings forth a world space, or, more poetically, a horizon ("hori-zone"). Of the two zones in each quadrant, one focuses on an "inside" understanding of the perspective represented by the quadrant that we label Zone 1. The other zone focuses on an "outside" understanding of the perspective represented by the quadrant we label Zone 2.[33] Wilber notes that colloquially we can think of Zone 1 as how the quadrant feels and Zone 2 as how the quadrant looks.

As Wilber illustrates each zone brings forth different information about the Kosmos and as such implies methodology unique to that zone. The combination of the eight methodologies is called Integral Methodological Pluralism (IMP). The basic idea of IMP is that researchers in all fields first identify which aspect of the Kosmos they want to research by identifying the quadrant in which their object of research arises and then the appropriate zone within that quadrant. Having done this they will then know to use methodologies that represent the quadrant and zone thus identified (what we could call the "research address" of their study). This should greatly increase the probability of avoiding the category error of trying to explore something with the wrong tool, which inevitably results in error. The best example of such error is when researchers try to explain away the experience of mind (upper-left quadrant) with results obtained studying the brain (upper-right quadrant).

You really can think of this simply: The four quadrants represent four perspectives on reality and thus four perspectives of your being (and your clients' beings). They are not dry, theoretical constructs—they are you and who isn't interested in learning more about themselves? That is what the perspectives (represented as quadrants) offer us—a way to learn about ourselves or, in the psychotherapy setting, a way to engage people who come to us for help. So, we've got four perspectives that are aspects of your being. Now the zones simply point to the fact that there are two ways to explore each aspect of your being: interior and exterior. Figure 2.2 summarizes the language associated with each of the four perspectives (quadrants) and Fig. 2.3 summarizes the two zones or ways of exploring each perspective (quadrant).

The powerful research tools that arise from these zones benefit all disciplines. Although all eight zones contribute to research and practice in psychotherapy, the use of both zones in the upper-left quadrant is particularly important to psychotherapy practice. Before we revisit the quadrants, zones and explore their relation to language; I want to clarify the relation of first, second, and third-peson language to perspectives.

	Interior	Exterior
Individual	"I" language	"IT" language
Collective	"WE" language	"ITS" language

Figure 2.2. Language of each quadrant.

	Interior	Exterior
	"I" language	**"IT" language**
Individual	ZONE-#1: Sense of "I" (how "I" feels) ZONE #2: Objective study of how "I" develops, evolves (how I" looks")	ZONE #1: Objective view of individual interiors ZONE #2: Objective view of individual exteriors
Collective	ZONE-#1: The feeling of "we" ZONE #2: The structure of "we"	ZONE #1: Communication between organisms ZONE #2: Networks of Exchange (Systems Theory)
	"WE" language	**"ITS" language**

Figure 2.3. Language of each quadrant and emphasis of zones in each quadrant.

A Note on the Relation of Language to Perspectives

Before going into this section I emphasize the difference between first, second, and third-person perspectives and first, second, and third-person language. Perspectives as indicators of cognitive ability are developmental achievements that expand the Kosmos and our experience of it. Each perspective gives rise to an experience of the world that we then seek to express with language. The limits of language come into play when we examine the language used to express the perspectives. Generally we summarize the language of perspectives as follows:

- First-person language is "I" language (the language of the person speaking) and has possessive expressions of "me" or "mine." These latter expressions will come into play in Chapter 4 when in the discussion of the self-system and the ways your "I" can own aspects of itself or its experience.

- Second-person language is "you" language (the person being spoken to)

- Third-person language is "it" or "its" language (language referring to the thing or things being spoken about)

There is also language of the first-person plural known as "we" language (the language of two or more people who share an understanding). There can be a second-person plural although English does not directly accommodate this and we compensate by using "you all" (y'all) or "you'se guys."[34] There also is nothing in the English language that directly represents fourth-, fifth-person perspectives, and so on. As seen in the next section, the way a client uses the language of first-, second-, and third-person can provide clues as to clinical interventions.

Equally important in this caveat is that people who have not mastered taking second- or third-person perspectives can and do use third-person language. When my son was 2 years old I was in the kitchen and saw him smear his peanut butter sandwich on the television in the living room. When I asked him if he did it he said, "No, it just got there." When I told him I saw him do it he said, "No you didn't—you are in the kitchen and it is here." Obviously, he was still struggling with second-person perspectives but he used (however imperfectly) third-person language (if you have kids try listening for their efforts to take perspectives—it is truly amazing). As becomes clearer, the ability to take perspectives is one thing, whereas the ability to accurately use language to express perspectives is another. It is in the difference that much clinical direction is provided.

REVISITING THE UPPER-LEFT QUADRANT

Recall that the upper-left quadrant represents your subjective, phenomenological world. Based on the last section of this, we can also say that the upper-left quadrant represents what we described as the experience of a first-person perspective. First-person language is usually "I" language ("I feel pissed off," "I don't understand you," "I had a dream last night"). Therefore, clinical work related to the client's experience of I is focused on this quadrant. This domain of subjective "I" experience has been labeled Zone 1 in this quadrant by Wilber. Simply put, Zone 1 takes subjective experiences at face value as just that-legitimate subjective experiences or how your "I" feels. So whatever you're noting in your awareness right now is Zone 1 territory.

But, how does your "I" look to an external observer? There is way of looking at this sense of "I"—Zone 2 in this quadrant that studies how "I" develops and in that development how it relates to everything that is "not-I." The establishment and evolution of "I" and the horizon that it reveals really are miraculous. Think about the incredible developmental achievement when a toddler establishes the sense of "I" that (however torturous their incessant "no!!!!" can be) consumes the toddler's world. With the advent of an initial sense of "I," the toddler's new "horizon" is a whole world of things for the "I" to experience ("again! again!"), and, in toddler-logic, dictatorially control ("now!!!").

The look of this developmental unfolding as well as the structure of this "I" is the focus of Zone 2 in the upper-left quadrant.

No one reading this page can deny the presence of a sense of "I" as they read. But, as therapists we are constantly using our theories and organizing frameworks to understand the structure of our client's sense of "I." In terms of ego development, we explore if the "I" is mature for the client's chronological age. From the perspective of ego psychology we explore how strong or stable it is. And, in the case of people suffering from severe mental/emotional disorders we help the person as they struggle with an "I" that is fragmented and easily overwhelmed. We also check if the boundaries of the client's "I" are healthy— meaning fluid enough to form a healthy "we" in relationship but strong enough to consistently discern what is "I" and what is "other." These assessments are just the beginning. When we include developmental considerations we gain a fuller appreciation of the complexity (and miracle) of our sense of "I."

Wilber has consistently pointed out that one of the great contributions of Western psychology is the discovery that our sense of "I" develops through predictable stages. I referred to this earlier in the chapter, noting that our sense of "I" stays with us and evolves throughout life. This is critical to understand: Our development can continue throughout life and does not stop when one establishes an "adult" sense of self. I want to repeat that last statement because it is tragically ignored in most psychotherapy training programs[35]—our sense of "I" can continue throughout life and does not stop when one establishes an adult sense of self. Although the subjective experience of "I" in the upper-left quadrant is the focus of Zone 1, the objective study of how the sense of "I" evolves and develops that is so critical to good psychotherapy is the focus of Zone 2.

In Integral Psychotherapy we lean very heavily on Jane Loevinger and Susanne Cook-Greuter's theory of ego development for a stage conception of how our sense of "I" evolves and increases in complexity.[36] The increase in complexity is characterized by a broader, deeper sense of "I" that increasingly is able to take the perspectives covered earlier in this chapter (second-, third-, fourth-person perspectives, etc.). So we can summarize the upper-left quadrant by stating that from the inside we feel our sense of "I" (Zone 1) and from the outside (Zone 2) this sense of "I" develops through predictable stages that can be assessed and understood.

Here is another way to distinguish between the two views of the upper-left quadrant provided by Zones 1 and 2. Psychologically healthy people are all aware of a sense of "I," you can feel it, talk about it, and reflect on it. Unless something has gone wrong, there is no denying your sense of "I." Conversely, unless you have studied how this sense of "I" develops, you are likely completely unaware of the stages your own "I" has gone through in development. There is nothing in your immediate experience comparable to Zone 1 that will tell you "hey, by the way, you just had a huge developmental leap in the structure of your sense of "I"—congratulations and pick up your door prize on the way out."

As a therapist, you obviously have this sense of "I" as does your client. By entertaining a second-person perspective you are trying to "feel into" or empathize with what they experience through their sense of "I." That is one thing you're doing. Another thing is you are trying to view their sense of "I" objectively to discern how "healthy" it is, their cognitive abilities, what they need, what they value, and so on. From Zone 1 you are perhaps using the Rogerian core conditions to establish relationship with your client and from Zone 2 you are discerning things like ego-strength and where on the spectrum of development your client identifies so that you can better meet them where they are at (remember Rule 1 of therapy: meet the client where they are at).

SUMMARY: THE CLINICAL UTILITY OF THE UPPER-LEFT QUADRANT

The clinical utility of the upper-left quadrant is in acknowledging, connecting with, and making an object of awareness the client's sense of "I." This includes honoring the phenomenology that arises as this perspective as well as learning and using validated stage theories to help elucidate the structure of a sense of "I" for any given client (as well as for the therapist). The theory of ego development is covered in Chapter 4 toward this end. The personality style or type is also something we may be able to assess about a client and this is discussed in Chapter 5.

Absurd as it sounds, we must remind some clinicians or professionals related to clients in secondary or tertiary ways that the phenomena one experiences from the upper-left perspective are in fact real and will drive client's behaviors, affect their relationships, and determine their ability to benefit from therapy. I recall working with a psychiatrist who would not address clients directly and insisted that the therapists (me in this case) accompany the client to medication checks. These clients all suffered from severe mental and emotional disorders but it was clear the psychiatrist (who was an exception in my experience) did not have the patience to wait for answers to emerge from the fog of the clients' disordered thinking. Although this may have been a time saver for the doctor, it was correlated with more medication noncompliance on the part of the clients than those seeing our other psychiatrist who was much more interpersonally skilled.

Finally, much of the divergence across theories of psychotherapy can be understood as the relationship between the therapist's sense of "I" and the client's sense of "I." From Freud's guidelines about how to preclude unresourceful gratification of the "I" (put the patient on a couch facing away from the therapists thus denying him an audience) to Gestalt's direct engagement and challenge of the client's sense of "I" ("show me this "I" who doesn't believe in himself") theories can also serve as reflections of their adherents' types and temperaments.

REVISITING THE UPPER-RIGHT QUADRANT

The upper-right quadrant represents the objective perspective of the individual or, all things that could be measured without you ever needing to say anything. The perspective of this quadrant is expressed primarily in "it" language and "it" language is referred to as third-person language (language that gives the impression the speaker is standing outside of that being described). "It" language has long been the language of scientific method and while this has distinct advantages, remember it is only reflecting one perspective and in Integral Psychotherapy we are interested in all perspectives.

Recall that the "mind–brain problem" summarized in chapter one has been the basis for theorists pitting the upper-left perspective against the upper-right perspective. From Gustav Fechner's own struggle with the extent to which subjective psychological experiences derive from brain function to the current "Rumble in Reno" conferences where pharmacologists and biological psychiatrists debate psychotherapists in a "zero-sum" format it would appear that we have learned little about mind or brain. I fully expect interdisciplinary wrestling matches when YouTube becomes our primary entertainment ("in this corner representing biological psychiatry and weighing in at 300 pounds . . ."). Integral Theory and Integral Psychotherapy in particular solve the problem by noting that both perspectives (upper-right—brain and upper-left—mind) are right about some things but not all things. It is unresourceful to try to prove that your "I" experience is *merely* a side effect of your "it" brain. You can properly be agnostic on that count as there really is not enough evidence for a final verdict. In the Integral Psychotherapy framework both arise together. This requires professionals of different disciplines to "play nice together."

Getting back to the "it" perspective of the upper-right quadrant, recall that this is third-person language and this quadrant embraces those aspects of your being that are best understood through this perspective. Just as with the upper-left quadrant we can explore the upper-right quadrant with our two zones. We start with Zone 2 (how this perspective "looks") because that is more intuitive. Zone 2 of the upper-right perspective is simply an "it" view experienced by (and used by) an individual. From behavior to the levels of serotonin metabolites in spinal fluid to things like blood pressure Zone 2 simply looks at the exteriors from a third-person perspective (what is "it" doing?) and describes what is seen in third-person language ("the test showed toxic levels of lithium in the client's bloodstream" or "the client manifested signs of fatigue and tearfulness during the session). This is the zone emphasized by strict behaviorism and biological psychiatry. What is interesting is that at different times both behaviorism and biological psychiatry have made absolutist claims about their disciplines. Although history has clearly proven such claims wrong regarding behaviorism, the same appears to be happening in biological psychiatry. Again, even Nobel laureate Eric Kandel has focused his research on the interactions of mind and brain—when we "decide" to do something, what changes can that cause in our brain and when our brain suffers a trauma, how does that impact the facility with which we make such decisions?

Now obviously the truths discovered exploring this quadrant with Zone 2 are vital to our understanding of clients and psychotherapy (as evidenced by the number of physical disorders that mimic psychological symptoms [e.g., thyroid conditions, multiple sclerosis, Addison's disease]). These truths are helpful but, taken alone, they are not as much help as some would lead you to believe.[37] Although there are still those who claim that all psychological symptoms are nothing but biochemical events, the claim has not received much support. Human beings are complex creatures and to do psychotherapy we need all four perspectives (with two zones in each) described here.

So how do the exterior aspects of the individual "feel" so to speak? The way Zone 1 explores the upper-right quadrant is a bit different. In Zone 1 of the upper-right quadrant we are asking, "What is the interior view of the objective aspects of the individual?" Learning theories, the study of language development and cognitive science, are all attempting to objectively map what is happening in people mentally. These disciplines try to create objective maps of our mental processes. Although most psychotherapists are generally familiar with learning theory and language development, cognitive science requires a brief overview. Cognitive science is a multidisciplinary field that explores mental processes from behavioral, functional, and physical levels. Behaviorally, cognitive scientists record the behavior in question. Functionally, cognitive scientists try to model how information is processed in order to produce the recorded behavior. Physically, cognitive scientists try to describe the physical structures that must be involved in such computations. The impact of cognitive science on psychotherapy is promising but still unclear. An interesting development though is that having gained some measure of specialization, many cognitive scientists are attempting to secede from psychology departments because they feel their field is unique and should not be a subdiscipline within psychology.[38] As my colleagues would say, "Here we go again."

SUMMARY: THE CLINICAL UTILITY OF THE UPPER-RIGHT QUADRANT

The clinical utility of the perspective from the upper-right quadrant includes the more obvious things like physical wellness of your client, medications they are taking, and behaviors relevant to therapy. The less obvious things include the way the client processes information, the client's neuropsychological pro- file, and the client's style of learning.[39] The importance of clients having a physical exam cannot be overrated. There are numerous cases where a client is engaged in months of therapy for anxiety or depression only to find that the root of the problem was a physical disorder that somehow caused psychologi- cal symptoms. It also is important to pay close attention to how interventions aimed at the body impact the mind. For example, there is very little research on clients' phenomenological response (upper-left quadrant) to psychotropic medications (upper-right quadrant). Laura Burns, a postdoctoral fellow at the Cleveland Clinic found in her dissertation work that clients will have widely divergent subjective experiences of antidepressants based on factors like how they understand their depression and how they felt about their relationship with the prescribing psychiatrist.[40]

Revisiting the Lower-Left Quadrant

The lower-left quadrant represents the perspective of *shared* subjective experiences. This includes the obvious shared experiences of culture that may be based in ethnicity, race, a family, or a subgroup or sect that has broken off from a larger group. The language that captures the perspective of this quadrant is "we" language ("we believe . . ." we have agreed that . . ." we will fight for . . ."). Whereas from the perspective in the upper-left quadrant the individual experiences the signifieds of language, the "we" of the lower-left quadrant experiences shared collective signifieds that contribute to what Wilber calls a predominant mode of mutual resonance.

An individual holon has a dominant monad defined as a governing capacity followed by all subcomponents (you get up for a beer and all your cells and organs follow). Although social holons do not have any dominant monad, the predominant mode of resonance reflects a shared understanding of meaning that then increases the probability of (but does not guarantee) the group moving, working, making meaning together—as a group (or couple, or trio, etc). Again, the difference is critical to understanding the difference between individual therapy and group or family therapy. Individual holons (e.g., individual clients) have a dominant monad. Families or groups have a predominant mode of resonance (or try to negotiate one in therapy). As some researchers have found, some clients in groups will actually become more egocentric in response to the norms of perspective taking in a group because of what the norms represent to them.[41]

It is important to practice mindfulness in that our species is riddled with labels that are intended to *reflect* some predominant mode of resonance but rarely do. This is a form of word magic[42] where an illusion of consensus or certainty (that in fact does not exist) is created with words. For the sake of example, a group of mental health professionals may all be referred to as therapists and not share a predominant mode of resonance. Imagine four mental health professionals having lunch: a biological psychiatrist, a social worker who works as a client advocate at an agency for indigent clients, a postmodern-oriented counselor who believes there is no such thing as objective reality, and a psychoanalyst. Imagine further that the waitress is having a slow day so is chatting with the group. When she hears they are all therapists she shares a story about her cousin who suffers from depression.

After hearing the story the psychiatrist says the cousin likely suffers from a chemical imbalance, the social worker asks if anyone has helped the cousin apply for disability, the psychoanalyst asks about the cousin's relationship with her father, and the postmodern counselor storms out of the lunch offended by the marginalizing mode of discourse expressed by her companions. Worse still, the waitress gets a lousy tip because the psychoanalyst never resolved issues with his mother, the psychiatrist got paged, and the social worker (although she advocated for a larger tip), doesn't make much money. Four people in the "same" type of profession with no predominant mode of resonance or more simply put: same planet, different universes.

All social holons from couples to families to political parties have a predominant mode of resonance that can shift if the members or membership of the holon change. Each member has her or his own center of gravity or altitude (described in Chapter 1 and elaborated in Chapter 3). The politics of all relationship is partially negotiating a predominant mode of resonance between and across the members of a social holon. Negotiating predominant modes of resonance is the underlying reality behind all forms of group politics. A political agenda requires finding ways of getting people who you believe share your predominant mode of resonance into positions where they have the power to make changes.

This is trickier than many people think. There is a universe of difference between sharing a label (e.g., Democrat; Republican) and sharing a dominant mode of resonance. This holds true from large political parties to a relationship between a husband and wife or a client and therapist. In relationship work in psychotherapy, therapists must identify each party's center of gravity and then determine the probability of negotiating a dominant mode of resonance and how to do that. Understanding your client's center of gravity and "languaging" your interventions accordingly is an important tool in cultivating the "we" of the therapeutic relationship. Once a "we" is established, client and therapist negotiate a predominant mode of resonance that is, ideally, something the client carries between sessions.

Perhaps the most intriguing aspect of the lower-left perspective is what Wilber calls "the magic of we," that is, the heart of the therapeutic alliance in psychotherapy. This "we" is a shared understanding between client and therapist. Using the quadrants, we might say that client and therapist come into the relationship as first persons trying to take a second-person perspective of the other to forge this "we" space in which the therapeutic work is done. Given that relationship factors have been estimated to account for approximately 40% of change in psychotherapy,[43] the "we" of the therapy session is important. Very little change is accomplished in therapy without a therapeutic alliance. This is either unknown or ignored by every advocate of court-ordered treatment who makes no provision for screening court-ordered clients for readiness to engage in therapy.[44]

Every theory of psychotherapy addresses the issue of the therapeutic alliance or the "we" of therapy and Integral Psychotherapy complements these with the therapist's understanding of development, use of perspectives, and functioning in a framework the ground of which is spirit. For example, the six core conditions of Rogers[45] are complemented in Integral Psychotherapy by expanding unconditional positive regard to infinity, supplementing the idea of therapist congruence and client incongruence with developmental altitude, and languaging the communication of empathy and unconditional positive regard in a manner that reflects the client's altitude.

Let me unpack those a bit. Expanding unconditional positive regard to infinity is similar to loving to infinity. Unconditional positive regard is described by Rogers as "the extent that the therapist finds himself experiencing a warm acceptance of each aspect of the client's experience as being a part of that client, he is experiencing unconditional positive regard."[46] Although warm acceptance may seem vague, think of the warm acceptance many adults have for young children whose behavior can be as annoying as it can be charming. For the accepting adult, it is all one package and although the adult may direct the child, he or she does not feel a need to judge the child. To the extent that a therapist's meditative or contemplative practices help that therapist practice equanimity and warm acceptance, the unconditional positive regard may radiate to infinity.

The idea of supplementing Rogers' concept of congruence with developmental altitude is really a fine-tuning of congruence. Congruence is the extent to which a person is freely and deeply her or himself. This applies to the therapist and the client. What we learn in Chapter 3 on ego development is that there are many centers of gravity that one can inhabit with regard to how one defines what is "I." Healthy identification of "I" is synonymous with congruence. However, it is not until the later stages of ego development that this sense of I one is comfortable with starts to become an object of awareness.

Finally, Rogers' sixth core condition for therapeutic personality change was that the therapist, to some extent, communicates their experience of empathy and unconditional positive regard for the client to the client. In Integral Psychotherapy we refine this through the perspective taking outlined in this chapter and then choosing language that reflects the client's developmental altitude.

HERMENEUTICS AND SEMIOTICS

Finally, the two zones of the lower-left quadrant use hermeneutics and semiotics. Hermeneutics in Zone 1 is the use of interpretation to facilitate what Wilber calls "the *actual felt texture*" of shared space—"the inside of a we . . . the we is formed when a first-person singular is converted to a first-peson plural by inclusion of a second-person."[47] Now from Zone 2 or the outside, there is a structure to that shared "we" space that includes a grammar, a syntax, rules, chains of signifiers, or what Wilber calls a semiotics that can be thought of as the structure of a symbol system. Part of working with couples, families, or groups includes learning or helping members negotiate the semiotics that exists or is forming in the "we" space. By facilitating the form of the "we" space, the therapist then facilitates different we feelings experienced by the members.

Summary: The Clinical Utility of the Lower-Left Quadrant

The clinical utility is rather neatly summarized by the two zones of the lower-left quadrant. From the inside view, clinicians and clients are aiming to forge an experience of "we" in the therapeutic setting. This felt texture of shared space becomes the spirit of the therapeutic container within which the clinical work is done. From the outside view, clinicians are aiming to understand the semiotics of couples, families, and groups so as to better facilitate the felt texture of shared space within couples, families, and groups. Supervisors can also work with the semiotics of the therapeutic relationship to help therapists in work with clients. From a professional view, the politics of mental health organizations can be examined from Zone 2 and experience of shared space (or lack of it) can be monitored by individual members as one indicator of the value of the organization.

Revisiting the Lower-Right Quadrant

The lower-right quadrant represents the *interobjective* perspective. The interobjective perspective represents the exterior aspects of collectives or groups—those aspects of groups that can be measured without hermeneutic dialogue. Things captured in this perspective include objective aspects of social institutions or groups, and systems theories that focus on the relation of the elements of units like families or ecosystems. Similar to the upper-right quadrant, the language used to express this perspective is what we call "its" language. In psychotherapy, systems theories are frequently used as examples of the perspective from this quadrant. *Systems theory* is a term for a multidisciplinary study of the structure and properties of systems in terms of relationships from which new properties emerge. The most common application of this is family therapy, which studies the structure and properties of the family system. As you may have guessed, the description of systems theory and family systems is a Zone 2 description. Family systems theory also studies the communication between the family members and this is the Zone 1 view of the family.

We might say that families are composed of individual members *and* the communication between those members. In Integral terms, the family is a social holon that is composed of individual holons. The communication between those individuals can be mapped out and studied. It is typically studied in relation to the "texture of shared space" that we charted in the lower-left quadrant.

There are certainly systems other than families that are relevant in psychotherapy. Everything from institutions that the client is involved with to the legal system that governs your practice to the group that wrote your code of ethics can be explored in the lower-right quadrant. In this quadrant, we identify any group an individual holon (client or therapist) is "inside of." We can then map the workings of the group (Zone 2) as well as the communication between its members (Zone 1).

SUMMARY: THE CLINICAL UTILITY OF THE LOWER-RIGHT QUADRANT

The clinical utility of the lower-right quadrant lies in application of its perspective to couples, families, or groups in the role of "identified client" as well as to understanding the groups to which individuals belong (by choice or coercion). The lower-right quadrant also provides the perspective and zones through which to explore the functioning of professional groups. This includes the actual organization of the group as well as the mode of communication aimed at creating the predominant mode of resonance in the lower-left quadrant. Like the upper-right quadrant, the language used to express the lower-right perspective is "its" language or language that infers an objective, third-person assessment. Neither the group- nor the individual-felt experience is captured in this language that, like the language of all quadrants, is what makes it partial. Useful, but partial.

This brings us to the end of the second part of this chapter. The first part focused on perspectives as reflections of the four Integral quadrants (and thus reflections of aspects of your being). We also have covered the language typical of each perspective and the two zones that can be used to explore each quadrant. Before moving on to the next section, I introduce another of Wilber's pioneering ideas and suggest an application to Integral Psychotherapy.

Perspectives Expressed in Language as a Reflection of Psychodynamics

In this section of the chapter, we summarize how perspectives can be expressed with language in such a way as to point to problems in the client. In this sense, we cover the way first, second, and third-person language are properly used and then how their improper use can point the clinician toward the problem (or part of the problem). To use perspectives in this manner in the psychotherapy session requires a general understanding of the self-system and the self-boundary in Integral Psychotherapy. Although this is covered in detail elsewhere,[48] a general summary suffices for this section on perspectives and language.

A Quick Tour of the Self-System in Integral Psychotherapy

In order to examine the relationship between language and psychodynamics, we must first have at least a general understanding of the Integral self-system, which is the topic of Chapter 3. The self-system in Integral Psychotherapy includes the proximate self, the distal self, the antecedent self, and the shadow. The antecedent self is first experienced as the ever-present witness but is actually the field of awareness within which all things arise. The proximate self is thought of as synonymous with what Loevinger called "ego" or what we might call our subject. Some of our subject we are aware of, some of it we are unaware of because it is the context we are "swimming in" (in other words it is not repressed, it is something we are embedded in). The primary dynamic of growth in one's "I" we call the subject–object dynamic. When you as a subject consistently make some aspect of yourself an object of awareness we say that aspect is no longer proximate but distal. Metaphorically, we might say we have moved it from the proximate part of the self-system to the distal part of the self-system.[49] Instead of being so close to it (proximate) that we can't really look at it, we gain some distance (distal) and are able to make it an object of awareness. This subject–object dynamic is the force behind healthy translation and transformation. In healthy translation, the subject broadens the scope of self and refines its ability to navigate with that sense. In transformation, the subject of one stage deepens to the point where it becomes the object for the subject of the next stage.[50]

THE SELF-BOUNDARY AND SHADOW

Recall the case of Linda, the client who wanted to "get outside of" her divorce. In these terms we would say that the therapeutic work we did with the genogram helped her make her role as wife and her marriage an object of awareness so she could move on with her life now that the marriage was over. At one point, Linda would say her whole identity was immersed in the waters of the marriage to the point where she took that context for granted. Once the divorce forced her out of that context she needed to psychologically, emotionally, and spiritually engage that reality.

The self-boundary is where you intrapsychically draw the line between what is self and what is not. Put another way it is your sense of what is self ("I") and what is "other." Each of us daily negotiates making decisions about what is self and what is other; sometimes accurately and sometimes inaccurately. For Linda, the sense of "I" was deeply tied up in being married. Recall also that in discussing Linda's case I noted that she not only had to make the marriage (the good and bad parts) an object of awareness but identify with it or *own* it. If she could own it then she was free to disidentify from it and move on. If she did not own it (identify with it) she would likely dissociate it or push it out of awareness. The breakup of the marriage also forced her to look at and own aspects of herself she would rather deny and push out of awareness. In particular, her anger was something that she spent a great deal of energy pushing away. In the parlance of the Integral self-system we call pushing something out of awareness making it "shadow" or "other." In this sense, we dress up as "other" something that is actually "I" in order to push it out of awareness. This sounds bizarre but we all do it in order to preserve a sense of self that, however false, we desperately want to be true. In this sense, shadow is composed of those things we lie to ourselves about.

In therapy sessions we can get clues about what aspects of the client's "I" they are lying to themselves about by the way they use first-, second-, and third-person language. In this sense, "I" language is the person speaking and in Linda's case when she talked about her marriage you would assume she would say things like "Well I am really angry about my husband's cheating and my marriage falling apart—I hate what he did." But, what she would say was things like "Well you know how it is, you get married and really commit, you put all this effort into it and it doesn't make any difference, none at all, it falls apart." When she would talk about the anxiety she would say, "It just comes over me—it is ruining my life."

IMPLICATIONS OF SELF-SYSTEM DYNAMICS FOR PERSPECTIVAL DISTORTION

Now these subtle distinctions are important. In talking about her marriage Linda would frequently use second- and third-person language referring to herself as "you" and the marriage as "it." Her anxiety was almost always an "it" that "just came over her." Don't get me wrong—this is how she experienced these things but this was part of the problem—she was dressing up parts of her "I" as "you" or "it" in order to preserve an unrealistic self-image.

Before we go further, let's make sure you are following how common this is. Have you ever done something you would condemn in someone else then spent the rest of the day rationalizing why it was right? This could include speaking badly of someone, cursing another driver on the freeway, claiming credit for something that wasn't really your accomplishment, and so on. To fully understand the driving force behind this subject–other dynamic, it is best to look at examples from your own life—you have to pull your humanness out as an object of awareness. The impulse I am referring to here is the impulse to explain away an action or thought that you authored but that you don't think is "like you." This is pushing away some part of your "I" that clashes with how you like to think of yourself.

Now let's go back to Linda's case. By using second- and third-person language, she was showing me clues as to what she was doing psychologically—pushing her marriage, her anger, her humiliation, and the years of life she devoted to being married away from herself. Now most of us would say, "Well sure, these are unpleasant things and it is natural to push them away." When you get served "maggots in the bread of life" it is natural to want to push them away. If it were possible to just push aspects of ourselves away with no consequences it would make sense and psychological life would be a lot easier. BUT, we can't and here is why.

From his earliest publications, Sigmund Freud developed what came to be known as the economic principle of the psyche,[51] which simply stated is that the psyche has a finite amount of energy to work with so energy that is being used to push some aspect of your "I" away, is not available to do something else. In Freud's system, when the energy related to this "subject–other" dynamic is freed, the person is supposed to be cured of a symptom and have more psychic energy available. Wilber, elaborating on the economic principle, uses the simile of psychic energy as a limited amount of money you have to work with. The money you consciously invest in subject–object work pays off dividends allowing you to continue growing. The money you invest in pushing things into shadow then is unavailable to you. Thus, cannot put money into the shadow account without loss of capital. The idea is that sooner or later you will need that capital to continue growing. When the content or extent of shadow begins to interfere with living your life, then you develop symptoms and end up in psychotherapy. Psychotherapy is the process of rediscovering the capital you've used to push aspects of your "I" out of awareness. To reclaim it you have to face the aspects of "I" you've been pushing away.

The "1-2-3" of Psychotherapy

In *Integral Spirituality*, Wilber noted that there are many *experiences* of God and these can be somewhat summarized through the language of the first-, second-, and third-person. The first-person experience of God is an identification with God (the "I am" experience), the second-person is God as the "Great Thou" (God as "other" to worship), and the third-person experience is God as an interconnected "it" (e.g., "great web of life"). A main point of *Integral Spirituality* is that all three are important facets of God. Similarly, these same three perspectives (the 1-2-3) apply to psychotherapy. We need all three perspectives for a healthy "we" and want to avoid getting overly focused on one to the exclusion of the others.

The evolution of approaches to therapy and corresponding theories is in one respect the discovery (or rediscovery) of one of these perspectives and the lobbying to bring it back into the understanding of therapists. Sometimes, this lobbying process gets out of control and the enthusiasts for the theory commit the category error of trying to account for all perspectives with just one. As Bert Parlee has written, "therapists have perceptual lenses through which they view the client's situation and personality, and the therapeutic process itself."[52] We might paraphrase by noting that therapists and clients have perspectival lenses through which they experience and make meaning of client symptoms, the therapeutic process, and the experience of suffering and change. Similar to

Wilber's 1-2-3 of God we can think of a 1-2-3 of psychotherapy. Echoing Wilber, I asserted in Chapter 1 that healthy translation includes being able to use as many perspectives as possible and balance one's own quadrants of experience. With that in mind, psychotherapists make use of all perspectives represented by the 1-2-3 shorthand without reifying any one perspective.

The "1" of psychotherapy can be thought of as varieties on the first-person experience including the first-person plural "we" of the therapeutic container. Integral psychotherapists strongly emphasize the notion of self as instrument. Although the maintenance of the instrument is the focus of ILP, Zone 1 mindfulness of the self from the upper-left perspective throughout the therapeutic process is the use of the self as instrument. This includes clinical judgment, empathic identity, experiences of countertransference, personal knowledge, and attunement to intuition, fantasy, and awareness of communion.

There are times when clinicians make the mistake of reifying the first-person perspective to the neglect of the others. One therapist, James, claimed to "work intuitively" to allow his soul total access to the session to facilitate what he called "deep healing." James interpreted any client dissonance with this approach as resistance and tended to regard all physical symptoms clients suffered from as metaphors for deeper psychological conflicts. James had several ethical complaints filed against him with the state psychology board. Although he had received one warning from the board, at the time of our last contact he had not broadened his approach.

Clearly, this is an extreme example that I use to make the point but many therapists harbor sentiments similar to James'. They may know better than to voice them, but they come out occasionally in supervisory discussions. Other than reification of the first-person perspective, another glaring problem with James' approach to therapy is a total neglect of Zone 2 in the upper-left quadrant. He was clearly well-versed in Zone 1 but his neglect of Zone 2 blinded him not only to critical developmental variables in his clients but to his own ego identification. Insight into the latter would increase the possibility that he might consider there are things related to therapy that *may not be* "on his radar screen" so to speak.

The "2" of psychotherapy can be thought of as variations on the second-person perspective and in particular what Martin Buber referred to as the "I–Thou" relationship. For psychotherapists, this I–Thou includes how the therapist approaches the client—with both head and heart. I once heard a story told about Swami Muktananda who was answering questions about how he worked with people. He told one questioner that he tried to behold every person as if that person were his favorite in all the world and today was this favorite person's birthday. This struck me as a wonderful way to practice Roger's unconditional positive regard. It was one cognitive technique that might flex the emotional muscle that opens one's heart space. This is a sacred approach the therapist can use to honor the "thou" of the client.

Certainly, this "2" of psychotherapy can derail for both therapist and client. Some therapists operating under what we might call the "myth of the objective observer" fail to fully account for their role in the therapeutic process and review cases as if each client were exposed to the "same" therapist operating in a same or similar manner. These therapists frequently believe in a "one-size-fits-all" science of psychotherapy devoid of art. They also neglect the intersubjective aspects that manifest differently as the subjects involved change. One acquaintance of mine was trained by a prestigious cognitive therapist and did only cognitive therapy in his practice. This was not as problematic to me as his assertion that cognitive therapy could be done with all clients as long as they were able to make psychological contact. Although he honored the variations he experienced as "you" in the client, he did not monitor his own reactions to and involvement in the therapy as a therapeutic variable of significant import.

Many times in therapy the client projects onto the person of the therapist a "sacred thou" that is really more projection than reality. This is one variation of what psychodynamic theorists would call transference but is also a distortion that can occur in the "2" of psychotherapy. Perhaps the greatest barriers to the sacred "we" of a therapeutic alliance are unrealistic perceptions of the therapist or the client. When a therapist or client is not seen to some degree as fully human, the "we" space is not operating from a predominant mode of resonance. Trying to create a "we" space without opening to the other is akin to building one's house on the proverbial sand.

The "3" of psychotherapy contains all the "it" and "its" elements that are part of any therapeutic relationship. Being able to take a third-person perspective of the relationship as in supervision or of the client (as in intake) is part of the work. The "3" of psychotherapy, reflecting the right-hand quadrants and their perspectives as it does, is still the perspective that can be used to, even temporarily, hijack the entire enterprise. Derailments related to the "3" of psychotherapy not only occur daily but are supported by large pharmaceutical lobbies and much of the consumer culture. When a client's personal, intersubjective narrative is reduced to a mythological "chemical imbalance" it not only does damage to the client but to the whole therapeutic culture. There is a great deal of effort being made to draw adherents to a predominant mode of resonance that reduces mind to brain and psychology to chemistry. Again, the 1-2-3 of psychotherapy is at least acknowledging the place of I/we, you, and it in the therapeutic process.

Concluding Thoughts

In this chapter I have elaborated on the use of perspectives in Integral Psychotherapy and offered four primary uses of them. First, understanding perspectives as indicators of cognitive development is important because cognitive development is necessary but not sufficient for ego development. Also, cognitive development gives therapists some idea of their client's perspective-taking ability. Second I reviewed the understanding of perspectives as expressions of the quadrants introduced in Chapter 1. From there we reviewed the two zones in each quadrant and the clinical utility of each zone and quadrant. Third, I outlined how the client' use of first-, second-, and third-person language can reflect psychodynamics that give therapists clues as to what a given client is threatened by or trying to push out of awareness. Finally, in summing up, I proposed a 1-2-3 of psychotherapy that again emphasizes the clinical utility of all three ways to conceptualize it.

3

The Self-System and Ego Development

R. Elliott Ingersoll

"There is always one too many around me"—thus thinks the hermit. "Always one times one—eventually that makes two." I and me are always too deep in conversation . . .[1]

—Friedrich Nietzsche

The Wiles of the Self-System

When we talk about psychotherapy we frequently refer to the self. Clients go to therapy to "work on themselves," while therapists try to assist clients in this amorphous task. We talk about self-esteem,[2] self-efficacy,[3] and self-injury.[4] What is this "self" that is so present in the literature but seems to vanish every time we try to point to it? In Chapter 1 I noted that at each level of development we can have real and false selves. This involves the self-system as well. The self is wily (yes—like the coyote in Roadrunner cartoons). If the self weren't wily it would not require a complex map to make it an object of awareness. We use the concept of the map of the self to help people gain insight and make an object of awareness of the way their minds work. This then helps clients make mindful choices about how to react to their experiences as well as increasing their level of self-awareness.

While founder of Gestalt Therapy Fritz Perls[5] believed awareness in and of itself is curative, we go two steps further in Integral Psychotherapy. First awareness *and* ownership of that which is an object of awareness is what *seems* curative (outcome research in psychotherapy is still a new field and it is hard to say which therapeutic factors are most operative case by case). I have said several times that this takes practice. If we have literally spent years pushing some aspect of ourselves out of awareness even when we become aware of it, this aspect of self can easily slip back into psychic oblivion. This can even happen when making it an object of awareness has been the cause of a powerful emotional release. After we can consistently make something an object of awareness, we

have to disidentify from it so we are free to move on to the next experience
of growth. This is the subject–object sequence wherein we (a) make aspects of
the client and/or their lives objects of awareness, (b) facilitate the work of the
client consistently owning or identifying with that which is made an object
of awareness, and (c) finally help the client disidentify with and integrate the
object of awareness. The Integral map of the self-system provides a framework
for understanding these dynamics and how, when things go wrong, we can
actually disown part of ourselves.

Every therapist needs a map of the self in order to structure what he or she
is doing with a client and where the therapist seems to be heading. The Integral
self-system is a map of the self, how our self-sense evolves and how we metabolize
experience through it. As Wilber noted several times, the Integral self-system is the
result of partial truths developed in numerous areas of psychology and psychotherapy. Particularly, the schools of depth psychology have pioneered our ability
to offer a self-system map that transcends sectarian jargon but integrates different
theories about how the mind works. Having said that however, I need to be clear
that I do not see it as necessary that a therapist adhere to explanations offered by
the schools of depth psychotherapy. I think that other pioneers like Aaron Beck
have made clear that one can appreciate the insights into how the mind seems
to work that depth psychologists have given us without necessarily abiding by all
the depth psychology explanations as to *why* the mind seems to work that way.
Put more candidly, it seems that Freud's brilliance was in observing and recording
psychological dynamics but not in explaining their etiology.

This chapter is divided into the following four sections:

- Describing the Self-System: In this section I provide a summary of
  the self-system including proximate, distal, and antecedent selves
  and then the shadow. I also discuss the notion of psychogenic
  pathology.

- Subpersonalities: In this section I cover what Wilber and other
  theorists have called subpersonalities, and review the subject–object
  and subject–other dynamics.

- The Self-System, Defenses, and the Threat Zone.

- Ego Development: This section is devoted to describing the
  proximate self as ego. I summarize the work of Jane Loevinger and
  Susanne Cook-Greuter, as well as offer clinical applications.

Describing the Self-System

As many thinkers in the wisdom traditions have concluded, the more intently
one seeks a self, the more ephemeral it becomes. Students of Zen who are

seeking "the way" are instructed by the Roshi to "please show this self that is seeking." The self is like the pattern of a whirlpool. It is consistent and ever changing, powerful yet dependent for its existence on forces around it like irregularities in stream banks or winds. Despite the fact that (barring brain damage) we can all refer to a sense of self, this "sense" is far from a unified thing. As anyone struggling over whether to eat a second doughnut can attest to, we are divided within and sometimes against ourselves. We argue against ourselves, talk to ourselves, and most importantly lie to ourselves. As Nietzsche wrote, the most common lies are those we tell ourselves. Wilber has noted that among the pioneering insights bequeathed us by Freud, the observation of how we lie to ourselves "tops" the list. Although the Integral self-system offers a map for understanding things like lies and other pathologies, it also provides a map of what is happening when we are healthy and growing.

Proximate, Distal, Antecedent, and Shadow

Wilber described the self as the navigator of life.[6] This navigator is nested in (and navigating) the AQAL matrix described in Chapter 1 (the quadrants, levels, lines, states, and types of the Integral system). Integral Psychotherapy relies on four aspects of the self-system that, although part of the same system, have unique qualities in relation to psychotherapy. The four aspects of the self-system are the proximate self, the distal self, the antecedent (or transcendent) self, and the shadow.[7] Although some of the foregoing description may sound a bit techni-cal, remember, just like the Integral quadrants, these aspects of the self-system are all aspects of you. The phrase *self-system* was first used in the interpersonal psychiatry of Harry Sullivan who coined it to describe the "organization of experience within the personality."[8] Jane Loevinger, who drew extensively on Sullivan's work in creating her theory of ego development, also preferred the label *self* or *self-system* to *ego*.[9] The proximate self is seen as synonymous with Loevinger's ego, which is the focus of the last section in this chapter.

A NOTE ON PATHOLOGY

In Integral Psychotherapy, the self-system can navigate normal development and the development of pathology. In normal development the navigational maps are accurate, in pathology the maps have been tossed overboard and the familiar reference points have all shifted. It is important to pause a moment to really define what I mean by pathology in this chapter. I am specifically referring to what appears to be psychogenic pathology, meaning, pathology that developed *primarily* (although not exclusively) through the psychological dynamics of the mind. This is an important point because currently there is much lobbying over the definition of "mental disease." Therapists using the *DSM* frequently are under the impression that all the disorders are somehow rooted in physiology.

As described in Chapter 1, the *DSM* is *categorical* in the way it organizes symptoms of psychological distress into syndromes.[10] These syndromes, however, are not diseases in the allopathic sense of the word (like bacterial infections are diseases). As the task force on the next version of the manual (*DSM-V*) has concluded, "the field of psychiatry has thus far failed to identify a single neurobiological phenotypic marker or gene that is useful in making a diagnosis of a major psychiatric disorder or for predicting response to psychopharmacological treatment . . . current classification in psychiatry therefore resembles the medicine of 50–100 years ago, before the underlying pathophysiology of many disease processes was understood."[11] The most obvious candidates for physical etiology are disorders like Schizophrenia that frequently show a common pattern of onset and present with pervasive symptoms throughout life. The latest theories of the origin of Schizophrenia lie in gene expression and neuronal migration/selection (the processes by which neurons, early in life, move into place to form brain circuits). Thus, we know that we cannot account for psychopathology solely through biological mechanisms despite promising but partial work by researchers like Nobel laureate Eric Kandel.[12] As noted in Chapter 1, pathology is an AQAL affair, but there are primary dynamics in the self-system, pioneered by the Western depth psychologists, which account for pathology that arises or is exacerbated by psychological factors.

My conclusions on this point are that because psychopathology is an all-quadrant affair, we cannot presume to reduce it to merely physiological dysfunction. Similarly, we cannot reduce it to only psychological dysfunction, cultural oppression, or social injustice. All of these factors may play a role. This is an important point as some of Wilber's writings have emphasized what is called the *spectrum of psychopathology*. This is pioneering work and my sense is that Wilber was simply trying to summarize the psychological aspects of pathology. Based on my reading of his work and conversations with him I do not feel he ever meant that spectrum to be taken literally or partially such as trying to account for things like severe autism or schizophrenia with only psychological variables. That said, however, there are still many in the integral community who lean too much on this spectrum of pathology neglecting to realize it is only one of many variables. Dr. Mark Forman has written a fair and balanced view of the spectrum and I recommend his book, which includes a rich presentation of that topic.[13]

THE PROXIMATE AND DISTAL SELVES

The proximate self (meaning close to or proximate to you) is what a person is most intimately identified with. As noted, it can be viewed as the same as what Loevinger (1976) described as "ego." Much of the proximate self is unconscious, not because it is repressed, but because the person is embedded in it.[14] Recall

Brigid's story from the first chapter. She was raised in a Christian framework and identified with that for a number of years until some other aspect of herself sought to be seen. When that other aspect of herself, her Goddess eye, arose, she grew into a new spirituality and the Christian framework no longer fit her. We could say that the Christian Brigid, who was the subject of her early life, became an object of awareness to the Pagan Brigid, who was the later young adult subject who could reflect back on the Christian period, own it, but no longer be embedded in it. The proximate-self is the lens through which we focus—the infinity of stimuli called life—and, similar to eyeglasses, the lenses need cleaned off and even changed every now and again.

LANGUAGE AND THE SELF-SYSTEM

Recall in Chapter 2, I discussed how dynamics of pathology might be reflected in the language that clients use. Speaking about oneself in the second or third person for example, can indicate that the person is pushing some aspect of themselves away. The self-system also allows for changes in language to reflect embeddedness and distal ownership. In Fig. 3.1,[15] the proximate self is reflected in the language of "I" and "I/me." The experience of "I" in the proximate self is one of embeddedness meaning whatever is considered "I" is mostly subject and not yet an object of awareness. For example, I currently identified as a therapist, musician, and university professor. I fully expect at some point one

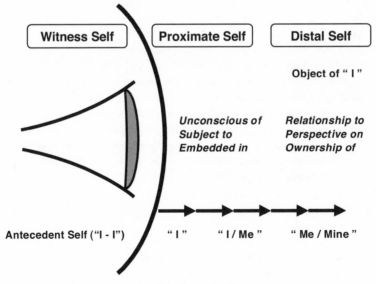

Figure 3.1. The Integral self-system.

or all of those identifications may change. If I am totally embedded in anyone of them any change in that identification will likely be painful. If I can make the identifications objects of awareness, I increase the chance of changing the identifications with less pain. As noted in Chapter 1, the main work of psychotherapy is to help clients make aspects of themselves and their lives objects of awareness. In this example, making one's proximate identifications objects of awareness is key to therapeutic growth.

In many cases, what needs to be an object of awareness is an aspect of the proximate self. In this model, when something the self identifies with consistently becomes an object of awareness, it is no longer labeled the *proximate* self but is labeled the *distal* self. In Brigid's case, her experience of self as Christian consistently became an object of awareness (or distal) during her experience as a Pagan. Based on this experience, she was very quickly able to make her Wiccan identification distal in the context of her "Goddess eye" that seemed to transcend all spiritual paths.

Going back to a key difference between Fritz Perls' view of awareness and an Integral view, just because something becomes an object of awareness does not mean that it is owned, integrated, and eventually disidentified with. This is one of the pioneering insights developed by Wilber in several publications. Many times, something becomes an object of awareness that a person experiences as threatening. In these cases the threatening part of self can be made "other" rather than being "owned" and made distal. Rather than the "subject" becoming "object," the "subject" becomes "other." When the subject is made object, owned and integrated we call that the "subject–object dynamic." When the subject is rejected and made other, we call that the "subject–other dynamic.[16] In other cases, something can be made an object of awareness, not made other, but equally not owned. Another of Wilber's pioneering insights is that sometimes meditation can hinder the owning, integrating, and disidentifying processes by making things objects of awareness and encouraging detachment (rather than embodied ownership) that can turn into dissociation.[17] For example the client who meditates and regularly watches his anger in meditation is no closer to owning it after the meditation than he was prior to the meditation.

So when development goes well, the distal self grows as aspects of the proximate self that were once the subject for you but from which you have gained some distance increase. This "gaining distance" is experienced by you as being able to accept and possibly own parts of yourself as just that—parts. In this case, you accept them as *part* of who you are but don't wholly identify with or become embedded in them. Embeddedness, the "fish-in-water" phenomenon, is characteristic of the proximate self. From the perspective of the distal self, things that were once experienced as subject (as the proximate self) can now be experienced as objects of awareness. In Fig. 3.1, the language of the distal self is described as "me/mine." For example a person who experiences his or her tendency to anger distally will say "that is a challenging quality of mine."

Wilber has described this as "a mode of self becomes merely a component of a higher-order self."[18] More recently, Wilber stated that the "I" of one stage ("that's just how I am") becomes the "me" of the next stage ("I used to think that was all there was to me").[19] From a psychotherapy perspective, making something that was "subject" an object of your awareness in the distal self frees you from unconscious embeddedness. This freeing expands your choices in how to navigate life.

Robert Kegan outlined similar dynamics. Kegan described shifts in our identity from proximate to distal self as an ongoing balancing between subject and object. He wrote that "subject–object relations emerge out of a lifelong process of development: a succession of qualitative differentiations of the self from the world, with a qualitatively more extensive object with which to be in relation . . . a natural history of . . . successive triumphs of 'relationship to' rather than 'embeddedness in.' "[20] In Integral terms, "embeddedness in" is the experience of your proximate self, whereas "relationship to" is the experience of your distal self. Kegan claimed that this notion of development is indispensable to psychotherapy because how we define what is "self" and what is "other" frames our experience and meanings.

ME AND MY SHADOW

So what happens when we refuse to own a part of ourselves? What happens to that part? This is one of the most amazing experiences (painful as it can be) of the human mind. We actually have the capacity to push aspects of ourselves out of awareness and pretend that they don't even belong to us—they are thus made "other." Here is an example. Tasha had come into therapy for depression. Although she met the criteria for Major Depressive Disorder, Single Episode, this told me little. It was in her narrative that I began to understand how Tasha's depression developed.

Tasha had a history of negative relationships with men. In most instances, she felt attraction to men who were more or less unavailable to her—married or otherwise committed men. Her "relationships" were always "affairs" for the men involved. She would construe their attention as meaning they would ultimately want to get divorced and marry her but she was very emphatic that she "didn't care" if that happened or not. She claimed to be a self-sufficient woman and was constantly annoyed by what she perceived as "emotional neediness" in others. Despite this, whenever the relationships ended Tasha felt used, rejected, and misunderstood. On top of that, the relationships usually ended with violent quarrels as Tasha would lash out and sometimes physically attack her romantic partner claiming he was "just another fucking liar." She would maintain these outbursts had nothing to do with "neediness" but the "fact" that the men were lying to her.

A few sessions into our relationship, Tasha described her relationship with her father as also one of constant disappointment. Her father divorced her mother when Tasha was 5 years old and rarely kept promises to meet Tasha after school or take her to special events. Tasha remained faithful that her father would eventually keep a promise until at the age of 13 when she began attracting the attention of boys from her school. She dated several boys and was somewhat promiscuous for the time (early 1980s) but never had what she would describe as a deep, satisfying, long-term relationship. In college she studied math and science, settling on a major in mathematics. She had affairs with two of her professors (both married at the time) while an undergraduate. She earned an advanced degree and now chairs a math department at a 2-year college.

Two months into our sessions, Tasha made a connection between the rejection she experienced from her father and the failed relationships that had become the norm for her. At the end of her last relationship she was having dinner with the man who ended the relationship before dessert. She was telling the story when all of a sudden she broke down in tears. She recalled waiting for her father at a restaurant when she was 16. She had gotten her driver's license and her father promised to take her to a really nice place for dinner to celebrate. Tasha's mother let her take the car and there she waited in the lobby for 45 minutes for her father. In the session she recalled the humiliation, pain, and rage she felt as if it were happening anew. It is fair to say that at that moment, the 16-year-old whose hopes had been dashed yet again appeared in the session and really became an object of awareness for Tasha.

Based on this abreaction,[21] Tasha clearly saw the patterns in her adolescent promiscuity (getting her father's attention in a negative way) and in her attraction to "unavailable" men. By pursuing unavailable men, the 16-year-old part of her believed she never again had to suffer the disappointment that came with being rejected. Although on the surface this may seem contradictory because all she felt in her relationships was rejection, the idea was that she was "beating life to the punch" in that she was trying to tell herself that the relationships she pursued would never amount to anything because the men were unavailable. This way, she didn't have to get invested and then suffer rejection.

After much emotional processing, we ended the 90-minute session and Tasha said she was going to go home and sleep, so exhausting was the emotional energy she had experienced. She did just that and the next session we processed her insight further. After that she was out of town for a week at a conference. The following week she came to the session and announced she had a new man in her life. As she described him I felt she was leaving out some important details: Where did he live? How had they met? Where did he work? Furthermore, Tasha did not look like someone who was excited about a new relationship. She looked more anxious than anything. I noted this and Tasha shared that the relationship had some complicated dynamics but she thought these would resolve once he was divorced. I waited a beat, two beats, and then her jaw about hit the floor. "What the fuck is wrong with me?" she said. In processing this return to the habits that weren't working for her, she had managed to push her insight about her father and what she really wanted totally out of awareness again.

Tasha's courageous work also illustrates the importance of practice and why, in some cases, therapy takes more time than others. It is probably unrealistic to expect anyone who has pushing something out of awareness for 15 years to consistently keep it in awareness after one 90-minute burst of insight. We spent three more sessions on Tasha's new insights and negotiated homework assignments to help her keep the insight in awareness. Through assignments like journaling Tasha began to own or identify with her need to feel loved by a man. She would practice ways of framing this need in strong, healthy terms (e.g., "I am strong enough to need a man's love and love freely in return"). Clearly, she could not push the need out of awareness as effectively as she had prior to therapy as evidenced by her anxiety in the session. After about 2 months, she really was able to own and begin integrating her emotional past. At this point, her energy level picked up and her symptoms of anxiety and depression remitted. When we say that psychotherapy is basically helping clients make things objects of awareness and own them we mean *consistently* make them objects of awareness and that takes practice. Once that is done, however, that object of awareness can be said to be safely distal and not consuming energy that the person can now use for more enjoyable pursuits.

Tasha's case illustrates three other important principles in Integral Psychotherapy—(a) the principle of the shadow, (b) the principle of subpersonalities, and (c) the principle of quasi-transformation in psychotherapy. Let's take these one at a time.

The Principle of Shadow

> there are certain things which we hate to tell anybody else, or which we
> are utterly unable to express at all . . . there are some other things which
> we hate to admit to ourselves, which we try to hide from ourselves and
> which, once they are accidently touched upon, we immediately endeavor
> to crowd out of our thoughts.[22]
>
> —Sigmund Freud

The shadow in Integral psychotherapy is not to be confused with Carl Jung's archetype of the shadow. Although there are similarities, the Integral construct is more straightforward and does not rely on the dubious construct of archetypes.[23] In Integral Psychotherapy, the shadow can be succinctly defined as things we lie to ourselves about and push out of awareness. We may use different defenses to become unaware of shadow material but the unifying factor is that the shadow material is in some way unpalatable to our image of ourselves so we simply push it away. In the language of the self-system, we make it "other" with the subject–other dynamic. Although we always have shadow material we can get better at catching ourselves pushing things out of awareness and better at using techniques to retrieve them once they are unconscious.

For 16-year-old Tasha, the rejection she felt from her father and the resulting image of herself as needy and "clingy" was pushed out of awareness. On one level, this makes sense and the younger we are, the fewer coping tools we have. At different points in our lives we need to push pieces of ourselves or our lives out of awareness. When we stabilize at a new stage of development, we usually push away what we identified with at the previous stage. This is fine as long as we go back eventually and recollect these pieces of self. If we don't, they can increase in psychic energy and maintain or create a distinct identity of their own.[24] These identities are referred to as *subpersonalities*. The idea of subpersonalities was thoroughly treated in a book of the same name by British psychologist John Rowan[25] but was not universally applied across psychotherapies until Wilber's explication of the construct in *Integral Psychology*.

Subpersonalities

Rowan noted that it is interesting that there are no systematic books on subpersonalities and the word does not appear in texts on personality theories. It is not in dictionaries of psychotherapy, yet many clinicians use the idea of subpersonalities. My own research turned up only one consistent use of the term prior to Rowan and that is in Roberto Assagioli's works on psychosynthesis. Assagioli describes a subpersonality as early as 1965.[26] One of Assagioli's students, Piero Ferruci, described *subpersonalities* as psychological satellites that coexist as a multitude of lives within the center of gravity of our personality.[27] Diane Whitmore, another psychosynthesis practitioner, describes subpersonalities as "autonomous configurations within the personality as a whole."[28] There is a good chance that the reason the term is not in general parlance is because it was initially associated with psychosynthesis and, because many theorists work in universities and have to get tenure, they frequently use the same construct as someone else but give it a new name.[29] Rowan's own definition of a *subpersonality* is "a semi-permanent and semi-autonomous region of the personality capable of acting as a person"[30] To me this seems to give too much coherence to the energies of these aspects of us. I think a better definition would be *a* semi-permanent and semi-autonomous region of the personality capable of acting as a person for short periods of time. A subpersonality can also be an aspect of self that is being (or has been) split off by being pushed out of awareness. This is the aforementioned subject–other dynamic in Integral Psychotherapy. The extent to which any aspect of self is split off is the extent to which it can *feel like* having the personality of another within our own but it does not act like another person except for short periods of time. We also need to note that subpersonalities require certain enabling circumstances to arise. As psychologists like Steven Hobfoll have noted, things like trauma affect levels of coping, use of resources and the extent to which aspects of self arise or conflict. People who are in toxic environments, like war zones, are focused on survival and the most efficient use of the proximate self.[31]

As Wilber has succinctly summarized, most people have a dozen or so subpersonalities that are semi-autonomous, semi-permanent aspects of the self.[32] Ferrucci offers an exercise to begin making your own subpersonalities objects of awareness. He outlined the following steps:

- Consider one prominent trait, attitude, or motive you have.

- Close your eyes and reflect on this trait, attitude, or motive allowing it to form into some image—don't try to force the image, just let it come.

- When the image appears give the character a chance to share something with you without interference or judgment on your part. Let the image talk and express itself. Find out its needs; get in touch with the feeling that emanates from it.

- After it has a chance to express something, have a dialogue with it. Find out more about its needs.

- Record all this in a notebook and give the subpersonality a name.

- Take your time and work on one at a time then be mindful of how they arise during the day.

Ferrucci makes the point that once you are able to make a subpersonality an object of awareness, you are then free to disidentify with it.[33] This disidentification is necessary to preclude feeling overwhelmed by the subpersonality—to the point where you believe that you *are* it. In Integral Psychotherapy, we agree with Ferrucci but add the two crucial steps described above. First we assist clients to embody or own the subpersonality before disidentifying with it. Then they can begin to integrate it—in essence, integrate the energy that was being used to hold the subpersonality together. Insight is one thing, embodiment is another. As Albert Ellis, the creator of Rational Emotive Behavior Therapy emphasized, most of therapy is practice, practice, practice.[34] As illustrated in Tasha's case, one high-powered insight in session is easily lost between the therapist's office and the parking lot. Once we have insights, we need to use will and intent to make those insights consistently objects of awareness.

Subpersonalities develop as a way to meet needs that we do not consciously own.[35] Understanding Tasha's subpersonality is easier once we see the impact of her making her emotional needs (not neediness) an object of awareness and owning them. Tasha spent years pushing emotional need out of awareness to preclude disappointment. This psychic or psychological energy did not simply vanish, however; it maintained its energy and grew the more Tasha pushed her emotional needs out of awareness.

A nice description of this growth—how the things we push out of awareness gain energy—is Stanislav Grof's idea of systems of condensed experience (COEX systems). A trained psychoanalyst as well as psychiatrist, Grof defined a COEX system as "a specific constellation of memories consisting of condensed experiences (and related fantasies) from different life periods of the individual. The memories belonging to a particular COEX system have a similar basic theme or contain similar elements and are associated with a strong emotional charge of the same quality. . . . Individual COEX systems have fixed relations to certain defense mechanisms and are connected with specific clinical symptoms."[36]

The dynamics of the COEX system are strikingly similar to what we are calling subpersonalities. Grof also emphasized that there is a law of attraction with COEX systems and we see this same law applying to subpersonalities. Once we start pushing things out of awareness we continue to push those things *and similar things* out of awareness. Using a gross spatial metaphor we could say all this energy goes to the same place—the "place" in Grof's system is the COEX system—in Integral Psychotherapy it is the subpersonality. It then may be expressed unconsciously as a projection.

Psychosynthesis therapists will use the subpersonality model to address multiplicity in the personality, limited identifications, and conflicting elements in the client.[37] For the Integral psychotherapist, the determination of a client's proximate self or ego will determine the usefulness of the subpersonality approach proper. Although we accept Assagioli's construct as useful, we also recognize that the later the client's level of ego identity, the more useful the subpersonality construct is likely to be. Tasha's center of gravity for ego was late conventional to early postconventional and as such she was a good candidate for this approach.

As noted, Tasha pushed emotional neediness out of awareness and then would frequently project her neediness in her "annoyance" with "emotionally needy" women. This is a classic case of projection or one way we pretend something we are feeling or experiencing isn't ours but someone else's. This was still the psychological energy of that devastated 16-year-old girl. The only safe expressions of it were criticizing it in others. When "it" would literally overwhelm her rising to the surface in fights over relationships, Tasha was emotionally 16 again. After the fight she might say "it just came over me" and in Integral parlance the "it" is the part of Tasha that she won't own but invests energy in keeping out of awareness. As Freud summarized psychoanalysis, "where it was, I shall become."[38] This exquisite statement really captures what we do when we help people consistently make disowned aspects of themselves objects of awareness, embody them, and integrate them.

This leads us the third important principle that Tasha's case illustrates: the idea of quasi-transformation. To fully understand this though we need an overview of what in Integral psychotherapy we call translation and transformation.

Translation and Transformation

We engage in translation and transformation using our self-systems. Translation is making sense of life with the tools and rules we have at hand. This can be thought of as balancing across the four quadrants wherever your various developmental lines may fall. This balance, addressing all four aspects of your being, is healthy translation. Transformation is when we actually add tools to our toolbox and decrease or add flexibility to our rules. Translation and transformation function in a way similar to what Piaget called assimilation and accommodation.[39] Translation is using the tools and rules you have to deal with incoming stimuli. Transformation is increasing your tools and decreasing or adding flexibility to your rules. Transformation becomes necessary when, for example, we have too many rules and not enough tools. The majority of work in psychotherapy is healthy translation. When you run into problems with something life is throwing at you, psychotherapy will typically help you translate first. On more rare occasions, long-term therapy results in an actual change in the ego or proximate self that we refer to as transformation. Transformation is the rare moment when a person moves into a new stage of development.

I noted that the third principle illustrated in Tasha's case is that of quasi-transformation.[40] This is when a subpersonality is consistently made an object of awareness, owned, integrated, and then disidentified with. It is the same process that we go through from proximate to distal self or from shadow to distal self.[41] I have already noted that a subpersonality can manifest in a way that assumes the characteristics of the age at which it was first split off by the person. In Tasha's case, the subpersonality was a 16-year-old girl. Once Tasha consistently made this subpersonality an object of awareness, owned it, integrated it, and disidentified with it, the energy was freed and immediately "caught up" developmentally to where Tasha was—in this case a 27-year-old woman.

We can translate in healthy or unhealthy manners. You can think of translation as metabolizing life. Healthy translation is extracting and integrating what we can from a life experience. Some life experiences take longer than others to metabolize. What we can't metabolize, stays in our system, undigested, and likely causing problems. If we can't metabolize it with our self-system we either try to make it "other" (subject–other dynamic) or we introduce something new into our system to help us. Tasha could not change who her father was and her yearning for closeness and love from him sat in her like undigested beef. She needed something to help metabolize her own needs and flush what she couldn't change from her system. She had translated her experience by denying her needs and giving the appearance of not needing anyone. This was not a healthy translation for her. She did need people and want to be loved. But to acknowledge this would be to suffer the pain of her father's rejection, which she had spent years trying to push out of awareness.

The Antecedent Self

The antecedent self is the pure witness that is present at all levels of development and was referred to as the transcendent self by philosopher Johann Fichte,[42] pure ego by psychologist William James,[43] and observing self by psychiatrist Arthur Deikman.[44] I already noted that your self-sense is connected to what you consider "I." At (and beyond) certain levels of development, people may be able to reflect on their ego as an object of awareness—beginning in a stage Cook-Greuter called "Construct Aware" or "Ego Aware" and continuing through the "Unitive" stage.[45] In Integral psychotherapy, the witness of the ego (or "I") is called the antecedent self and what Ramana Maharshi[46] referred to as "I–I" since it was an "I" that could observe another "I."

The antecedent self has clinical implications as both a state and as a level of development. Because the antecedent self is ever-present, clients can learn techniques (e.g., meditation) to experience the antecedent self as a temporary state. This is only advisable for clients with relatively healthy ego boundaries who are not suffering from dissociation. Because even a state experience of the antecedent self is one of nonattachment, this state can give the client a feeling of "I" or "self" that is free from problems. In this sense, the state can provide temporary respite from the suffering that comes from attachment. Training in such states is called appropriately "states training." This is discussed in more depth in Chapter 4 and 6, distinguishing state stages from structure stages.

As a level or stage of development, the antecedent self is the part of the self-system with which one can identify if ego becomes an object of awareness. If ego is an object of awareness rather than something one is embedded in, the issues brought to counseling likely are to be qualitatively different than issues requiring stabilizing identification with the ego. Experiencing the ego at a distance is an aspect of many spiritual experiences. Although people can have spiritual experiences or *states* at any level of development, there are also ego-transcendent, spiritual *levels* of development that unfold after the ego has fully matured. One of the most important contributions of Integral Theory is to understand the life of the mind and spirit and understanding these later stages accessible to the self is one way.

Whether as state or level, the antecedent self is central to a full understanding of how spirituality can be integrated into counseling. The inclusion of the antecedent self in Integral Psychotherapy allows clinical use of temporary states of identification with it as well as maps of human development that allow for growth well beyond healthy ego functioning toward spiritual actualization. Many clinicians use the antecedent self in therapy. The most common expressions of this are the wise mind in Dialectical Behavior Therapy by Marsha Linehan[47] and Mindfulness Cognitive Therapy promoted by Jon Kabat-Zinn[48] and others.[49]

The Self-System, Defenses, and the Threat Zone

Integral Psychotherapy includes the important work done on psychological defenses beginning with Anna Freud[50] and ending with the work of George Vaillant.[51] In Integral Psychotherapy, we use the idea of the self-boundary to describe the boundary between what a person considers self and what the same person considers other. When something crosses the self-boundary, the self must decide quickly whether it is self or other. When the proximate self (ego) is disturbed by something crossing the self-boundary, we say the person's threat zone is triggered. The threat zone marshals defenses to protect the self from whatever has crossed the self-boundary and is experienced as emotionally disturbing or dissonant. The idea of a threat zone is helpful in identifying and calling attention to a client whose defenses are mobilizing to push something out of awareness. Consider the following example.

Marcus and his wife were in couples counseling for infidelity. In a relationship where monogamy was the arrangement, Marcus was the offending party and his wife, Janice, the offended party. They had hit an impasse because Marcus, like most heterosexual males in his position, wanted to move on while Janice needed to process her emotions in order to decide if she wanted a divorce or wanted to try to maintain the marriage.[52] One Integral approach for dealing with impasse is to use the four quadrants and have each client write the stressor for the couple in each of the quadrants. It becomes an AQAL hotspot sheet for the couple (or the marriage if you will) rather than a single member. As we reviewed the lower-left quadrant, the dynamic of betrayal was the main topic. For Janice, this changed the relationship into something she no longer recognized. For Marcus, although it was a mistake he made, he felt it was time to move on from it. Each time we began to discuss the betrayal, Marcus' body language closed tightly and he would let out a long, disapproving sigh.

When this would occur I learned the best approach was to talk with Marcus about his threat zone. Marcus' idea of betrayal was not congruent with his image of himself even though he admitted the word fit the topic at hand. What we would discuss, rather than focusing on definitions, was his experience of threat. For Marcus, the discussion of betrayal reminded him of many negative family dynamics he experienced growing up. Marcus' father left when he was 3 years old and his mother always said, "You can't trust men—they always betray you." Although Marcus' infidelity certainly seemed to be a re-enactment of some of his father's behavior, he wasn't ready to process it yet. So we stayed with the idea of a threat zone. Basically, we paired his agreement that it was important for Janice to be able to process her feelings with the need to discuss her sense of betrayal in the context of helping Marcus relax his posture and remain physically open. In so doing, we were really helping him relax his threat zone not so he could be attacked, but so he could more readily engage in the process. Now imagine if every time Marcus folded his arms I said something like "there you go, getting defensive again." Although most therapists don't blunder quite so openly, by focusing on defenses proper, many of them fall err to interpreting too early and thus only exacerbating the very condition they seek to diffuse.

The Threat Zone and Development

Counselor Willow Pearson has described the threat zone as that which "the self will avoid at all cost in order to maintain a workable self-boundary. It is the threat zone that demarcates the ever-fluctuating boundary between self and other."[53] The challenge here is to allow the threat zone to be triggered and for the client to stay with that long enough to begin identifying what it is in the threat zone that is doing the triggering and its relation to self and other. Although many things can enter and trigger a client's threat zone, one of the more common dynamics is for the stage a client has recently left to be a threat as he or she is stabilizing at a newly entered stage. As Pearson has written "Humans do not focus their fears on that which is out of range and out of awareness. People are afraid of the self they have just recently transcended because they fear slipping back down the ladder of development."[54] Because the self-system is sliding in nature, this dynamic of pushing away that which you have just left is ongoing. Based on this, we next move on to a review of the sliding nature of self-identification.

The Sliding Nature of Self-Identification

Proximate self-development occurs at the self-boundary. As I have already written, the self-boundary is where each person negotiates what is self and what is "other." We may think of the self-boundary shifting with each decision about what is self and what is other. When the self is feeling relatively safe, the self-boundary is more likely to expand to include more elements in what is considered self. When the threat zone gets triggered, the self-boundary contracts and fewer elements are identified with self.

Andre Marquis[55] described how the self uses differentiation and integration to journey through levels of development. Babies differentiate (make an object of awareness) their body from the body of the caregiver then, at the self-boundary, integrate their body into their self-system. For toddlers, the body is eventually experienced as distal self and they differentiate (make objects of awareness) their emotions from the emotions of those around them. They then integrate the newly discovered emotions into an emotional self. This process can continue throughout development to the point where one's ego is differentiated and integrated allowing the person to transcend and include the ego, but not be embedded in it. With each differentiation and integration the person moves up a rung in the development of the overall self. The rungs remain as tools in our developmental toolbox but the views from these rungs are replaced.

These examples of ongoing differentiation and integration also reflect Kegan's sequence of subject–object balance described earlier. As Wilber summarized, as development occurs, the "I" (subject) of one level of development becomes a "me" (object) of the subject of the next level of development. The self identified as "I" in adolescence, becomes the object ("me") of a more expansive "I" (subject) in adulthood.

THE SUBJECT–OTHER DYNAMIC IN DEVELOPMENT

The Integral understanding of how psychogenic pathology occurs is when development (subject–object balancing) derails or is incomplete. In contrast to the subject–object balancing of healthy growth, the subject–other dynamic is when a part of the self remains identified with a view from a level of development the self has left behind and potentially becomes a subpersonality like that described in the case of Tasha. That part of the self "left behind" so to speak, interferes with the overall self's ability to translate in a healthy manner and ultimately transform. On these occasions, the person becomes the proverbial "house divided against itself."

For example, for any given person healthy sexuality requires experiencing it in the first person ("my sexuality"). As the person moves to stages of development where postpubescent sexuality emerges, this requires that the prepubescent views be transcended and included and replaced as the proximate self moves on into puberty. One client, Shannon, had internalized many prepubescent prohibitions around sexuality. Shannon's parents were members of a reformed sect of the Church of Latter-Day Saints. Although well intended, both parents had negative sexual experiences in their youth and dealt with them by pushing much of their own sexuality out of awareness. Shannon recalls being shamed at an early age for touching her body and learning that anything related to the body was sinful. When Shannon was confronted with her sexuality at the self-boundary, rather than integrating it as "I," sexuality triggered her threat zone and she made her sexuality "other."

Because some part of Shannon still identified with the prepubescent views, she split off emerging sexual capacities prohibited by these earlier views. For Shannon, this resulted in severe problems translating her postpubescent body and mind into a world where such things held no positive quality. This led to a crisis at age 24 when her first marriage ended because of what her husband called her "frigidity." Basically, Shannon had a lot of rules about sexuality, but no tools to learn how to express it. Shannon came to therapy for treatment of depression but the depression was clearly rooted in the divorce. At age 24 she was again single and, having left the church, she felt as though she had no place to turn. She believed her depression stemmed from the "degenerate" state of society. What Shannon was experiencing were projections of her own sexuality. Whenever sexual thoughts or feelings breached the self-boundary they would trigger her threat zone. Because she preferred the image of herself as sexless, any sexual ideas or feelings had to be quickly pushed out of awareness or explained by projecting them outward. This Shannon accomplished through eloquent tirades about devolving morals.

As discussed in Chapter 2, the manner in which a threatening aspect of self (sexuality in this example) is made "other" can show up in how a client uses first-, second-, and third-person language. The first-person perspective (subject–object balancing) reflects the healthy experience of acknowledging and owning any given issue as part of the self. In Shannon's case, healthy development would have allowed her to own her sexuality ("my sexuality"). When a part of the self is not owned and is threatening, the self identifies it as "other." For Shannon, it was projected onto men she knew ("They only want one thing") and society in general ("It's a perverted society we live in").

Even when Shannon would allow herself to be attracted to a man, the attraction became a threat that sparked an inner dialogue ("That man is attractive, why don't you try to get to know him?" "No, that wouldn't be right."). We got to a point where Shannon could experiment with this in voice dialogue. The second-person "other" also can be dissociated to the extent that it is projected externally onto others as when Shannon believed that men only want "one thing." Perhaps most disturbing is when a part of self is so dissociated that it threatens to overwhelm the proximate self. For Shannon, this would take the form of severe anxiety prior to and during the few dates she went on following her divorce.

The interesting point about Shannon's work is that she came to therapy, one part of her at least, really ready to deal with this. She had left the church because she outgrew the beliefs. Part of this seemed rooted in family conflict because family and church were really one and the same thing for Shannon. Her real break was when she divorced her husband (also a Latter-Day Saint). For this she was "shunned" although at that point the shunning didn't have much effect because Shannon was not on speaking terms with her family. Shannon wanted to do spiritually inclusive therapy and, because of her issues with sexuality, she wanted her therapist to be male. This was a huge step for her. Over the course of a year, she began to own her sexual feelings and to experiment with ways to allow them. She got to the point where she could enjoy being with a man at dinner and maybe kissing without a lot of the previous feelings taking over.

As this progressed, however, an interesting transformation occurred: Shannon became increasingly critical, not only of religion but also of spirituality in general. She began reading books like Sam Harris' *The End of Faith*,[56] Richard Dawkins' *The God Delusion*,[57] Charles Templeton's *Farewell to God*,[58] and Christopher Hitchens' *God is not Great*.[59] She became positively outspoken in her conclusions that religion was based in primitive superstition and that no reasonable person could possibly subscribe to it. I reminded her that she chose therapy with me because she wanted a spiritually inclusive approach. She laughed and said, "See how sick I really was?" What was happening was the subject–other dynamic described in this section. Shannon not only had challenged dysfunctional psychological scripts, she had grown into a new level of development. This new level, however, was more focused on her uniqueness as a person, rather than on how she fit in to a prescribed group. To begin to stabilize and translate life from this new level, she needed to make sure the previous level did not interfere and so would violently push away any sort of association with it. The most obvious way of doing this was through her intellectual attacks on religion.

On the one hand, these attacks and distancing herself from all things religious or spiritual were necessary for Shannon to continue to allow herself to grow into her womanhood. On the other hand, Shannon will ultimately have to make peace with her religious background and decide what are genuine spiritual interests. We have discussed this briefly and I feel she is leaving the door open, however, should she slam it shut again, the chances are that this vitriolic hatred of religion will simply develop into a subpersonality because of the energy she is expending to push it away from the self.

In the first part of this chapter we traversed the map of the self-system and some of the related developmental dynamics. Although the map in Integral Psychotherapy is large, it is important to get as specific as possible. Toward that end, the rest of this chapter focuses exclusively on the proximate self or, as Loevinger labeled it, the *ego*. In focusing on the ego, some of these self-system dynamics are given a concrete form in what we know about proximate self or ego development.

Ego Development

> There is a subtle but widespread misapprehension among many students and much of the general literate public . . . that all psychologists doing laboratory experiments or using complex statistics are, ipso facto, reasoning rigorously, whereas all those concerned with personality as a whole are incapable of reasoning rigorously because their thinking is vague or sentimental.
>
> —Jane Loevinger [60]

> I been in prison, in college, and in the work force. I got a real handle on people. There aren't different kinds of people—there are different kinds of views they take. The problem is most people think every view (other than their view) is fucked-up. That's the problem.
>
> —48-year-old male client

"Vague," "sentimental," fuzzy-headed," and "daffy" are all words I heard my psychology professors use when describing personality theories compared with the more "manly art" of experimental psychology. Beginning my study of psychology in the late 1970s, there was still a patriarchal feel to most departments with lots of "*t*-test envy" and unresolved "variance complexes." As an unmotivated freshman I became captivated by philosophy, but one of my philosophy professors[61] helped me figure out that I really belonged in psychology. In one of our meetings he said to me "hell Ingersoll, if you're still in love with philosophy as a psych major you can always study personality." And so I did. My early studies of personality theory read more like philosophy texts—the constructs were almost poetic and hard to test empirically. Just when I was about to consign all personality work to the trash heap I came across Loevinger's work.

Integral Psychotherapy relies on Loevinger's work (as well as that of other respected developmental psychologists) for good reason. The constructs she developed have proven to be robust across time partly because, as she so often points out, they were developed as a way to make sense of data. As she wrote "Ego development is related to and based on observation, but it is not directly observable."[62] Because there are valid and reliable tests to explore her constructs (the Washington University Sentence Completion Test [WUSCT] and the Sentence Completion Test Integral [SCTi-MAP]),[63] they can be researched in relation to similar constructs like moral development. To the layperson, this may not mean much but it is important. If you go to the self-help or psychology sections of your local bookstore you'll find reams of books claiming astonishing insights into human behavior and how those insights will help you solve your problems. The biggest problem is many of them are based on nothing more than speculation, the charisma of the author, and sexy titles. Ego development is a solid construct and that is why I use it as the primary example of a self-related line of development. Ego development is not without its critics but I have yet to see a criticism so penetrating that it would lead me to abandon ego development.

The researcher who has done the most to extend Loevinger's work into the 21st century and Integral Theory is Dr. Susanne Cook-Greuter.[64] Her work has supported her hypothesis of later levels of ego development (referred to as postautonomous or postconventional) and offered a theory of how these later stages may contribute to transcendent realization.[65] In this final section of the chapter I provide an overview of proximate self or ego development, summarizing the work of Loevinger and Cook-Greuter and pointing the reader to the primary resources and related studies. These resources are important for me as an academic and a clinician.

In academia, the world of ideas must be fleshed out slowly with dialogue, debate, and evidence to support one's hypotheses. In the clinical realm, what is done in the psychotherapy session should have some theoretical and empirical support if effective treatment is to be more than a "fluke" or an elaborate placebo. Furthermore, clinical observations should inform theory and help it evolve. This has been the case with ego development, making it a rare gem in the treasure chest of personality theories. I use the word *ego* to describe this self-related line, although that is certainly not the only (or best) way to describe it.[66] Ego development is different than cognitive development in that it is interpersonal and happens in the "real world." To understand ego is to understand how a person is navigating life. As Cook-Greuter stated, our sense of self or ego is the story we tell ourselves about life. As our sense of self evolves, the story evolves. This illustrates another strength of the construct: You can say what ego development is in one breath. Some competing constructs are so psychometrically elaborate that the face validity is obscured by the jungle of statistics growing up around them. There is always a trade-off between psychometric checks and balances versus the clarity with which the construct can be understood by clinicians and laypeople. If there are multiple lines of development (which is explored in the next chapter), then the hypothesis that self or ego is a separate line is nicely supported by the research on ego development.

Ego as Proximate Self

Think of someone you know well; someone whose view of the world you understand. How would you describe that person's view of life? Perhaps you would describe them as a "rational" person, or perhaps as someone who is "traditional" in their view of things. Let's suppose for the sake of argument that you're right in your assessment of the person. How is it that you came to understand this person and how he or she "sees" the world? Furthermore, is there a common vocabulary you drew on as you thought through your description? These questions are critical in psychotherapy. When we come to know clients, we learn the view they hold of themselves; the view of self that is proximate (close) to them. Thus, Integral psychotherapists refer to ego as the proximate self. When we form a sacred "we" with clients, ego development provides a common language (and theory) to facilitate our perspective taking of the client's subjective experience in the world. Furthermore, ego development provides us a sense of where the client "has been," where they "are," and where they "are going."

In this section, I describe levels of ego identity and explore how Integral psychotherapists can use ego development to assess and treat clients. This is a newer area in terms of therapeutic application and there is still a need for more literature. One of the pioneering studies on this was conducted by Gil Noam and the reader is encouraged to study the work he has done.[67] In Chapter 2 on perspectives, I summarized two "zones" that one can use to explore each quadrant or perspective in the Integral Model. Recall that the subjective sense of self or "I" in the upper-left quadrant is explored through Zone 1. How the unfolding of your sense of "I" would look to an external observer is what we explore with Zone 2. Loevinger and Cook-Greuter can be thought of as upper-left, Zone 2 researchers who have gifted us with a map of ourselves and it is to that map we now turn.

Ego Development, Health, and Illness

First let's clarify the relationship between ego and mental health. As soon as someone supports a stage theory with levels of development, there are people (especially in the United States) who want to know the fastest route to the "highest" level (recall that the United States is the birthplace of "accelerated" college programs, "fast-tracking," and of course "power yoga"). So here is the hard part. In Integral Psychotherapy, *where* a client is on the ego spectrum is less important than *how* they are on that spectrum. We don't refer to "higher" and "lower" stages of ego development, but rather "earlier" and "later" stages. Remember, a primary goal in Integral Psychotherapy is to meet clients where they are developmentally and help them translate reality in as healthy a manner as possible. As I summarize later, being able to feel the wisdom of this position is in itself something people seem more likely to experience at later stages of ego identity. This is in marked contrast to most people's ideas of intelligence, which appears to be a quite different line of development than ego.[68] Certainly there is overlap. Our personalities defy the slicing and dicing of categorization. However, even if we think of different lines of development as overlapping domains, we can see areas where one may be quite far along in one domain (say cognition) and just getting started in another domain (say self or ego). In biology this is referred to as heterochronic change.[69]

Recall that healthy translation means balancing the aspects of one's being reflected in the four integral quadrants. People can be anywhere from healthy to unhealthy at most of the levels identified by Loevinger and Cook-Greuter.[70] So are people at later stages of ego identity healthier than those at early stages? Loevinger was quite clear that this is not the case. She wrote "ego development is a dimension conceptually distinct from the health–illness dimension . . . the distinct relation between ego development and mental health, adjustment, or pathology is found only at the low end of the continuum."[71] She also noted that "[a] person of any ego level may become a patient, though there may be differences in the kind of pathology or presenting symptoms characteristic for different levels."[72] This aligns with what Noam found in his study in that it does seem that different levels of self-identity (and when trauma occurs at different levels) different therapeutic approaches are called for.

In Integral Psychotherapy, complexity brings with it gifts and burdens. Put simply, the more complex something is the more things can go wrong with it. Think about cars you have owned. The more "bells and whistles" a car has, the more things can go wrong with it. There is a reason auto manufacturers still make hand-crank car windows—electric ones tend to break more frequently because they have more moving parts (and trust me, living in Ohio, a broken window mechanism is one "king-hell bummer"). This relationship goes for people too—the greater the complexity we employ to translate reality, the greater the margin of error (and as to whether or not that can result in a "king-hell bummer" ask anyone who has suffered from existential depression).

This is not to say that later stages don't bring advantages to the person who identifies with them. Researchers have found that later ego identity is correlated with better preventive health care among the elderly,[73] higher levels of support and understanding of children in mothers,[74] greater strength in couples' relationships,[75] competence and decision-making ability among managers,[76] lower symptom severity among psychiatric patients,[77] and higher client satisfaction among psychotherapists.[78]

Clearly, the research on ego development has turned up many positive correlations. One way to interpret this is to look at the entire self-system as a toolbox. The more tools you have in your box, the more depth and breadth of jobs you can take on. If you doubt this, try changing your watch battery with an ice pick. It might work and it might leave your watch faceless and timeless (not in the Nirvanic sense). In the next section, I describe the levels of proximate self or ego development as well as the "tools" each level adds to our box.

The Dialectic of Ego Development

Before discussing the various stages of ego development it is important to address the dialectic of growth where ego is concerned. A point Loevinger made in 1976 is still valid: We don't really know how ego develops; how or why it changes; how it assimilates and accommodates. These are all metaphors that can be clinically useful but of course are still metaphors. They are metaphors that hold up as we try to interpret data related to subjects in study. But, we are still making interpretations. Here we see a connection to the theorists discussed in the next chapter on developmental psychology. Theorists like James Mark Baldwin (even with his literary flaws) help us conceptualize how one's sense of self evolves. His ideas still survive in the dialectic model of personality development. The dialectic of growth is still a primary theory of how our sense of self develops.

The dialectic model of self development was most recently elaborated by Sidney Blatt and Golan Shahar.[79] In this model, the authors point out that our ego or proximate self is intimately linked to our experience and internalized representations of significant others. Drawing on Erikson's model of psychosocial development, these authors saw the self evolving dialectically through three general interpersonal levels of development: basic trust, cooperation, and intimacy. The inability to negotiate these developmental levels has implications for emotional and behavioral dimensions. This is very similar to the attachment theories of John Bowlby and Mary Ainsworth. Failure to establish early relations of trust leads to an emotional sense of worthlessness and inhibition of behaviors of initiation. In plain English, this means that when we do not learn to trust we feel worthless and fail to start things because of that feeling. Moving from trust to a capacity for cooperation depends on the child's ability to develop a sense that he or she is autonomous and capable of participating in cooperative relationships such as those found in play. Finally, this capacity to engage in cooperative relationships leads to further refinement of self and identity that then make it possible to engage in intimate relationships (much in the same way that Karen Horney's treatment required the person to relate to others on the basis of changes made in awareness of wants, needs, and values). Thus, "the sense of self and the quality of interpersonal relatedness develop in a reciprocal, mutually facilitating, dialectic transaction."[80]

Got Ego?

So what is this ego anyway? Simply put it is what each of us considers "I." Whenever we say "I am . . ." or "The way I see it . . ." we are referring to our ego. Loevinger compared the concept of ego with Alfred Adler's "style of life" [81]and what Harry Sullivan called interpersonal integration.[82] We are embedded to some extent in our egos. They are ego syntonic and for this reason may not be objects of awareness. Consider the following cases.

> *Ned suffers from what classical psychoanalysts might call introjective depression. He suffered neglect from both parents early in life and lives*

his adult life with a harsh inner critic and fear that his wife and children will abandon him. Ned has defined his role as parent and husband to be the provider. Outside of that he shows little interest in his family. After engaging in two extramarital affairs, Ned's wife filed for divorce. Ned interprets this as evidence that people you love will always abandon you.

Jenna suffers from what analysts might call anaclitic depression. She also experienced abandonment early in life and was raised in a series of foster homes. Her approach to relationships is needy and fear-based. Her fear also is that the love object will abandon her. Despite her difficult life she has risen to a vice presidency at a large investing firm and says forthrightly that she has relied on achievement rather than relationships for satisfaction. Despite this, as her 38th birthday approaches, Jenna feels lonely. She has tried online dating and even set up a timetable for meeting someone, including scheduled activities where she might meet eligible men.

David suffers from a fatalism that manifests as depression about the human condition. The nonprofit human services agency he worked for recently closed its doors after 40 years due to funding cuts at the state and federal levels. David is angry with, Karen, his wife of 5 years, for her criticism of the way the agency handled its money. The fact that Karen is the main income earner in the household is fine with David. His criticism of the work she does is wearing thin on her, however. She is a pharmaceutical representative for GlaxoSmithKline and specializes in the area of psychotropic medications. Karen earns $82,000 per year to David's $19,000. David wonders aloud if he hasn't renounced all his values in "marrying the enemy." Karen is not only concerned about David's depression, but also their marriage. She married David because of her attraction to his charisma in leading others but lately her image of him is of a spoiled child who "refuses to get his hands dirty in the real world."

Sharissa suffers from what might be called existential depression. She is a yoga teacher and has studied Ashtanga yoga for 20 years. She holds herself lightly in the sense that she has a fluid sense of self. Lately she has had experiences of the enormity of suffering in the world and feels overwhelmed by it. During these experiences her self-sense contracts and she says she feels like an impotent wee mouse confronting a holocaust.

What is fascinating is that our current diagnostic nosology (the *DSM-IV-TR*) could very well lead us to diagnose each of these people with Major

Depressive Disorder, Single Episode. What is missing in the diagnosis is just about everything unique to each person. It is the diagnosis of the stranger in that it only tells you the bare minimum about the symptoms causing distress or impairment. In particular, each person's ego identification gives us clues as to how we might treat their symptoms differently. Even if the same treatment is applied, it will be tailored to each person largely on the basis of how they see themselves; on their ego identity. I return to these cases as we go through the levels of ego identity.

Levels of Ego Identity

The theory of ego development is considered a stage theory because the research on it largely confirms that these levels or stages unfold in one direction and that people don't skip stages. This is the essence of a stage theory. Although there dozens of self-help books touting different "lines" of development, few of them have the research to support their claims. Again, ego development has extensive research support making it a critical construct in learning about people and tailoring treatment to fit their needs.

Many readers may wonder why, if ego identity is such a strong construct, more clinicians don't use it in their practices. The primary reason is that to be able to assess clients across the known range of ego levels, extensive training is recommended in both the theory and use of the projective sentence completion tests. Additionally, once trained, these protocols may still take up to an hour to rate and summarize. Training is available from Cook-Greuter & Associates (www.cookgreuter.com). Many clinicians prefer shorter inventories that are easier to work with. As I emphasize in the next chapter, however, these come at a cost and the cost is what makes the individual unique. There is still mixed support for the idea that personality can be assessed outside of life narratives[83] and inventories that reduce the number of factors (like the Five-Factor Model introduced in Chapter 5) do so at the expense of getting a taste of the individual client.[84] Although we know the WUSCT and the SCTi-MAP have good reliability and validity, we also are conducting research to determine whether clinicians trained in the theory of ego development, can discern a client's level of ego identity by listening to 30 minutes of a recorded psychotherapy session with that client. Again, this is an area that requires more research but research is occurring that may give us a more definite sense of the clinical usefulness of ego development.

I already noted that clients may be psychologically healthy or unhealthy at most of the known ego identity stages. Thinking of earlier and later stages of ego development, we know that beyond the earliest stages, each one can be a very nice stopping off point in the journey of life and some are so nice that people settle there. For reasons we don't fully understand, many adults (perhaps a majority) settle into a level rather than continuing their journey. Loevinger wrote

> with regard to ego development, however, the vast majority of the population stabilizes at some stage far below the maximum compatible with their intellectual and other development. This fact implies equilibration to hold them steady at that stage. Moreover, the very fact that people do not indeed proceed to higher stages or perceive the need or possibility to do so suggests that it would be costly for them to change further. The question of why apparently normal people stabilize in their ego level far below their hypothetical maximum level, as contrasted with the tendency to approach the maximum in cognitive level, has been insufficiently researched or even discussed.[85]

Clearly, from an Integral perspective, events that arise in other quadrants can influence the sense of self in the upper-left quadrant. As Cook-Greuter stated,[86] Loevinger began her work in the 1950s prior to the consciousness-raising of women. At that time, the majority of women tested at earlier stages than after the consciousness-raising movements of the 1960s and 1970s. Here, events in the lower quadrants clearly correlate with the way women respond to sentence-completion stems on ego-identity tests. It stands to reason (Gottfried Leibniz noted that actuality implies probability) that similar dynamics are currently taking place as traditional social structures are cracking apart and new, more fluid structures are rising from the rubble. If we are in a period of intense transformation, the map provided by ego development theory can give us a sense of our next stop on the journey.

Now we are going to examine those stops in some detail. There are three general levels of ego identity that we work with and can rate on sentence-completion tests. The first is preconventional and includes Impulsive and Opportunist. We estimate that approximately 10% of adults test out at these levels. The conventional stages are Expert, Diplomat, and Achiever and we estimate that 80% of adults test in this range. The postconventional stages are Individualist, Strategist, Magician, and Unitive. On the minimal data available, it appears approximately 10% of adults would test at these levels. All levels of ego identity are described in the following pages using examples from sentence-completion tests that are typical for that level.

PRECONVENTIONAL STAGES [87]

With regard to perspectives in Chapter 2, people whose ego identity falls into the preconventional levels operate primarily from a first-person perspective.

They may have intimations of the second person's wants or needs but they do not incorporate these intimations other than to process them in terms of what they can get from the second person. The focus is primarily on self and others are seen as potential threats or sources of gratification.

THE IMPULSIVE STAGE

Most summaries of ego development begin with the Impulsive stage.[88] Prior to this, the individual has not differentiated enough from caregivers to have a stable sense of self. We all move through the Impulsive stage developmentally and it is quintessentially seen in toddlers. The two words that characterize the Impulsive stage of toddlers are "no!" and "mine!" When a 2-year-old pastes the television with peanut butter or poops in a hat (I've really seen this done) we tend to be somewhat indulgent. When a 20-year-old does the same thing we are less forgiving. When children are neglected and living in toxic environ-ments[89] the characteristics of the Impulsive stage of ego identity may actually help them survive. At this stage, individuals' conscious preoccupation is bodily feelings. They are vigilantly focused on the separation between themselves and the rest of the world, making their interpersonal style very egocentric and, as the label for the stage attests, impulsive. At this stage, people are understood in the very simplest dichotomies (e.g., good vs. bad). In adult sentence-completion protocols, responses from Impulsive people are primarily hostile or sexual in nature. For example:

"When I am with a man . . . *I get hot.*"

"Men are lucky because . . . *they can screw girls.*"

"When I am with a woman . . . *I like to fuck the shit out of her.*"[90]

Because the dichotomized worldview of a person with this identity cannot be easily communicated in terms of single responses, at this level people will tend to repeat themselves giving the same answer to multiple stems.

"A good mother . . . *is nice.*"

For a woman a career . . . *is nice.*"

The Impulsive person's attitude to the world is one of passive dependence and they frequently complete sentence stems communicating this:

"A good father . . . *should give his daughter anything she wants.*"

People who identify at the Impulsive level of ego frequently suffer from negative moods and reactions far more often than people who identify with later levels. This is why at this level we do see more psychopathology as well as self-medicating with alcohol and street drugs. Integral psychotherapists working in chemical dependency settings frequently encounter clients who identify as Impulsive or the next stage, Opportunists. Finally, because people who identify at the Impulsive level are more concrete in their thinking, they often reduce their limited emotional range to physical states.

"When people are helpless . . . *they feel bad.*"

"Usually she felt that sex . . . *is good to me because I get hot.*"

Although the percentage of adults who fall into this segment of the population is small, they constitute a significant portion of court-ordered clients. It is unlikely to find too many people with Impulsive ego identities outside of correctional or other institutions. These people are typically labeled as the "forensic population." Therapists working in these arenas would do well to understand the perspective of these clients to tailor interventions in a way that the clients are more likely to hear and engage.

THE OPPORTUNIST STAGE

The next level of preconventional ego identification is the Opportunist. A key issue that separates Opportunists from Impulsives is control. Opportunists are more "on guard" to control themselves and situations. In exercising this control, they increase their chances to remain in mainstream society, whereas the Impulsive person, lacking control, is more at risk for things like incarceration. Opportunists are so labeled because they are always on the look out for and may even "have a nose for" opportunity. The opportunities may be criminal in nature (noticing a weak link in a security guard's routine) or working in business to pursue deals "without reflection or delay."[91] The Opportunist still sees the world from the perspective of her own needs and lacks insight. What this person has that the Impulsive does not have is the ability to try to exercise control to protect the self. Opportunists differentiate between inner wants and desires and can fashion what Cook-Greuter calls a "false face" that is used for protection and to fulfill desires.[92] This frequently takes the form of manipulation or deception and the shadow side of course is fear of being manipulated or deceived.

In chemical dependency counseling, this false face is the one that memorizes the rules of the program (usually a court-ordered program that is the only alternative to incarceration) and says all the "right" things about wanting to "be clean." These "right things" sound a little "too right" to experienced therapists. Interns and newer therapists who identify at much later ego stages may, for a time, take the Opportunist at his or her word and misconstrue the false face as dedicated engagement in treatment. Most therapists learn quickly how to craft interventions to include helping the Opportunist client set realistic goals. These interventions include setting strong boundaries, letting the person know who is "in charge," and making sure the client knows what he or she will get out of the treatment. Opportunists want the quickest gains possible so the goals are usually short-term in nature and may include behavioral shaping techniques to help keep the client motivated to stay in treatment.

Opportunists do not yet have the ability to take responsibility for their actions or the consequences and will frequently frame problems as "getting into trouble." Again some examples:

"My conscience bothers me . . . *if I feel someone is watching me.*"

"What gets me into trouble is . . . *being caught while doing bad things.*"

In the last example we also see that the Opportunist has what Cook-Greuter calls "expedient morality."[93] What the Opportunist does is only bad if he or she gets caught and punished. If these individuals do get caught, they are unlikely to show regret or remorse and likely to express anger or frustration at getting caught.

Another characteristic of Opportunists is humor that is hostile in nature. As Le Xuan Hy and Loevinger note, the humor is more sarcastic than humorous. At the very least, it may reflect a "slapstick" humor that views another person's misfortune as funny.

"When people are helpless . . . *I laugh.*"

"I just can't stand people who . . . *bug you to death to finish their damn survey.*"

This style of humor can be a real problem in group work. In one chemical dependency group, a member was discussing a recent relapse that included riding a bicycle into a telephone pole. Two of the other members thought this so funny they had to be asked to leave the group because they were laughing so hard. Another group member (in a different group) used to fart very loudly and then say "this group stinks" before dissolving in laughter.

In therapy, Opportunists tend to be highly guarded because "the more people know about me the more they can take advantage of me."[94] Using the Integral perspective-taking abilities discussed in Chapter 2, therapists can easily imagine how difficult Opportunists find the world. They must either outwit and dominate or protect themselves from those who wish to dominate them. This is a very fear-based experience. Although many beginning therapists think Opportunists would respond well to Carl Rogers' six core conditions,[95] that is only possible if the Opportunist sees therapy as somehow working to his or her benefit. Without this sense of getting some direct gain from therapy, however, it is unlikely that the Opportunist will engage and the most a therapist can do is basic behavioral shaping that will produce, at best, temporary results until the client is off court order or "out of trouble."

Regardless of the theory with which the therapist is working (and an Integral framework is going to offer the greatest number of options), the therapist must set clear limits with the client and assert him or herself as being "in charge" in terms of the relationship and the treatment. Again, this is necessary because the Opportunist sees the world in terms of dominance and submission and, while not wanting to be dominated, is more likely to respond to a structure that makes sense to him or her.

As Bill Torbert noted,[96] every stage from Opportunist onward has, generally speaking, a bright and dark side. The bright side of the Opportunist is being able to "cut to the chase" without the necessity of reflection and courageously embarking on paths others may be fearful of undertaking. The dark side for the Opportunist is the use of deception and manipulation in the short term and not accepting responsibility for one's actions.

The Conventional Stages

The conventional stages are so-named because they are what industrial and postindustrial cultures aim for in developing individuals. They reflect the conventions of the society. These conventional stages are where most adults who take the sentence-completion tests are rated. As noted earlier, we estimate that 80% of adults in Western societies would test at this level. This is based on meta-analytic research as well as the trends over time in thousand of protocols.[97]

THE DIPLOMAT STAGE

The earliest conventional stage is that of the Diplomat. This stage describes adults who are learning to become rule-oriented and, as such, are interested in understanding the second-person perspective. Cognitively, Diplomats are still more concrete but at the next conventional stage (Expert), cognition becomes more abstract until at the latest conventional stage (Achiever) meaning-making is based in formal operational thinking.[98] A main difference between Opportunists and Diplomats is that the former are struggling alone against the world, whereas the latter have aligned themselves with a group that provides much of the identity and protection that characterize this stage. So for the Opportunist, it is "me against the world" but for the Diplomat it is "us against the world."

In healthy development, the Diplomat's rule orientation occurs because one desires to be accepted by a larger group be it the family, one's peers, or one's religious community. Therefore, one wants to look, act, and appear "right" based on whatever the group one wants to be accepted by defines as "right." On sentence-completion tests, even though the Diplomat's responses are conceptually simple, they reflect the sense that the group is more important than the individual. For example:

"Being with other people . . . *is good for everyone.*"

"A good mother . . . *teachers her children about good and bad.*"

"I am . . . *easy to get along with.*"

For Diplomats, acceptance is gained by following the rules and in this sense, the world becomes less hostile and the Diplomat repays this gain with loyalty and obedience. Instead of the Opportunist's experience of "me against the world," Diplomats see the world as "us versus them." Diplomats are no longer alone and have the support of the group (if of course they follow the rules). Whereas Opportunists lacked the ability to be comforted by the company of others, Diplomats take great comfort in their "sameness" with others in the group. The author Kurt Vonnegut wrote that much human misery can be alleviated if people have groups to join, whether they are bowling clubs, political parties, or knitting circles. Vonnegut, of course, warned that some groups were more dangerous than others.[99] One of the crises facing human beings now is traditional groups with clashing ideologies possibly getting weapons of mass destruction.[100]

Diplomats want to keep everyone "happy" and present as overly upbeat and positive. They thrive on service to the group and do not want to stand out from it. Diplomats will internalize norms without question and allows themselves to basically be defined by others. As noted, however, this has payoffs that make the arrangement worthwhile. Responses of Diplomats on sentence completion tests include generalizations like:

"Being with other people . . . *is good for everyone.*"

"Women are lucky because . . . *they can get any man.*"

As Hy and Loevinger noted, Diplomat virtues are conventional and the faults or problems they do acknowledge show up as minor or as backhanded compliments.

"A wife should . . . *be faithful.*"

"I just can't stand people . . . *who brag or lie.*"

Generally speaking, the bright side of the Diplomat experience is the qualities of loyalty, reliability, and morale-raising good will. The dark side is avoiding conflict or valuing the "smoothing over" of differences rather than engaging in possibly uncomfortable dialogue to genuinely resolve differences. This can come across as the Diplomat dismissing what others experience as legitimate concerns. Although the goal is to maintain harmony, this also can produce alienation.

It is important to emphasize yet again that in terms of mental health, Diplomats (and all other conventional and postconventional levels of ego identity) can show up anywhere on a continuum from unhealthy to healthy. One therapist I supervised identified as a feminist therapist and, in terms of ego development, as what I describe as a Pluralist later. She was seeing a client who clearly identified as a Diplomat and was suffering from a great deal of anxiety about a family crisis. The client was referred to the therapist by the pastor of her church who thought the client might benefit from some techniques to deal with anxiety. The client's husband had recently lost his job due to an extramarital affair with a co-worker. The family practiced a conservative Protestant Christian religion that had a great deal of impact on how they defined themselves and their roles in the world. The client was distressed feeling that she had failed in providing the emotional strength and comfort necessary to keep her husband from straying from their monogamy. The counselor offered that there were many ways women could define themselves and perhaps this was an opportunity for the client to change her self-definition. This was not at all what the client needed from the therapist. In this case, the therapist failed to meet the client where she was (remember Rule 2 of therapy from Chapter 1?). The client was basically a healthy Diplomat and needed to translate the current crisis with the tools she had. Once the therapist reoriented her approach she was able to help the client with her anxiety and the pain of her husband's infidelity.

THE EXPERT

The next conventional ego identity is called the Expert. Originally, this was conceived of as a transition stage between Diplomat and Achiever,[101] but in time it became clear that it was a stage in itself. The Expert stage marks the real beginnings of abstract thinking with regard to oneself and others. It is this thinking and the growing appreciation Experts have regarding how they are different from the group that differentiate this stage experience from the Diplomat stage. Experts have access to a third-person perspective that, although not fully developed until the next level, allow individuals to reflect back on themselves and in so doing come to acknowledge and enjoy the ways in which they stand out from the group. Some research has supported the claim that Expert was the modal level of ego identity in the United States at the end of the 20th century.[102] This increased ability to use abstract cognition manifests in responses where Experts can see multiple possibilities where Diplomats are likely to see one or two "correct" approaches:

"A good mother . . . *comes in many packages.*"

"A man's job . . . *can be anything.*"

"Rules are . . . *made to be revised.*"

Whereas Diplomats rely more on mutually exclusive categories, Experts begin to think about the role of the situation, including things like exceptions and comparisons. Such responses are still general in nature until the Achiever stage, when specifics become more characteristic. Consider Expert responses compared with Achiever responses to the same stems:

	Expert	Achiever
"Raising a family . . .	*can be difficult for working women*	*is a challenge even for mature adults*
"Rules are . . .	*good if fairly administered*	*needed when people don't exercise self-discipline or good judgment*
"When I am criticized . . .	*it depends on what it is about*	*I try to find out if it is justified.*

Because Experts are beginning to appreciate what makes them special—meaning different from the group—they are more comfortable standing out from the group. The shadow side of this is a new experience of loneliness or being alone. The bright side of the Expert experience is a newly found future orientation, the joy of hard work for the sake of completing something well, and a willingness to accept feedback from those the Expert considers "masters" in the field. The shadow side for the Expert is not being a good team player, an appearance of (and possibly legitimate presence of) competition that is not seen in Diplomats, and their rejection of feedback from those outside their field. The latter may make them appear closed to feedback ("my way or the highway").

In therapy, Experts may frequently present as eager to learn the therapist's areas of expertise and training. Because Experts are just beginning to discover the ability to view themselves as objects of awareness (from the third-person perspective) and are increasingly interested in sharing their inner nature,[103] refining these abilities becomes a useful activity in therapy. If they are seeking therapy on their own initiative, they will frequently accord the therapist respect as having skills they themselves do not yet possess. However, if they are reluctant clients, they may devalue therapy particularly if it has not been a part of their professional life and what they themselves are good at. One such client was Larry who came to therapy only under the threat of divorce from his wife. Larry suffered from depression and would self-medicate with alcohol. Although not alcohol-dependent, he met the criteria for alcohol abuse. This topic however was off limits in the therapy because, in Larry's words, "I know how to handle drinking. How can you even make a determination on what works for me? I'm the expert on my life." Granting Larry this expertise was crucial to the therapeutic alliance. It was only after producing a small white paper on how alcohol use can exacerbate depressive symptoms that Larry would entertain discussing ways to curtail his alcohol use—at least until he was through the depressive episode.

THE ACHIEVER

The last conventional stage of ego identity is the Achiever. What differentiates the Achiever from the Expert is a mastery of the abstract thinking that the Expert is just beginning to use. Achievers have refined the third-person perspective blossoming in Experts to the extent that they can think forward and backward in time across many years. Where Experts want to stand out, can be dogmatic, and may choose "efficiency over effectiveness,"[104] Achievers are able to juggle time demands to attain effective, long-term results. Where Experts value decisions on their technical merit, Achievers can embrace complexity and how decisions (regardless of their technical merit) will impact the larger system. Finally, whereas Experts will typically only accept feedback if it comes from someone they consider a "master" in their field, Achievers can accept a broader range of feedback. Although the value accorded feedback broadens for the Achievers, they will typically not use it to adjust their perspective. In other words, they do not expect to use feedback to change the frame they are using to work out an issue. Their tenacity in holding to their frame of reference reflects their assumptions that reality is "out there" and that one need merely study the facts of a problem to come to the best solution.

As noted, the abstracting ability of Achievers allows them to make full use of an expanded third-person perspective. They are interested in cause–effect relationships and value the ability to predict the consequences of actions. The use of time becomes more important to Achievers and they try to manage it effectively. As Cook-Greuter has written Achievers "become interested in the truth about themselves through feedback and introspection."[105] Achievers were probably what psychotherapists had in mind in describing the stereotypically "perfect" client. Such a client was called the YAVIS (young, attractive, verbal, intelligent, and successful) client. Achievers can be genuinely introspective, making them good candidates for psychotherapy. Because Achievers value living by their own *chosen* standards, guilt over not having done so can be a prominent issue in therapy. Again, Cook-Greuter: "When aggression is turned inside, self-criticism can be severe. [Achievers] fall prey to hypercritical, neurotic self-criticism especially easily because their plans and intentions are so single-minded and high-aiming."[106]

Because Achievers place such a high priority on rational analysis, they are particularly good candidates for a variety of cognitive-behavioral therapies. Regardless of the theory used, however, the therapist will want to emphasize psychoeducation with Achievers and teach them the skills of therapy that can be self-applied. Recall the vignette of Jenna earlier in this chapter. When Jenna completed her therapy, she commented that the most helpful thing was learning tools to combat irrational thoughts and how the irrational thoughts related to underlying dysfunctional schemas that had developed as a result of her poor attachment in childhood. Although this was certainly true and Jenna benefited greatly from these things, there was another benefit that she did not see right away. In a 6-month phone follow-up, she commented on how she had thought more and more about how some aspects of life responded very well to her highly organized, motivated style and others did not. She began to consider that things like falling in love happened "outside of time" rather than inside a timeline designed to complete a project. What Jenna was expressing were the first beginnings of an Pluralist experience of life. After another year, Jenna crossed that threshold and came back to therapy to explore what this meant for her life.

The Postconventional Stages

The postconventional stages are so named because these are the stages wherein people grow beyond the conventions of their society. In a very Integral manner, they transcend and include the conventional stages in broader, deeper mean-ing-making stories.

THE PLURALIST[107]

The first postconventional stage is the Pluralist. Where conventional stages are gratified by similarity and stability, postconventional stages "increasingly appreciate *differences* and participating in ongoing, creative *transformation*." [108] Postconventional stages emphasize less the internal perspective or frame of mind that limits a person's choices and more the multiple external perspectives and the ability to choose from them to make decisions. This ability to take multiple perspectives is reflected in the sentence-stem responses. When compared with the responses of Achievers, one can see the broader span of perspectives the Pluralist can take.

	Achiever	Pluralist
"Raising a family . . .	*is wonderful but sometimes stressful*	*is a source of great pleasure, lasts too short a time and is unpredictable.*
"When I'm criticized . . .	*I get mad but still appreciate it*	*I try to listen, don't like it sometimes, and try to evaluate it fairly.*

As far as sentence-completion test responses, at the Pluralist stage responses become increasingly unique and less like those seen in the manuals. Pluralists make distinctions not found at earlier stages. They distinguish feelings from thoughts, outcomes from process, and intentions from outcomes. Particularly, interpersonal relationships become very important, psychological causality can be recognized for what it is, and emotions are reported in greater depth. The fact that the same situation can have different meanings for different observers makes interpersonal relations richer and more satisfying. Identities are not "swallowed whole" without reflection, conventional values are deconstructed, and Pluralists turn inward "in search of their unique gifts or pursuing their own burning questions."[109] The bright side of the Pluralist is the ability to entertain so many perspectives, whereas the shadow side is degenerating into relativism. This shadow has been particularly pronounced in academic settings where the ability to deconstruct was not followed by an ability to recreate and led to some of the more bizarre manifestations of multiculturalism, postmodernism, and political activism in the classroom.[110]

The Pluralist begins being able to take what we call a fourth-person perspective. As noted in Chapter 2, this underlies the ability to deconstruct because the person can psychologically "stand outside of" things and realize that what is "seen" depends on the position of the observer. As Cook-Greuter notes, "Thus the idea of the participant-observer, the observer who influences what he observes, is now becoming a conscious preoccupation. One can never be totally detached and 'objective' " as the Achiever once believed.[111]

Although Pluralists retain the ability to be mindful of the past and the future, the present moment is of more interest to them. Although they watch to learn how things unfold, their interest "turns from outcomes and deliverables to an interest in the processes, relationships and nonlinear influences among variables."[112] It is no coincidence that the psychotherapies that borrowed heavily from the Eastern wisdom traditions in their emphasis on spontaneity and the present moment (e.g., Gestalt therapy, encounter groups) rose to prominence during a period where the effects of the Pluralist worldview were dominant in Western societies.

In psychotherapy, Pluralists will frequently struggle with the shadow side of that ego identity which, as previously stated, is relativism. In the case of David summarized earlier in this chapter, we see a man with contradictory values. On the one hand, he is a vocal proponent of diversity and pluralism. On the other hand, there seems to be no place in his definition of diversity for his wife who works in corporate America. David and his wife opted for couples counseling, which was wise because the relationship issues seemed so interwoven with his depression. Working as a couple they are struggling to grow together as David struggles to own his "shadow," which manifests as his scorn for is wife's work while at the same time he relies on her income.

THE STRATEGIST

Resolving the inertia that can result from being able to honor multiple perspectives is what the Strategist excels at. Just as the Achiever enlarged the third-person perspective that emerged in the Expert stage, the Strategist enlarges the fourth-person perspective that emerges in the Pluralist stage. Whereas Strategists can still resonate with possessing a psychological "community of selves," they do not get lost in that community as Pluralists might. Strategists are particularly skilled at owning and integrating the different parts of themselves and recognize their "power to generate meaning and to tell a new story."[113]

Whereas Achievers and Strategists share some general similarities, the depth of meaning-making in Strategists allows broader and deeper levels of acceptance, which frees up more energy to work. As Torbert and his colleagues learned, where Achievers will tend to discount feedback that does not fit into their preconceived frame of reference, Strategists easily change frames of reference when they deem it resourceful. Where Achievers believe there is an "objective world out there," Strategists can readily use the role of observer as "co-creator." Whereas Achievers rely on the structure of organizations, Strategists are more likely to "test the limits of their organizations' and their superiors' constraints and to create new spheres of action for their subordinates and for themselves."[114]

Where Pluralists honor individuality, Strategists can accept it in the context of relationship and the developmental process. This breeds a broader, deeper tolerance than the Individualist's tolerance of diversity with qualifications. Strategists see that others must make their own mistakes as surely as making these will contribute to growth. Although Strategists value autonomy, they also understand its limits and the value of emotional interdependence.[115] In stark contrast to Achievers, Strategists are open to rethinking their positions or frames of reference. Strategists can hold multiple perspectives and make decisions about which ones will be most resourceful for particular groups in particular situations. As Torbert notes the Strategist "sees purpose in life beyond meeting his or her own needs. Continuing development of self and others is a primary concern,"[116] Although global concerns appear for Pluralists, Strategists are more likely to include spirituality as part of their identity.

Where Pluralists may feel threatened by cynicism when they achieve adequacy at deconstructing dynamics like power, Strategists accept such things with humor as part of the human condition. Where Pluralists are threatened by becoming more serious, Strategists move more in the direction of sincerity. This is the beginning of a dynamic that deepens in later postconventional stages of holding oneself lightly. The relativism that is so problematic for Individualists evolves into "personal commitment and responsibility for creating one's own meaning."[117] In psychotherapy, Strategists may find that they are more skillful at owning their shadow for the same reasons they can accept the shadows in others. Difficult emotions become easier to metabolize once they are acknowledged, which Strategists can do quite fluidly. Recall the discussion of the self-system in which the subject–object and subject–other dynamics were discussed. Because pushing aspects of one's self away takes energy, being able to accept and own these frees energy. In this sense, Strategists have far more of their psychic energy available to them because they can spot their own shadow material more quickly and accept it more readily than those at previous stages.

Sentence-completion protocols from Strategists "display a richness and variety of topics" that cannot be illustrated in categorical format. The responses characterize conflicting dynamics as simply aspects of multifaceted life situations.[118] Strategists feel inner conflict fully because they accept it more readily than those at earlier stages. Rather than resist inner conflict, Strategists cope with it, transcend it, or reconcile themselves to it.[119] Overall, there also is a richness and complexity in Strategist responses that mirrors both their abstracting ability and their willingness to accept what is:

> "When a child will not join in group activities . . . *it may mean he has an inner strength and sees a different world.*"

> "When people are helpless . . . *they need help. The tricky parts of this equation are offering appropriate help and accepting it.*"

In terms of holding oneself lightly, where Pluralist responses can show an almost tortured cognitive regression, Strategist responses show a humor and spontaneity that resolves the regression by, again, accepting it.

> "The worst thing about being a man . . . *is often the best thing about being a man—women!*"

"Sometimes he wished that . . . *he had things he would not be happy with if he had them.*"

So you may be wondering what Strategists struggle with. One area is a fear of not fulfilling potential. Although this sounds like an Achiever theme, the potential spoken of here is more ontological in nature. Equally, Strategists fear not living by the value system they have forged in the crucible of development. "Depression is often based on loss of courage, loss of self-agency and guilt for not having fulfilled one's unique human promise."[120] Strategists also need solitary time for reflection because the self is "experienced as unfolding and constantly reappraised."[121] Although Strategists value their lives enormously, they also value the lives of others as equal expressions of the Kosmos. As such, they are intensely interested in helping others grow and this is a powerful motivator for them. "Psychologists, coaches and consultants often inhabit this stage, as do effective executives and leaders."[122]

Strategist breakthroughs in psychotherapy often relate to embodying the true authorship of one's life. Diplomats believe their life scripts are best written by a central committee, Experts realize they may have a unique destiny written by another, Achievers seek out mastery through a linear plot line, and Pluralists recognize they could "hire" any number of writers for the life script. Strategists are really the first one's who take full responsibility for authorship of their lives and experience great joy as a result. Strategists are more open to their creative energies and allow their thoughts to soar past the boundaries of the known into the mysteries of life. While authoring their lives, Strategists may also glimpse the field of awareness within which the authoring becomes an object. Intense curiosity about or accidental identification with this field gives rise to a new dilemma, which is this: To what extent is the Strategist (as object of awareness) related to the field of awareness within which the whole journey appears to be arising? And if the Strategist is not just the object in the field of awareness but somehow the identified with the field itself what does that mean in terms of identity? The extent to which Strategists pursue questions like these is the extent to which a new disequilibrium arises that can manifest as the next stage.

THE MAGICIAN

The Magician (referred to as the Alchemist by Torbert) is one of the latest stages to be confirmed by Cook-Greuter's research.[123] She also has described this stage as Construct Aware and Ego Aware. These latter names give insight into how the Magician experiences the world. Magicians have "become aware of the pattern of development that encompasses an ever broader realm of experience and thought." This also illustrates what the Magician has that the Strategist doesn't.

Although Strategists can "play" in and choose from among multiple perspectives, they still experience "realities" to choose from without consistently deconstructing things like the role language plays in construction of all these realities. Magicians realize that the "ego" has functioned both as a central-processing unit for all stimuli and as a central point of reference and self-identity.[124] Once this "ego-centricity" is made an object of awareness, it begins to feel as a barrier to further growth rather than the facilitator of growth. Magicians increase the complexity of their thought structures to where they are taking fifth-, sixth-, seventh-person perspectives, and so on. Magicians are similar to many long-time practitioners of spiritual disciplines in that they recognize the ego's efforts at self-preservation. When the ego itself becomes an object of awareness, final knowledge is experienced as unattainable because knowledge is put into forms the ego can understand and these forms, by definition, are not complex enough to reflect the realities the Magicians are beginning to experience.

Torbert has associated the Magician with figures such as mystics and the founders of religions and asked "Why are there so few people who experience life in this manner?" His research included studying six people who appeared to be Magicians and some patterns emerged. These individuals were less likely to compartmentalize their lives into work and play but rather experience life as "workplay." He noted that these people tended to live both "symphonically" and "chaotically." They were able to fluidly shift from urgency to leisure to efficiency to playfulness.[125] Magicians are characterized by "moment-to-moment inquiry into the source of the life and love that he or she practices."[126] Torbert concluded that Magicians practice vulnerable power that includes using their own charisma to challenge rather than charm and to engage rather than rule.

Magicians are particularly aware of the constructed nature of language and thoughts—what Cook-Greuter[127] calls the *language habit*. Magicians are continuously exploring the way experience is metabolized in the mind and heart. They try to remain aware of the fact that words co-create or limit the extent to which reality can be conveyed but they also embrace that limitation playfully as some responses to sentence completion stems illustrate:

> "Raising a family is . . . *a sacred commitment like tending a wonderful pot of stew in which you are one of the ingredients.*"

> "When I'm criticized . . . *I like to respond like a sea urchin that has been poked, or maybe curiosity, humor, or with the unfolding of growth.*"[128]

The situation of a Magician presenting for psychotherapy illustrates the importance of therapists understanding ego development. First, as Loevinger said, "each stage of ego development embodies a view of human motivation and interpersonal interaction consonant with its own functioning. The ego or self-system screens out observations of interpersonal interactions that do not fit with its frame of reference."[129] To this she added "those of (earlier) ego level can only translate the motives of persons of (later) ego level into their own terms, thus misunderstanding them."[130] Thus, it is difficult for a therapist with a conventional ego identity to treat a client with a later-stage postconventional ego identity. It is not a statement about the skill of the therapists but rather what the therapist can see as possible in the human condition. This type of statement is of course anathema in academic circles where relativism prohibits discussion of levels but nonetheless the evidence is there to support the stages.

Problems that would be psychological in nature and common for Magicians include feeling there are few people (or no people) who they can really connect with and be fully seen and heard by. As Cook-Greuter wrote, "It is a fact of life as a (Magician) that there are few other people like them. They may fear that almost nobody understands them in their complexity and sympathizes with their experience, and fearing this, they feel culpable of hubris, of feeling 'better' than others."[131] She adds that although Magicians sometimes experience a sense of envy at the simplicity of earlier periods they typically arrive at "a dynamic and hopeful balance within these fundamental conflicts."[132] In the example of depression, their depression "is about man's essential aloneness and inability to create lasting meaning through the rational enterprise."[133] Although everything we detailed in our example pathology of depression can apply to Magicians, the way to treatment must take into account both the cognitive ability and their struggle to live within and outside of the limits of rational thought and language.

It is worth noting that the tools that come with the Magician experience of the world are very useful for psychotherapy. Magicians "have access to their own past ways of meaning making in a much deeper way than earlier stages. This allows the to effectively tailor their interactions to the recipient."[134] While not presuming to understand every aspect of a client, they can feel a kinship with clients from various levels while at the same time languaging things in a way that is meaningful to the client.

THE UNITIVE STAGE

Cook-Greuter has begun the structure for a stage beyond the Magician, which she calls the Unitive stage (referred to as Ironist by Torbert). As she notes,

> From the ancient wisdom literature to recent research in higher stages
> of consciousness there is evidence of many more stages beyond the
> rational, personal realm or postconventional tier of meaning making.
> How many such stages exist depends on the literature consulted
> and the criteria by which stages are defined. The data from using

a Sentence Completion Test as a gathering tool did not allow me to make any finer distinctions in the ego-transcendent realm. My description of the Unitive stage thus confounds several distinct higher levels of consciousness into on catch-all level. Still, the characteristics were carefully taken from actual utterances from individuals who did score at this highest stage of the SCTi measure.[135]

Thus, we enter the boundary realm of ego and what is beyond ego. At the Unitive stage, ego is consistently an object of awareness. The primary dynamics of seeing the world through the ego are that of the self's perspective via language. At the Unitive stage, individuals can "take multiple points of view and shift focus effortlessly among many states of awareness. They feel *embedded in nature*—birth, growth and death, joy and pain—are seen as natural occurrences—patterns of change in the flux of time."[136]

There are similarities between a person at the Unitive stage and Maslow's unitive consciousness. Maslow described this as "the ability to simultaneously perceive in the fact—the *is*—its particularity *and* its universality; to see it simultaneously as here and now, and yet also as eternal, or rather to be able to see the universal in and through the particular and the eternal in and through the temporal."[137] Maslow noted that any reader of mystical literature would know what he is talking about. Although this may be true it is a pretty good bet that most students of psychotherapy would not know what Maslow is talking about. Although we have made great strides integrating ideas of a "farther reach" or highest potential of human nature, such ideas are still outside the mainstream. One of the greatest contributions of Integral Psychotherapy is a map of human experience that clearly includes the spiritual without overemphasizing it to the exclusion of everything else. Now that we have a working model for perspectives, the self-system, and the ego, we need to tackle the difficult question of whether or not self or ego constitute lines of development and whether or not there really are such things as lines of development. That is the topic of the next chapter.

4

———————

Lines and Levels of Development

DAVID M. ZEITLER

Nature does not promise us an orthogonal universe, a world arranged in rows and columns, where every distinguishable trait is statistically independent of all others.

—Jane Loevinger[1]

Some developmental lines have omega points, and thus are pulled; some are more causal, and thus are pushed; some are spiral, and run in circles; some are mandalic, and unfold from within. But the self—the poor lonely self—has to juggle them all, to the degree it can.

—Ken Wilber[2]

There Is No Psychograph

I address the obvious first. In many of his pioneering works, Wilber has stated that if there are multiple lines of development a graph that could plot a given client's progress in the different lines (a psychograph) would be enormously useful clinically. Across the country in multiple Integral Psychotherapy seminars, when polled, one of the top interests for clinicians was the psychograph. So where the last chapter elucidated the self-system and detailed ego development, this chapter reviews a great deal of developmental psychology and explores the evidence for and against actual lines of development. I offer three understandings of the much-talked-about psychograph while also emphasizing that until we can establish that there are such things as lines of development and then measure them, we'll have to wait for a valid and reliable psychograph.[3]

The three types of psychographs I refer to in this chapter are theoretical, clinical, and empirical. A theoretical psychograph is, as the name implies, an artifact of Integral Theory. It assumes that lines of development do exist and it can be used for thought experiments aimed at understanding human behavior. The clinical psychograph accepts lines of development at the very least as a metaphor that can be used with clients in therapy. For example, in the case of Tasha in Chapter 3 some of the therapy work involved Tasha discriminating the difference between emotional impulses coming from her 16-year-old subperson- ality and those from her adult self. With this model she could make sense of the difference between her emotional life, her cognitive ability, and what she was doing in therapy. The third and final type of psychograph is an empirically valid one. This would require first validating the constructs of multiple supposed lines of development (e.g., cognitive, ego, interpersonal, emotional), then (if the constructs are valid) developing tests for each line and finally making sure those tests retained validity and reliability when given as a test battery. As you can imagine, an empirically valid psychograph is a Herculean undertaking.

Psychology and psychotherapy are young disciplines. This is good news and bad news. On the one hand, it is exciting that new horizons are always being met. On the other, it is daunting to consider that, for example, we have only begun to realize just how complex the development of consciousness is. Collective discovery in psychology and psychotherapy is like a group nature walk. What lies ahead at first appears to be a general grouping—"trees," "water," "mud"; but as you continue, things become clearer, and you can differentiate—"pine trees and oak trees and maple trees, . . ." "a stream, a puddle, a lake, . . ." "dark mud and light mud and gold flakes." Walking this path we refine our methods and models. We hope that we are following the "gold flakes" that lead to a vein of truth. Developmental psychology is an important component in Integral Psy- chotherapy, but developmental psychology proper has yet to be integrated into the psychotherapy mainstream. We rely on constructs like cognitive ability but rarely do we realize how slippery they are and how much we take for granted. The notion of developmental lines is a good example.

Readers of Integral Theory may be surprised to learn that in general, the concept of developmental lines is not a dominant one in developmental psychol- ogy. The actual concept of developmental lines proper is hard to find browsing the index of introductory text on developmental psychology. You'll find reference to developmental stages, developmental pathways, developmental achievements, and developmental tasks but rarely developmental lines. Run a literature search through psychological research databases like PsychInfo, PsychInfo Historical, and Psychological and Behavioral Sciences using the phrases "lines of development" or "developmental line" as part of article titles and the result is about a dozen loosely related entries (compared with the phrase "developmental stages," which yields about 200 entries). The phrase "developmental lines" actually yields only 20 entries written between 1974 and 1994, almost all of which are psychoanalytic in nature. Given this, it is fair to conclude that the concept of developmental lines is not a mainstream construct in psychology or psychotherapy. That does not prohibit use of the construct but provides important context that requires us to offer a summary of what we mean by developmental lines before discuss- ing their place in Integral Psychotherapy.

To accomplish this goal, the chapter is organized into the following parts:

- The History of Developmental Lines: Anna Freud's Metaphor: This section looks at the researchers who first noted that the concept of lines has validity.

- Is Development "Sloppy?": This second part addresses the notion that development is uneven.

- Five Research Questions Regarding Developmental Lines: This section looks at the main questions implicated by lines research that are relevant for clinicians. It also looks at current research and practice in developmental lines.

- Principles of Development for Integral Psychotherapy: This fourth section looks in detail at the five main questions relevant for clinicians, and offers a new way for organizing lines of development.

- Putting it All Together: This section will look at the implications that emerge for clinicians who take the notion of developmental lines as valid.

The History of Developmental Lines: Anna Freud's Metaphor

Developmental lines are sometimes described as a metaphor conceived of by Anna Freud to illustrate the continuous and cumulative nature of child development. Anna Freud introduced the concept of developmental lines using what she called psychoanalysis' prototype of a line that progressed toward an adult sex/love life. According to her, mature functioning in this line of development depended on interaction and integration of four factors. The first she called *drive maturation*, which determines the location of erotogenic zones and supplies the energy toward seeking satisfaction. The second she called a *ripening of ego* function that allows recognition and attachment to the object of the drive (the beloved). The third was *super ego* ("over-I") action that provides checks and drive control. Finally, the fourth factor is *environmental influence*. Anna Freud noted that normal development in the line of adult sex/love life depends on the intactness of each of the four factors as well as, ideally, their simultaneous development.[4] She later referred to many aspects of growth (from a psychoanalytic perspective) to be lines on which pathology may occur (these include intellectual, moral, and social growth; growth of drives; and growth of object relationships).[5]

So here we have a metaphor for what is a developmental balancing act. It seems hard to imagine that the balancing is actually done well in most cases. Anna Freud's point was that clinicians needed to distinguish between pathology caused by conflict versus pathology caused by developmental delay or derailment. Unfortunately, she does not say how to do this. Psychiatrist Peter Neubauer tried to clarify the point concluding that developmental lines were conceived to be units of interaction between the "it" ("id") and the "I" ("ego"). He also referred to lines of development that are similar to ego function, libido, and other units.[6] In this sense, the phrase "lines of development" does not imply a linear progression and Neubauer acknowledged that using the word "lines" may be misleading. Anna Freud chose the word in the sense of an axis or line that cut across the usual psychoanalytic references to id, ego, superego, and economic/dynamic processes. In her later writings she also described a line composed of "steps on a ladder" with each step representing a different level of integration and the ladder standing for links between these levels.[7] This is more akin to Wilber's metaphor of "ladder, climber, view" wherein the farther the self proceeds up the ladder (or "out into" the developmental wilderness) the broader/deeper the view. Neubauer asserts that Anna Freud never intended the concept of developmental lines to be a meta-psychological construct and he is probably right because she was addressing the psychoanalytic community with no apparent intention of drawing together different theoretical perspectives. With that in mind we now review earlier theorists' views of development that contributed to what we are calling "lines" in Integral Psychotherapy.

Johan Tetans

Some date the beginning of developmental psychology with the work of Johann Tetans in 1777 with the publishing of "Philosophical Essays on Human Nature and its Development." This recently rediscovered thinker was a mathematician, physicist, and philosopher.[8] Yet his most enduring comments are those regarding development of the psyche, and the difference between studying a phenomenon empirically, versus observationally:

> While Tetans had a firm belief in the value of what was at that time called the empirical method, he saw very clearly the fallacy of reducing psychology to terms of mechanics or physiology; he maintained firmly the doctrine that the true method for psychologists is the *psychological method.* . . . Experience is the basis; the modifications of the soul are to be accepted as they become known through inner experience; they are to be repeatedly observed, with variations of circumstances; their origin and the action of the forces which produce them are to be noted; the observations are to be compared and resolved, so that the simple capacities, with

their operations and interrelations may be sought out; and these are the essential parts of a psychological analysis that rests on experience. This statement . . . accepts the whole spirit of science without confusing the notions of inner and outer reality . . . the whole question of physical development runs parallel with that of mental development, from birth to death: embryology, physiology, evolution and epigenesis are here discussed as relevant topics, but always with the proviso that it is a matter of analogy (the relations within the material series being equivalent to the relations within the other [i.e., mental or subjective] series).[9]

We might say that in differentiating physical and psychological experience, development, and methods for studying each, Tetans had stumbled on the notion of different lines. He also created a life-span developmental theory that distinguished between what we experience as subjective and what we experience as objective. Here again he noted the need for multiple methodologies lest future researchers collapse or reduce domains that he believed were irreducible. One can only wonder how he would feel if he could see biological psychiatrists going through the mental gymnastics of trying to explain psychological experiences via brain processes. Finally, Tetans' model was tripartite—where cognition, volition, and affect (emotion) work equally in the human soul but, again, may develop in different ways at different rates.

Charles Darwin

Charles Darwin and his theory of evolution have had (and continue to have) enormous impact on the field of developmental psychology. His work sparked decades of research aimed at identifying biological bases of behavior and the relationship between evolution and development. Current developmentalists are ambiguous about his presence in the history of developmental psychology primarily because previous researchers hit so many dead ends with erroneous assumptions. Consider the impact of belief in Lamarkian principles that was based in erroneous thinking about genetics. The belief that parents can genetically pass on traits acquired during their lifetime to their children was partially accepted by Darwin. Later writings, however, emphasized that natural selection influenced the frequency and distribution of germplasm (a zone found in egg cells) but not its content.[10]

Psychological historians Dwayne and Sydney Schultz sum up four influences Darwin had on psychology.

1. His work brought about a focus on animal psychology that formed the basis of comparative psychology (rooted in the idea that there was a substantial evolutionary continuity in some mental functions between animals and humans).

2. Darwin's work emphasized functions rather than structures of consciousness.

3. Darwin accepted the methodologies and data from many disciplines, and developmentalists have continued this practice.

4. Darwin's work influenced developmentalists to focus on the description and measurement of individual differences (which was to have a huge impact on developmental psychology and American Functionalism).[11]

Darwin made quite an impression on Sigmund Freud who passed on a theory of development rooted in his own psychoanalytic thinking. Historian of science Frank Sulloway published an entire volume called *Freud: Biologist of the Mind* in which he argued that Darwin had a profound influence on Freud. Darwin wrote about several ideas that Freud carried into psychoanalysis including unconscious mental processes, hidden symbolism in behavior and the importance of sexual arousal. According to Schultz and Schultz, Darwin's theories affected Freud's ideas regarding childhood development. Darwin had apparently given notes and other unpublished material to George Romanes (a pivotal figure in comparative psychology). Romanes later published two books based on Darwin's notes about mental evolution in humans and these two books were found in Freud's library with many of Freud's notes in the margins.[12]

Granville Stanley Hall

For students of American psychology, the name G. Stanley Hall is a familiar one. Hall studied with William James at Harvard, receiving the first doctoral degree in psychology in America. He then studied with Wilhem Wundt in Germany (where he coincidently found himself living next to Gustav Fechner). He was developing the psychology program at Johns Hopkins University when he received an offer to serve as president of Clark University. While at Clark, he established several psychology journals and, in 1892, organized the American Psychological Association and served as its first president. He remained at Clark for the rest of his career, making great strides in having women and minorities not only admitted but able to earn degrees. While president of Clark, he also conducted research on individual differences in children and adolescents.

Hall also was greatly influenced by Darwin, an interest that led him to study children. He developed a theory that our mental history (ontogeny) recapitulates the history of our species (phylogeny). This was the thesis of his two-volume work on adolescence. His later works included life-span theories and works on aging or senescence. Hall is of interest because many Integral scholars and popular theorists still retain traces of the idea that mental history to some extent mirrors the history of the species. Wilber noted that Jurgen

Habermas "begins with the observation that the *same structures of consciousness* (his phrase) can be found in the individual self (UL) and its cultural setting (LL)."[13] Wilber adds that neither he nor Habermas started with an assumption of ontogenetic–phylogenetic parallels but came to the conclusion after studying structures of the self, morals, notions of causality, and cognition. Hall came to similar conclusions. It is important to emphasize that these conclusions (Habermas' and Wilber's) are only regarding mental life and are not to be confused with the discredited theory of embryological parallelism first set forth by Ernst Haeckel. Hall's variation on this (which he called a theory of *maturationism*) seemed closer to Haeckel's and has thus faded from the scene. Regrettably, Hall's works on adolescence fell into disfavor in his own time because of his treatment of sexuality. In our time, Hall is not read because his version of recapitulation is too close to the discredited version of Haeckel's embryological parallelism. What is one of his lasting contributions though is his sociobiological conception of childhood. This conception parallels Integral thinking in that Hall pointed out that "growth brings changes in cognition, memory, emotions, symbolization and social behaviors."[14]

James Mark Baldwin

The next developmental psychologist to advance the field greatly was James Mark Baldwin,[15] whose work later received attention and refinement by Jean Piaget. Baldwin developed a concept that something akin to lines of development exist in human beings, driving us in symmetrical and asymmetrical ways simultaneously. Here is where we see some of Baldwin's idiosyncratic use of language. He referred to these lines of development as "modes" of consciousness with "coefficients of control." He seemed to think these corresponded with specific sets of behaviors, skills, and talents:

> [Baldwin] proposed a comprehensive genetic[16] epistemology embracing various modes of experience organized into sequential stages of logical, scientific, social, moral, religious, and aesthetic consciousness. . . . These various strands intertwined in a series of dualisms, such as inner versus outer, mind versus body, and self versus not-self. Each fresh form of meaning arose systematically and dialectically out of the failure of previous modes to do justice to concrete everyday experience. [Each mode is] in turn integrated into the manifold of consciousness through the struggle for personal coherence . . . transforming the mind and self into a qualitatively different whole.[17]

If Baldwin's "modes" can be thought of as lines of development, they are important to psychological growth and development and Integral Theory.[18]

The main groupings of Baldwin's *modes* are precisely the *Big Three* of Integral Theory—art, morals, and science; or I, We, and It. It may turn out, after a century of research and debate, that Baldwin may have had this much right.

Jean Piaget

Piaget, who used many of the concepts conceived by Baldwin, also understood that development is a disparate affair. Piaget's theory is often referred to as cognitive structuralism. But Piaget was not a grand theoretician; he was an empiricist who wanted to know how children understood the universe from *their own* point of view, not the point of view of the adults raising or teaching them. How did they self-generate an understanding of the world around them? Sadly, for all of his sensitivity to children's ways of knowing, Piaget may forever be equated with a stoic, ladder model of development. It is important to note that there is evidence that Piaget himself viewed his stages not as an end in the theoretical sense but as a heuristic to explain the process of equilibration.[19]

Piaget also studied the morality of children, the rules that they themselves generate and to which they hold one another in agreement. He was particularly interested in games that had little adult co-creation, like marbles, because it was in such games that he could see a morality that was not brought upon the child, but which they bring upon one another. And after years of studying morality, Piaget concluded that we cannot avoid the fact that some intelligent people inflict the worst suffering on others:

> Piaget is aware of a deep social question raised by his work. Although moral judgment develops in certain regular ways, it is by no means obvious that adult behavior lives up to the idealized norms of which children are capable. There are various plausible ways of understanding this disparity. For example, it may be that all mature adults are capable of high levels of moral judgment, but not necessarily of moral behavior, given the pressures of an often irrational and corrosive society. Or, it may be that living in such a world eventually erodes the capacity for moral judgment and even for rational thought. These questions lead to another theoretical issue, the relation between practical reason and pure reason. The main line of Piaget's position is to insist that thought grows through action, but at the same time that actions of a given stage are determined by the intellectual level then achieved by the child. This position allows for minor disparities or *décalages* between thought in one domain and another, such as logico-mathematical thought and moral judgment . . . whether or not research eventually shows a strong correlation between higher types of moral judgment and the

achievement of formal thought, no one can afford to blind himself to the historical facts: some of the world's most intelligent people have inflicted a great deal of evil on their fellow human beings.[20]

Piaget understood that overall development may not be a ladder affair; but he could not get beyond the stage sequence of cognition in terms of logic, math, and reason. Those *décalages* or disparities may be the summarized 25%–50%–25% breakdown of responses in developmental research[21] (Wilber's claim that people will generally answer 25% of the time from levels immediately prior to, and in advance of, the level they currently occupy; I explain this in detail later).[22] Piaget may not have been able to generalize his findings in cognition to his experiences with the world but he was a master at revealing the underlying structure stages[23] that give rise to expressions at all levels. For that and much more, all developmentalists owe him a debt of gratitude. Certainly, no theorist escapes criticism and Piaget has, like Baldwin, been criticized for using the same word in different ways. Webster Callaway asserts that Piaget's theory is Hegelian metaphysical philosophy "dressed up as" psychology. Calloway claims that Piaget's references to and multiple definitions of the "Absolute" are problematic.[24] Having reviewed some history we now move into the question: "Is development sloppy?"

Is Development "Sloppy?"

Is development sloppy? Yes. The discovery that we develop in disparate fashion may belong to Baldwin, but the clear elucidation of how that might occur belongs to Anna Freud. Consider the following two quotes that suggest Anna Freud was a developmentalist with an eye for the future. It is worthy to quote her at length here: "Developmental lines . . . are historical realities which, when assembled, convey a convincing picture of an individual child's personal achievements or, on the other hand, of his failures in personality development."[25] Furthermore:

> If we examined our notions of average normality in detail, we find that we expect a fairly close correspondence between growth on the individual developmental lines. In clinical terms this means that, to be a harmonious personality, a child who has reached a specific stage in the sequence toward emotional maturity (for example, [Piaget's/Mahler's] object constancy), should have attained also corresponding levels in his growth toward bodily independence. . . . We maintain this expectation of a norm even though reality presents us with many examples to the contrary. There are numerous children, undoubtedly, who show a very irregular pattern in their growth. They may

stand high on some levels (such as maturity of emotional relations, bodily independence, etc.) while lagging behind in others (such as play where they continue to cling to transitional objects, cuddly toys, or development of companionship where they persist in treating contemporaries as disturbances or inanimate objects). . . . Such imbalance between developmental lines causes sufficient friction in childhood to justify a closer inquiry into the circumstances which give rise to it, especially into the question how far it is determined by innate and how far by environmental reasons. . . . The disequilibrium between developmental lines which is created in this manner is not pathological as such. Moderate disharmony does no more than prepare the ground for the innumerable differences as they exist among individuals from an early date, i.e., it produces the many variations of normality with which we have to count.[26]

Here, Anna Freud suggests an outline of developmental lines that allows for their disparate development and the fact that disequilibrium is inevitable and even healthy. Perhaps her position outside the Piagetian approach lent itself to a more comprehensive view on structures of development. Whatever the case may be, the sad conclusion is that we are only minimally closer to understanding lines of development than Anna Freud was in1965. The evidence we do have is that development is sloppy and if separate lines of development exist, they are not going to progress at the same pace.

Remember Jenna, from chapter 3 who suffered from anaclitic depression? Jenna had to orchestrate a great deal of complexity in her position as vice president, which was evidence that she had access to at least formal operational cognition. In terms of a clinical psychograph, if we accept that there are emotional and interpersonal lines of development we might view her crippling and rigid dependence on romantic partners as evidence that these lines were either lagging in development compared with her cognition or, perhaps, getting hijacked by a subpersonality. One of Jenna's defense mechanisms was projection, which showed up as intense jealousy in her relationships, fueled by her paranoia that her romantic partner might abandon her. In therapy, Elliott worked with her to use her cognitive capacities to reframe distorted feelings and assumptions. However, the hidden splits of Jenna's subpersonalities limited the sustainability of cognitive techniques in the absence of the therapist. Therefore, Elliott used Gestalt techniques to address interpersonal and emotional projections.

It is hard to know where theory and practice meet. Generally, after you gather enough data, you try to discern patterns, particularly when generalizing your data to other models or theories. This is not normally a problem in the first place. But what if the patterns "found" are merely *artifacts* of something else? What if the exceptions to the rule prove to *also* be consistent? Well, at that point, "exceptions" become "variables to study." And that, in a nutshell, is where we stand with the theory of multiple lines of psychological development.

As far back as Piaget, developmentalists have struggled to understand how their data could be so consistent when it came to studying how people make sense of their world, yet so inconsistent with exceptions like really "smart" people being doing very "bad" things. For example, when looking at morality from within a "moral perspective," yes, there is consistency and patterns that repeat. Tasha's moral choices about having sexual affairs with married men were consistent through much of her adolescent and early-adult life. But when looking at morality as compared with cognition, there were consistent inconsistencies for Tasha. Her case exemplifies the idea that not everyone who *can* achieve a moral complexity or view actually *will* achieve that complexity or view. For Tasha, the necessary moral complexity followed therapeutic insights about why she pursued relationships with married men.

There are apparently many variations in how humans develop, only some of which can be ascribed to cultural variation. Smart Nazis were also genocidal. Less controversially, entire books are written by leaders in the cognitive-behavioral field of psychology as to why otherwise smart people do extremely dumb things.[27] Emotionally gifted artists often cannot throw a football. Exceptional mediators also may put their faith in the predictive power of sun-sign astrology. These situations are the result of exceptions to otherwise generalizable data from developmental studies. One guideline to understand such developmental disparity is called the "25%–50%–25% guideline," after Wilber. This guideline asserts that although the *majority* of responses from developmental tests gravitate around a single stage of complexity, roughly 25% reflect the stage below, and 25% reflect the stage above.[28] This is one of the patterns in a valid ego development protocol. This makes intuitive sense because development is a complex, gradual, and graded process. We are "all over the place"[29] and "we live much of our lives out of balance."[30] This also means that early researchers were likely confounded as to whether or not the disparate responses as summarized in the 25%–50%–25% guideline (vertical differences) could *also* account for the fact that there were disparities across cognitive, moral, interpersonal, emotional, and ego development (horizontal differences). The answer is, "yes" and "no." It depends on what you are studying and how you study it. Wilber came to a similar open-ended conclusion in an essay titled *Ontogenetic Development*, published later as the chapter "Structure, Stage, and Self," in the book *Eye to Eye*.[31] In fact, this issue has plagued developmentalists for almost a century: It is the difference between vertical and horizontal development.

So, this is an example of the kind of issue that leads researchers and clinicians alike to conclude that people operate differently depending on the *content* of a situation, regardless of *context*. Furthermore, people respond to psychometric instruments from three different stages regardless of the *content* they are producing (i.e., their *context* of interpretation is shifting).Previous to the emergence of Integral Theory (particularly Wilber's notion of the *Integral Psychograph*) there were many "level/line fallacies."[32,33]

This seems more complicated than it is. Physicist Arthur Eddington referred to the playful concept of a *wavicle* (the concept also has been credited to Neils Bohr), which helped quantum physicists understand the paradoxical nature of matter and energy (that they can be measured as both a waves and a particles).[34] My analogy of stages and lines with wavicles uses the "wave–particle duality" interpretation (i.e., matter is simultaneously—and separately—composed of waves and particles). In developmental psychology, stages can be thought of like waves and lines can be thought of like particles. Whether researcher or clinician, it is useful to know that what is "actually" happening is both wave and particle. We, however, need to differentiate them in order to understand them. Researchers can know that they are studying *particles*, but this makes their research extremely specific, and it is unclear how much of their evidence we can plausibly generalize to stages. Likewise, because there is much consistency across an individual's responses on any given measure, researchers can be confident that they are also studying *waves*; but this makes the application of developmental principles unclear, which is something important to psychotherapy. Knowing specifics about development allows us to understand someone's "position," but *not* where they are headed. Knowing a general stage allows us to understand where someone may be headed, but *not* where they are "right now." This is how developmental research has been, and it is why evidence from *particles* is often mistaken as arising from *waves*. With the dawn of Integral Theory, it is becoming clear why developmentalists, despite a century of outstanding evidence, often are confounded about whether they are viewing a line or a level in an individual at any given time. Therapists, too, lay grids of perspectives over their clients but should never lose sight of the fact that reality is a continuous wavicle.

Most major advances in research methodology are precipitated by a new view; a model is created that can account for the greatest amount of evidence, and once again the path of research is undertaken to further differentiate and refine our knowledge base. Wilber's model of Integral Psychology is a new view that accounts for these confounding variables that result from a level/line fallacy. From an Integral perspective, development is stratified, but in a fairly consistent way. If lines of development "exist," Integral Theory expects that they will progress at varying rates, but as Kohlberg predicted, cognition seems to be necessary but not sufficient for development in other lines. Loevinger, at times, seemed to support the view that cognition is necessary but not sufficient, and at other times, she seemed to support a consistency view. Ultimately, Loevinger saw cognition as a pacer of development (leaving the notion of lines as *structures* open to for future research). In fact, it is likely that among the "cognitive-related" lines of development there is a particular sequence of unfolding: cognitive (the complexity of *your* thinking) to interpersonal (*who* you consider) to moral (*how* you consider them) to ethical (*what* your considerations involve). So what can Integral Theory do to help us clear up these confounding issues?

Five Research Questions Regarding Developmental Lines

I suggest that there are five research questions that need to be addressed to clear up the confounding issues:

1. To what degree is a line relatively *independent* versus relatively d*ependent* on other lines?

2. Can we measure e*nduring* deep features versus *transitional* surface features?

3. Can we identify in clinical situations disparate development versus regression?

4. To what extent is line development impacted by biopsycho *affinity* versus sociocultural *selection?*

5. Can we confirm line construct validity?

To be sure, these are challenging questions. But in the end, the claim that we can generate empirically valid psychographs (as opposed to *clinically* valid or *theoretically* valid psychographs) rests on our capacity to refine our understanding of lines of development. If the hypothesis of multiple lines of development is correct, then there is likely a combination of structural and sociocultural reasons for disparate development (Question 4). If lines develop with some form of independence (Question 1), then the manifestations of structural differences across the lines should be amplified by the sociocultural factors (again, Question 4). As psychologist Jerome Kagan points out, historical conditions (lower-left and lower-right quadrants) play a fundamental role in those traits or characteristics that are valued, assessed, and thus developed within a society. This is similar to what Anna Freud and Howard Gardner cite as main factors. Just as the industrial revolution gave rise to what Kagan calls "the friction of intelligence," so too is our emerging information society calling upon people to develop new *forms* of intelligence, or at least new *skills* from the same intelligence (Question 5).[35] So even if lines are indeed independent they *might appear transitional* (Question 2), depending on the degree of sociocultural influence that stimulates their growth and their biological and psychological foundations (Question 4).

Kohlberg and Loevinger each asked whether developmental lines were independent. Both agree it is an issue for future research, with Kohlberg leaning towards independence, and Loevinger leaning towards dependence.[36] Both of these psychologists understood that context, content, behavior, and cognition all exert a force on the self-system, which makes the study of line independence or dependence difficult. Not much in the way of understanding the uniformity and décalage of development has changed since their developmental models were created. The field of developmental psychology became embroiled in the defense of hierarchically arranged organization for several decades, and only now are we beginning to unearth this latent issue. So where do we stand, as research-practitioners? In the next sections, I discuss how current psychologists see this issue, and I begin with a figure who looms large over the debate of developmental lines, Howard Gardner.

Multiple Intelligence Theory

The question of the independence of lines brings us to Howard Gardner, whose theory of multiple intelligences (MI) has impacted the way that lines are understood in Integral Theory. MI Theory is a primary source that Wilber has looked to for his theory of multiple lines of development, one of the five main components of the AQAL model. A brief summary of Gardner's thoughts on MI is useful before moving on to current research.

Gardner believes multiple intelligences to be universal, with culture *mediating* the development and expression of intelligence through education and vocation. Gardner's work speaks directly to another major issue in lines research: bio-psycho affinity versus sociocultural selection. Gardner believes that the universality of multiple intelligences is due to the fact that they arise from the brain (bio-psycho affinity). This also is why he believes the intelligences are independent. Gardner does not qualify this notion, even though he understands that future research may reveal that the intelligences "overlap."[37]

According to MI Theory, human intelligences go through four stages:

Stage 1:   "raw patterning ability" (i.e., of the physical world and people);

Stage 2:   "symbol system" (e.g., language);

Stage 3:   is "notational system" (reading, math, musical notation);

Stage 4:   is "vocational and avocational pursuits" (i.e., the master expression of our resonate intelligence in work and play).

Gardner's MI Theory aligns well with the quadrants of Integral Theory. For example, Gardner sees "intelligence" as a biopsychological potential (upper-left/upper-right quadrants), "domain" as the discipline is practiced or integrated in the society (lower-right quadrant), and "field" as the cultural determinants of merit for any intelligence (lower-left quadrant).[38] Gardner also sees the core of each intelligence as differentiated from their "attendant psychological processes," which appears similar to Wilber's notion of *translation*.[39] Nevertheless, Gardner views biology and particularly brain structures as the primary component for the intelligences.[40]

Yet Gardner writes "while multiple intelligences theory is consistent with much empirical evidence, it has not been subjected to strong empirical tests within psychology."[41] Furthermore, Gardner also sees MI Theory as descriptive, rather than functional—he understands that the evidence gathered has been for purposes of identification of intelligences, rather than understanding the structure of intelligences. Thus, although Gardner identifies the surface features, the deep features of developmental lines (Question 2) have not of themselves been measured. It also seems unclear as to whether or not the lines have even been identified. Gardner goes on to say that "considerable ingenuity will be required in creating formulations that are faithful to the scope of these intelligences and yet lend themselves to some kind of objective assessment."[42]

Little has changed with regard to his definition of what constitutes intelligence since his book *Frames of Mind*. Although he is clear that his theory of MI is merely descriptive, it sometimes unnecessarily devalues evidence: "the abilities used by a scientist, a religious leader, or a politician are of great importance. Yet, because these cultural roles can (by hypothesis) be broken down into *collections of particular intellectual competences*, they do not themselves qualify as intelligences."[43] It seems from this passage that Gardner errs on the side of the sociocultural selection processes when it comes to certain forms of "descriptive intelligence" (i.e., spiritual intelligence or political intelligence), but the bio-psycho affinity for others (his other intelligences as biologically based). Gardner gives no thorough reason for such decisions. This touches on another issue, which is that Gardner posits no organizing self-system whatsoever. This seems to be a continuation of his reductionist bias: "The phenomenal experience of an executive sense of self . . . does not appear to be an imperative of successful human functioning."[44] This is another version of David Chalmers' "hard problem of consciousness,"[45] which Gardner explains away. Yet Gardner also maintains that the "total is greater than the sum of the parts" when it comes to the combined use of our multiple intelligences.[46] This appears to be a problem with MI Theory, for how can there be "synergy" with no center?. Also missing from Gardner's considerations are lines for morals, spirituality,[47] and art. Nevertheless, Gardner has shown many people that *intelligence* is much more than the capacity to manipulate logic internally.[48] Table 4.1 contains a list of Gardner's intelligences.[49]

Gardner's MI Theory touches in different ways on the five research questions about multiple lines of development. Lines can be independent in Gardner's model, because there is no self-system organizing them, and because the intel-ligences emerge directly from brain structures. This clearly would not work in Integral Psychotherapy because there is a posited self-system that is doing the juggling. Because of this, lines for Gardner develop in disparate fashion—"In the work of Piaget's follower Kurt Fischer, there is a welcome recognition that development may not occur at the same rate in diverse domains."[50] Regression happens when brain damage occurs, or when the sociocultural selection process devalues the natural emergence of someone's inborn affinity for an intelligence. Another issue with MI Theory has to do with states of consciousness. In Integral Psychotherapy, the surface features of levels are linked with states of consciousness in the form of level specific interpretations. This is particularly true of religious or spiritual experiences. These are concepts that are explored in more detail in Chapter 8. Basically, some states of consciousness appear to stabilize with sustained practice (e.g., meditation). Integral Theory calls these stabilized states *state-stages*, and they are distinguished from levels and lines of development. Integral Theory is entering a new phase, where the simplicity of the five elements (quadrants, levels, lines, states, and types) is assisting scholar-practitioners who want to use a parsimonious model that can also account for the complexity of body, mind, and spirit.[51]

So far, there are no clear deep features to intelligences, other than brain structures; but the surface features are readily identifiable and in need of study. In Integral Psychotherapy, surface features give something of the flavor of both the client's temperament (or type if you will) as well as their sociocultural context. Recall the case of Brigid in Chapter 1. She clearly had a willful temperament, but growing up embedded in her family's conservative religious culture ignited her type. Even when Brigid made a break with that culture and became Wiccan, her willfulness made her question more conventional Wiccan interpretations.

There is a tacit recognition of structure-stage groupings of lines in MI Theory. Gardner is aware that certain intelligences blossom early, where others

Table 4.1. Gardner's Multiple Intelligences

- Linguistic Intelligence (e.g., a poet)
- Logical-Mathematical Intelligence (e.g., a scientist)
- Musical Intelligence (e.g., a composer)
- Spatial Intelligence (e.g., a sculptor or airplane pilot)
- Bodily-Kinesthetic Intelligence (e.g., an athlete or dancer)
- Interpersonal Intelligence (e.g., a politician or teacher)
- Intrapersonal Intelligence (e.g., individuals with accurate views of themselves)
- *Naturalistic Intelligence* [Postulated]
- *Existential Intelligence* [Postulated]

---

take time to bloom, and that this seems to be true universally. In other words, our ability as psychologists to effectively treat or research specific level/line group-ings depends on the natural associations that lines have for each other (I call this "line relatedness"), and the structure-stage organization of those level/line groupings (I call this "level regulation"). The relatedness of lines of development is the *organization of processes*. Line relatedness is likely an all-quadrant affair, as explained later. For now, it is enough to know that sociocultural selection and bio-psycho affinity is one way of attempting to understand line relatedness. Gardner's reducing of lines to brain components (and the associative proper-ties of neuroanatomy) that respond to sociocultural selection (ala Anna Freud's hypothesis) provide a solid premise for using the quadrants to map these four correlated forces. The structure-stage dependent activity of using the capacities in lines is the *process of organization*. Each grouping of lines (line relatedness) appears to have an optimal window for development and activity. Next, I explore the implications of line-relatedness (organization of processes) and level-regula-tion (process of organization). Gardner shows some indications that he, too, saw certain lines growing together, while others awaited the right amount of sunshine and water. However, unlike Integral Theory, MI Theory does not see morals, spirituality, or art as distinct lines of development.[52] As far as I can tell, this seems to be an arbitrary decision on the part of Gardner, which goes back to Question 2: what are deep features (structures), and what are surface features (aggregate qualities that appear to be structures, but are in fact merely the activity of several lines).

Key to understanding Gardner's selection of certain lines and his under-standing of whether or not skills transfer is the concept of *distribution*. Intelligence is distributed within the person just as it is distributed within a culture—we aggregate our skills together. Thus, artistic intelligence is a combination of distributed intelligence within the person (and culture) that is applied to the aesthetic domain. Morality is a combination of distributed intelligence within the person (and culture) that is applied to the ethical domain. And spiritual-ity (if one accepts it as a line of development) is a combination of distributed intelligence within the person (and culture) that is applied to the domain of ultimate concern. Kurt Fischer has a similar view of "distribution," taking the view that *every* skill potentially represents an individual line within a self-system (a line being a "domain" where the "skill" is being used in context); the tasks learned in context can be generalized across domains, particularly when the environment supports generalization of learning.[53]

OTHER DEVELOPMENTALISTS

Robert Kegan can be thought of as a developmentalist who is a "quadruple threat"—therapist, coach, empiricist, and educator. He takes a more fundamental view of cognitive-developmental structures, stating that *every* line occurs within and is under the influence of a specific order of consciousness with specific subject–object dynamics that govern those lines in a primary fashion.[54] This brings up the issue of control. Control has to do with deep features versus surface features. If surface features are expressions of a level, then they are not developmental structures, they are *not lines*. If, on the other hand, the intelligences, domains, skills, capacities, or lines are enduring structures that generate surface features, which are wholly replaced with each new level, then they are lines, *but how would you ever discover this?* Furthermore, would it make a difference for psychotherapists to know this information?

Relying solely on self-generated verbal and written communication is a window into a specific and reproducible aspect of one's subjectivity. For Piaget, it was the way to understand the *cognitive dissonance* that reveals the limits of logico-mathematical operations as indicated in the communications. For Kohlberg, it was the way to understand the *moral dilemmas* that revealed the relationship of self and meaningful behavior embedded in the communications. For Kegan, it is the *emotionally charged recent history* that reveals the subject–object dynamic that gives rise to each communication. For Loevinger and Cook-Greuter, it is the *everyday experiences* that best reveal the meaning identity of the self behind the completion of sentences. For Robert Selman, it is the *golden rule* (and other role-taking measures) that reveals the interpersonal capacity inherent in the communications. For Kurt Fischer, it is the way into discovering the *motivation* of the individual, which reveals the complexity underlying the communications.

It is a new century, but the issues facing developmental psychology with regard to isolating and studying the different human capacities and how they grow are the same as they were almost 100 years ago. Which begs the question, "What can allow us to go beyond what came before?" To be sure, this is a necessary step for the advancement of the field. But does it compare, say, to understanding that socialization itself is precipitated by the development of consciousness to a particular level of development? I believe the answer is "yes." Because the promise of multiple lines research is that everything from psychotherapy to coaching, education, and parenting will benefit from the understanding that even though we are intelligent in different ways, all of those ways nevertheless deserve the support and challenge necessary to determine expertise, to elicit excellence, and to map areas of concern.

Currently, there are several researchers taking the notion of developmental lines seriously. Howard Gardner is one. Others include Theo Dawson, Fischer, Cook-Greuter, and Kegan. They all take slightly different views on the notion of lines of development (different labels, different emphases, and different views on the dependence or independence of line growth). I have already discussed Gardner's views at length. Fischer studies human skills, and the development of those skills. This is part of the issue with defining a line of development—are they more *skills*, or are they more *structures* of consciousness? As mentioned, Fischer takes a view similar to Kegan's, in that there is an upper-limit—which for Fischer is cognitive capacity. Beyond cognitive capacity there is no independent domain growth. Dawson created the Lectical Assessment System (LAS), a method that she claims measures the condensation of different skills defined within human domains (e.g., leadership, morality, cognition).[55] Kegan sees lines as relatively *dependent*, not relatively independent. In his model, the cognitive, emotional, interpersonal, and intrapersonal lines are activated differently, but they are equivalently "ordered" within the self's meaning-making. In Kegan's view, disparities can be explained by the constant "out-of-balance" states (recognizing that we are *never* fully at any one level, but are always in-between meaning structures), or by the occasional regression to a previous way of meaning. Cook-Greuter studies human identity, leadership, and linguistic complexity in her SCTi-MAP, an updated version of Loevinger's WUSCT. But although Cook-Greuter acknowledges differential development, her psychometric does not actually study differences *between* lines.

I have often said to students and colleagues that creating a *true psychograph* would require 5 years and $50,000. Of course I am only half joking—it would probably be more like 10 years and $500,000. The issue at hand is that there are no umbrella psychometrics. The LAS is the first ever effort at creating a single psychometric that claims to measure different lines of development. Yet the scope of the LAS depends on linguistics, and therefore seems to highlight cognitive-regulated levels and the linguistically related lines. In other words, the LAS apparently does not measure prepersonal or transpersonal levels, nor does it measure line groupings other than the linguistically related lines (Wilber, personal communication, January 29, 2008; *Journal of Integral Theory and Practice* conference call).

The work done by Dawson is groundbreaking in terms of the scope and ambition of the research. Furthermore, all developmental psychometrics currently rely on language and communication. However, the vision provided by Integral Theory goes beyond existing methods, even if we have yet to develop psychometrics that match the theory. Over a century ago, James Mark Baldwin provided a vision for which Jean Piaget would begin empirical study. Wilber has provided a similar vision, and hopefully it takes less than 50 years for researchers to understand and implement that vision.

Lines as Processes

As noted earlier, Sullivan said that the self-system is the *organizer of experience*. It may be helpful to consider that the overall level of the self-system, with respect to *lines*, is the aforementioned *organization of processes*. This can be thought of as similar to (if not coextensive with) someone's center of gravity. A recently achieved level of development, by making more perspectives available, will increase the organization of processes. The lines in this analogy are the "processes." The self-system is still the organizer of experience, but each new level brings *more* experience from background into foreground. But developmental lines are not *merely* processes to be organized by levels. Lines also exert forces on development (as noted, cognition appears to run ahead of overall development). Lines are the *processes of organization*. In other words, the *process of organization* (all line activity) will influence the meaning constructions of the individual, influencing what moves from background to foreground (Piaget called this micro-accom-modation). This dance is similar to what occurs in a corporation—the larger corporation is the "organization," like the level; individual departments within the organization are like lines, they are the "processes" that run in parallel. But they do not always run concurrently—in fact, healthy, sustainable corporations know that their "processes" should be running asynchronously, depending on the larger financial realities and internal needs. Developmentalists may not know *exactly* how levels and lines relate—but there is a dance going on, and it involves the *organization of processes* (how levels, acting like filters, exert an influence on lines) and the *processes of organization* (how line activity exerts influence on levels).

In Integral Theory, *eros* is the force of transcendence and integration. As such, it appears that eros may be showing up in us as the *organization of processes* (level transformation). Agape is the complementary force, of differentiation and embrace. As such, it appears that agape may be showing up in us as the *processes of organization* (line activity). Our differentiated capacities, whose affinities and associations the self-system must manage. For years, Integral Theory has been highlighting the fact that the self-system must manage the *organization of processes*, the transcendence and integration that occurs from level to level. But implicit in Integral Theory is the notion that lines reflect agape, and the self-system differentiates and embraces its very own capacities according to life conditions (which can be mapped on quadrants). Integral psychotherapists can thus plot healthy eros (and unhealthy phobos) along the organization of processes; likewise, they can plot healthy agape (and unhealthy thanatos) along the processes of organization. Elliott and I will explore this notion further with a visual aid that I created called the *Integral Psychotherapy Cube* (see Chapters 7 and 8 for examples.)

Principles of Development for Integral Psychotherapy

What would it mean for Integral psychotherapists to use the latest research on developmental lines in their practice? I have so far suggested some of the main issues for psychology with good potential for application. I now look at how this research directly affects therapy. The first point is that a defining characteristic of achieving development is *simultaneity*. It is the capacity to *simultaneously* take perspectives that mark transformations in self-identity. As a clinician, this capacity for simultaneous perspective taking will show up in how the client frames certain situations. Jenna, for example, was able to readily frame several cognitive perspectives on why she has trouble maintaining relationships; it was not until she could release her jealousy by taking second- and third-person *emotional* perspectives, however, that she could mitigate her suffering (which means granting both herself and her partner the integrity necessary for continuous connection).

Deep Features, Surface Features

Some lines of development fall into the category of deep features (those shared by a group), and some fall into the category of surface features (what particular groups do across different cultures). What does it mean to have a line that generates only surface features? Is that actually a *structure* of consciousness, in the Piagetian sense of the word "structure," that can be reliably measured as such? Or, are we to follow Gardner, Loevinger, and Kegan, and see the phenomenological expression of these surface features as being an amalgam of interactions across the four quadrants? Therapeutically speaking, *surface features* are likely to be easier as potential objects of awareness; *deep features* will likely take more time to become a part of the client's distal self. Identifying deep and surface features can help the integral psychotherapist delineate a timeline of sorts (and the line affinities that I suggest here also may assist in this process).

In other words: Are "lines" that generate surface features actually "lines?" The best example is the relationship between morals and ethics, both of which have been highlighted as lines of development in Integral Theory. Being lines, they have quasi-independence. Presumably, moral development precedes ethical development (our moral "ideals" or "talk" logically precede our ethical "actions" or "walk"). Morality is a line of development whose surface features are entirely jettisoned upon successful overall transformation by the self-system from one stage to the next. Many also presume that cognition is necessary but insufficient for interpersonal development, which is necessary but insufficient for moral development, which is necessary but insufficient for ethical development. So it makes sense that these developments are related, because our own psychic metabolism seems to match this process. If I have the ability to take others into my thoughts, I can identify with a family or some group larger than myself, which allows me to extend ethical considerations to that group. This becomes transparent to people who are identified at the Strategist stage, where learning the many ways that we lie to or "hide" from ourselves becomes fodder for growth—like learning a better *system* when identified at the Achiever stage, or converting others to our favorite *rules and roles* when identified at the Expert stage.

Yet if the moral processing is wholly replaced (and, according to Kohlberg, Kegan, and Wilber, that is what happens), then how much sense does it make to say that we are studying a "line" of development? Presumably, a "line" of development is a series of levels or stages that occur in an invariant sequence. Given this, does the study of a line reveal the method of growth and activity that arises from transformation (and by implication, from regression as well)? The guilt and shame of holding selfish moral or ethical opinions is important for clinical approaches to assessment. Is a client regressing or is the client's moral line less developed than the rest of his or her self-system? If morality is merely a combination of cognition, interpersonal, emotional, and socialization lines (as just one alternative example), then wouldn't it be better to study those four lines in combination, than to study "morality," if our goal is to understand what makes a line, a line? Preliminary evidence has shown that morals and ethics are likely distinct elements of human nature. However, this same preliminary evidence does not reveal if such differences are structural or artifactual.[56]

This can be a useful distinction in therapy, particularly because morals and ethics loosely fall into the tools (ethics) and rules (morals) of a client's self-identity. Another clear example, and a leverage point in therapy, is the intrapersonal line: Is your client applying his or her well-developed sense of morals and ethics to themselves? This is often an entrée for therapeutic intervention, particularly for individuals who are identified at the Diplomat stage of self-identity. Such therapeutic intervention has a firm foundation because decades of research has supported the validity and usefulness of Kohlberg's research.[57] Even if morality is not truly a line of development, it is still a manifestation of consciousness that displays developmental complexity with respect to overall self-system transformations. So I am not suggesting that we abandon the study of morality. What I am suggesting is that if we want to generate psychographs, we had better be clear that we know what we *are* doing, and what we *are not* doing.

And according to most developmental psychologists, development happens in the way that Wilber described in numerous texts (see *Transformations of Consciousness* and *Integral Psychology*).[58] Table 4.2 summarizes steps the self-system (discussed in Chapter 3) takes highlighting those aspects relevant to the topic of lines.

This process is like being pushed out of the nest directly following emergence from your shell. I say this because metaphors like "shedding old skin" or "emerging from the cocoon" are too *clean*, and fall short of the anguishing subjective experience of transformation. Of those seven steps, the two I am most interested in exploring for the topic in this chapter are *negation* (Step 5) and *reintegration* (Step 6). According to Integral Theory, surface features are *negated*, whereas deep features are *reintegrated*. The idea that many aspects of who we are burn away in the fires of transformation makes intuitive sense to most people, and often is seen in clinical contexts as a client feeling like they no longer know themselves, "one experiences, even literally, being beside oneself."[59] Make sure that your client is not differentiating from a worn-out self-identity before you assume that they are dissociating. After all, we are not who we were last week, last year, or last decade, to differing degrees. Degrees that are in large measure the result of *negation* and *reintegration*. And so it would behoove us to get a firm understanding of those lines that fall under the rubric of deep or enduring features, and those that fall under the rubric of surface or transitional features. This can help us to create better theory and therefore better clinical interventions.

Surface features are generated by the self-system as it identifies with a new level of complexity. A metaphor that I have found useful with my students is a stained-glass window. Each new level of complexity can be thought of as having more panes, with more brilliant colors, revealing a more sophisticated scene. The deep features are like the metal strips that are reintegrated into each new, more sophisticated image. Creating more strips allows for more colors to be used (surface features), and a finer grade of detail can be achieved (deep features). Therefore, not only can the scene be more accurate, it can also be more beautiful.

If one of my lines of development grows beyond my cognitive abilities, my self-system may not be able to generate the translations or surface features from the more complex level until I transcend more fully into that level. I may only have intuitive access to the more complex translations. This may in fact be the structural basis for Wilber's *basic moral intuition*, the notion that we have intuitive access to more developed morals, even if we cannot self-generate the "view" from that perspective (cognitive development). This is something that we may never be able to measure, but can be potent in clinical situations. For

Table 4.2. Six Steps to Transformation in the Self-System's Lines

1. The self-system identifies with a stage of consciousness.
2. The self-system "translates" or "metabolizes experiences" according to that perspective, that view (i.e., "worldview").
3. The self-system eventually experiences dissonance between experiences and the capacity to make sense or meaning out of the experiences.
4. The self-system begins to "view" experiences from a radically different, more complex perspective which marks the beginning of transcendence to the higher stage.
5. The self-system simultaneously enjoys the greater fullness at the later stage, while sometimes negating the previous identification (often experienced as self-disgust).
6. Ideally the self-system reintegrates those aspects of being that continue to benefit thriving and growing.

example, if a young child shows a lack of empathy for his or her sibling, who shows great care and empathy in return, we are not interested in whether or not they can *cognize* their empathy. It may very well be that the cognitive line is coextensive with the basic structures of consciousness.[60] But even if this were to happen, it is likely to remain an intuition, and therefore difficult if not impossible for our cognitive-linguistically based developmental psychometrics, and therapies that do not look for unconscious processing (e.g., most cognitive-behavioral therapies).

Disparate Development, Regression, and Independence Versus Dependence

Does the self-system maintain coherence in every context, or over time within a single context? What about the idea that people regress—temporarily in service of the ego, or pathologically in service of subpersonalities (fixations/regressions)?[61] Remember Marcus, who viscerally contracted whenever it was suggested that his marital infidelity represented a betrayal? Marcus could not believe that he had done to his wife what his own father had done to his mother. It was simply too much, and the somatic reactions and emotional denial he exhibited indicated a deep split in his self-system. Helping Marcus to relax somatically and turn his threat zone from a wall to a permeable boundary resulted in the emergence of some painful feelings. Not surprisingly, when Marcus recontacted some of those splits, his posture, tone of voice, and meaning constructions changed dramatically. This form of regression can be healing if care is taken, as the self-system is circling back to embrace a split. When done correctly, more "energy" is freed up from the developmental coffer. Marcus did not only want to "move on" from the infidelity because of the natural guilt and shame—he wanted to move on because he was protecting himself from himself. That is what splits of consciousness do to us. Being unconscious, we cannot see them; arising during early development, they are simple but powerful sign on the door that says "keep out!"

   We know from more than a century of depth psychology that the psyche is often fractured, split, fragmented, and compartmentalized, and that the earlier the pathology, the greater the disturbance it causes. And so this begs the question—is the "asynchronous development" of lines the result of *natural disparity* (line independence) or is it rather of *everyday neurosis* (normal regressions)? These two issues are so closely related that I deal with them simultaneously. "Everyday neurosis" helps us to understand that as humans we are all fragmented in some way, which may in fact be the reason that we appear, developmentally speaking "all over the place,"[62] or "out of balance."[63] Kegan claims that he "holds to a 'consistency assumption' but not a simple-minded one."[65] He is referring to the fact that although he maintains a position that the disparities of asynchronous development can be explained by temporary regressions, he understands that there are cognitive, moral, interpersonal, emotional, and intrapersonal "domains" (i.e., lines) of development.[66] For Kegan, it is the subject–object shifts that precipitate each stage that *thereupon* "similarly organizes the different phenomena (cognitive, affective, and so on [i.e., domains]) of the same order of consciousness."[67] Marcus, then, would be regressing entirely—a temporary but total return of the self-system to a previous view. This is like deep-sea diving—we use modern equipment (therapy) to look at all the ancient life forms (splits).

When people experience regressions or are otherwise seemingly operating from an earlier "order of consciousness," Kegan claims that their most complex order of consciousness is still at work. This is evidenced, according to Kegan, by the fact that the experience they have will spontaneously be self-evaluated in negative terms. In other words, barring severe pathology, they will experience this as a deviation from normal operations. In fact, it would be *not* constructing such experiences as deviations that would indicate being "in over our head," rather than a disparity of development.[68] Which begs the question, are the elements of pathology pointing toward cohesion or disparity? Is it regression—normal and pathological—that is giving "false-positives" for the independence of lines, or is psychological pain itself the proof of multiple independent lines, whose differentials of health and pathology cause symptoms? Again, it is worth quoting Kegan at length regarding splits of consciousness:

> Cognitively, they can cause distortions; affectively, they can generate painful symptoms; biologically, they drain off energy that goes into keeping the parts separate . . . [because] the self seeks consistency even if it cannot always achieve it. . . . What principle of organizing is expressed in the defenses that sustain this lack of integration within the self? On logical grounds alone it would be counterintuitive to conclude that defenses that sustain this relationship could be *less* complicated than our most complex way of organizing. But I believe we also see it clinically demonstrated that the defensive structures that maintain the dissociation bear the mark of . . . the self's most complex way of organizing.[69]

Perhaps Kegan is correct in assuming that we bring our baggage with us each time we reorganize subject and object; or perhaps Wilber is right in that our subjective splits of consciousness remain where they are, affecting us in different ways as we grow. This is where clinical empirical evidence is required to help differentiate the issue. However, it could be that Kegan's Subject–Object Interview fosters the self-generation of subconscious issues that people are carrying around with them, as opposed to the deep-seated issues brought forth in traditional depth psychology. After all, the Subject–Object Interview is a tool that asks respondents to dialogue with an interviewer about a recent, emotionally charged issue. Perhaps this method gleans the painful *sub*conscious issues that are present day translations, but whose true source lies in unconscious split-off subpersonalities. Kegan is therefore correct in pointing out that splits of consciousness are defended against using the self-system's most complex resources. But that does not mean that those defenses are the only one's being employed, or that the issue being defended against is the *deepest form* of the issue itself. It could mean that the subconscious always interfaces with the self-system at its current level of self-identity, and that therefore the defenses employed will be from the current level of self-identity. In other words, it could very well be an artifact of his psychometric.

Earlier, I stated that the issue of levels and lines can be summed up as the *organization of processes* and the *processes of organization*. This commonsense approach also is what informed the hypotheses of disparate development and regression as candidates for *why* human beings are "all over the place" in their development, particularly with regards to cognition versus everything else. I agree with Wilber that there is evidence for the existence of multiple lines of development. However, there is of yet almost *no* robust evidence that the lines of development are "quasi-independent." In fact, the evidence so far tells us that the lines are "quasi-*dependent*." This is for sure a matter of degree, and not kind. Loevinger, due to her exacting scholarship, attention to detail, brilliant empirical mind, and sensitivity to all the major issues of psychological development, nevertheless struggled with the notion of disparate development in her seminal *Ego Development*:

> One of the central themes of this book has been our contention that there is but one major source for all of the conceptions of moral and ego development, one thread of reality to which all of the conceptions give varying access. Kohlberg, on the other hand, sees ego development as prior to moral development. Although Selman has appeared to side with Kohlberg on this issue, his own data now appears to support our view. His data provide no evidence that interpersonal perspective taking leads moral development. Some data suggest the opposite relation, but because the results are mixed, the hypothesis that they are both aspects of a single variable cannot be rejected.[70]

It is worth mentioning LAS. The LAS grew out of the work of Michael Commons' General Stage Scoring System and Fischer's research in skill theory.[71] The LAS measures the acquiring of skills where complexities are measured using linguistic data analysis. The differentiation of skill sets is defined by corroborating with experts in particular fields (i.e., moral acumen is abstracted by consulting with leaders in the field of morality; leadership acumen is abstracted by consulting with leaders in the field of leadership. *Abstraction* here refers to the process of applying the generalized complexity as measured through linguistics to the specific "domains," which represent lines). As to whether or not the differentiation of development between lines can be measured through the analysis of skill acuity and abstraction of elements that are generalizable across domains, I save for later. For now, it is worth noting that this is the first pioneering effort to attempt to differentiate the disparity of development across lines using empirical methods.[72]

Bio-Psycho Affinity and Sociocultural Selection

Anyone familiar with Integral Theory will immediately see that the quadrants are well represented in this issue of lines. Any discussion of the epistemology and ontology of developmental lines would do well to have a clear understanding of where the map and territory come together. Here, the work of developmentalists like Gardner, Kegan, Erikson, and Anna Freud are most relevant. According to Wilber, the self-system must organize the many lines of development. Wilber here is following psychoanalysis, self-psychology, and object-relations theory; fields that may not have used the notion of lines of development, but adopted Freud's notion that the "ego" is twofold in its functions: self-cohesion and the locus of identity. Although Gardner does not postulate a "self" that organizes anything (instead reducing the multiple intelligences to brain structures), he does note the importance of sociocultural selection. He is in accord with Anna Freud's own view, that the sociocultural matrix, and the parents (as representations of the sociocultural matrix), exert selection pressures as to which developmental lines will be highlighted within the growing psyche. The seeking of approval and the avoidance of punishment are powerful forces early in life, and children learn quickly to highlight and downplay their capacities according to the responses they receive from parents. There is a *coupling* that takes place.

On the other hand, both Wilber and Gardner acknowledge that there is also an *affinity* that each individual will have for certain lines/intelligences. Without speculating as to why this is the case, I instead point interested readers to Gardner's extensive research into savants, brain-damaged individuals, and exceptional cases.[73] There is no need to speculate as to why we have certain affinities for specific lines (and perhaps for groupings of lines, as I discuss later). What researchers need to account for is the fact that this is a hypothesis that already has some evidence to support it, and what therapists must remind themselves of is the extensive anecdotal evidence from almost every parent on the planet who finds their child interested in particular things *despite* sociocultural pressures. I will not even begin to talk about Mozart, but I think it is pretty clear that his affinity for the musical line of intelligence overwhelmed his self-system as much as his sublime music has overwhelmed the human race since the flowering of that line.

We can say the same for exceptional *athletes* in the bodily kinesthetic line; for exceptional *thinkers* in the cognitive line; for exceptional *politicians* in the interpersonal line; for exceptional *actors* in the intrapersonal line; for exceptional *gurus* in the spiritual line; for exceptional *empaths* in the emotional line; for exceptional *architects* in the spatial line; for exceptional *pandits* in the ethics line; for exceptional *philosophers* in the existential line; for exceptional *mediators* in the perspectives line; for exceptional *translators/multilinguals* in the linguistics line; for exceptional *seond-person spirituality* in the faith line; for exceptional *third-person spirituality* in the witness line; and for exceptional *first-person spirituality* in the spiritual line.

Earlier, I mentioned that sociocultural selection and bio-psycho affinity are examples of how the life conditions in which lines are called forth or neglected can be modeled. This is also called *tetra-enactment* in Integral Theory. This is also likely the most difficult area for clinicians with respect to whether or not the notion of developmental lines has any utility. Following Anna Freud and Gardner, I believe that it is a worthwhile pursuit. This tetra-enactment of perspectives, then, can also serve as our guide, and may prove to be a critical element for Integral psychotherapists that wish to use all three forms of psychographs—theoretical, clinical, and empirical.

Line Construct Validity

This is something that we must decide together as a community of scholar-practitioners. I first give a brief overview of current research, and then list those lines that I think and feel are worthy of our best efforts. I end with a list divided into three parts: lines that have empirical evidence; lines that have anecdotal evidence; and lines that make theoretical sense for future study. Table 4.3 lists possible lines, differentiated by empirical evidence that is so far available to us, and the individuals behind the research. Table 4.4 lists lines with anecdotal evidence as reported by various researchers. Finally Table 4.5 lists some lines of interest for those working with Integral Theory.

Pulling It All Together

Based on Wilber's notion that the self-system will have an *affinity* for particular line groupings, as well as the "necessary-but-insufficient" clause,[79] combined with the idea that the complexity of our identifications goes from body to mind to soul to spirit, I have come up with what I believe is a helpful way of parsing out existing data given by psychometrics for the creation of psychographs. Having a model that can organize future data from psychometrics can be of service to integral psychotherapists, psychologists, educators, and researchers.

Decades ago, Gardner quipped that many of his lines "do not lend themselves to measurement by standard verbal methods, which rely heavily on a blend of logical and linguistic abilities."[80] Nevertheless, all current developmental

Table 4.3. Lines with Empirical Evidence

Lines With Empirical Evidence:	As Studied By:
Logico-Mathematical Operations	Piaget
Linguistic	Vygotsky,[74] Chomsky[75]
Self-Identity	Kegan
Perspectives	Cook-Greuter
Psychosexual Stages	Freud, Ferenczi, A. Freud
Interpersonal Development	Vygotsky, Perry, Selman[76]
Moral Development	Kohlberg
Values	Graves
Ego Development	Loevinger

Table 4.4. Lines with Anecdotal Evidence

Lines With Anecdotal Evidence:	As Reported By:
Bodily-Kinesthetic	Gardner
Musical	Gardner
Emotional	Goleman[77]
Needs	Maslow
Spiritual	Wigglesorth
Faith	Fowler[78]
Intrapersonal	Gardner

Table 4.5. Lines of Interest

Lines With Promise:	As Proposed By:
Naturalistic	Gardner
Spacial	Gardner
Spacetime	Gardner
Existential	Gardner
Witness	Wilber
Nondual	Wilber

psychometrics use language and cognition in one form or another. What we need is a vision that allows the robustness of language, without being limited by linguistics. After all, empirical study is fundamentally about *observation*, not linguistics. There will always be confounding factors, because we live in a universe of whole-parts, and there will always be *interpretation* for the same reason. Clinical psychographs are important for the Integral psychotherapist because language is merely one aspect of clinical work. There is much more to the "conversation" than what is spoken, and in fact what is spoken can often be the red herring that someone uses to defend against healing. That being said, nothing is stopping us from making new lights for observation and interpretation.[81]

The following proposed model is informed by and consistent with Integral Theory, but adds some pieces from existing developmental research. In the end, what we end up with is four main levels of *Regulation*, and four main groupings of line *Relatedness*. The first notion is the idea of "regulation." Certain levels of development appear to be "regulated" by specific processes in the self-system. For example, as Piaget said of the sensorimotor stage (inspiring Wilber to abandon his romantic leanings) "During the early stages the world and the self are one; neither term is distinguished from the other . . . the self here is material, so to speak, and only slightly interiorized."[82]

Using a combination of Wilber, Kegan, Loevinger, and Cook-Greuter, I submit that the next set of levels is socially oriented. Freud himself maintained that this next phase of development, beyond egocentrism, was the formation of the Superego, the internalized representation of the social world. Beyond this phase, the self-system becomes exquisitely cognitive, and therefore we may follow philosopher Sri Aurobindo in highlighting these levels as being regulated by the mind. Finally, following Aurobindo, Wilber, Cook-Greuter, and Kohlberg, we can say that the levels beyond the mind are spiritually regulated. Table 4.6 summarizes how these *regulations* line up nearly perfectly with the existing groupings of preconventional, conventional, postconventional, and transpersonal.

Please note two things: Those labels are also *lines*; and, those lines, barring any upper-right organic or severe upper-left pathology issues, *continue to develop from birth until death*. What "regulation" refers to here is this: The self-system during this phase is expressing growth and development in these terms. There is a lot of research being done by Elizabeth Spelke[83] at Harvard, and Karen Wynn[84] at Yale, showing that infants possess innate abilities for recognizing "impossible" situations. One of the biggest implications is that there is some sort of proto-mathematics happening. Yet the research protocols are occurring physically, kinesthetically. It is the *gaze* of the baby that informs researchers that the infants are processing information. And it is physical objects that are being manipulated to present the "impossible" situations in the first place. It is entirely kinesthetic.[85] This is not to say that the math itself is kinesthetic but we cannot truly know this, for we are relying here on interpretation. I am inclined to believe that it is kinesthetic, following Piaget's notion that the self is material at the sensorimotor level.[86]

This brings me to the next notion, that of line affinity or groupings. One of the reasons that I used line labels for the developments that are highlighted during the phases of preconventional, conventional, postconventional, and transpersonal, is that it is these line groupings that I believe are *necessary but*

Table 4.6. Regulated Level Groupings

Preconventional Phase:	Kinesthetic—Regulated Levels
Conventional Phase:	Interpersonal—Regulated Levels
Postconventional Phase:	Cognitive—Regulated Levels
Transpersonal Phase:	Spiritually—Regulated Levels

insufficient for acquiring authentic information about stages. In other words, if levels always occur within lines, and lines occur in semidifferentiated groupings, whose developments are quasi-independent (and therefore, quasi-dependent), then any psychometric that seeks to gain a window into the phases of development must skillfully access the self-systems natural line-relatedness in order to get the best information available on development. Table 4.7 illustrates the affinities.

For the Integral psychotherapist, this model of the relationship between the *organization of processes* and the *processes of organization* allow for a general scheme of clinical tracking. For example, if you suspect that your client's main concerns are showing up somatically, yet their personal style and life conditions appear to not be factors, then you may be dealing with the preconventional phase, and therefore you might *begin* your intervention by highlighting the bodily related lines. Likewise, accounting for confounding factors from style and life conditions with a client who feels that they are always using schemas that don't line up with their loved ones, you might *begin* your intervention by highlighting the linguistically related lines. Figure 4.1 summarizes the previous three tables.

Framing Therapy

So far I have gone over the past and present of research into lines of development, which in my opinion is one of the least understood and least researched aspects of Integral Theory. This is understandable, due to its overlap with another irreducible element of the AQAL model, levels of development. In addition to *Regulated Levels* and *Related Lines*, we must consider how to *Frame* therapy accordingly.

Table 4.7. Related Line Groupings

Preconventional Phase:	Bodily—Related Lines
Conventional Phase:	Emotionally—Related Lines
Postconventional Phase:	Linguistically—Related Lines
Transpersonal Phase:	Lines of Ultimate Concern

For the Kinesthetically Regulated Levels and the Bodily Related Lines, *let the body be your guide.* Eye movements, full body movements, aggressive and passive stances, orientation to a room, manipulation of physical objects, and reaction to light/dark can all provide windows into the Zone 2 complexity of a human. As with the Cognitive-Regulated Levels and Linguistically Related Lines, there is *always overlap.* In framing therapy where Interpersonal-Regulated Levels and Self-Related Lines seem to be at the source of suffering, we let the persona be our guide. The self-generation of meaning is paramount at these levels—this is the reason why Kegan's Subject/–Object Interview was deftly able to reveal the fact that *early formal operations* is the basis for an entire stage of development, whose themes revolve around mutuality, affiliation, and the internalization of socialized roles (the third-order of development, in his system). Many developmentalists attempt to explain these unique, level-specific issues as being the subphase of another level, stemming from either full concrete operations on the one hand, or full formal operations on the other.[87] The same can be said for ego-development theory, which differentiates two stages from early formal operations cognition: the diplomat and the expert. These issues are germane to therapy because at these levels, meaning constructions generally revolve around romantic relationships and relationships with those we follow, our "leaders." This is also when we are only beginning to understand the concept of "self-esteem." Self-esteem is something that we *learn* from experiences of *other-esteem.* As with all development, a process that was "outside" moves "inside"—our self-efficacy and the evaluations from others (especially romantic relationships and leaders) will form the basis for our self-esteem capacities at the achiever level of self-identity. Therapists who look for high or stable self-esteem in people who are only beginning self-generate this developmental achievement are committing what Grof calls a *crime of omission,* and according to Kegan are placing them *in over their heads.*[88]

With the Spiritually Regulated Levels and Lines of Ultimate Concern, we let the soul (if there is such a thing) be our guide. Here more than anywhere lies the greatest promise and the most issues in attempting to go beyond what has come before. But sensitive, intelligent scholar-practitioners from all disciplines have broached the subject of spirituality as a valid phenomenon, and not necessarily to be reduced to physical processes. It makes sense that with the Cognitive-Regulated Levels and Linguistically Related Lines, we would let the *mind* be our guide. But spiritual development has been done in many ways, and is largely tradition-specific. The *Bodhicaryavatara,* for example, is a guide to the development of spiritual adherents in the Madhyamika tradition. In studying this text, it became clear to me that it combines growth in vertical stage self-identity with growth in horizontal state-stage freedom. Another example of the wisdom traditions and their grasp of development comes to us from the *Lankavatara Sutra,* which is a codified system of development

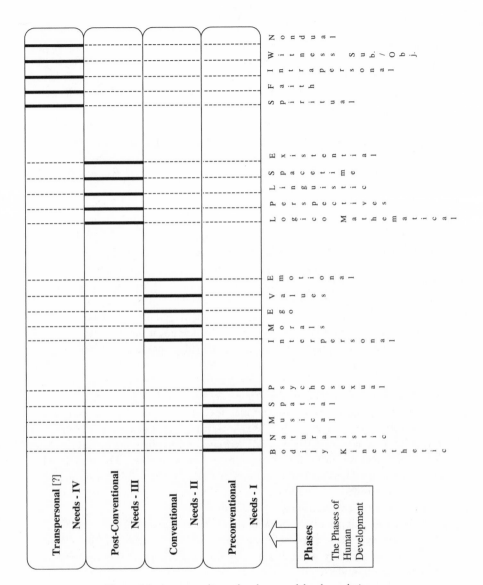

Figure 4.1. Aggregate line relatedness and level regulation.

in both vertical and horizontal dimensions as well. Many traditions naturally fall into this category of combining stage specific self-identity and state-stage development, for they were less interested in proving the discreet stages of growth as they were in achieving spiritual enlightenment. In that way, these traditions were not so different from Western researchers, who also collapsed structure-stage and state-stage developments.[89] As Wilber has consistently maintained throughout his efforts at integrating Western and Eastern approaches to growth, both spiritual traditions and developmental psychology are interested in transforming subjects into objects. Both attempt to facilitate the process of emptying our *attachments* (Eastern view) that represent our *fusions* with the world (Western view).

More recently has been the work of Cindy Wigglesworth, who takes the concept of spiritual intelligence, places it within Wilber's AQAL model, and compares and contrasts it with the developmental tasks of emotional intelligence, moral development, and the evolution of the culture at large. Her pioneering effort is aimed at understanding just how related and independent those four constructs are in the developing human. Her definition of spiritual intelligence is the ability to behave with compassion and wisdom while maintaining equanimity regardless of the circumstances.[90] Of importance is Wigglesworth's highlighting of actual behavior as an important factor in determining spiritual intelligence (and therefore, spiritual development). Unsubstantiated or grandiose claims regarding spirituality are and have been readily abused by people with pathologically *asynchronous* development, and combining behavior with intention is crucial for empirical observation. The ability to measure spiritual intelligence as an actual construct whose qualitatively different manifestations may be observed, recorded, and repeated seems far off. What Wigglesworth offers is a way of starting the conversation of how to relate and differentiate spiritual intelligence, and to do so in a way that can foster future research. It is possible that such research will give us a clinical language, and perhaps even clinical tools, to address spirituality in levels of self-identity, in addition to those means that are currently available for general states and state-stages (see Chapter 8).

We still grapple to understand the differences between learning a skill or behavior, and the growth of innate constructs; to understand how certain developmental skills are generalizable, whereas others appear to be context- or task-specific; to understand continuous versus discontinuous change; and to understand domain-specific versus domain-general growth and development.[91]

For the clinician, the only psychograph that matters is the clinical psychograph. Clinicians have been using and will continue to use various forms of these instruments, which are basically an extension of their clinical judgment regarding specific areas of focus in the therapeutic occasion. I have presented a way of looking at psychographs that will hopefully begin to bridge theoretical, empirical, and clinical psychographs, that they might inform and enrich one another in the landscape of therapy.

Where Do We Go From Here?

If a line exists, it exists as phenomenon; if it exists as phenomenon, it can be observed and measured. The hypothesis generated by Integral Theory is that multiple lines of development are always developing in asynchronous fashion, and the self-system seeks homeostasis across lines, generating an overall level of self-identity. Too much asynchrony, and it appears that the result is neurosis, anxiety, and feeling torn apart. Too much homogeneity, and it appears that the result is depression, arrest, and regression.[92] Piaget looked at reality from the child's perspective, changed the field, and added solid research that backed what Tetens and Baldwin had articulated since the 18th century.

We find ourselves in a similar situation, with Integral Theory leading the vision for new and creative ways of discerning the issues that have daunted developmentalists for decades. There are promising signs that a corner has been turned. The Integral Sentence Completion Test, the Lectical Assessment System, and the Subject/Object Interview all offer more nuanced and specific information as to how human beings have differentiated capacities that develop. The tests themselves cannot relieve suffering (although, it would not surprise me if a pharmaceutical company attempted to market just such relief in pill form). As with most theories and models, the clinical context compels us to discard developmental considerations as the dominant interpretive mode; rather, your self-as-instrument is *always* the most important instrument. But these theories and models *can* be running like an operating system, one that makes appropriate suggestions in a timely fashion, whereupon you note and close the window, that you might get back to being a human in relationship with your client.

My offering also is necessarily flawed: How can so much interpretation, necessary in the absence of spoken or written communication, lead to robust evidence? How can we study something like "spirituality" as something *different* from morality, perspectives, or unverifiable experiences? These questions and many more are entirely valid, and also are no reason to continue to try and draw the cognitive line of development into every other line.

We have the opportunity to create psychometrics and clinical approaches that take specific perspectives and combinations of perspectives into account. Developmental psychology is a field that has suffered from a dearth of creative vision, limiting itself to written and verbal information. Yet nowhere is it written that this particular form of self-generated data is the *only viable* form of self-generated data. Paul van Geert's lament that developmentalists lack the vision necessary to embrace dynamic systems modeling should be remembered here! In addition to the infant studies by Spelke and Wynn, there are several animal models that use nonverbal structures to glean information about animal consciousness. Furthermore, for almost 100 years clinicians have used mainly nonverbal assessments with young children; there is no reason that we cannot use similar means for adults with early development issues (as in attachment theory), nor why we cannot import some of these nonlinguistic means for psychometrics. Why have developmental researchers not tapped into this rich vein? Perhaps because there was no *Integral Methodological Pluralism*.

Integral Theory gives us a way to begin making sense out of the data in developmental research. The study of psychological development—be it of levels or lines or both—is about the ways that we change over time. The field of psychology has also created many perspectives on the opposite phenomena: The ways that we *don't* change over time. The study of personality types likely began when humans started assigning characteristics based on the order of birth. Theories on how we are *stable* over time—our "type" or style—have had much more influence on popular culture (and certainly business management theory) than developmental psychology. From the problematic concept of developmental lines, then, we move now to an equally problematic concept: types.

5

Types and Styles

R. Elliott Ingersoll

The greatest barrier is probably set up by teachers who know a little more than the public, who want to exploit their fractional knowledge, and who are thoroughly opposed to making the least effort to learn anything more.

—Ezra Pound[1]

Thus far in this book we have talked a lot about tools and rules, but in this chapter we talk about styles. As we grow, particularly in ego identity, we have more tools and fewer rules, but what about style? Styles can shift as we grow or they can stay relatively constant—that's what makes them different than stages like ego identity or cognition. What do you see as your style of moving through life? Are you more internally or externally focused? Do you prefer to experience things sensually or are you more of an intellectual? Have you experienced a shift in your style as a result of transformation? One client, a university professor named Eric, considered himself an intellectual. He preferred to spend his time reading books and writing scholarly papers rather than interacting with other people. He was quite content to sit in his study for days at a time. Eric was in therapy because his wife was not so content having him sit in there for days at a time and the two were being seen for couples counseling. Although Eric's style of being in the world was not in and of itself a problem, it became a problem in a relationship with a wife who had a different style.

There do exist, however, styles of being in the world that cause the person with that style (and those around him or her) a great deal of suffering. These styles are referred to in psychiatric jargon as *personality disorders*, although that label may change because of its negative connotation.[2] The first person to suggest shifting from the phrase personality disorder to *personality style* was psychiatrist Len Sperry.[3] As Sperry rightly pointed out, what is referred to as a personality disorder that doesn't work for a person may, in therapy be crafted into a personality style. Most people don't respond well to being told that the essence of who they consider themselves to be is dysfunctional; however, if they understand their personality as a style, the stage is set for an alliance wherein that style may be crafted or modified.

Consider the case of Marsha, who was in therapy for severe depression. She had suffered all the severe symptoms for 3 weeks following the end of a romantic relationship. An integral intake[4] showed hotspots in her lower-left quadrant. She seemed to have a string of volatile and disastrous relationships in which her emotions swung from ecstatic love to venomous hatred in the same day. Her lovers found her sometimes stifling and needy but at other times violently jealous or hateful. Most of them left because they couldn't tolerate Marsha's insecurity. Marsha suffered from a personality style referred to as Borderline Personality Disorder.

Marsha's "style" seemed to stem from a childhood of sexual abuse and abandonment. Developmentally, it appears that she never successfully differentiated her emotional self from her physical self. We might say that part of Marsha was still 2 years old. Her first therapist told Marsha her problem was that she has "a personality disorder." As can be imagined, Marsha was less than thrilled with that feedback. When she first came to see me for her depression, I was aware that she had a history of negative relationships, would have difficulty with trusting people, and believed most people were going to abandon her. After we made some progress with her depression using dialectical behavior therapy[5] Marsha gained some trust in our relationship and we were able to discuss how her style of life was not getting her what she wanted. We worked for another year on skills to help her express herself, strengthen her self-boundary, and learn what to look for in people that conveyed trustworthiness. Although cases like hers are rare, they are important to include in a chapter on psychological styles or types. Marsha's style developed to keep a young child safe in a world where she had few tools and many harsh rules. Although the style might have kept Marsha safe as a child, it really proved dysfunctional as an adult.

Why Typologies Are Popular

a man hears what he wants to hear and disregards the rest.

—Paul Simon

As in all things Integral, Integral psychotherapists must keep an open mind with regard to new developments in psychology, including typologies. In psychology there is a dictum named after space engineer James Oberg (Oberg's Dictum). The dictum is "keeping an open mind is a virtue, but one's mind should not be so open that one's brains fall out."[6] There are always fads in any helping profession that are not only unhelpful, but can hurt clients. As seen in Chapter 8 on spirituality and psychotherapy, there also are aspects of the human experience that are difficult to map with the tools of science and require different technologies. Typologies fall somewhere between the tools of science and the experiential approaches necessary in understanding things like spirituality. Typologies can be used appropriately, as metaphors that the client resonates with to make things objects of awareness. They can also be used destructively, as "gospels" that offer temporary states masquerading as solutions that the client believes will solve a complex problem. As psychologist James Hillman wrote, the way type was used in the original Greek "gave it the meaning of an empty or hollow form for casting, a kind of rough-edged mold. From the beginning of its use by Plato and Aristotle the word had a sketchy, incomplete relief, or outline character that emphasizes a visible shaping rather than a sharply struck definition."[7] In this sense then, if we hold type lightly, we can derive ethical clinical use from the models I review in this chapter.

Typologies can be a foot in the door for clients to start looking at themselves or typologies can merely be used as another distraction from the truth. Consider the case of Jerry, a 45-year-old owner of two sandwich shops in the Midwest. Jerry was in the midst of a divorce that, although he wanted for 5 years, he couldn't face. His wife had an extra-marital affair and he felt betrayed but didn't want to lose her. The truth, he said, was that he had a poor self-image and couldn't imagine that anyone else would have him.

At one point, he and his wife went to a couples counselor who gave them each a personality inventory based on a theory of typology. She then counseled them (at $150 an hour) solely on the typology profiles. Initially, Jerry felt greatly relieved. The differences between himself and his wife were merely differences of style and the counselor claimed she could help them both communicate better given their style. Jerry and his wife spent $1,000 for sessions but never resolved their issues. In the eighth session, Jerry confessed that he didn't really feel the couples work was helping him deal with his feelings about the affair. The counselor said this was just Jerry resisting healthy communication. The initial relief he felt on learning about typology and style gave way to increasing frustration as he felt that the therapist, in her devotion to typology work, was ignoring some very difficult issues and painting Jerry and his wife into a typological corner. The counseling sessions ended when his wife filed for divorce. When I asked him what kept him in the couples counseling he said, "the belief that I'd hit upon a simple solution to a complex problem. I guess it was wishful thinking. I really hate my wife for what she did but I wanted an easy way out."

People will go to great lengths to avoid fear and other types of emotional pain. If someone is willing to tell us something that will help us believe what we want to believe, many of us will queue up, credit card in hand. From

astrology to phrenology to personality assessment, entire industries have been
built on our willingness to hear others say what we want to believe or to
believe what some charismatic expert says. As noted, this is not to say that the
constructs of types and typologies have no redeeming features—but it is to say
that types must be handled with ethical clarity and presented for what they
are: speculative interpretations of how a person navigates the world. Again, the
beauty of the Integral framework is that this is always one of the assumptions,
that types (and all the other AQAL components) are merely one aspect of a
person and a full understanding of the person requires a complete AQAL map
of who they are.

Understanding Types and Styles

In Integral psychotherapy, styles are treated as synonymous with psychological
types and some psychological types are promoted on the basis of temperament,
character, or both. Because of the paucity of research supporting types, allowing
a broad range of type-like systems gives us more flexibility in conceptualizing
the way a person navigates life and offers a broader range of tools for therapy.
In fact, the difference between "styles" and "types" is not so great. Personality
types have been described as a style of personality that is defined by a group
of consistent, related traits. Psychological types (also called personality types in
academic psychology)[8] have been described by Wilber as "types of orientations
possible at each of the various levels" of development.[9] He describes types
as horizontal in nature referring to the fact that a certain type or style *could*
maintain itself across different levels of a person's development (but in many
cases do change).

Wilber rightly cautions that although we have great confidence in many
of the stage models of development like Loevinger's model outlined in Chapter 3, we have no such confidence in typologies. As psychologist Lou Hicks
wrote, "It would be safe to venture that most American behavioral scientists
are strongly disposed to reject typological approaches."[10] Wilber concludes that
typologies simply outline some of the possible orientations that may be found
at any particular stage and in this sense, types can be of value when working
with clients. I agree with Hicks that the use of typologies should really follow
the client's preference or serve some global purpose where the type has research
support.

Most academic psychologists and psychotherapists would agree that a
personality type refers to people who have several traits in common.[11] The
most debated research question is to what extent any typology is useful in
psychotherapy. If we are looking at people who have several traits in common
how do we avoid the risk for overgeneralizing? However, if certain types of

work require particular traits (like police and firefighter jobs) shouldn't we try to measure goodness of fit by looking at the prominent types in a job and then assessing job candidates for that type? Well, the answer to both questions is "it depends." When types are used (as metaphors) to join with or engage the client in his or her work of making things (objects of awareness) they serve a useful purpose. When types are zealously advocated with starry-eyed mania clearly the advocate has gone round the bend and requires sedation and a long recuperative stay in the country. This chapter provides the broadest possible overview of typologies, their strengths and weaknesses and then illustrates how, in an Integral Psychotherapy, they can play an important role. We explore the speculative, the ridiculous, and the more current models that try to create typologies through statistical analysis of assembled traits.

Many psychologists relate the traits that cluster together forming types to attitudes toward life and such attitudes can be found in philosophical works. Beyond Plutarch's Apollonian/Dionysian artistic dichotomy[12] and Hippocrates' theory of humors, the first Western philosopher to explore this area systematically was Freidrich Schiller who tried to summarize two typical attitudes toward the external world that he believed arose through evolution. Schiller's attitudes were summarized as the realist and the idealist.[13] The realist was focused on the outer world and the idealist on the inner interpretations of the external world. Setting one type or attitude against another in the process of evolution, Schiller argued, was the best means to develop the manifold capacities of humanity[14] thus these attitudes evolved into preferences that then were refined by being pit against their opposites. As seen later, Schiller's work had a strong influence on Carl Jung's system of types.

Typologies and Psychology

Aside from challenging whether or not psychology is a "real" science, there is no more explosive topic to psychologists than the validity of typologies. Academic psychologists view most popular typologies on par with astrology (apologies to Dr. Richard Tarnus) while advocates defend them with crusade-level zealousness. Certainly, types predate psychology proper to at least the time of Aristotle's successor at the Lyceum, Theophrastus. Theophrastus' book *The Characters* presents an outline of 30 moral types that are said to reflect a good deal about the nature of life at that time but little about human nature.[15] The controversy over types began in part with the work of psychologist Walter Mischel. In 1968, he published a critique of all personality assessment (including typologies) and concluded that only a small amount of the variance in a person's behavior can be accounted for by personality tests.[16] Like Integral Psychotherapy, Mischel made the commonsense point that human beings are far more complex than most of the subjects in experimental psychology (rats, mice, or monkeys) and that complexity had not been captured by psychological assessment. This critique rippled through the psychological community and called into question the legitimacy of personality theories and personality assessment.[17]

Mischel's work, however, is hardly noted—if even known—in the training and personal-growth industry. The norm in the personal-growth industry is to eschew any peer-review of its practices or objective follow-up on its methods.[18] Many so-called "trainers" heavily rely on partial knowledge about the inventories they use as well as the history of the inventory. Numerous corporations employ tests used by "consultants" even though the tests have no evidence of reliability or validity. Although there is a vast gray area between the personal-growth industry and psychology/psychotherapy, nothing highlights this gray area like typologies. Many typologies blend seamlessly with occult schools, palmistry. and astrology because these practices were among the first efforts to "type" personality beginning more than 3,000 years ago[19] (and to be clear these are not credited as having scientific value).

This chapter is divided into seven sections as follows:

- Historical Effects: In this section I review some of the history behind typologies and illustrate how many ancient (and mistaken) notions of type are still with us.

- Type and Temperament. I review efforts at typing people by temperament.

- Typology Proper. The third section focuses on types proper spawned in various psychological theories.

- Popular Typology Tests. This part uses the example of Jung's typology and the Enneagram in describing the movement from types to tests for those types.

- Factorial Models of Types: The Big Five and Seven-Factor Models. Building on the theme from the previous section, this part reviews factorial models where tests are constructed from analyzing how the traits in various types cluster together. In this section I review the Five-Factor Model and psychiatrist Robert Cloninger's Seven Factor Model.

- When Styles go Wrong: Typology as Pathology and Personality Disorders. This section focuses on personality disorders and how typologies based on symptoms form the historical lineage for today's understanding of these dysfunctional styles.

- Masculine and Feminine Approaches to Type: From Typing to Sexual Identity. The final section discusses the pros and cons of masculine and feminine approaches to type.

Although I offer a broad overview in this chapter, there are dozens of efforts at typologies in the history of psychology and psychiatry. What I have included represents a sample that illustrates the different ways this daunting task has been attempted as well as ways these can be used in psychotherapy.

Historical Efforts

Most students of psychology and many laypeople are aware that the ancient Greeks attempted to correlate physiological fluids or humors (humours) with personality types. The four primary humors (yellow bile, black bile, blood, and phlegm) were thought to correspond to the four elements of earth, water, fire, and air. From this correlation, in the fourth century BCE, Hippocrates proposed (and Galen later elaborated) four temperaments (choleric, melancholic, sanguine, and phlegmatic) that corresponded to the humors and supposedly to the elements the humors represented. Hippocrates also asserted that disease stemmed from some imbalance between these humors—his may have been the first of many incorrect theories of "chemical imbalance."[20] Although we may regard these early philosophers as naïve, their terminology is still part of our language as in calling someone "good humored." Despite the invalid nature of the humor theory of personality and disease, Hippocrates and his followers used objective observation and deductive reasoning in an attempt to separate medicine from superstition.[21] They did fairly well considering they had no library databases or Internet.

The early classical philosophers also explored the idea that body structure was associated with personality. Aristotle is thought to be the first to record the idea of physiognomy that proposes personality characteristics can be identified by outward appearances. This led to the 18th-century system of morphology and the regrettable phrenology of Franz Gall. Ernst Kretschmer, in a monograph called *Physique and Character*,[22] later explored morphology at length. In this book, Kretschmer proposed that people with a round-bodied (*pyknic*) physique were predisposed to what today we would refer to as bipolar I disorder (manic depression). He further proposed that average people with somewhat athletic builds possessed balanced (*syntonic*) temperaments. Psychologist William Sheldon followed up Kretschmer's work proposing endomorphic (heavy set and happy), ectomorphic (thin and irritable), and mesomorphic (muscular and even-tempered) body types and creating an *Atlas of Men* wherein the reader could use a rating system to describe not only pure types but mixtures of types on a graded scale.[23] Sheldon's morphology (like many typologies today), although exciting the public and the media, fell out of favor for lack of evidence and, in the post-World War II era, for its too-proximate relationship with physiognomic ideas that were the basis of the Third Reich. Also, Sheldon's enthusiasm for researching types by amassing a large library of photographs of nude men was viewed with suspicion by many of his colleagues.

In the last paragraph, I noted that Gall's phrenology was regrettable. This was because, as a neuroanatomist, Gall made important contributions to thinking about the mind–brain relationship. First he proposed that mental processes had biological underpinnings or, as we would say from an Integral understanding, were correlated with biological events. Second, he proposed that the cerebral cortex had distinct regions that governed specific functions. Gall was misguided in his association of discrete mental functions with specific parts of the brain and in the belief that the areas of the brain most used would push the skull outward forming bumps and that from these bumps one could discern information about the personality of the patient. The result, phrenology (also called "bumpology" by early detractors like William James) took the European and American public by storm winning such lifelong adherents as Walt Whitman who decided as a result of his phrenology examination to pursue writing (but remember, everyone is right about something—just not equally right about everything).

The point of including the invalid examples of morphology and phrenology in this chapter is to draw a parallel. Both morphology and phrenology had zealous followings and there were "scientific" papers and entire journals devoted to their exploration. These publications gave both an air of validity until more critical thinkers conducted studies to test the claims. Both the claims of morphology and phrenology were unsupported.[24] Today we have similar dynamics particularly in the personal growth industry where pseudo- and quasi-scientific claims about personality go unchallenged and some systems publish their own "scientific" journals. So let the reader beware: There are no systems of typology that have clear support in the research and at best, the efforts I review here provide the Integral therapist with a treasure chest of metaphors that can be used to facilitate the therapeutic alliance and work—metaphors, not scientific systems.

One more caveat: As we all know, people are free to believe whatever they want to believe—they may not be free to speak their beliefs, but they are free to hold them (as evidence a contemporary reader need look no further than the latest 2012 hype, which seems strikingly similar to hysterical and equally wrong Y2K, Harmonic Convergence, and the Hale-Bopp Comet phenomena). Nowhere in psychology is this freedom exercised more than in the area of typologies. Many people approach typologies with a faith that is religious. In Integral Psychotherapy, our aim is to meet clients where they are. If that includes using the framework of a typology as metaphor, we do that. As I discuss in Chapter 7, a person's psychological address can provide clues as to who may and who may not value such typologies. Either way, as trained, licensed therapists, we are expected to know the difference between a well-constructed and a poorly constructed test; between a well thought-out construct and a construct based on faith. Although the whole state of California may file suit against me, there simply is not much scientific support for most of the systems or tests discussed in this chapter (particularly the Enneagram). In fact, many of them may actually be the 21st-century equivalents of phrenology.[25] Be that as it may, there can be a place for these typologies (and perhaps their tests) in therapy if they help clients with the work of making aspects of themselves or their lives objects of awareness.

Type and Temperament[26]

Many psychologists and psychotherapists have tried to create typologies based on a person's temperament. Temperament has generally been thought to be based in the body and is currently described as innate, genetic, and constitutional influences, including how gene expression facilitates the production and actions of brain chemistry.[27] Although some have tried to postulate temperament from things like the shape of the body (e.g., morphology) others (particularly American psychologists) thought that temperament reflected heritable factors that could be discerned from observing behavior. William McDougall is perhaps the best-known American psychologist in this area. Working at the dawn of the 20th century, he proposed eight "tempers" based on the way combinations of three dimensions manifested in behavior. The three dimensions were intensity (strength and urgency), persistency (inward as opposed to outward expression), and affectivity (emotionalism). High-intensity people were active and low-intensity people were passive. High-persistency people were extroverted and low-persistency people introverted. High-affectivity people were susceptible to pleasure and pain, whereas low-affectivity people were far less so.[28]

There were European efforts similar to McDougall's. German psychologist Ernst Meumann focused on eight fundamental qualities of feeling. He included two dimensions or polarities of pleasure versus displeasure and activity versus passivity. This resulted in another elaboration of the Hipporcratic humors with active-pleasurable people being sanguine, active-displeasurable people being choleric, passive-pleasurable people being phlegmatic and passive-displeasurable people being melancholic.[29] Hungarian psychiatrist Jeno Kollarits derived character types in a similar manner using dimensions of pleasantness versus unpleasantness and excited versus calm. He would refer to "calm depressives" or "calm euphorics" in an effort to describe clients he treated. As with Meumann,

Kollarits related the dimensions to the Hippocratic humors with calm-unpleasant being sanguine, excited and unpleasant being choleric, and so on.[30]

In the mid-20th century, Salvatore Maddi proposed a theory that focused on the activity–passivity dimension used by Meumann. For Maddi, activity is operationalized as wanting to influence one's environment, whereas inactivity is trying to avoid the stimulation of one's environment. Maddi approximated 24 different temperaments using this one dimension, but focused on four primary types: high- and low-activation types each subdivided based on the presence of internal or external traits that are similar to introversion and extroversion. A high-activation person who is an extrovert will be seen as a "go-getter," whereas a high-activation person who is an introvert would be more geared toward seeking intellectual challenges. Low-activation extroverts would tend to seek out routines and conform, whereas low-activation introverts would tend to carefully avoid excesses and tend to function in a stable manner.[31]

Typology Proper

There have been multiple attempts to create personality typologies in psychology beginning in Europe in the late-19th century. French psychologist Theodule Ribot created a typology similar in structure to botanical classifications. He came up with types based partly in temperament like the humble, contemplative, and emotional characters.[32] At the same, time Frederic Queyrat postulated nine normal character types through permutations of three dispositions: emotionality, meditation, and activity.[33] Interestingly, one of the founders of experimental psychology, Wilhelm Wundt, was among the first to suggest a possible correlation between the humor theories of Hippocrates and Galen and personality or more precisely temperament. Prior to this point, the humors were thought of as discrete categories—you either belonged to one or you didn't. Wundt was perhaps one of the first to realize this was clearly not true (an argument that, as is seen here, has yet to reach enthusiasts of the Myers-Briggs Type Indicator [MBTI]). Wundt suggested that melancholic and choleric types shared strong emotional reactivity, whereas sanguine and choleric types shared changeableness. Wundt created from the four Greek temperaments, two intersecting dimensions of personality as depicted in Fig. 5.1.

So Wundt dealt with the problem of exclusivity by delineating two dimensions on which one could be rated. This allowed for possessing more or less of the two dimensions as each case allowed (as illustrated in Fig. 5.1). Without realizing it, one of the founders of experimental psychology had contributed unwittingly to one of the least scientific aspects of psychology. In all fairness, we must understand Wundt's context compared to early 20th-century American psychologists. Wundt was embedded in a European tradition that was far

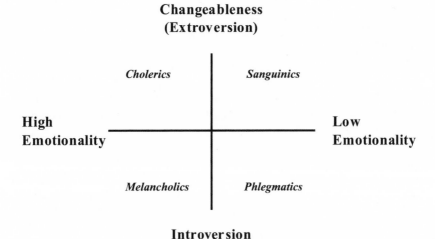

Figure 5.1. Wundt's two dimensions of personality type.

closer to what we are calling Integral in that scientific problems were viewed within a complex and broad philosophical framework that included meaning and the purpose of life. American psychology, in contrast, has always aimed at simplifying problems to search for practical applications.[34] Recall from Chapter 3 that American psychologists were so zealous to be considered scientists that they would interpret European psychological works like Freud's changing words like "it" to the Latin "id" in the hopes of sounding more scientific.

Popular Typology Tests

Jung's Theory of Psychological Types

Perhaps the most well-known theory of types is that of Swiss psychiatrist Carl Jung. Both Wundt and Schiller's work inspired Jung to take up the issue of types with an eye to understanding how his clients were translating reality. Healthy translation for Jung laid the base for a process of Individuation, which he felt was a potential that lay dormant in most people but could be awakened through access to the total personality. For Jung, the total personality was captured in the archetype of the Self.[35] The Self, which provides balance and stability, is the midpoint of personality around which all the other elements revolve. In

Jung's system, for the Self to emerge in an individual, various components of personality must become co-developed or equally developed. If David's message in Chapter 4 about development being sloppy made sense, you will understand how challenging this co-development is.

Of these components, Jung (following Schiller and Wundt) proposed the primary attitudes or orientations called *introvert* and *extravert*.[36] These are both present in all people, but one is dominant and conscious, whereas the other is subordinate and unconscious. Additionally, Jung proposed four psychological functions: Thinking is how people make sense of the world, feeling is how they evaluate it, sensing yields concrete facts about the world, and intuiting relies on subconscious contents to search for the essence of life. Jung claimed he arrived at exactly four functions on empirical grounds that could function in orienting people similar to the way latitude and longitude orient geographers.[37] As with attitudes, each person possesses each of the four functions, however, one is more differentiated than the others. This differentiated function is called the *superior function* and is what the person leads with consciously. The least differentiated function is the *inferior function,* which is unconscious and expresses itself in dreams and fantasies. Both the superior and inferior functions have auxiliaries that act as backups in case the function in question is prevented from working.

Like both Wilber and Kegan, Jung wanted to understand how people deal with subject and object. Recall that in Wilber's model of healthy growth (the subject–object dynamic of Chapter 3) the subject of an earlier stage becomes the object of the subject for a later stage—if all goes well. We also represent objects based on the tools we have as subjects. This relates to what is called *object relations* where an "object" usually refers to another person, typically a significant other or caregiver.[38] The person with the extravert style is more tuned in to the experience of the significant other. The person with the introvert style is more tuned in to the internal representation of the significant other. Representing objects also is related to what we know about sensation and perception. As seen later in the chapter, males and females have biological differences that affect how they map external objects. Jung described the relationship between a subject and an object to be one of adaptation and, based on the person's type "every relation between subject and object presupposes the modification of one by the other through reciprocal influence."[39] This notion was later adapted to a psychodynamic dialectical model of self-development where the style of the proximate self was sculpted developed through interactions with other "objects" in the environment.[40]

As noted earlier, the introvert, according to Jung, is far more interested in the inner world of her mind and prefers to direct her energy inward for abstracting. In Jung's words, the introvert places more energy in the subject (the proximate self) and withdraws energy away from the object for fear of being overwhelmed by it. The extravert has a more positive attitude toward objects and directs her energy outward and allows her attitude to be oriented by the object. This is far from absolute as Wundt concluded earlier. As most psychologists will point out, some introverts can be very externally focused in certain situations and some extraverts can be internally reflective under the right circumstances. Although Jung saw this as a starting point, he felt a two-category scheme for classifying complex human beings was too simplistic. Jung elaborated his system to the point where it represented eight types that were made up of combinations of attitudes and function (extraversion, introversion, thinking, feeling, sensing, and intuiting). Despite the fact that his original system proposed eight types, he is quoted as saying there was nothing magical about eight and there could be any number of types we wished—even hundreds and hundreds.[41]

In describing the complementary relationship between conscious and unconscious, he wrote the following:

> It may be gathered from what has been said in the previous section that a purely objective orientation does violence to a multitude of subjective emotions, intentions, needs, and desires, since it robs them of the energy that is their natural right. Man is not a machine that one can reconstruct, as occasion demands, upon other lines and for quite other ends, in the hope that it will then proceed to function, in a totally different way, just as normally as before.[42]

Jung believed that the compensating attitude of the unconscious creates a psychic equilibrium but never thought of type as a stable thing. He saw personality moving toward individuation[43]—a way of being where a person can draw from all his or her typological faculties depending on the situation. For Jung, this is not a linear type of development, however; he really conceptualized it as a movement toward the center of one's being. It might be depicted as all four functions placed equidistant from each other around the circumference of a circle. The center would represent the synthesis of all four differentiated functions. In Integral Psychotherapy, we would be more inclined to describe this as a combination of state and stage growth. The state of individuation takes one to the center of his or her being but this is transitory. The later stages of self-development as outlined by Cook-Greuter (Chapter 3) are the pathway to a stage where individuation occurs.

FROM THEORY TO TEST: THE MYERS-BRIGGS TYPE INDICATOR

So what does all this really mean for the average person? That question was taken up in the early 1940s by Isabel Briggs Myers and her mother Katherine Briggs. They both were interested in Jung's type theory and began creating what would become the Myers-Briggs Type Indicator (MBTI) for personnel selection.[44] Isabel Myers believed that personality type and job performance were related and that goodness of fit could be assessed by mapping the requirements of the job, assessing the personality type of the job candidate, and making the best match possible between the two. The result of this belief and her immersion in Jung's writings was the MBTI. Myers, armed with a healthy dose of family financial support, made it her life's mission to develop and disperse the MBTI. In 1957 the Educational Testing Service (ETS) began using the test for research purposes and, after an unfavorable internal review of the test, decided not to pursue further development or use it in any test batteries. ETS worked internally with the test until it broke off relationship with Isabel Myers (whose tenacity had worn relations quite thin).

The MBTI was discovered in 1968 by Mary McCaully, a psychologist on the faculty of the University of Florida and one of the few academics to be enthused about the test. In 1972, McCaulley and Myers founded the Center for Applications of Psychological Type (CAPT) and in 1975 Consulting Psychologists Press acquired the right to sell the MBTI and it has been successfully marketed since. According to some, the key word in the last sentence is "marketed." As one of my colleagues remarked, "there is type, and then there is hype—hype sells type."[45] McCaulley remained president of CAPT until 2001, two years prior to her death. Throughout the years of their collaboration, McCaulley worked closely with Isabel Myers on the development of the test and the manual.[46]

The current versions of the test have approximately 90 items.[47] The items are forced-choice items, meaning the person being tested has to choose one of two possible answers. This is one of the criticisms of the test because forced-choice items are designed to push responses from the middle toward the extreme (in psychometric language this means the items have good *midpoint discrimination*). This is a problem because Jung himself felt most people fall closer to the midpoints on his typological traits. More recently, psychologist John Barbuto proposed reconstructing the MBTI with continuously measured items to more accurately reflect Jung's types.[48] When a client's MBTI is scored he or she is assigned a four-letter code that represents the client's personality style. For example ENFJ would stand for extravert, intuiting, feeling, and judging. There are 16 possible types one can get on the MBTI.

Whether the MBTI represents type or hype depends on whom you ask. Some psychologists use the test in clinical practice because they find the psychological reality of the types helpful in making clients' styles objects of awareness and then using that awareness to help that client translate reality.[49] This clinical use is holding the type lightly but honoring it as the style that the client "resonates with." By that I simply mean the style that the client feels most comfortable with or most comfortable *identifying with*. In this sense, the inventory is only as good as the dialogue that follows it.[50] If the client feels that his or her resulting type is a good fit, then it can be clinically useful. If on the other hand, the client says "that is not the way I see myself at all," the therapist would do best to move on. This raises one of the problems with the MBTI. Some researchers have found that people can simply read through the types and fairly accurately choose their type without taking the inventory.[51]

All psychological tests must have some degree of what is called *validity* and *reliability*. Validity simply means the test measures what it claims to measure. In the case of the MBTI, the claim is that it measures personality types. Reliability is the extent to which a test consistently measures what it claims to measure. For example, according to some studies, 50% of people who take the MBTI twice will end up with a different type code from each testing.[52] Some researchers have even suggested that type will vary with the time of day the person takes (and retakes) the test.[53] To complicate things, there are multiple methods for assessing validity and reliability, some more important than others when one is seeking to generalize from a test to understanding a person. For example, face validity means the items and descriptions look like what the test is supposed to measure. This accounts for why many people can simply read the description of the types and pick the one they resonate with. Face validity, however, is not useful in judging the quality of the test.[54]

As you might guess, much of the debate regarding the MBTI and other typologies concerns what sort of methods to use to check the test's validity and reliability. Those who use the inventory favor tests run by MBTI enthusiasts who support its reliability and validity. Those who feel the test is useless, focus on the many studies outside of the MBTI organizations that have not supported the test's usefulness. As noted previously, the MBTI has good face validity. The construct validity of the MBTI, however, is less robust. Construct validity basically means that research supports the idea that personality falls out into the 16 types on the test. This has not been consistently supported. Psychologists Robert McCrae and Paul Costa concluded that four of the five personality characteristics in their model (discussed later) accounted for most of the 16 MBTI types.[55]

Critics of the MBTI claim that although there is some validity to aspects of the test, the extent to which type is fixed or fluid heavily depends on the state in which the person takes the test.[56] We return to this point in Chapter 7 on states. There also is the question of whether or not the "types" of the MBTI are really discrete—meaning they are exclusive categories with no overlap.[57] Because the test makers suggest that people are primarily either introverts or extraverts, one would assume that samples of subjects would fall primarily into one of those two categories. This is not supported in many of the studies done on the MBTI. Instead people score between these two extremes as if they were on a continuum.[58] So a person whose primary style is extravert may have a personality profile very similar to someone whose primary style is that of an introvert.[59] This is congruent with Jung's own writing on the large number of people who fall somewhere between extraversion and introversion:

> There is, finally, a third group, and here it is hard to say whether the motivation (primary attitude) comes chiefly from within or without. This group is the most numerous and includes the less differentiated normal man.[60]

It also is important to note that Jung's response to the MBTI was muted at best and he declined to meet Isabel Myers after she sent him the test. Critics feel that the MBTI does not really measure what Jung intended when he wrote of psychological types. The developers of the test added the functions of Judging and Perceiving that did not appear in Jung's theory, which he claimed to have created based on empirical observation.[61] Other researchers have suggested that instead of 16 types there are really three general factors studied by the test.[62]

Psychologist Hans Eysenck tried to correlate Jung's introverted and extraverted types with mental stability and instability. Although he found some correlations suggestive of Hippocrates' ancient theory of humors,[63] he also recognized that "it is too easy to read into historical writings what one wishes to see."[64] Finally, Jung viewed types in the context of individuation described as the impulse each of us has to distinguish ourselves as a single and separate person. This includes conscious and unconscious reactions, but the MBTI is heavily weighted toward the conscious reactions.[65] Finally and perhaps most problematic, it is estimated that between 33% and 50% of the published material on the MBTI has been produced for conferences at the CAPT (which provides MBTI training) or as papers in the *Journal of Psychological Type* (which is edited by Myers-Briggs enthusiasts).[66] The MBTI is still viewed unfavorably in the vast majority of the academic psychological community. It is viewed more favorably in the clinical community as evidenced by a recent survey of doctoral-level psychologists.[67]

The reason for reviewing this research is that millions of people have taken the MBTI and had different expectations for what the results meant. Toward that end, I offer a maxim of Integral Psychotherapy: In Integral Psychotherapy, a test is only as good as the dialogue that follows it. Although the MBTI may be weak on some statistical points, there can still be a clinical utility to its use. This depends on the ethical application and use by psychotherapists. As Jungian analyst John Beebe pointed out, one can use a limited inventory in a way that resonates with the client and furthers therapeutic work.[68] One example is Janessa, a client who had taken a great many workshops on the MBTI, administered it appropriately to clients, and strongly resonated with being an ENFJ. One of the qualities of the ENFJ has been referred to as "the teacher." Janessa had wanted to pursue a PhD because she felt a calling to teach at the university level. Using her understanding and the language of the MBTI typology facilitated more efficient use of the therapy time and helped Janessa feel safer when confronting the inner conflict that thus far had prevented her from pursuing the degree. It is important to note, however, that on ego identity, Janessa tested at the Achiever level and this, along with her desire to teach, seemed to be more primary to her career shift than the MBTI type.

So what is so attractive to so many people about the MBTI type? Writer Annie Murphy Paul gives a good summary of this dynamic. At the management level, she concludes, conflicts that may be rooted in differences of race or gender can be reconceptualized (even if artificially) as differences in type. Anything that sorts people is likely to be welcomed by companies and similar organizations. As she notes:

> the Indicator's unfailingly positive tone blends seamlessly with the language of corporate political correctness and with our society's emphasis on promoting self-esteem. The euphemistic blandness of the Myers-Briggs, its mild vocabulary of 'fit' and 'gift,' is the key to its success.[69]

She continues, however, stating that "under this banner of respect for individuality, organizations are able to shift responsibility for employee satisfaction onto that obliging culprit, 'fit.' There's no bad worker and no bad workplace, only a bad fit between the two."[70] In Integral parlance we might say that MBTI types are attractive to Pluralists who may dislike differentiating performance on quantitative criteria.

As for the individual, Paul notes that the MBTI comes along at a point in many people's lives where they are uncertain, in transition, and struggling in a confusing world. She notes that the idea of belonging to a group type, or having a type that "explains" things comes as a great relief. Recall the case of Jerry earlier in the chapter. He (and apparently his wife) felt "relief" to have an explanation for their problems. Jerry, in particular, was more relieved at not having to confront his demons, of having a convenient external explanation of a difficult fit between himself and his wife. Such convenience, however, frequently comes at a cost.

As asserted Chapter 1, one of the primary aims of Integral Psychotherapy *In Integral informed ways.* is that the therapist meet the client where the client is at. In Chapter 7, I discuss what is called the client's *psychological address*. A primary component of that address is the altitude of the client's proximate self as outlined in Chapter 3. The issue of types and the MBTI in general raises the question: To what extent is the test actually measuring aspects of ego development rather than type? This is not easily discerned, but many of the conclusions shared by MBTI enthusiasts could just as easily be interpreted as levels of ego identity rather than type. This also would account for the studies that find more than 50% of the people retaking the MBTI come out with a different type. The National

Research Council's studies of the MBTI led the organization to conclude that anywhere from 24% to 61% of test takers who retake the test will end up with a different type.[71] The conclusion of these researchers was that the MBTI should not be used for career counseling until its validity and reliability is supported by further research. Ultimately, it is recommended that the Integral psychotherapist can use type as a vehicle for dialogue but nothing more. If it helps tune into what a client values about him or herself, that is fine. If it is looked to for direction in how the therapy should proceed, that is a poor choice that borders on being unethical.   *not for direction but vehicle for dialogue*

The Enneagram

No discussion of types and testing is complete without an exploration of the Enneagram, another typology that is widely hyped, widely used, and widely misunderstood. Many advocates of the Enneagram assert that it is of a mysterious "spiritual" origin emerging from the mists of pre-recorded history. Probably the most mysterious thing about the Enneagram is why so many people find it useful. The answers appear to be similar to the same reason so many people adore the MBTI—because it offers simple explanations for the complexity of human beings and does it in many cases, cloaked in a faux aura of occult mystery—a cloaking that does a great deal to attract those seeking to validate their egos or styles as having metaphysical import.

Despite being widely used for 20 years, as of 2009 there were only two peer-reviewed publications of the reliability and validity of the Enneagram. These studies found little support for the nine discrete types of personality supposedly measured, but, like the MBTI, noted that the Enneagram can be useful if the client is enthusiastic about using it—in other words, it can provide a vehicle for dialogue with the client and that can be useful for helping clients make things objects of awareness.[72] Most papers and studies on the Enneagram skip right over reliability and validity and give anecdotal claims by enthusiastic users[73] or begin with a biased assumption that the Enneagram is a useful tool regardless of its psychometric properties.[74] A number of researchers doing doctoral studies on the Enneagram do not even report their findings in abstract form through the dissertations database. This is certainly suspect in the academic world.[75]

Despite the lack of evidence that the Enneagram is a rigorous instrument, some coverage of it is important because of its widespread use. Also, as noted, in Integral Psychotherapy we meet the client where he or she is. If the client resonates positively with an Enneagram type, it behooves the therapist to use that in the sessions, even if the validity of the type is questionable. Therapists who adhere to the Enneagram notion of type may also have different approaches to therapy. Chilean psychiatrist Claudio Naranjo convened a seminar of nine such therapists (embodying nine different Enneagram types) who all had different perspectives on how the Enneagram could be used therapeutically. This little-known work is still important in that the thrust is to work with the client's (and therapist's) perceived style without putting too much reliance on any magical qualities that the Enneagram has per se.[76]

MYSTERIOUS ORIGINS

As with most occult traditions, the history of the Enneagram is a bit of a soap opera. Initially, Don Riso and Russ Hudson wrote that the Enneagram was a synthesis of several ancient wisdom traditions[77] whose origins have been lost in history.[78] This type of "origin" is fairly common practice in those claiming to have some special occult knowledge and who are usually anxious to exploit that knowledge for the right fee[79] (what I referred to in Chapter 1 as a "for-profit-prophet"). To be fair, Riso recanted on the idea that the Enneagram came from an ancient oral tradition and admitted it appears to be a contemporary system.[80] Despite this, these highly suspect occult origins have been enthusiastically reported as late as 2007 with authors still citing Riso as the source of this information even though he has since recanted.[81]

The introduction of the Enneagram to the West has been attributed to Armenian self-proclaimed teacher George Gurdjieff (via his disciple Petry Ouspensky) but the actual figure associated with it today seems to have originated with Chilean teacher Oscar Ichazo[82] in the 1960s (Ichazo later rejected the enneagram in favor of his own Arica training.)[83] Helen Palmer, a student of Claudio Naranjo, claims to be carrying on the esoteric oral tradition that Riso and Hudson have turned their back on.[84] Interestingly, Oscar Ichazo sued Palmer in 1992 for copyright violations but lost. Palmer seems to have used Ichazo's ideas of enneagon and ego fixations and changed the labels to Enneagram and personality types.

The label Enneagram comes from the Greek words for nine (*ennea*) and something written or drawn (*grammos*). In geometry an enneagram is a nine-sided star polygon (Fig. 5.2).

Figure 5.2. Nine-sided star polygon

The logo familiar to users of the Enneagram today is a nine-pointed geometric figure on which each point represents a personality type. This is the figure used in the "fourth way teachings" of the Enneagram (Fig. 5.3), a phrase coined by Gurdjieff's disciple (and later competitor) Ouspensky.[85]

Figure 5.3 is composed of three parts: a circle that supposedly represents wholeness, a triangle that represents the trinity or lack of duality, and finally the hexad, which is found by tracing lines between points numbered 1, 4, 2, and 8. The nine personality types fall on the circumference of the circle and are connected to each other by the other lines.

How the types are defined varies depending on who you ask. Some claim they represent an individual's fundamental weakness, whereas others maintain they represent a fundamental energy that drives a person's entire being. Still others define them by the relative presence of three drives: self-preserving, social, and sexual. Followers of Gurdjieff (who himself claimed to have studied Sufi tradition) refer to the three drives as mental, emotional, and instinctual. Oscar Ichazo spoke of imbalances or ego fixations at each of the nine points. These were based on the seven deadly sins of Christianity plus fear and deceit.[86] Despite this The U.S. Bishops Secretariat for Doctrine and Pastoral Practices condemned the Enneagram in the National Catholic Reporter as having no scientific import or use for those seeking to live by Christian doctrine.[87]

To further complicate matters, there are at least four Enneagram inventories, including one by Thomas Zinkle,[88] one by Helen Palmer,[89] one by Jerome Wagner,[90] and one by David Daniels and Virginia Price.[91] The most frequently used is the fourth, the Riso-Hudson Enneagram Type Indicator (RHETI). The RHETI is the version that researcher Rebecca Nugent studied in her 2001 dissertation research. Although Nugent did a good job exploring questions of

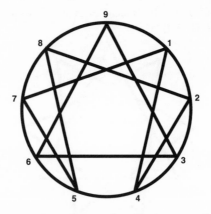

Figure 5.3. Enneagram used in fourth way teaching.

reliability and validity of this version of the test, her work did not support the construct of nine types and suggested that in fact the nine types may (like the MBTI types) be manifestations of the "Big Five" personality traits, which is the subject of the next section of this chapter. Although Nugent's overall conclusions were modest at best, this did not stop Riso and Hudson's Enneagram Institute from claiming the following:

> In March, 2001, the Riso–Hudson Enneagram Type Indicator (RHETI Version 2.5) was officially validated by independent research . . . Dr. Nugent concluded that the RHETI is scientifically "valid and reliable" as a test instrument with "solid psychometrics" . . . with these findings, the RHETI has become the most widely used Enneagram-based questionnaire to be independently validated by an impartial researcher.[92]

If you choose to read the dissertation you'll see that Nugent concluded "results of this investigation provide mixed but general support for the general research hypotheses."[93]

THE "TYPES" AND CONCLUDING THOUGHTS ON THE ENNEAGRAM

Table 5.1 lists the different versions of the Enneagram types from Ichazo to Palmer to Riso and Hudson.

If Integral psychotherapists can dissociate themselves from the general nuttiness of the politics surrounding the Enneagram and tolerate the paucity of psychometric studies, they may find it useful as a springboard for dialogue. This is only recommended, however, if the client is already an enthusiast of

Table 5.1. Correlations between different versions of the Enneagram

Type Number	Palmer Labels	Associated Sin	Riso=Hudson Labels
1	Perfectionist	Anger	Reformer
2	Giver	Pride	Helper
3	Performer	Deceit	Achiever
4	Romantic	Envy	Pluralist
5	Observer	Avarice	Investigator
6	Trooper	Fear	Loyalist
7	Epicure	Gluttony	Enthusiast
8	Boss	Lust	Challenger
9	Mediator	Sloth	Peacemaker

the test. Otherwise, it is akin to putting the proverbial legs on a snake. A case example of how it can be useful is that of Francis, a 51-year-old Anglican priest who identified with his primary type of "helper" and who definitely had shadow material around pride. For Francis, the Enneagram provided a framework that allowed us to move right into shadow work rather than having to spend time negotiating how we were going to talk about his issues.

Factorial Models of Types:
The Big Five and Seven-Factor Models

One of the more statistically rigorous models for discussing types or styles is the Five-Factor Model. The first mention of this model was by psychologist Louis Thurstone in his 1933 presidential address to the American Psychological Association.[94] Subsequent research led to two separate but similar models. One is referred to as the Five-Factor Model and the other "the Big Five."[95] Although these are technically two distinct conceptual models, I generalize both of them here as a single model for the sake of discussion. The Five-Factor Model also derives in part from the work of psychologist Raymond Cattell, who refined the practice of using factor analysis to explore personality traits. Traits are considered basic units of personality structure but vast disagreement persists over what traits should be included in taxonomies and what influence the situation has over what traits are expressed and how they are expressed.[96]

Cattell built on the work of psychologist Gordon Allport. Because Allport believed that any personality traits of interest or importance would be represented in language, he and colleague Henry Odbert scoured an unabridged dictionary and compiled a list of 17,953 words that represented traits. They then reduced the list to 4,504 adjectives they believed to refer to observable and relatively permanent traits.[97] This is referred to as the lexical hypothesis of personality or style and is attributed to Sir Francis Galton. Cattell then reduced Allport and Odbert's list to 171 items by deleting synonyms. Then he used rating systems and factor analysis to condense the list to just 16 factors. He developed the 16 Personality Factor (16PF) to create a set of traits common to personality but that were weighted differently in different people. Although his theory is considered a great contribution to psychology, it has never been fully replicated and later analyses found there was little support for the 16 original traits he thought were central to each person's style.[98] Despite this, it refined the path on which the later discovery of the Five-Factor Model was made.[99]

The five factors (represented by the acronym OCEAN) are openness to experience, conscientiousness, extraversion, agreeableness, and neuroticism. For the most part, I refer to these as "Goldilocks Factors" in that it is optimal if one possesses not too much and not too little of each. Openness to experience is just what it sounds like. It is typical of people who lead with extrovert styles and also has been correlated with greater growth in ego identity.[100] Basically, openness to experience increases the probability of moving into experiences that are "disequilibrating" in nature and such experiences have been correlated with growth in ego identity.[101] Conscientiousness is conceptualized as a tendency toward self-discipline, achievement, and a preference for planned rather than spontaneous behavior. As Loevinger pointed out, this is only one description of conscientiousness and very general and bland compared to her ego developmental level of Conscientiousness (also referred to as "Achiever" in Chapter 3).[102] Extraversion is a trait typified by having high energy, seeking out the company and stimulation of others, and generally what we would call an agentic orientation. Agreeableness has been generally summarized as a tendency to, as Karen Horney wrote, move toward others.[103] This "movement toward" manifests as compassion rather than suspicion, cooperation rather than antagonism. Finally, neuroticism is an index of vulnerability to unpleasant emotions like anger, anxiety, and depression sometimes interpreted as emotional instability.

In the model, a client's general personality is conceptualized as the combined expression of these factors. The five factors are not types in the strict sense. As noted previously, one of the main problems with types is that they typically do not show up in people as exclusive categories and the ones that do tend to change over time.[104] In both the MBTI and the Enneagram, there is mixed support for the idea that a person has a psychological type that is consistent across both states and developmental stages. For the same reason that in Integral Psychotherapy we think broadly of types as synonymous with styles, the five factors in the Five-Factor Model are really a set of trait continua representing factors that are more or less present in a given person. Again, this is similar to the approach Wundt proposed to allow for representation of the degree to which a person possessed a given trait.

Because the traits or factors are on dimensions, they can reflect greater or lesser emphases in different people. As noted, in the MBTI, the forced-choice test format will represent a moderate preference for extraversion in the same way as it represents a strong preference—there is no middle ground reflected in the final type. The tests based on the Five-Factor Model (described later) offer the test taker five choices on a continuum (what in testing is called a Likert scale.)[105] There also appears to be some evidence that these five traits or factors are stable over a long period of time (45 years in one study).[106] Some initial research is beginning to support the hypothesis that these traits may have heritability factors, meaning, they can be shown to result from some genetic influence.[107] Although gene expression is always an interaction between genes and the environment, the initial studies looking at genetic correlates are opening a promising research area.[108] There also is some evidence that knowing one's placement on each of the factors facilitates the process of psychotherapy.[109]

In many ways, the Five-Factor Model of personality assessment provides a framework functionally similar to the Integral framework in that it appears to transcend and include many theories of personality allowing for some orienting generalizations without the emotional baggage present in those who champion one particular theory. The shadow side of this is that many critics feel that the Five-Factor theory is far too simplistic to account for personality.[110] Personality psychologist Jack Block summarizes the criticisms of the Five-Factor Model and reviews the possibility that the five factors are really two higher-order factors: one representing the socialization process and the other representing something akin to personal growth.[111]

Psychologists Gerard Saucier and Lewis Goldberg argued that most personality-related adjectives could be subsumed into the Five-Factor Model.[112] Although other researchers disputed this,[113] some have suggested that the types in the MBTI and Enneagram seem to reflect traits captured in the Five-Factor Model. From an Integral perspective, the Five-Factor Model provides a partial but useful part of the human story. Although the title of the model is not as sexy as the Enneagram or anything linked to Jung's theory, the evidence for reliability and validity is good.

The most commonly used tests to assess how a client embodies and expresses the five factors are the NEO-PI-R (NEO Personality Inventory Revised) and the NEO-FFI (NEO Five-Factor Inventory). These are later generation versions of the NEO-I, which stood for the Neuroticism Extroversion Openness Inventory, which measured only three of the five factors. The acronym "NEO" was retained for later versions of the test, although it is now merely a prefix because the later versions measure all five factors. Psychologists Robert McCrae and Paul Costa developed the tests. The NEO-FFI is a shortened, 60-item version and has good evidence of reliability and validity.[114]

Even though the statistical robustness of the NEO tests surpass that of the MBTI or Enneagram, the Five-Factor Model and its tests share with the MBTI and Enneagram a history of intense political lobbying to get the constructs and tests into popular use.[115] Costa and McCrae have been criticized for putting their enthusiasm for a product ahead of scientific evaluation.[116] Other criticisms of the test are that it uses no lie scales to detect if respondents are being truthful,[117] it does not account for the origins of personality, and it assumes that "human beings are fundamentally rational.[118] Additionally, the five factors are far from an in-depth understanding of the individual, don't really predict behavior, disregard the context of human experience, and fail to provide compelling explanations for human behavior.[119]

Using the Five-Factor Model in Integral Psychotherapy

As with all other inventories, psychotherapists are ethically bound to hold tests lightly and use them only as part of an assessment. As noted earlier, a test is only as good as the dialogue following it and the tests based in the Five-Factor Model are no different.

As Dan McAdams pointed out in his critique of the model "the Five-Factor model is essentially 'a psychology of the stranger,' providing information about persons that one would need to know when one knows nothing else about them."[120] There are times when such an approach is useful for example when screening candidates for high-stress, potentially dangerous jobs like police work. Therapist Matt Cappazutto uses the NEO-FFI in screening applicants to police departments around Cleveland, Ohio. Trained in psychoanalytic and object relations theory, Cappazutto says that the NEO-FFI gives one a general feel for how a person measures on the five factors compared with successful police officers in the field. This is just the beginning, however, and only one of three inventories that he uses. After the inventories are complete comes a clinical interview where the client can ask any questions about the inventories and then Cappazutto's final evaluation based on all that information.

Another use of the model is in trying to assess for personality styles that do not work for the client (personality disorders—the next topic in this chapter). Several researchers have found that the tests based in the Five-Factor Model show statistically significant differences between those who meet the criteria for a personality disorder and those who do not.[121] There is also some effort to correlate the profiles of clients who suffer from disorders like mood or anxiety disorders with particular types of scores on the Five-Factor Model tests.[122] An Integral psychotherapist who feels the client is suffering from his or her personality style but not yet ready to make it an object of awareness can use the NEO-FFI to confirm the clinical hunch. Again, although the test does not give a diagnosis proper, it can give the clinician a sense of what might be happening, thus informing clinical decisions. Finally, in an Integral framework, the Five-Factor tests of personality might be useful with so-called "normal" clients who are seeking growth-oriented therapy or coaching, however, more research needs to be done on this.[123]

Final Thoughts on the Five-Factor Model

One of the more eloquent critics of the Five-Factor Model has been Loevinger, whose work was the basis of the second half of Chapter 3. In a Distinguished Contribution Award piece in the *Journal of Personality Assessment*[124] titled "Has Psychology Lost its Conscience?" Loevinger tears into the Five-Factor Model. Trained initially as a statistician, Loevinger points out that no test probing the structural nature of personality can accomplish that task with what are called factorial methods. All the tests discussed thus far in this chapter were accomplished with such methods and that, according to Loevinger, is their greatest weakness. Factorial methods are statistical tests (factor analysis) that look for item responses that cluster together. If the responses that cluster together are similar to the traits that the test makers hoped to represent, we say that the results support the validity of the test.

As Loevinger noted, however, it is not difficult to assemble a list of items containing adjectives that will cluster together; however, this type of thinking will always miss the complexity of personality. Her example centers on the use of the term *conscientiousness*. This of course was her term for what we refer to as the achiever level of ego development in Chapter 5. Loevinger points out that the Five-Factor trait conscientiousness, is really a limited understanding that is similar to the type of conscientiousness parents hope to instill in their children: "be on time, keep your things neat and in order, and do what your teacher tells you."[125] In ego development, such traits are found in the conformist or Diplomat levels. As Loevinger wrote, she was not taking exception to the research findings as much as the assumptions they are based on. Her point was that all the factors in the Five-Factor Model by virtue of their successful factor analysis cluster narrowly around a small range of adjectives and, as McAdams also noted, this will reveal very little about a person. As she concluded:

> There is no reason to believe that the bedrock of personality is a set of orthogonal (independent) factors, unless you think that nature is constrained to present us a world in rows and columns. That would be convenient for many purposes, particularly given the statistical programs already installed on our computers. But is it realistic?[126]

Cloninger's Seven-Factor Typology

A valuable dynamic that mirrors the aim of an integral approach is when researchers build on previous efforts and begin considering more variables. As their models increase in complexity they begin to map more of the Kosmos. Psychiatrist Robert Cloninger's Seven-Factor Model is one example in the realm of types and styles. Cloninger uses the biopsychosocial approach (described in Chapter 1) to combine temperament (believed to be body-based) with character (believed to be psychologically based but influenced by temperament). He explored these using Thurstone and Cattell's factorial approach and the result is a seven-factor model (and test) that assesses four aspects of temperament and three aspects of character. Whereas the Five-Factor Model is based on factorial classification of personality-related adjectives in the English language, Cloninger's model is rooted more in a psychoneurobiological understanding of personality.

Cloninger sought to bring the partial truths of brain and mind to bear on the problem of traits and how they translate into styles. He operationalized temperament as the result of gene expression (which always occurs in relation to the environment) and how it results in preconceptual biases in memory

	Interior	Exterior
Individual	*Self-concept*	*Gene expression*
Collective	*Social effectiveness*	*Impact of environment on gene expression*

Figure 5.4. Cloninger's trait construct in the four quadrants.

and learning of behavior. He operationalized character as the development of self-concept and the influences of personal/social effectiveness by insight-based learning. What is fascinating about this is reflected in Fig. 5.4, which shows the positioning of his concepts within the integral perspectives or quadrants.

Additionally, Cloninger allows for a developmental curve in the way that self-concept and other character traits evolve over time. The seven factors Cloninger derived from factor analysis are summarized in Table 5.2.

Table 5.2. Cloninger's Seven Factors

Factor Label	Aligned with Character or Temperament	Brief Description
Novelty Seeking (NS)	Temperament	Measured as behavioral activation
Harm Avoidance (HA)	Temperament	Inhibition of behavior for safety
Reward Dependence (RD)	Temperament	Maintenance of behavior
Persistence (P)	Temperament	Persevering in pursuit of goals
Cooperativeness (C)	Character	Being able to work/play with others
Self-Directedness (SD)	Character	Sense of being an autonomous individual
Self-Transcendence	Character	Experiencing self as a part of the universe as a whole

Also of interest from an Integral perspective is the factor of self-transcendence. As noted in Chapter 3, this should correspond to later-stage ego identity as well as state training in contemplative or meditative traditions (Chapter 8). Although the Five-Factor Model appears to have better replication, the basis of the Seven-Factor Model appears to have more clinical utility.[127] In particular, the Seven-Factor Model seems to be more predictive of dysfunctional personality style, which is the topic of the next section. Cloninger has developed an inventory with the hope of accurately measuring temperament and character variables for use in clinical settings. The inventory, the Temperament and Character Inventory-Revised (TCI-R) shows promising reliability and validity. If further studies replicate this, the TCI-R should prove useful in clinical settings[128] and more integral in nature than tests based on the Five-Factor Model.

Before completing this survey of type and style models, let's attempt an integral summary of the partial truths that the better efforts have yielded. Figure 5.5 attempts to capture a snapshot of how these truths fit together integrally.

This figure represents one heuristic summary of how many variables there are to choose from when deciding to use a typology of some sort. For example, a clinician may be working with people suffering from personality disorders. In particular, they will want to know about the client's openness to experi-

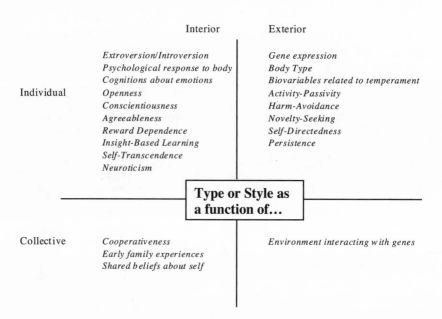

Figure 5.5. Quadratic heuristic of typological constructs.

ence, agreeableness, neuroticism, and early family experiences. In that sense, the Five-Factor Model would be a good choice to work with for these clients. In other settings such as employment screenings, clinicians may be screening clients for things like self-directedness, cooperativeness, and persistence. In those cases, Cloninger's Seven-Factor Model may be more useful. Generally, however, clinicians can review the heuristic, isolate the variables of greatest interest to them based on the client, then choose and inventory or interviewing protocol that reflects the variables chosen. Assuming the client has not come to therapy with a preferred typology (e.g., MBTI or Enneagram), the clinician can also exercise ethical decision making regarding the importance of validity and reliability when making the choice.

This leads us to the final section on dysfunctional types or styles of personality. This section derives in large part from a psychodynamic heritage of clinicians who sought to characterize client's styles by the symptoms they suffered from. Linking the symptoms to their own theories, they came up with taxonomies of character or personality disorders.

When Styles Go Wrong:
Typology as Pathology and Personality Disorders

Recall the case of Marsha at the beginning of this chapter. Martha desperately wanted love and acceptance but when she got close to it, it seemed too good to be true. Being raised in an abusive home and then a foster home that was not much better, she learned two things: First, don't count on anything except other people leaving; and second, sex is a way to feel close even if only for a moment. Imagine going through life with this set of rules about relationships. It is not a very happy prospect and it certainly wasn't for Marsha. Her life was a series of efforts to avoid real or imagined abandonment, swinging between idealizing her lovers and denigrating them, recurrent suicidal thoughts, and a constant sense of emptiness. When she met a potential lover she would immediately divulge the most intimate aspects of her life (what we might call pathological openness to experience in the Five-Factor Model) and then become enraged when the other person would feel overwhelmed by everything Marsha shared. As an adolescent, Marsha began cutting herself when she felt overwhelmed, which was often. She still bears the scars of using pencils, razors, and virtually anything available for cutting when she felt emotionally vulnerable. She said that this had a "grounding" effect, although she wished that she could stop. She had one suicide attempt at age 21 and now at age 29, she just felt very depressed wondering what life was all about.

This is a fairly typical portrait of someone who meets the criteria for what is called borderline personality disorder (BPD). The last sentence is intentionally awkward. I always train my interns that you do not treat "a borderline," you treat a person who has a borderline style or a person who meets the criteria for BPD. Because people with this style of personality are so hard to treat, the actual label becomes a signifier to many therapists to stay away from the client. Although these people are hard to treat, they can benefit greatly from therapy that is attuned to their needs while still setting up healthy boundaries.

Personality disorders are described as enduring, pervasive, and inflexible patterns of inner experience and behavior that deviate significantly from the expectation of culture. They are thought to be "set" in late adolescence or early adulthood and, like all disorders in the *DSM*, are sources of distress or impairment.[129] In the current diagnostic manual for psychotherapists (*DSM-IV-TR* mentioned in Chapter 1), there are three clusters of problematic personality styles or disorders. These "clusters" are supposed to represent disorders that are generally similar. "Cluster A" disorders are thought to present as odd or eccentric and include Paranoid, Schizoid, and Schizotypal Personality Disorders. "Cluster B" disorders are thought to be dramatic or emotional in nature and include Borderline, Antisocial, Histrionic, and Narcissistic Personality Disorders. Finally "Cluster C" disorders are thought to be anxious or fearful in nature and include Avoidant, Dependent, and Obsessive-Compulsive Personality Disorder.

Types as Character Syndromes: Origins of Personality Disorders

Yet another way that psychologists and psychotherapists have tried to type human beings is through their symptoms and it is these efforts that most directly led to the current conceptions of personality disorders. Freud and Karl Abraham created the bases for psychoanalytic character typology. These syndromes were thought to be the result of frustrations or indulgences of instinctual drives at particular stages of psychosexual development. Thus, examples of oral character types are the oral-dependent and oral-sadistic types. The former is happy go lucky as a result of an overly indulgent sucking stage, whereas the former was frustrated at the biting phase of the oral stage and as a result is pessimistic, distrustful, and tends to blame the world for his or her problems. Similarly, there are anal and phallic character types.[130]

Freud also postulated a simpler version of types in people whose mental life was dominated by the "I," the "over-I," or the "it." Those whose lives were dominated by the "I" would be so self-absorbed that they would be considered narcissistic types. Those whose lives were centered around the energies of the "it" would be erotic types. Finally, those whose intrapsychic lives revolved around the "over-I" would be compulsive types. Freud also described mixed types where a combination of two elements outweighs the third.[131]

Other psychodynamic clinicians and theorists added to the psychoanalytic notion of character types. Wilhelm Reich is credited with cementing the current psychoanalytic formulation of character. Reich saw psychosexual conflicts as leading to neurotic conflicts that restructured a person's defensive style and effected a total formation of character that becomes character armor. As the armor hardens, the response to earlier conflicts becomes transformed into chronic attitudes and automatic modes of reaction.[132] In addition to Reich, Otto Fenichel contributed to the psychodynamic understanding of the origins of character types.[133] Fenichel felt that descriptions of character syndromes were confusing because there were so many potential conflicts that there was a great deal of overlap in the types (the same problem that cropped up in other typologies necessitating dimensional representation). He classified traits into two types. Where instinctual energies were developmentally congruent with the "I" (mistranslated as ego) they would be expressed as conflict-free patterns, thus of the "sublimation" type. Where the instinctual energies aim was blocked by the "I" and requiring conflict-resolving defensive measures, Fenichel labeled the resulting character "reactive" with two subtypes of avoidant and oppositional. He then went on to describe phobic, hysterical, compulsive, cyclic, and schizoid characters—all reactive types in his schema.

In creating typologies from syndromes observed through the lens of a particular theory, we must recognize the work of Kurt Schneider, Harry Stack Sullivan, and Karen Horney. All three aimed to develop descriptions of personality types that were atheoretical and based on observation. It is this atheoretical nature that Robert Spitzer emphasized when he pioneered the categorical diagnoses that are now known from *DSM*.[134] Schneider, perhaps best known for his work in delineating what are now called positive and negative symptoms of schizophrenia,[135] wrote a text on psychopathologic personalities in which he described 10 such personalities seen in psychiatric work.[136] Schneider's types are outlined in Table 5.3 (next page).

What is interesting is that Schneider's observations appear accurate in that many of his descriptors continue to exist in current descriptions of *DSM* personality disorders.

Like Schneider, Sullivan also developed a typology of 10 personality styles that were central to his interpersonal psychiatry.[137] Sullivan's types were less complete than Schneider's but are outlined in Table 5.4 (next page).

Finally, Horney attempted to describe types of people based on the solutions they gravitated toward to solve life's problems. Throughout her writing, she used many different terms to describe these types but generally they can be summarized by three broad modalities of relating to others: moving toward people, moving away from people, and moving against people. Individuals who are moving toward people are more compliant in nature seeking to please others. Those who are moving away types are more detached and their primary goal is avoidance of others. Moving against types of individuals are aggressive, expansive, and narcissistic.[138]

Table 5.3. Kurt Schneider's Personality Typology

Schneider Type Label	Brief Description
Hyperthymic	Active, Impulsive, undependable
Depressive	Serious, skeptical view of life with little capacity for joy
Insecure	Ruminate excessively and chronically uncertain of self
Fanatic	Expansive, uninhibited, querulous and litigious
Attention-Seeking	Heightened emotional responses, excess enthusiasm, showy, boastful
Labile	Characterized by abrupt and volatile mood changes and impulsivity
Explosive	Impulsively violent, combative without warning
Affectionless	Distance and indifferent to friends and strangers alike, alexithymic
Weak-willed	Docile, unassuming, easily duped by others
Asthenic	Hypochondriacal and preoccupied with bodily functions

Table 5.3. Harry Sullivan's Personality Types

Sullivan Label	Brief Description
Nonintegrative	Fleeting involvements with others, failure to profit from experience, superficial
Self-absorbed	Autistic, wishful thinking, see relationships as either wonderful or horrible, usually end relationships with disillusionment
Incorrigible	Hostile toward others and pattern of unfriendly, threatening behavior
Negativistic	Much insecurity but refusal to subscribe to view of others, passively resist social norms
Stammerer	Not well defined in Sullivan's typology
Ambition-ridden	Frequently exploit others, competitive and manipulative
Asocial	Detached, lonely, unable to establish relationships
Inadequate	Needs guidance from a strong other, use clinging as adaptation to life
Homosexual	Again, not well defined by Sullivan
Chronically adolescent	Constantly seeking to achieve ideals but rarely able to do so

The Problem With the Concept of Personality Disorders

The concept of personality disorders as rooted in development and character was pieced together by many theorists (from Freud and Abraham's character types,[139] Reich's character analysis, Fenichel's sublimating and reacting types, Horney's character disorders).[140] Each of these theorists contributed to our current conception of personality disorders but, like all efforts at typing, the personality disorders have their own problems. To detail the problems with personality disorders (and their predecessors) I focus on one of the most prevalent of the current personality disorders—BPD. The label *borderline* goes back to the later 19th century referring to clinicians who "had patients who seemed to inhabit a psychological 'borderland' between sanity and insanity."[141]

Otto Kernberg elaborated on this description in what he called borderline personality organization. He used the word *organization* to reflect enduring ways of thinking, behaving, and experiencing interpersonal situations. He emphasized that although not psychotic, these people could become more cognitively disorganized than most others when under stress. Finally, he noted that people with borderline personality organization could not maintain a balanced view of self or others and frequently would "split" their representations into all bad or all good.[142]

BPD is one of the most prevalent disorders and is thought to manifest in 20% of inpatient and 10% of outpatient clients.[143] One prominent feature of BPD is the tendency of people who meet the criteria to use primitive defenses. Because they heavily rely on denial, projection, and splitting when they regress, they can in fact be hard to distinguish from a person suffering from a psychosis. An important difference between a person suffering from psychosis and a person with BPD is that the latter will show responsiveness to the therapist (even if through negative emotions). Another area where there are similarities and differences between people with psychosis and BPD is in their experience of proximate-self. If a therapist asks either client to describe their personality, they may both be at a loss. The person with BPD will tend to dismiss the therapist's interest in the complex nature of the self.[144] People with BPD struggle with insight. They cannot observe their pathology or problematic style in the same way as someone suffering from depression or anxiety can. This again is what we call an ego-syntonic problem. The problem is so much a part of how the person navigates life that they never considered changing it. As Nancy McWilliams notes "they just want to stop hurting, or to get some critic off their back."[145]

Can a person's "personality" really be disordered? This is still a matter of debate. Even the term *personality* is ill-defined (as evidenced in the last section about personality assessment). Psychologist Gordon Allport, writing in the early 20th century, noted "the term personality is a perilous one for [the psychotherapist] to use unless he is aware of its many meanings. Since it is remarkably elastic, its use in any context is seldom challenged."[146] It is safe to say, however, that a person's style can be so ineffective at getting them what they think they want that the style can cause significant distress and impairment.

There are many reasons to question whether there really are such things as personality disorders per se. Among them, the level of interrater reliability is among the lowest for any disorder in the *DSM*. This means that when three different clinicians try to diagnose a particular client, in the case of BPD, they may likely come up with three different diagnoses. Second, the personality disorders do not have as much validity as other disorders in *DSM*. Recall that validity is the extent to which a diagnosis describes a particular syndrome and the diagnosis of BPD "can most charitably be described as less than impressive."[147] Finally, all personality disorders have high comorbidity with other personality disorders including those in other clusters. In layperson's terms, this means that if a client is diagnosed with one personality disorder, there is a high likelihood the same client will meet the criteria for one or two additional personality disorders.[148] That said, many clinicians find the existing clusters meaningful as styles or structures going back to the analytic tradition and these styles or structures can be generally described psychodynamically so that treatment can be tailored to the client.

An Integral Approach to Dysfunctional Styles

So based on this what is an Integral guideline for treating a person who meets the criteria for a personality disorder? Because each type of disorder, manifesting uniquely in each individual requires tailoring of treatment, I use BPD for an example. First, therapists should realize that most clients who meet the criteria for this disorder will come to therapy for other symptoms, usually mood or anxiety symptoms. Second, therapists must rely on the "self as instrument" to discern if their reaction to the client is accurate and whether the client seems to match the *DSM* criteria. On the heuristic of typological constructs (see Table 5.4) clients with BPD will likely show strong extraversion (from the Five-Factor Model), a great degree of openness, and low levels of insight-based learning. All the latter appear in the upper-left quadrant. Also, clients who meet the criteria for BPD will have a history of significant problems in early family life (which may be endorsed on Marquis Integral Intake) as well as poor attachment in childhood (lower-left quadrant). Finally, clients who meet the criteria for BPD may be low in harm-avoidance (upper-right quadrant). Most of this can be gleaned from an intake or dialogue with the client but if the clinician wants to check her intuitions, an inventory based on the Five-Factor Model may be helpful. Also, there are standardized structured interviews that have some validity and reliability in confirming the existence of personality disordered characteristics (but not a particular disorder per se).[149] In the final section of this chapter, we revisit a final typology that shows up frequently in Integral Theory: masculine and feminine types.

Masculine and Feminine Approaches to Type: From Typing to Sexual Identity

Men tend to be power-driven. They measure their lives by their accomplishments. Women are more relationship-driven. They tend to define episodes of their lives by the men they are with.

—Jenna Jameson[150]

Typing as masculine or feminine, although broad, is important because these types clearly occur as a result of integral interplay between biology, psychology, culture, and society. In one sense, these types persist in the psychological literature because they have roots in what we call biological dimorphism.[151] In another sense, masculine and feminine typing is fraught with inconsistency, political agendas, and questions about the usefulness of the constructs. This final section of the chapter reviews the psychological exploration of sex and gender typing and its usefulness in therapy. In particular, I hope to convey the immense guidance an integral approach to type offers us as we contend with challenging issues like the extent to which biological differences may lead to differences in psychological translation and possibly transformation. In psychology and psychotherapy we focus on sex and gender differences but, as I conclude at the end of this chapter, we are best to nest them in the context of sexual identity.

What may seem an easy task at first can become an all-quadrant nightmare. What is sex? What is gender? Are they synonyms, antonyms, or complementary terms? Gender and sex differences can be set out as distinctions or biological/physiological characteristics typically associated with males and females. From an integral quadratic perspective there are clear biological (upper-right quadrant), cultural lower-left quadrant), and social markers (lower-right quadrant) that impact psychological functioning (upper-left quadrant) whether we use the words *sex* or *gender*. From a sociological perspective, these are two words that are consistently *misused*. Sociologists Nancy Greenwood and Margaret Cassidy wrote the following:

gender roles are socially learned and reinforced and are amenable to change. "Sex roles" refers to biologically-based aspects of the behaviors of women and men, such as lactation or erection, and are essentially unchangeable by social forces. [152]

Sociologist Mary Reige Laner elaborates on the problem, writing:

We have known for quite some time that the gender/sex link is
far from perfect. That is, not all men are stereotypically masculine,
and not all women are stereotypically feminine. In fact, Spence
and Helmreich's (1978)[153] study, *Masculinity and Feminity,* showed
that men and women vary greatly in terms of their gender characteristics. According to their findings, 60% of men who score high
on conventional masculinity include 32% who also score high on
femininity. . . . Similarly, women who score high on conventional
femininity (59%) include 27% who also score high on masculinity.
Socialization into conventional gender identities, as these data show,
is not fully effective. Moreover, virtually equal proportions of men
and women (40% and 41%, respectively) score high on the characteristics conventionally attributed to the *other* sex. Clearly, gender
and sex do not have the same referent most of the time. To put it
another way: with very rare exceptions, we know what sex we are.
However, our gender identity is not at all as certain.[154]

Although it is tempting to simply use *sex* or *sex-role* where biologically
based aspects of behavior are concerned, the problem from an Integral perspective is that these arise together with sentient identification shaped by powerful
cultural and social forces. Problems of terminology are equally present in the
psychological literature. One of the most prominent researchers on sex or gender
typing is Sandra Bem. She described sex-typing as a function of the readiness an
individual has to organize information about the proximate self and the world
in terms of cultural definitions of maleness and femaleness that come from a
society's gender schemes.[155] At some points, Bem seems to align with the sociological understandings of sex and gender just noted. In 1985, she wrote that
"human behaviors should no longer be linked with gender, and society should
stop projecting gender into situations irrelevant to genitalia."[156] Bem has been
very transparent about the goal of her work which is reducing the influence
of biological sex in the way individuals and society co-construct identity,[157]
however, recent neuroscience research makes such bifurcations speculative at
best. Ironically, there is substantial evidence that her psychological measure,
the Bem Sex-Role Inventory[158] (BSRI), has actually led to cementing the idea
of psychological sex-typing rather than reducing it.[159]

One problem is we don't really know the extent to which biology (sex)
influences what some would refer to as differences in gender. For example,
neuroscience researcher John O'Keefe, beginning in 1971, executed a research
agenda to determine how cells in the hippocampus register information about
the space surrounding an organism. He demonstrated that pyramidal cells in the

hippocampus of rats respond specifically to differences in the space the animal is put in.[160] O'Keefe later extended his research on spatial orientation to sex differences in humans. What he found is that men and women orient themselves to the space around them in very different ways. In giving directions, women use more local cues ("drive straight ahead and turn right at the filling station") whereas men rely more on an internalized map ("drive north 3 miles then head west on Route 224"). Brain imaging illustrated that different parts of the brain were activated when men and women were asked to give directions.[161] As Eric Kandel queries, "Are these differences innate, or do they stem from learning and socialization? It is in questions such as these that biology and neuroscience can provide us basic guidance for far-reaching social decisions."[162]

Although the BSRI is one of the most widely used psychological inventories to research masculine and feminine roles and the extent to which men and women have internalized these roles, there are multiple problems with it. First, but certainly not least, is that the test manual provides two ways to score the inventory that researchers have shown will produce widely divergent results.[163] Second, the ideas about which items represented masculinity and femininity have not been updated since the test's creation in the 1970s. In a follow-up study by counselors Rose Hoffman and Diane Borders, only two items showed the required 75% agreement on being specifically masculine or feminine (these were simply the words *masculine* and *feminine*).[164] Bem had originally proposed androgyny as an escape hatch from the more constricting notions of masculine and feminine in that the androgynous individual could express both masculine and feminine traits. This is based in Bem's gender-schema theory which, like the items on her inventory, appears in the 21st century as an invalid artifact of 20th-century feminist psychology.

Other problems with BSRI include the fact that there exist both long and short forms of the test. Although the short form (30 items) has the most psychometric support, the long form (60 items) is the one researchers and clinicians must purchase if they wish to use the test. Additionally, the test appears to have poor construct validity partly related to the fact that Bem was never entirely clear on what the test was measuring. Although she claimed the test measured one's global masculinity or femininity, she also admitted that it measured the extent to which one used gender as a lens to view the world.[165] In responding to critics, Bem added that the test partially measures instrumentality and expressiveness (thought to be masculine and feminine, respectively).[166] Finally in factor-analytic studies, the BSRI, masculine and feminine do not emerge as primary factors from the items on either the long or short form.[167] So like most efforts at psychological types that exist in sex or gender roles, efforts to operationalize definitions and create inventories are for the most part failures. However, just as in other typing efforts, this does not mean that there are no successes in the endeavor.

From an Integral perspective, we can see numerous successes and clinical uses in Bem's work. First as we embody the Integral attitude ("Everyone is right about something but not equally right about everything") we can ask, "What is Sandra Bem 'right' about?" First, she is clearly "right" that regardless of the extent to which sex influences gender, culture and society play huge roles in how people conceptualize what is "manly" and what is "womanly." From an Integral perspective, this is simply common sense but because that is not the case for conventional society, Bem's work has given us constructs to play with as we "think outside the box" and constructs that challenge conventional rigidity about the roles of men and women.

As we think outside the box, we realize that the ways in which culture and society craft male and female roles can result in oppression, inequity, and violence. We also can credit Bem with giving us a way to make an object of awareness out of just how much some people want to control the most intimate aspects of others' lives—namely their sex lives. As Bem wrote in 1995:

> what I am—and have been for as long as I can remember—is someone whose sexuality and gender have never seemed to mesh with the available cultural categories . . . my central passion has always been to challenge the longstanding cultural belief in some kind of a natural link or match between the sex of one's body and the character of one's psyche and one's sexuality.[168]

This is an important challenge to consider for all who experience their sexuality and gender as "outside the box" and the therapists who are treating them. We have made much progress deconstructing gender in psychotherapy but little progress in understanding sexuality that is best described as poly-sexual, meaning those individuals who can find and express sexual pleasure across the boundaries of heterosexual, homosexual, and bisexual.

One of Bem's other driving passions has been to make objects of awareness out of how "historically-constructed cultural lenses embedded in the social institutions and cultural discourses of society . . . insidiously make their way into our individual psyches and thereby lead us to become unwitting collaborators in the social reproduction of the existing power structure."[169] This relates to the dynamic of internalized oppression that we see in people whose sexual orientation or gender identification fall outside what is considered the "norm" (e.g., heterosexuality and gender bifurcation).

Consider the case of the Rev. Mel White. Rev. White is a gay Christian minister who could only accept his sexual orientation when the only other option he could see was suicide. Early in his life, Rev. White was embedded and highly placed in the American Christian Evangelical movement and worked as a ghostwriter for people like Jerry Falwell and Pat Robertson. Although he married and raised children, he knew that his orientation was gay but that there was no way to live that openly in his cultural/social context. After resorting to every kind of bogus treatment claiming to "change" sexual orientation (including electroconvulsive therapy),[170] the reverend met a counselor who helped him through the difficult journey of embracing and living who he was sexually. Rev. White has written an autobiographical account of his journey[171] and has founded *Soul Force*, a nonprofit organization aimed at supporting lesbian, gay, bisexual, and transgender individuals in freedom from religious oppression through nonviolent resistance.[172]

In 1995, Rev. White was the keynote speaker for the American Counseling Association conference. I had the opportunity to meet him there and he discussed at length the importance of having mental health professionals who are versed in issues of sexuality—even if the therapeutic concern revolves around gender. This is where an Integral approach is critical. Rev. White discussed the countless therapy sessions he endured at the hands of therapists who were claiming to be able to change his orientation. Sexual orientation, the predisposition of sexual attraction to one or both sexes, is only one aspect of the broader construct of sexual identity. Sexual identity also includes gender identity (the sense of self as male/female and/or masculine/feminine) and intention (what one desires to do to a partner or have done during sexual activity). Variations in gender identity and intention are the only things that can be diagnosed as mental illnesses that cause significant impairment or distress (e.g., Gender Identity Disorder or Pedophilia).[173]

It also is noteworthy that many of the taboos in our society around frank expression of sexual ideas are reflected in training programs for therapists. Not one accrediting body for mental health professionals mandates a course in sex counseling or psychotherapy leaving the topic to the whim of elective offerings. Although Integral psychotherapists appreciate the successes and contributions of exploring sex or gender typing, it is recommended that they treat sex and gender in the context of sexual identity even in cases where the therapist is particularly concerned with the client's masculine and/or feminine qualities. The context of sexual identity is a far more integral concept and less likely to lead to an emphasis on partial truths in therapy. Again, using the quadrants as a schematic, Fig. 5.6 (next page) represents the critical elements of sexual identity.

Figure 5.6 shows how to work with clients in a way that includes and transcends what we know about sexual identity. If the client is struggling with gender issues and, for example, fearing that developing more of his feminine traits will alter his sexual orientation, two obvious areas can be made objects of awareness. The first is educating the client about what we know regarding sexual orientation and how prenatal variables like germ cell differentiation and levels of testosterone contribute to sexual orientation.[174] Second, the issue of internalized oppression is raised by the "fear" the client may have about his sexual orientation changing. Even if this were possible, what does the fear represent? The client's psychological address, particularly his ego identity, will determine

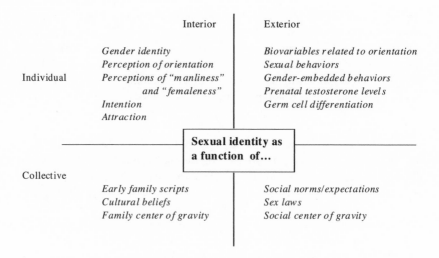

Figure 5.6. Quadratic heuristic of sex-typing constructs.

how to proceed with both issues. A client who identifies as a diplomat and adheres to a conservative Christian viewpoint will require a different approach than a client who identifies as a pluralist with a neo-Pagan worldview.

Concluding Thoughts

As noted throughout this chapter, there is no shortage of typological systems in psychology and psychotherapy. There also is little to support them, in and of themselves, as valid or reliable constructs. This is to be expected to the extent that typologies are synonymous with the Greek understanding of type as merely a roughed-out sketch rather than a definitive picture. Integral psychotherapists must understand how the constructs they use have been researched and how strong they are as maps that reflect the complexity of any individual human being. On the other hand, Integral psychotherapists can and do benefit immensely from the use of type as clinical metaphor. We have a rich legacy of such metaphors in typologies and, as long as we use them mindfully, they can be important vehicles in helping clients make aspects of themselves or their lives objects of awareness. Understanding types as styles gives us the flexibility to work with more rigorously researched trait inventories as well as metaphors like the Enneagram and the MBTI. Where "know thyself" was the Delphic motto, a less succinct but important motto for Integral psychotherapists is "know your typology and how to use it resourcefully clinically."

6
_____

States of Consciousness and Psychotherapy

R. Elliott Ingersoll

There is a reality other than the one that science and common sense—a workable definition of naturalism—set before us, and it is more exciting by every standard that can be invoked.

—Huston Smith[1]

The idea that brains produce consciousness is little more than an article of faith among scientists at present, and there are many reasons to believe that the methods of science will be insufficient to either prove or disprove it.

—Sam Harris[2]

It takes a certain amount of intelligence and imagination to realize the extraordinary queerness and mysteriousness of the world in which we live.

—Aldous Huxley[3]

States are a critical component of all psychotherapy and coaching, although it is rarely phrased that way by clinicians and researchers. The most obvious state in the psychotherapy relationship that we aim for is one of emotional connectedness, or in Wilber's words, the magical "we" of the therapeutic alliance.[4] In psychotherapy, clients come to us because of symptoms that express themselves as states. States of psychosis, states of depression, states of anxiety, and states of suicidality—all are states that, for the most part, clients want to rid themselves of. That said, there also are states we chase after (despite being ill-advised in most spiritual disciplines).[5] States of ecstasy, states of pleasant intoxication, states of adrenalin-induced surge, and states of what I call competence—all are desirable. Life coach Tony Robbins has emphasized that all motion is e-motion.[6] We do things because we want to *feel* a certain way and this can almost always be framed as achieving a desired *state*. People pursue states in ways that range from the resourceful to the disastrous. Although we

197

are always aiming for an AQAL embrace of the client, states have paradoxical place in psychotherapy. Some states are frequently the presenting problem clients arrive with and want to get rid of. Other states are just as frequently the key to relief of the symptoms.

The use of states by therapists has a long and at times sordid history. Harry Sullivan, founder of Interpersonal Therapy, used to prescribe a drunken state for his clients for up to 10 days before engaging them in therapy.[7] Most of the physiological treatments designed to bring about cessation of severe symptoms all had in common the induction of different states sometimes by drastic means including insulin coma therapy, electroshock therapy, and severe fever induced by infecting patients with diseases like malaria.[8] Thankfully we have advanced beyond these techniques and now employ trances (shamanic and hypnotic), daydreaming, imagery, and dream states in the service of psychotherapeutic aims. There are still government-sanctioned studies on the therapeutic and spiritual effects of psychedelic states,[9] particularly with terminally ill clients.[10]

This is not to say that all therapists are in agreement about states. There is some compelling literature suggesting that some "therapeutic states," such as hypnosis, are in fact nothing more than a tacit agreement between therapist and client that gives the client permission to act in a less defended manner.[11] Despite this, there is still plenty of research about the clinical utility of states whether they are in fact altered or variations of waking consciousness.[12]

Rules About States

Let's start with the obvious—like other things covered in this book, there are "rules" that apply to states and states can certainly be used as tools. First some rules. There is still much about states that remains unknown to psychologists and psychotherapists. We have found some rules about states that can be bent and some that can be broken. The first general rule is that states are thought to be exclusive. As Wilber noted, one cannot be sober and drunk at the same time.[13] In psychotherapy this is well illustrated in the treatment of phobic anxiety and panic disorder. In these cases, anxiety or panic states[14] have diminished the client's satisfaction with life to the point of causing marked distress or impairment. One of the first things we check with clients is their ability to engage what physician Herbert Benson called the relaxation response.[15] Some studies have confirmed that this response is a state of relaxation that is exclusive of other states like aggression[16] or anxiety.[17] Although few hypotheses of this sort ever find uncontested support, this one holds up well enough clinically to get the point across to the client. There are things one can do to induce relaxation because they are antithetical to anxiety.

But are states really exclusive? This is a rule that can be bent depending on how states are defined and used in psychotherapy (and psychology proper).

As psychologist Imants Baruss concluded, when we include the subjective, phenomenological experience of states (upper-left quadrant) in our studies, we lose all baselines for what might be considered normal waking states and altered states. Baruss wrote, "one person's ordinary waking state could be someone else's altered state."[18] States can be classified as "normal" or "altered" but they vary widely. In Integral Psychotherapy we make use of a wide variety of waking states including daydreams, guided and nonguided imagery, and powerful emotional states that arise from these. Given the wide fluctuation of states across categories and how little we really understand them, Baruss preferred to discuss consciousness and alterations of consciousness (rather than "altered states"). This makes sense from an integral perspective, so I follow Baruss' lead and when I feel I can adequately categorize discrete states (e.g., waking vs. dreaming, ordinary vs. chemically altered) I refer to discrete categories. When dealing with the variety of waking states of consciousness I confine myself to Baruss' phrase "alterations of consciousness."

Second rule: States are transitory. This rule seems more consistent in that even within a given state there are alterations that make the person feel closer to or farther from whatever the state is. Like all sacred things, this is a blessing and a curse. When I worked the midnight shift on a suicide hotline, one of our primary strategies was to keep the suicidal caller on the phone through the night and give the person a follow-up plan for the morning. I would tell the caller that his or her current state of depression/suicidality, although it may come back, cannot last forever because it requires correlated brain/hormonal activity and the structures supporting those activities will tire out and need to re-energize. In most instances, the client would finally get tired, fall asleep, and awake with the action plan we worked out—still depressed but, at least temporarily, out of the suicidal state because it had temporarily exhausted itself.[19] The curse of the transitory nature of states is that sometimes clients will experience things in transitory states that they rate as more pleasurable than what they experience in the normal waking state. If you doubt it, compare your last orgasm with the experience of driving through inner-city Baltimore. This of course can be the genesis of psychological or physical dependence on a drug.[20]

Third rule: States are likely to unfold in a sequence when particular training methods are undertaken. A classic example of how meditative states fall out developmentally is the work done by Wilber, Daniel Brown, and Jack Engler in *Transformations of Consciousness*.[21] Their chapters validate stages of mindfulness meditation. This led to another pioneering insight of Wilber's that David discussed in Chapter 4—that structure stages (or levels of development) are very different than state stages. State stages are experienced in states training that fall out in an invariant order but are *not* reflective of the *levels* of a person's development (e.g., cognitive or ego). One can receive state-stage training at almost any point on the ego-identity spectrum[22] but this does not necessarily change the person's developmental center of gravity.

While we work with meditation in psychotherapy, the depth of state stages we are aiming at is usually more focused on earlier stages of states than that seen in traditional state-stage training. For the most part, we are teaching clients skills like how to access a witnessing state or how to enter a hypnotic state. There also appears to be an efficacy one can develop in entering states of hypnosis or other nonordinary states like those seen in Eye Movement Desensitization Reprocessing (EMDR) therapy. Integral psychotherapists should understand the scope of state stages but also know that the majority of their work with clients will focus on a small part of that spectrum.

There is another question of state stages that is as yet unresolved. The question is "What is the place of popular technologies in inducing predictable sequences of state stages?" Both the Monroe Institute and Bill Harris' Centerpointe Research produce binaural beat technologies and claim a certain progression in states training through the use of these technologies. Harris has set forth his views in one book that is more technical than spiritual.[23] Robert Monroe wrote three books over the course of his lifetime[24] that detail what he initially described as out-of-body experiences (OBEs). His three books detail the terrain he explored in this state and the different focuses or states his Hemi-Sync recordings are supposed to induce in listeners. Monroe sought objective labels for his states and relied on "focus" combined with a number. For example, Focus 3 is mind and body in harmony. Focus 10 is mind alert and awake, body asleep. There are some similarities to spiritual literature but perhaps the most striking similarities are between Monroe's descriptions of his states and scientist John Lilly's description of mental states induced in sensory deprivation tanks both with and without mind-altering chemicals.

Lilly invented the sensory-deprivation tank, wrote numerous books[25] and conducted peer-reviewed research on this as well as human communication with Cetaceans.[26] Lilly was trained as a medical doctor in brain science as well as a psychoanalyst. While using LSD-25 and ketamine (a drug that induces states that feel like OBEs), Lilly seems to have come across terrain and beings similar to those described by Monroe. For example, while Monroe talks of "nonphysical third parties" that "radiate a warmth of friendliness that evokes complete trust."[27] Other of Monroe's entities seem to be curious nonhumans who themselves have had a human experience. The beings Lilly encountered particularly while using ketamine in the isolation tank, included a different (higher? deeper?) aspect of himself that frequently had OBE meetings with two other beings who were interested in the evolution of consciousness on earth.

According to Lilly's account, there are beings over these who are less interested in what happens on earth. For these interested beings, however, there is an evolutionary speed limit that should be adhered to. The beings create coincidence to speed evolution up if the species is lagging behind, or other events to slow it down if evolution is careening out of control. Most of this is done through an agency Lilly described as the Earth Coincidence Control Office, which is overseen by a Cosmic Coincidence Control Center.[28] Lilly himself never committed to an explanation of these encounters allowing that they may be actual encounters conducted in an OBE state or they may be simply aspects of his brain creating scenarios in response to isolation, ketamine, or both. I mention binaural beat technologies and Lilly's studies because an Integral approach to psychotherapy implies openness to developments in the upper-right aspect of our being, which is reflected in the technologies we develop for internal exploration.

Getting back to the rules about states, a fourth rule is that apart from a developmental spectrum of states (state stages), we also know that there are types of states. I have already noted that in the human experience there are natural and altered states (also referred to as ordinary and nonordinary). The altered states may result from physical activities like sex or exercise, psychoactive drugs acting on the nervous system, or peak experiences sometimes called "flow" experiences[29] that come on for reasons we may not understand. Even within a therapeutic school, different types of states can be identified. Ericksonian hypnotherapist Kay Thompson listed six types of hypnotic states based on the motivation of the person entering the trance (all hypnosis is self-hypnosis). In clinical trance states, the aim is self-control or self-help. In experimental trance states, the motivation may range from money to self-knowledge to contributing to science. In demonstration trance states, the goal is learning and teaching. In forensic states, the motivation is to recall past events. There also are spontaneous trances like "highway hypnosis" where a range of motivations (from boredom to self-control) may operate. Finally, Thompson notes entertainment trances where people enter trance states as part of a show.[30]

Perspectives and States

In psychotherapy, there are many perspectives on states and we can safely say these diverse perspectives can be organized into a "1-2-3" of states. The "1" of states is using or trying to understand a client's first-person experience of states. This is the classical phenomenological perspective used by psychologists like William James. In the phenomenological perspective, mental phenomena are considered in and of themselves without effort to attribute them to something else (usually the brain). This method requires introspection on the part of the individual to discern her or his own states.

The "2" of states refers to the reports of others who are observing the person who is supposedly having the state as well as dialogue between people who may be experiencing similar or different states. For example, in LSD psychotherapy, psychiatrist Stanislav Grof always had multiple observers or "sitters" with the client who was under the influence of the drug. These sitters were able to make observations sometimes of a purely physical nature and at other times record things the client was saying that, when metabolized after the session, turned out to have psychological significance.[31] Grof later continued using sitters when he and his wife Christina developed their nonchemical method of inducing altered states called Holotropic Breathwork. In integral psychotherapy, the clinician is usually the sitter if the client is guided through or spontaneously enters into an altered state. How the clinician guides the client is very important, as seen later in this chapter.

Finally the "3" of states refers to the physiological and cognitive perspectives on states. The physiological corresponds to research Zone 1 in the upper-right quadrant from Chapter 3. It is the "outside" of a third-person view of states where physiological processes involved with states are studied with neuroscience technologies and methods from the biological sciences. Some groundbreaking work researching consciousness in infants has been done tying behavioral repertoires and eye tracking to preferences infants develop very quickly.[32] Other work from this perspective includes Michael Winkelman's model of trance states. Winkelman's first systematic attempt at a model argued that various trance induction techniques "lead to a state of parasympathetic dominance in which the frontal cortex is dominated by slow wave patterns originating in the limbic system and related projections into the frontal parts of the brain."[33] More recently, Winkelman concludes that serotonergic-acting psychedelics (which he calls psychointegrators) disinhibit the serotonergic neurotransmitter systems resulting in the loss of their inhibitory effects on the mesolimbic temporal lobe structures and these actions result in the common effects.[34]

The cognitive perspective on states is the "inside" of a third-person view and is concerned with cognitive processes involved in states discerned from observation of verbal and physical behavior as well as rational inquiry. Cognition must go beyond perception to meaning. As Daniel Robinson noted, perception is denotative, whereas cognition is connotative. "Perception has recognition as its primary object. Cognition, on the other hand, is most closely associated with meaning."[35] As Baruss has noted, no one of these three perspectives (the "3" the "2" or the "1") is enough in and of itself and in working with states therapeutically we must be mindful of all three.

The Politics of States

States also are politically explosive—and not just drug-induced states. From an Integral perspective, the lower quadrants abound in quandaries regarding states. In psychotherapy, the role of states in both pathology and healing is strongly debated mostly by those who hold partial views of states. For example, when Roland Griffiths and colleagues published their findings that psilocybin did seem to occasion mystical experiences,[36] there were four commentaries on the paper in the same edition of the journal. This is highly unusual as far as commentaries go as well as the fact that all four commentaries were supportive of the work. Those immersed in biological bases of behavior focus on the physiological correlates to states of mind.[37] Those immersed in cognitive therapy and cognitive science try to understand how cognition and brain circuitry combine to create desirable and undesirable states.[38] Depth psychologists (from the Freudian[39] to the transpersonal)[40] focus on how the psychological dynamics correlated with past traumas (in this life or supposed others) manifest as pathological states. All of these approaches to states have something to offer the integral psychotherapist. The key is knowing how to work with all the available evidence.

It goes without saying (but I'll say it anyway) that if politics is the art of controlling your environment, then states are potentially threatening to anyone seeking control over others. The development of religious traditions based in states is dependent on who has the power to sanction and name those states. On numerous occasions, I have witnessed the same phenomenon packaged with different labels and interpretations. The phenomenon in this case is an emotional catharsis (replete with crying, shaking, and screaming) that gives way to a feeling of peace and bliss. In the yoga ashram it was attributed to the movement of prana. Quaker founder George Fox referred to this as "an opening." In the Pentecostal Church it was attributed to the movement of the Holy Spirit. At the Gestalt intensive it was attributed to healthy contact and at Dianetics auditing it was attributed to releasing of engrams and movement toward being "clear." Ultimately, we may have faith in our labels but we cannot test them with any confidence.

The Art of State Induction

This power of state induction is abused in almost every cult group I have studied. Similarly, many in the personal growth industry tread dangerously close to what is seen in cults. One primary difference between much of what passes as the personal-growth industry and psychotherapy, is that psychotherapists are ethically held to render treatments that generalize outside the treatment setting and have some basis for efficacy. Bottom line: State induction is not enough and in itself constitutes unethical practice. In other words, where many personal-growth gurus excel at inducing temporary states, psychotherapists must engage the client in the process of state induction as well as teach the client, to the extent possible, how to induce the state without the therapist. It is not hard to induce a temporary state in willing participants who want to believe the answer lies outside them. It is more challenging to help clients make objects of awareness out of how they stop themselves from changing their states. Finally, therapists are ethically accountable to monitor how well the client seems to be generalizing either the state or what was learned from it outside of the therapy sessions.

The most positive development in the personal-growth industry was the beginning of a coaching ethic that requires the same thing of personal coaches.[41] Our aim is always to take the mystery out of states. To do this, we are back to breaking taboos first discussed in Chapter 1 and perhaps the biggest taboo in conventional Western society is that the conventional waking state is all that is "real." For example, many children are told, "you think too much." I frequently heard this when I would stare off into space contemplating whether or not there was a God, what the meaning of my life was, and why when going stale hard cookies would get soft but soft cookies would get hard. The center of gravity of one's society is attended to by adults and there is a reason we refer to it as "conventional." As noted in Chapter 4, it is because it reflects the average conventions of the society that spell out what behaviors are expected of individuals. Adults aim to bring the awareness of children within the parameters of whatever the center of gravity is. Most adults are innate behaviorists when it comes to "tuning in" reality. As stand-up philosopher Robert Anton Wilson has said, we don't know about being or non-being all we know is what we tune-in. What we don't tune-in doesn't necessarily not exist—it is just not tuned-in.[42] If you tune-in things that deviate from the center of gravity in your society you have to keep it to yourself. This seems to be a dominant taboo regarding states.

State induction has been summarized concisely by psychiatrist Roger Walsh who, drawing on the work of Charles Tart, cited three general stages of induction:

1. destabilization of the initial ordinary state,

2. transition to a new state, and

3. stabilization of the new state.

In the first stage the "destabilizing forces disrupt usual brain–mind function. Destabilizers can be sensory, physiological, or chemical."[43] In the second stage, when destabilizing forces are strong enough, the transition to a new state begins. As Walsh writes "The contours of this new state will depend largely on the combination of 'patterning forces' operating on it, forces such as specific organization on brain-mind function and thereby induce a corresponding state of consciousness."[44] In the final stage, consciousness settles into the new state that may be transitory or endure as a stable state or trait of consciousness.

States and Existential Artistry

Nothing demonstrates our artistic abilities like the states we can create with mind and brain. Take states that can be induced by music. Writer Hunter S.

Thompson noted that music is fuel.[45] Most of us can be moved to deep emotional states listening to and performing music. These states can be rapturous and ecstatic. Of course the downside is that states artistry can be ill-used by us at times producing irrational states of fear, paranoia, or hate. In analyzing the history of attempts at "brainwashing," author Dominic Streatfield documents the uses of music to induce different types of states to wear down possible informants.[46] We can invoke a kingdom of inner daemons to work ourselves into a broad spectrum of states.[47]

As I noted previously, an ability to induce temporary states for profit is probably one of the oldest cons used by psycho-spiritual hucksters (for-profit prophets). When I met Ericksonian hypnotherapist and psychologist Ernest Rossi, he told a story of one of his first meditation retreats. He was a young man in the 1970s going to the retreat center of a well-known guru in southern California. A beautiful woman dressed in a flowing, white silk gown greeted him. All the "attendants" were equally beautiful and Rossi spent a lovely time sitting on a cushion, sipping hot tea while ephemeral flute music played and he chatted with these lovely women. He said by the time the guru showed up he was ready to be sold almost anything. Being a scientist at heart he noted that no real "enlightenment" was had but he still counts it as one of the nicest days of his life.

Now, some 40 years later, Rossi is contemplating another benefit to the experience other than lining the guru's pockets. As we now know, genes express at different speeds.[48] Some are locked in to a particular time table (e.g., those related to pubertal changes), whereas others may begin or cease expression in relation to environmental stimuli within a period of time as short as 90 minutes. Rossi's research suggests that states that are interpreted as numinous, awe-inspiring, or otherwise rich in pleasant sensations and psychological meaning may constitute a stimulus sufficient to shift the ways in which gene blueprints are expressed that in turn lays the base for long-term changes. He believes this to be the link between things like spiritual experiences or psychotherapy and lasting change. Although he admits many self-professed teachers, gurus, and therapists are adept at inducing temporary states, most do not understand what they are doing or how to follow up to increase long-term changes.[49] His hope is that understanding psychologically numinous states and their correlated physiological shifts will move us toward a replicable technology of therapy or at least a technology refined to highlight those things more likely to induce positive changes at the cellular level.[50]

Integral Psychotherapy and States

Integral psychotherapists aspire to an AQAL view of states. This sets us apart from most other approaches to psychotherapy because we honor the truths offered by disciplines as diverse as cognitive science, spiritual practices, shamanic initiation, and natural state-inducing activities like exercise. Wilber has consistently pointed to three states all human beings have access to that are recognized by spiritual traditions—waking, dreaming, and deep sleep. He has also discussed at length fourth and fifth states that usually are only experienced by those in states-training programs.[51] For the most part, Integral psychotherapists spend most time with clients dealing with states of waking ("normal" and "altered") and dreaming states of consciousness.

As I mentioned previously, there is no hard and fast line between defining a normal waking state or an alteration of the normal waking state. The university administrator who meditates regularly may find herself sitting in a meeting in a profound altered state that is a result of her meditation practice. Such a state might be experienced as her self-boundary expanding to the point where she feels she is herself *and* the other people in the room. Clearly, states can be generally induced by different psychoactive substances.[52] I wrote "generally" because mind-expanding substances seem to act as nonspecific amplifiers of intrapsychic contents. In those cases, we won't know the effect of the drug in advance; just that it will amplify whatever is psychologically happening with a given individual. Alternately, consciousness constrictors (e.g., alcohol) will tend to focus attention and what the focus is on will, to a large extent, qualify the state as positive or negative.

In Integral Psychotherapy, we hope that the clients will be masters of rather than slaves to their states. This is a powerful goal and in this sense psychotherapy includes states training aimed at waking and dreaming states. I frequently have clients try to *catch themselves* feeling ways they *want* to feel (e.g., satisfied, powerful, content, sexy). This is a variation of cognitive-behavioral journaling where clients carry a small notepad with them and, when they are experiencing the target feeling, they note the feeling, time, and what was happening. From there we work on sculpting the client's life—aiming at healthy activities[53] that bring desired states and decreasing the influence of those things that bring the opposite.[54] One of the most liberating experiences a client can have is knowing how to change their states of mind and heart. Because Integral Psychotherapy is such a comprehensive map, clinicians and clients are able to work more effectively decreasing undesirable states and increasing desirable ones.

Although many undesirable states can be eliminated with treatment (e.g., major depressive states) others are part of life and must be tolerated and mastered if the client is to thrive.[55] Thus another maxim of Integral Psychotherapy is that states in and of themselves are neutral. What is desirable or problematic depends on the clients' psychological address and the impact of the state on the clients in the context of their lives. Some approaches to therapy focus on states (e.g., Ericksonian hypnosis and EMDR), whereas for others states are peripheral.

So what exactly are states and how do we deal with them in Integral Psychotherapy? The following sections will tackle those questions:

- Defining States: This section offers working descriptions of normal and altered states,[56] consciousness and discusses criteria about what makes a state "pathological" or undesirable state versus "healthy" or desirable.

- Waking States in Integral Psychotherapy: In this section, I provide an overview of waking states in psychotherapy.

- Dreams and Psychotherapy: This section focuses on dream states in Integral Psychotherapy. The primary focus of this chapter is on waking and dream states because those are the ones clients typically present with.

- Chemical Alterations of Consciousness: Chemically Induced States and Integral Psychotherapy: In the fourth section of this chapter, I discuss entheogens[57] and what they have taught us about the bridge between psychotherapy and spirituality. I reserve discussion of meditation and contemplation in psychotherapy for Chapter 8 on spirituality in integral psychotherapy.

Defining States

what consciousness is, we know not; and how it is that anything so remarkable as a state of consciousness comes about as the result of irritating nervous tissue, is just as unaccountable as the appearance of the Djin when Aladdin rubbed his lamp, or as any other ultimate fact of nature.

—Thomas Huxley[58]

materialism has been content to set up baseless hypotheses regarding the dependence of mental functioning upon physical process; or it has been concerned to refer the nature of mental forces to some known physical agency. No analysis has been too halting, no hypothesis too visionary, for its purposes.

—Wilhelm Wundt[59]

To define states of consciousness do we first have to define consciousness? Thankfully the answer is "no." Entire volumes are devoted to describing consciousness and, as of yet, we have no fixed definition or source for what is clearly the characterizing quality of our species—sentience or self-awareness. Noted psychological scholar Daniel Robinson also made a strong case that we barely understand (at least in psychology) what the parameters are within which we should define consciousness. His is the latest psychological treatise that effectively combats the partial view that consciousness is merely a side effect of something physical—namely the brain. Reviewing arguments from Aristotle to cognitive science, Robinson writes:

> Consciousness thus understood is a mode of deliberation distinct from awareness. To be aware is to be in contact with the present. To be *consciously* aware is to be disposed toward all that might follow based on all that has preceded. One of the roots of "conscious" is *scio*, alerting us to the epistemic element that, when removed, leaves only awareness in its wake. It would be tempting to reduce all this to an equation: *Consciousness = awareness + knowledge.* This is haphazard. Consciousness has a focus and is therefore not in any way a passive state. It is rather a state of what might be called *directed awareness,* and in this respect would seem to have a volitional component, itself needful of knowledge, no matter how minimal.[60]

Robinson concludes, stating:

> Neither the single cell nor the entire participating choir of cells offers any evidence whatever of consciousness. That turns out to be a property of mine—and yours. To ask just *how* so many cells bring this about begs the question. From all that is now known about cells, in isolation and in networks, the scientifically responsible position should be that there is no clear evidence or coherent theory warranting a physicalistic explanation.[61]

The actual phenomenon to be described by reference to consciousness is not agreed on. From Aristotle to David Chalmers, the description particularly depends on whether you define the organism as separate from the environment. As many luminaries from William James to Lev Vygotsky to John Dewey have suggested, this is not an accurate description. The organism or self-system, as we easily see through an integral lens, is embedded in a context or nested in the four quadrants, as described in Chapter 2. Allowing for this sort of organism–environment relationship allows for some operational definitions or descriptions of consciousness. Second, an Integral description of consciousness allows for fluidity between the intentional and mental aspects of consciousness and the physical–behavioral aspects of consciousness. Again, we do not reduce one to the other but see them co-arising in relationship.

With these qualifications in mind let us move on to descriptions (rather than *definitions*) of consciousness. Baruss[62] offered four such descriptions of consciousness from a review of the psychological literature. The first is consciousness as the registering of information and acting on that information in a goal-directed manner (here we see Robinson's awareness and knowledge). You see this book on the bookshelf, register the title, become aware of an interest in it, and plan to reach for it. A second description is behavioral consciousness wherein you explicitly demonstrate knowledge of your situation, state, and environment behaviorally. Building on the previous example, you pick up this book, thumb through it, purchase it, and carry it home (here we see Robinson's volition). The third description of consciousness is the stream of subjective events that occurs for you as you are viewing, picking up, thumbing through, and purchasing the book. This is the experience William James described in his *Principles of Psychology*, as thought going on. He wrote "we must simply say that *thought goes* on."[63] He then describes five attributes of this subjective description of consciousness that include thoughts being experienced as personal, consciousness as always changing, thought being sensibly continuous, and that consciousness chooses some of the things in the stream of thought over others. Finally, a fourth description is the sense of existence of the subject having the experiential stream. In this case you sense yourself as existing while purchasing the book and experiencing the stream of consciousness while doing so.

The 1-2-3 of Consciousness

Similar to the 1-2-3 of states, we can define consciousness in different ways by examining the perspective used to experience or study it. From a neuroscience perspective (upper-right), consciousness has been described as the effect of interactions in neural systems that, as Robinson artfully and skillfully points out, have yet to be clearly defined.[64] From a cognitive science perspective, consciousness can be reported (upper-left) and brain functions can be monitored before, during and after the reporting (upper-right). From the clinical or psychotherapeutic perspective (upper-left) conscious contents are related to states that clients report (summarized in the symptom lists in the *DSM* and inventories to measure such self-reported states). Reportability appears to be the most widely used operational definition of conscious contents.[65] Of course, as illustrated in Chapter 5, states may be reported but their underlying cause (subject–other dynamic) may be unconscious.

Each of these descriptions gives us partial truths that, if we overstep them, quickly become drawbacks. For example, neuroscience is vitally important in helping us understand that, as neuroscientist Andrew Newberg points out, neurons that fire together, wire together.[66] Just as our environment and state of mind affect our gene expression, they also affect which parts of the brain are working and *how* they are working. As noted, however, to reduce all phenomenological state experiences to being a "side effect" of the brain, you would have to show *how* the brain creates these states through the physiological mechanisms described. Science writer John Horgan has dubbed this the "Humpty-Dumpty problem."[67] Like all the King's horses and all the King's men, once we've "taken apart" consciousness, we have no idea how to put it back together again.

Many psychologists and psychotherapists rely on first-person descriptions of consciousness as synonymous with awareness—to be conscious is to be aware of things.[68] As noted in the quote from Robinson, this leaves out the epistemic and intentional aspects of consciousness. Certainly, in Integral Psychotherapy we help clients make aspects of themselves or their lives objects of awareness and states can alter what clients are aware of. Thus, states can become desirable or undesirable objects of awareness for clients. But what about knowledge and intent? These are critical to successful therapy. We try to help clients "stay with" states that arise and understand them (knowledge) and sometimes even understand how to induce them and stop them (intention). The further issue of what to do when the field of awareness within which states arise becomes an object for the client will be addressed more thoroughly in Chapter 8 on spirituality in psychotherapy. Suffice it to say here that although some clients will request assistance with what to do when ego becomes an object of awareness, they will be a minority consisting for the most part of state-stage practitioners or people in later, postconventional, stages of ego identity (Magician or Unitive).

How States Become Healthy and Unhealthy

The most straightforward way to understand the relative health of the state is to ask, does it help the client balance across the quadrants? This is akin to William James Pragmatic position on ideas and feelings—look at the "fruits" not the "roots." Recall in Chapter 1 that one way to define healthy translation is whether it helps the client balance across the quadrants. The "fruits" of healthy translation is balancing across the quadrants. The same holds true for states—by their fruits you can rate them. Consider a person who has a powerful transformative state in a religious service and then goes on to found a destructive cult or a person who, in the midst of a heroin high has a vision for service that transforms his life. Both states are legitimate (roots) but the outcomes are different (fruits). Although the roots of states occur in the upper-left quadrant, how they impact and are reflected in behavior, shared beliefs and community, and their relations to society all are "fruits" that contribute to understanding a state as health or unhealthy.

Another way to understand the relative health of a state for a particular client is set forth by Roger Walsh in his key dimensions for mapping states of consciousness. Here he offers 10 dimensions that we can use to help understand whether a state is helping a client balance across the quadrants (healthy translation) or whether a state seems to be consistently disrupting the ability of the client to balance across the quadrants. Walsh's 10 dimensions are summarized in the following 10 questions for clinicians[69]:

1. To what extent does a client have control over the state? The degree of control and the response to states where there is little control give us a sense of whether a state is helping or hurting a client.

2. To what extent is the client aware of the environment when in the state? To the extent that a client is not aware of the environment, the state should be supported with a sitter or therapist depending on the situations.

3. Is the client's concentration fixed, fluid, or fragmented or some combination of the latter three in the state? Psychedelic sessions may move a person through all three, whereas hypnotic trances tend to produce fixed concentration.

4. To what extent can the client communicate while in the state? Communication may be impaired due to the method used to induce the state (e.g., ingestion of intoxicating substances) or the state may produce ineffable experiences where the limit is the vehicle of language rather than a problem communicating per se.

5. To what extent is the client energized or aroused in the state? The higher the arousal, the more the need for a sitter or therapist. The arousal may be anything from emerging shadow material to ecstatic trance.

6. To what extent does the client experience calm while in the state? As Walsh notes, this is more than just low arousal but implies a minimum of agitation and distractibility. Agitation can certainly be anything from an idiosyncratic response to a psychoactive agent to an eruption of shadow material. The Integral psychotherapist needs to be familiar with the symptom clusters most likely correlated with a large amount of painful shadow material (e.g., Dissociative Identity Disorder, BPD, PTSD).

7. What is the dominant affective flavor of the state? Are the dominant emotions pleasurable, painful? The total balance of the experience should be taken into consideration when answering this question. For example, many states designed to bring about catharsis of shadow material start very painful but can give way to an ecstatic bliss in the best-case scenarios.

8. What is the client's sense of identity during the state? As Walsh asserts, this can vary widely in shamanic trance and I would

assert equally widely in therapeutic applications. For example, in one hypnotic session a client identified with a plant being rooted and having beautiful blossoms with seeds that spread the beauty throughout the cosmos.

9. Does the client report any OBEs? Although these occur more frequently in shamanic trance, they are not unheard of in psychotherapy trance states. One client with whom I worked claimed to leave his body and go to another world where beings assisted him in making emotional meaning out of his difficult life. Another client would dissociate and report OBEs whenever she perceived a threat to herself. She learned this as a sexually abused child. In the former case, the OBE was healthy, in the latter unhealthy. Why? Because in the former case, the OBE helped the client balance across the quadrants; whereas in the latter case, the OBE short-circuited the client's efforts to balance across the quadrants.

10. Finally, what is the nature of the client's inner experiences during the states in question? Walsh notes three distinctions, including the degree of organization, the sensory modalities employed, and the phenomenological rating of intensity.

These questions can be a useful guide for gauging, relative to the client, the health of the altered state. These questions should be thought through for even the most common means of inducing alterations in consciousness. For example, meditation is widely used as a complement to or technique in psychotherapy and is one of the most researched techniques related to therapeutic states.[70] Granted, there are varieties of meditation techniques and it is hard to operationalize what is meant by the word.[71] Despite this, meditation, used in the wrong circumstances (or by the wrong client), can cause negative events for clients including exacerbation of schizophrenia,[72] anxiety, depression, and other symptoms.[73] Similarly, one has only to review the literature to find diverse perspectives on the use of just about any state in psychotherapy. Although this situation is not peculiar to states as techniques (it has been suggested that 3% to 6% of clients worsen as a result of psychotherapy),[74] state induction as a clinical technique requires appropriate training and supervision.

Although I have written extensively elsewhere about the limitations of the *DSM* classification system, to some extent Integral psychotherapists can use the *DSM* criteria as a general heuristic for what constitutes a "disorder" when thinking about states. The *DSM* editors wrote the following:

> each of the mental disorders is conceptualized as a clinically signifi-
> cant behavioral or psychological syndrome or pattern that occurs

in an individual and that is associated with present distress (e.g., a painful symptom) or disability (i.e., impairment in one or more important areas of functioning) or with a significantly increased risk of suffering death, pain, disability, or an important loss of freedom. In addition, this syndrome or pattern must not be merely an expectable and culturally sanctioned response to a particular event, for example, the death of a loved on.[75]

All therapists must remain mindful that deciding whether a client's symptoms or states are clinically significant always is a matter of clinician judgment. Having written that, however, we must recognize that in therapy, the aim of inducing certain states is going to be to help clients make aspects of themselves or their lives objects of awareness. Given this, the state may temporarily induce distress as the client becomes aware of something that was previously repressed. This is not always the case, but is certainly one of the possible dynamics we see using states in clinical situations. With these caveats in mind, let's move on to an overview of waking states in Integral Psychotherapy.

Waking States in Integral Psychotherapy

Alterations of Waking States

In this section, I summarize what has been done with alterations of waking states in psychotherapy. The focus in this book is always to come back to the clinical realm. As such, a common clinical theme is that the alteration of a state or the induction of states is nothing special. It is what is done during the alteration, the follow-up, and the ability to learn from the states that is critical and requires clinical skills. As religious scholar Huston Smith noted in an interview with Jeffrey Mishlove, "the object of mysticism is not altered states but altered traits."[76] Similarly here, clinicians are ethically bound to know the parameters of states they are altering or inducing, how to work with clients in those states, and how to follow-up so that the client can generalize from the state to everyday life. My clinical experience has been that the client's psychological address, and particularly the client's level of ego development, is critical to forecasting how he or she may respond to a particular state. In most personal-growth seminars offered by nontherapists, there is little or no effort to discern this, just a request that the client sign a waiver of liability.

In addition to the literature of mediation and contemplation, we have a vast literature on the varieties of altered waking states. Some of these are related to what Wilber[77] and Roger Walsh[78] describe as nature mysticism (e.g., shamanic identification with a totem animal), others are variously referred to as peak or flow experiences,[79] and still others have primarily been developed as therapeutic tools like trance states used in clinical hypnosis and niche therapies like EMDR. Although entire books have been written on this topic, I define an altered state of consciousness using the work of psychologists Charles Tart and Baruss.

As early as 1969, Tart pointed out that it is difficult to define normal versus altered states of consciousness. He wrote:

> there is a multitude of philosophical and semantic problems in defining just what "normal" consciousness and "altered" states of consciousness are, yet at this instant I have not the slightest doubt that I am in my normal state of consciousness. Yet there have been a number of occasions in my life when I have not had the slightest difficulty in realizing that I was in an altered state of consciousness. . . . Thus . . . an altered state of consciousness for a given individual is one in which he clearly feels a *qualitative* shift in his pattern of mental functioning.[80]

Tart goes on to describe that these qualitative shifts include mental functions that ordinarily do not operate or perceptual qualities with no normal counterparts. He later concluded that these qualitative shifts are experienced as *radically* different from the way one ordinarily functions. The perspective of qualitative shifts is clearly Zone 1 in the upper-left quadrant.

Baruss noted that "we can define altered states of consciousness more generally by specifying changes to the ordinary waking state along any number of dimensions . . . altered states of consciousness are stable patterns of physiological, cognitive, and experiential events different from those of the ordinary waking state."[81] Again there is the Zone 1, upper-left qualitative shift implied in Baruss' description. Finally, when we reflect on clinical situations, it is safe to say that the majority of altered states are evoked. One could make the circular argument that they are always evoked even if by something we cannot sense but without going that far, I use the following categories. Altered states can be evoked by the following:

- external events;
- specific self- or other training (state-state training like meditation);
- external persons (like a therapist using hypnosis); and
- ingestion of psychoactive substances.[82]

CASE EXAMPLE: WAKING STATES AS SYMPTOMS AND TREATMENT

Sami (an Americanization of his Hindu name) comes to counseling because he suffers from states of severe anxiety similar to panic disorder.[83] He is a graduate teaching fellow at a midwestern, urban university and is studying business. Since his first weeks in the United States he has noted his anxiety has been quite high. Sami's "style" of anxiety[84] is particularly physiological, resulting in excess perspiration, stomach cramps, dysentery, and migraines. He has a small Hindu student community but, as in most urban campuses, the students are dispersed across a 50-mile area, leaving little time for anything other than work, school, and commuting. Although Sami did not met the criteria for panic disorder without agoraphoabia, his hotspots were in the lower quadrants more than the upper-right might as would bd expected with that diagnosis.[85] In Sami's case, he has been living in an area with a high crime rate populated by predominantly blacks. The community has not exactly welcomed Sami with open arms and he is frequently verbally abused walking from his apartment to the bus stop. On top of it, the verbal abuse seems rooted in Anti-Arabic sentiment and Sami is both frightened and angry because of course he is no more Arabic than his harassers.

In Sami's case, his states of anxiety were what brought him into the university's counseling center. Although his therapist did not identify as "integral" in her orientation, to her credit, she worked with him to basically balance across the quadrants. First she realized that Sami's perception of his environment (upper-left) as unsafe was confirmed in consensual reality. She knew the area Sami lived in (lower-right), its demographics and the cultural center of gravity (lower-left). While addressing his psychological distress she also figured out a way to move to a residence where he felt safer. She worked with him and the International Students Office on campus to match him with a Hindu family who rented rooms to students and had a recent opening.

Therapeutically, the therapist also discovered that this experience was triggering traumatic memories of Hindu–Pakistani violence Sami experienced in his home country. The therapist worked with Sami who was actually suffering from a form of PTSD. Although Sami did not have prominent symptoms, once he moved from the problematic residence, he did suffer from nightmares and anxiety states triggered by witnessing angry encounters. He was able to learn to control these through Mindfulness-Based Cognitive Therapy (MBCT),[86] which included processing in dialogue many of the incidents he witnessed growing up. The mindfulness techniques helped relax him while the dialogue helped him metabolize traumatic memories.

Sami's case illustrates how states can be the focus of the symptoms and the treatment. As far as clinical interventions, mindfulness-based variations on the traditional CBTs are being referred to as the third-wave of CBT (the first wave being behavioral and the second being cognitive-behavioral).[87] In the therapeutic sense, the state of mindfulness is described as a process of nonjudgmental awareness and acceptance of subjective intrapsychic experiences traditionally viewed as distressing.[88] Although this is only one component of the way mindfulness is described in spiritual practices, it appears to have clinical effectiveness divorced from any such practice.[89]

Sami's case also illustrates the importance of balance across the quadrants, and most important, the role of the therapist's center of gravity. I was part of a supervision group where this case was presented. The therapist treating Sami appeared to have qualities we associate with postconventional ego identity (the topic of Chapter3). She was able to entertain multiple perspectives while not getting bogged down in them. Two of the therapists in the group focused *only* on the cultural aspects. Ludicrous as it sounds in retrospect, they actually began suggesting that Sami should learn more about the culture of those with whom he was living. They almost began suggesting that remaining in an area that seemed unsafe for Sami would be a good cultural experience! These two therapists reified culture as if it were an ultimate reality and sounded like Pluralists mired in relativism.

Sami's therapist was able to head-off this discussion with her perspective probably because, as a Black female, she had the "cultural capital" respected by the other two therapists. The other therapists also were surprised as they learned about Hindu–Pakistani violence. Having never been there, they seemed to idealize places like India as havens of spiritual realization (as is regrettably common among many who identify with the center of gravity Wilber refers to as derailed green). Sami's therapist, although not fully aware of the situation, seemed more able to take it in stride and move on. I would attribute this to her center of gravity being far closer to Strategist than Pluralist. After several discussions, she took one of our externally scored research protocols that included the SCTi—sure enough, she tested out at solid Strategist.

Hypnosis, Daydreams, and Imagery

Integral Psychotherapy can make use of hypnosis, daydream, and imagery as needed. These are alterations of waking states that can have a great deal of overlap in the umbrella category of trance states.

HYPNOSIS

Hypnosis is "an altered state of consciousness wherein the patient's focus of attention is concentrated or narrowed"[90] and it is perhaps best described as selective attention to some things and selective inattention to others.[91] The word hypnosis is really a poor descriptor. James Braid (1795–1860) coined the term indirectly and then renamed the then-scandalous mesmerism *neurohypnology*.[92] As seen here, Braid deserves much of the credit for reviving the therapeutic use of trance states after the wreckage of the Mesmerism movement. The word *hypnosis* is derived from the Greek *hypnotikos* for sleep inducing. Hypnosis is very different from sleep both phenomenologically and neurologically. Hypnosis is a vague term that likely refers to a range of altered states involving selective attention.[93] This selective attention is a trance state and some people in trance states are open to suggestions.

There are competing theories about what the hypnotic state actually *is* but those are beyond the necessary scope of this section. Suffice to say that all hypnosis is self-hypnosis. People, alone or with the guidance of a therapist, enter freely into trance states. Trance states cannot be coerced against a person's will (this conclusion is supported in Dominic Streatfield's overview mentioned earlier). It is important to note that because hypnotic states require the assent (whether conscious or not) of the client, the clients who are most responsive to hypnosis are those highly motivated to overcome a problem.[94]

Hypnosis plays a pivotal role in psychotherapy because of its inextricable presence among the practices used by the pioneers of depth psychology, beginning with Franz Anton Mesmer's work in "animal magnetism."[95] Mesmer held the mistaken view that disease was the result of a "misalignment of the corpuscular properties of the body" related to magnetic induction. He developed a technique of stroking the limbs of an afflicted patient with a metal bar to achieve "realignment." Well, one thing built on another and Mesmer came to believe that he was the chosen vessel through which these "realignments" occur. As psychological historian Daniel Robinson summarizes, Mesmer is "criticized hip and thigh" and is eventually hounded out of Vienna. He moved to Paris where he took up a practice that would turn today's new-agers green with envy (pun intended). Mesmer donned robes, danced around the patient, and became a figure of great celebrity and greater controversy giving "hypnosis" a "black eye" in the process (although he would have fit in well at many contemporary New Age Fairs).[96]

The French authorities gave Mesmer's claims a hearing with a committee chaired by Benjamin Franklin, who concluded the committee was under no burden to accept Mesmer's theory but that he did achieve clinical efficacy in some cases. Hypnosis was introduced to Jean-Martin Charcot by Charles Richet who rediscovered the hypnotic practices of Mesmer's few disciples.[97] Charcot, of course, was observed using hypnosis by Freud who offered to translate some of Charcot's works into German for the modest fee of getting some tutelage from Charcot on topics including hypnosis. We know Freud used hypnosis but gave it up likely because he could see no way to connect it to neurological events. We must remember that Freud's scientific training was in the shadow of greats like Ernst Mach and that Freud's ultimate aim was to be able to understand psychological phenomena physiologically. This aim culminated in "Project for a Scientific Psychology," which Freud later dropped concluding that he simply did not have the tools for the time to reach such conclusions.

Hypnosis has clearly recovered from Mesmer's showmanship and even its abandonment by Freud in part because hypnotic phenomena point toward the unconscious, which is the specialization of depth psychology. Currently, hypnotic

states also are part of the neuroscience research regimen conducted with tools
Freud could scarcely dream of. The neuroimaging studies confirm that there are
brain activities correlating with the phenomenological state of hypnosis. Neural
changes in the frontal lobes and specifically the anterior cingulated cortex and
the dorsolateral prefrontal cortex. Phenomenologically, hypnosis is associated
with focused attention and relaxation.[98]

Is there anything that is unique to Integral Psychotherapy in the use of
hypnosis? If anything, it is the depth and breadth of knowledge and awareness
that the clinician brings to the session. The therapist provides the parameters
within which clients' experiences are facilitated and which, to a large extent,
clients make meaning out of their therapeutic experience. The aim of an integral
approach is to embrace those possibilities that emerge from the hypnotic state
without concretely clinging to any one beyond what research and experience
can confirm. I allude here to the popular phenomenon of past-life regression
therapy. Based on several studies, psychological researchers have raised questions about the extent to which therapist suggestion and predisposing beliefs
play a part in the subjective intensity of what a person considers an experience
of a former life.[99] A more integral understanding of the past-life experience is
to honor it as an upper-left phenomenon, again however, without concretely
attaching to any particular interpretation of it. An example of this is psychologist Jenny Wade's exploration of subjective similarity between reported past-life
experiences and near-death experiences.[100] In her pilot study, Wade found that
the similarities and differences between the two experiences suggest a new (and
more integral) avenue of research without confirming any particular interpretation of what these experiences are.

Is this an important distinction? Absolutely. This is the difference between
an approach that is able to embrace the research methods of the day and
explore a phenomenon without attaching to explanations for the phenomenon
that are sure to alienate those clinging to particular explanations (e.g., the idea
that past-life regression is indicative of actual past lives and should be uncritically accepted as such; e.g., see the past-life regression hypnotherapy program
advertised at http://www.ravenheartcenter.com/). This difference distinguishes
Integral Psychotherapy as a promising new approach that can be implemented
in mainstream practice. In contrast, consider a recent survey of founders of
the transpersonal psychology movement and historians of psychology. The
researcher concluded that transpersonal psychology has made almost no impact
on mainstream psychology in part because of accentuating differences with
mainstream psychology and lack of inroads to psychotherapeutic practice.[101]
The Integral psychotherapist puts no hard and fast parameters on what is possible but practices discernment and mindfulness of their desires regarding what
they want to be real.

Daydreaming

Daydreaming shares many similarities to hypnosis and in fact may be a form of trance state or even a form of hypnotic trance that focuses on attending to spontaneously arising images. Several researchers have correlated hypnotic responsiveness ("hypnotizability") with aspects of daydreaming.[102] The essence of daydreams (as opposed to hypnosis per se) is their spontaneity. This was noted as early as the late 19th century by William James. Baruss points out that until recently daydreaming was viewed pejoratively as wasting time. More recent research has shown that "Daydreaming is a channel of information about ourselves to ourselves"[103] that helps us understand what we want, what we fear, and perhaps what we do not want to know.[104] As such, it is a state relevant to Integral Psychotherapy.

We can use the self-system outlined in Chapter 5 to form a sketch of a model for understanding daydreaming. In Integral Psychotherapy we want to know about client's daydreams as these can give us insights into the client's desires, particularly stifled desires. In this sense, daydreams are an important sense of information about self-systems. Are there styles of daydreaming supported in the literature that can help give shape to using this state in therapy? The answer is "yes." Psychologist Jerome Singer[105] noted that there appear to be three styles of daydreaming. The first is called *positive-constructive daydreaming* and is described as frequent, vivid, playful, and wish-fulfilling in nature. People who fit this style of daydreaming appear less hampered by psychological conflict and might be described as "happy daydreamers."[106] In clinical practice, positive-constructive daydreaming seems correlated with later-stage ego identity and the extent to which the person has learned how to explore their shadow in psychotherapy. I have found in coaching and in psychotherapy, positive-constructive daydreamers can use their daydreams as a blueprint for reaching desired outcomes.

Singer's second style is called *guilty-dysphoric daydreaming*. People who tend to express this style engage in daydreams with repeated themes having to do with ambitiousness, heroic deeds, fear, failure, hostility, guilt, regrets, and aggression. Here it appears that shadow material is largely fueling the daydreams. Therapists may use the daydream material to explore shadow elements that are emerging as projections and reaction formations.[107] There also is a correlation with this style of daydreaming and PTSD. The reliving of the trauma in daydreams, as well as daydreams exacerbating the sense of survival guilt, also are typical of these cases. Here we may say that the trauma has so impacted the self-system that it is perpetually in crisis response.[108]

The third type of daydreaming is called *poor attentional control* and is characterized by those who have difficulty concentrating and are anxious and distractible. Again, therapists may want to explore shadow elements that may be too anxiety provoking to bring to awareness. In that instance, the distraction is serving as a barrier to making the repressed contents objects of awareness. Frequently, such distraction may be a symptom of acute or posttraumatic stress. In children and adolescents these signs are frequently misinterpreted as attention-deficit hyperactivity disorder but are actually related to trauma or one of the anxiety disorders. Exploring what the client is distracting him or herself from in these instances is resourceful.

Daydreaming styles also have been explored in relation to the traits of the Five-Factor Model introduced in the last chapter. As might be guessed, scoring high on the factor of openness is correlated with the positive-constructive daydreaming style. Scoring high on neuroticism is correlated with the guilty-dysphoric daydreaming style. Finally, scoring low on conscientiousness is correlated with the poor attentional control daydreaming style. There have been no studies to date of daydreaming style and one's level of ego identity. Integral psychotherapists can assume, however, that the readiness to disclose daydream content likely is also correlated with ego identity. The earlier the level of ego identity, the less likely one would be to disclose daydreams just as on sentence-completion protocols, the earlier the level, the more guarded and unelaborated the responses.

IMAGERY AND VISUALIZATION

Imagery (also referred to as visualization)[109] is the use of intrapsychic images, spontaneously experienced or evoked, in therapy. This is a broad area in the states literature that includes types of meditation, psychoneuroimmunology,[110] and directed and nondirected imagery techniques from Jungian schools[111] to the visualization of symbols used in psychosynthesis.[112] Imagery or visualization can take the form of concentration on an image (similar or synonymous with concentration meditation), watching and reporting what emerges while listening to direction, or simply watching and reporting what emerges spontaneously. Imagery work is used for a variety of purposes including counseling the dying,[113] medical patients,[114] patients undergoing treatment for cancer,[115] and clients living in nursing homes.[116] Imagery or visualization is a variety of waking state that reflects a natural skill that most of us use on a regular basis. Some people seem to have a natural talent for visual imagery, whereas others can improve what ability they have through practice.

There is a great deal of overlap in the literature on daydreams, hypnosis, and imagery. Clients can work with guided or nondirected imagery in hypnotic states or states that are similar to daydreaming. If all hypnosis is self-hypnosis we might even posit the question of how we can really discern if a daydreaming subject is or is not in a hypnotic trance state. This is not as important as understanding what these states can and cannot do reliably. One of the most controversial results of hypnosis and guided imagery has been so-called recovered memories of sexual abuse. Although the debate is ongoing, what is clear is that memory is not like a camera. Images that appear during imagery or hypnosis should not be assumed to refer to consensual reality although in rare instances they may.[117]

Although imagery can be used with clients in the waking state, they also occur hypnogogically and hypnopompically. Hypnogogic imagery occurs when one is going to sleep and hypnopompic when one is waking. The images usually are visual but can have aural, kinesthetic, or even exosomatic (out-of-body) qualities to them.[118] Hypnogogic and hypnopompic imagery lead us now to dream work in Integral Psychotherapy.

Dreams and Psychotherapy

dreams have accordingly in all ages been regarded as revelations, and have played a large part in furnishing forth mythologies and creating themes for faith to lay hold upon.

—William James[119]

In weaving an Integral approach to dream work, it is helpful to review some of the influences and current literature on the topic. Dreams have been explored for millennia, so perhaps it is proper to begin with Aristotle the psychologist and his view of dreams. Robinson has claimed that Aristotle's psychology is as complete a system as Westerners have had and includes speculation about dreams and imagination. Aristotle wrote that the imagination and dreams have much in common such that "in both cases, activity persists in sensory systems long after the removal of the instigating stimulus. Such persistence is the basis of imaginings, for dreams, and for the aftereffects produced by long exposure to a moving or a colored stimulus."[120] So here we see a Western understanding of dreams that is to persist in scientific psychology[121] but that serves only as a minimal guideline in theories of psychotherapy.

Dream work was the province of Romantic philosophers in the mid-19th century who maintained that in dreams the soul was freed from the body to wander the astral planes. We see variations of this philosophy in many New Age or New Thought approaches to dreams. The positivism of the later 19th century returned to Aristotle's observations that the sense organs were the source of dream images. Positivists explored some of the Romantic view of dreams such as the idea that the blind could see in dreams when freed from the defective body. In 1888, Joseph Jastrow published a study exploring visual imagery in 58 blind subjects. Of the 32 who became blind before age 5, none reported visual images in their dreams.[122] This is consistent with contemporary research that supports a cognitive perspective of dreams in which mental imagery abilities develop between ages 4 and 7.[123] Thus far, no compelling case has been made for visual images in the dreams of the congenitally blind.[124] As also might be expected, deaf persons communicate in dreaming by sign language and do not report aural stimulation, but they do report far more vivid visual imagery.[125]

The first major psychological works on dreams predate Freud's *Interpretation of Dreams*[126] by several decades. Freud advanced what is now referred to as a disguise-censorship hypothesis of dreams where the manifest content (what the dream appears like to the dreamer) is merely a disguised version of the latent content (the wishes the dreamer is expressing that, in their original form, are too threatening to bring to consciousness). Freud's theory is original as a synthesizing theory but relies in part on numerous predecessors. Freud, being the careful scholar, cites all the influences discussed here in his dream book. The first influence on Freud's dream work is Karl Scherner.[127] Scherner's book *The Life of the Dream* was published in 1861. In his book, Scherner discerned three ideas that survived in Freud's book on dream interpretation. First was the idea that psychic activity is directly expressed in the language of symbols, thus the possibility of interpreting them. Second, Scherner held a middle ground between the romantics and the positivists, holding that some symbols were of a spiritual origin and others of a bodily origin. We also see here a precursor to Jung's "small" and "big" dreams. Finally, Scherner made a case that certain dream symbols correspond to parts of the body such as flying alludes to the lungs, traffic to circulation, and towers, pipes, and so on, to the penis.

Alfred Maury's book *Sleep and Dreams* was published the same year as Scherner's but was far more popular. Maury trained himself to write the dreams down as soon as he awoke and connected the hypnogogic hallucinations with dream content. Maury also experimented with sensory stimulation in relation to dreams. In one instance, he arranged to have his assistant daub his pillow with perfume after Maury had retired. Sure enough, that evening he dreamed of being in a Cairo perfume shop. Ellenberger notes that through such experiments, Maury inaugurated the study of experimental stimulation of dreams. Maury's studies confirmed, among other things, that memory plays a far greater role in dream imagery than is suspected. He maintained that his evidence supported the idea that the mind may draw images for dreams from very early parts of our lives.

A third major influence on Freud was Hervey de Saint-Denis who spent a lifetime exploring his own dreams. He eventually learned to become aware he was dreaming and voluntarily direct his dreams (what I refer to later as lucid dreaming), learned to wake himself at will to record a dream, and refined the ability to concentrate on any part of the dream. Inspired by Maury, de Saint-Denis conducted ingenious experiments. In exploring dream conditioning, he spent 2 weeks in a picturesque part of the French countryside, sleeping each night with a daub of perfume on his pillow. Upon returning, he instructed his assistant to randomly choose a night over the next month and to come in after de Saint-Denis fell asleep and daub the pillow with the same perfume. The assistant picked the 12th night after his return and sure enough de Saint-Denis dreamed that night of where he vacationed.

De Saint-Denis set forth several important dream work principles in his book *Dreams and the Means to Direct Them.* The first was his discovery of the plasticity of the dream process. In Integral Psychotherapy we may routinely instruct clients how to influence their dreams little knowing that we owe de Saint-Denis for the approach. De Saint-Denis also attempted to address the question of where dreams come from. He agreed with Maury that dream images are in large part drawn from memories that may have long since passed from conscious memory. Here we see a seed of Freud's idea that early impulses may survive in the manifest images of dreams. De Saint-Denis identified forgotten memories in his studies that he referred to as "snap-shot" memories because of their connection to an emotionally arousing event that may later be repressed. De Saint-Denis also confirmed to processes in dream work he called abstraction and superimposition but that we recognize as Freud's constructs of displacement and condensation.[128]

The final influence on Freud that I mention here was F. W. Hildebrandt who focused on the use of dreams in every day life. He outlined four approaches in this regard. First he felt that the beauty of some dreams worked as a comfort to the dreamer. Although Freud would interpret this as a form of wish fulfillment, it could more loosely be a form of sublimation. Second, Hildebrandt believed dreams gave the dreamer a magnified image of her or his moral tendencies. This is important both as Freudian wish fulfillment and what we are calling the emergence of shadow material. Third, Hildebrandt believed dreams could give dreamers insights into dynamics that are not clearly perceived in waking life. Finally, like Aristotle, Hildebrandt felt that some dreams may announce the onset of illness.

Returning now to Freud's theory, it is important to understand that even in his own time (as now), his theory was one of many. The disguise-censorship hypothesis of dreams basically posits that dreams are compromise formations fueled by wish fulfillment. The compromise is between expression of a repressed wish and the need for sleep. In other words, Freud's theory sees the mind to some extent working in service of the needs of the body. Freud's theory of course also extends to slips of the tongue (parapraxes), bungled actions, and what would come to be called neurotic symptoms.[129] The repressed wish in Freud's theory is the psychological equivalent of a biological drive (what Wilber calls the archaic unconscious) and the content of this drive may become attached to elements of current memory or residues from the day. The drive can be discharged when adequately disguised.

The disguising is in part to make the wish conform to the world of the familiar. Psychoanalyst Emil Gutheil noted the following:

what we recall as "dream" is the end product of an evolutionary thought process which begins in the unfathomable depths of the unconscious and ends with complete wakefulness and consciousness . . . under the influence of growing lucidity, the prelogical, amorphous thought material gradually obtains shape and content, until it conforms to the rules of logic, becomes fully intelligible and relates to situations which are thinkable.[130]

That this new form differs dramatically from the original impulse is of course the point. From an Integral perspective, we might say that the analytic dream process is the ultimate "subject–other" process whereby a part of ourselves is masterfully disguised as some "other."

We know that Freud's contemporaries and the therapists that came after him posed radically different approaches to dream work with clients. Jung saw dreams as normal creative expressions of the unconscious. He wrote that he had no theory of dreams meaning that he had no preconceived notion of what a dream should mean as opposed to Freud who claimed it was always wish fulfillment. Although Jung did not approach dreams with preconceived interpretations, he did have assumptions that include viewing the dream as compensating the dreamer's conscious situation. When defenses are relaxed in sleep, Jung felt that a door was opened to a world that consciousness did not accept but that wished to express itself nonetheless. In this he is accepting that the dream says what it means and can hold a message for the dreamer. In this sense Jungian dream work is more geared toward possibilities for growth rather than analysis of the past.[131]

Contemporary Jungian dream work has been summarized as a four-step process:

1. Use associations to the original dream image (rather than chain associations) to form the foundation for interpreting dreams. The therapist continually brings the dreamer back to the original image until something "clicks."

2. The dreamer is to look for parts of the inner self that are represented by the images. These parts in Jungian therapy include the archetypes.

3. The dream is interpreted in light of the first two steps as a message for the dreamer from the unconscious.

4. Rituals are developed to make the dream more concrete for the dreamer and thus aid the dreamer in owning the parts of self emerging from the unconscious.[132]

Alfred Adler, founder of Individual Psychology, approached dreams as purposeful rehearsals for future events as well as functioning to preserve the

unity of personality and one's sense of self-worth. As a result, Adler felt dreams
dealt with aspects of the individual that were currently poorly understood as
well as the prospective dreams that sought to explore the future. Adler was clear
that he did "not hold the view that the dream is a prophetic inspiration, that
it can unlock the future or give knowledge of the unknowable. My extensive
preoccupation with dreams has taught me one thing, which the dream like
any other psychic manifestation comes into being through powers inherent in
each individual."[133]

Adler noted that most clients are striving for certainty of future event
(what Eckhart Tolle calls a compulsive belief in a future that promises salvation),
thus many dreams are preparing the individual for engaging "actual difficulties
encountered by the dreamer's lifeline."[134] Adler concluded this leaves us with
two types of dreams; one where the person is preinterpreting how to solve a
problem and another initiating what the dreamer desires to do in a given situation. One of Adler's assumptions (which holds no support today) was that the
less social interest a person had, the more that person would dream because
dreams also served a self-deceiving function of selecting the demands of the
dreamer's lifestyle over what is demanded by common sense.[135] Although not
tying ourselves to the self-deceiving function related to social interest, it is clear
that as a subject–other dynamic, the self-deceiving function may serve to bring
the dreamer closer to what otherwise would appear repulsive. What is perhaps
most noteworthy in Adler's work is his supposition that dreams achieve their
purpose through employing emotion over reason and mood over judgment.
Adler called dreams the factory of emotions suggesting that dreams create an
emotion that helps the dreamer solve a problem.[136] In this sense, he was most
aligned with the contemporary "continuity theory" of dreams that posits that
dreaming is similar to waking thoughts.[137]

Fritz Perls, founder of Gestalt therapy, also emphasized a growth-oriented
approach to dream work in psychotherapy. Whereas Freud saw dreams as the
royal road to the unconscious, Perls saw them as the road to integration. Perls
approached every dream as if it represented the whole person. "Perls was of the
opinion, like Jung, that every dream has an existential message for the dreamer,
especially if dreamers will allow themselves to discover it freshly from within
themselves and not in response to an external authority's 'interpretation.' "[138]
Perls would instruct the dreamer to recount the dream as if it were happening
in the present moment from a first-person perspective. The dreamer is then
helped to play out aspects of the dream as aspects of her or his existence. Again,
the focus is on the present rather than past history. One of the best-known
aspects of Perls' dream work is viewing the dream as a projection—all aspects
of the dream are part of the dreamer. Again, as I noted with regard to Freud's
theory dreams may be thought of as the ultimate "subject–other" dynamic. As
the dreamer can own aspects of herself by owning aspects of the dream she is
broadening her experience of self in the world rather than fragmenting it.[139]

Dreams in the Current Psychotherapeutic Literature

So what has happened since the heyday of depth psychology and the advent of the humanistic psychologies? Well for one thing an enormous amount of research, some of which confirms what the early dream researchers speculated about and some of which clearly refutes earlier understandings. Dream interpretation almost disappeared from view entirely in American psychology in the early 20th century. At that time it simply did not fit American ideas of "practicality" in therapy as well as the emerging behavioral paradigm. Psychologist Rosalind Cartwright believes it made a comeback in part due to advances made in technologies that increased what we could learn from sleep laboratories and how much we could help clients in sleep clinics.[140] Clara Hill adds that interest in internal phenomena again became "permissible" after the initiation of the cognitive revolution.

To practice ethically, the Integral psychotherapist should have a review of current literature and an understanding of how that literature relates to an integral approach to dreams. This section is designed to provide that review. Much of this review draws on the work of psychologist Clara Hill. Hill has distinguished herself both as a researcher of dreams and as a clinician who works with dreams.

Updates: Freud (Again!)

There have been numerous attempts to test and explore Freud's theories about dreams and dreaming. Contemporary analytic approaches hold that the manifest dream content is directly a representation of waking life.[141] So rather than distorting hidden impulses, "dreams are thought to reflect waking issues and to further waking efforts at problem solving and conflict resolution."[142] As Maury and Saint-Denis both noted in the 19th century, contemporary analysts still see memory as playing a large role in dream images. To the extent that our issues have origins in our childhood, our dream images will draw up memories from that period. As Hill concludes "even though dream content may be stimulated by current concerns, these concerns are characterized by the dreamer's personality, which had its foundation in childhood."[143] Free association is still used widely in analytic approaches to dream work. The associations themselves frequently prove useful in therapy and interpreting resistance can help therapist and client understand why the client has barriers to associating.

Updates: Gestalt and Humanistic/Existential Approaches

Dream work in Gestalt and other humanistic/existential/experiential approaches to therapy has continued and one model that summarizes these therapeutic approaches is by Erik Craig and Stephen Walsh. These two psychologists offer a two-stage approach to phenomenological (upper-left) analysis of dreams. The first step is explication where the dreamer describes different parts of the dream as well as parts that emerge (likely via priming) during the description that otherwise would remain forgotten. Like Perls, these therapists like to have the client present the dream in the first person as if it were happening. Therapists in this approach support and listen as the client tells the dream and do not offer an interpretation.

In Craig and Walsh's second stage, elucidation, the therapist works with the client to make meaning in what the dream presents. This is done without reference to a theoretical framework or system of symbols. Craig and Walsh feel that dreams images may be primary (refer to themselves), secondary (to the kinds of images they are), or tertiary (to corresponding elements of waking life).[144] As Hill notes in her analysis of this method, the therapist listens for what is attended to and what is *not* attended to, finding resourceful ways to make the latter an object of awareness without foisting an interpretation on it.

It is important to note that counselor Phil Barrineau has developed a person-centered (or client-centered) approach to dream work, building on the earlier theories of Rogers. Barrineau suggests that a dream model has not been developed in Rogerian work because it was somewhat antithetical to the non-directive, co-explorer role of the therapist. Near the end of his career, Rogers wrote openly about a role for nonconscious or unconscious processes stating "our organisms as a whole have a wisdom and purposiveness which goes well beyond our conscious thought."[145] Rogers' original research led him to conclude that as therapy progressed "feelings which have previously been denied to awareness are now experienced with immediacy and acceptance" rather than being "denied, feared, or struggled against."[146]

In client-centered dream work, the client presents a dream and the decision to explore a dream is the client's alone. The dream work is a process of the client discovering the meaning of the dream in the moment as the client presents it. Barrineau uses various types of questions and responses crafted in the Rogerian tradition. Two types of questions are clarifying and exploring questions. Clarifying questions help the therapist complete his or her understanding of what the client presents. Exploratory questions are

> intended to facilitate the client's exploration of the waking-life meaning of some element(s) of the dream. The assumption is that the dream is a symbolic or metaphorical representation of some reality in the dreamer's world, so the key to the dream's meaning is in the client's translation of the symbolic language into his or her individual and personal conscious, waking awareness.[147]

Responses Barrineau crafted include reflective, idiosyncratic, and cumulative. Reflective responses are paraphrases in the Rogerian tradition aimed at supporting the client in their exploration. Idiosyncratic responses are those in which the therapist expresses uniquely individual feelings and understandings that grow out of empathic understanding (one of the six core conditions in Rogerian work). Finally, cumulative statements are those that draw on data previously revealed in earlier sessions that may have a bearing on the dream being explored. Although Barrineau realizes that some client-centered therapists feel his model is too directed, he makes a good case for it being well within the client-centered tradition.

Related to the client-centered tradition is Eugene Gendlin's focusing technique as a way to explore dreams. Focusing grew out of Rogers' therapeutic approach but is unique in its emphasis on staying in touch with experiences, particularly at the body level. Gendlin developed a technique to facilitate awareness of inner experience (called *focusing*).[148] Focusing is a process through which clients focus on what is directly felt in the body and waiting for meaning to emerge from that felt sense. The idea is that this is body–mind thinking allows for the definition of mind to encompass the wisdom of the body.[149] Focusing-oriented dream interpretation works with focusing on the body while working with the dream and waiting for a "felt shift" to occur that signals resolution.

Updates: Cognitive Approaches to Dreams

As cognitive and behavioral theories reached a peak, it was only a matter of time before they would produce approaches to dream work. Two of the better-researched approaches are those of Rosalind Cartwright and Hill. Cartwright's method is labeled RISC and focused on research suggesting that people have more dreams (and more bad dreams) when in crisis. Each letter stands for a step in the process. "R" stands for the first step—that of recognizing you are having a bad dream, which really requires that clients develop a lucid dreaming ability. The "I" represents the second step, which is when the dreamer identifies what in the dream is related to feeling badly. Usually these are feelings of weakness, vulnerability, threat, or inadequacy. The "S" represents the third step and stands for stopping the bad dream. This requires not only a lucid dreaming ability but also the acceptance that you really are the writer, producer, director, and star of the dream. Finally, the "C" stands for changing the negative dream dimensions to their more positive antithesis.[150]

Hill has done extensive research and clinical application of her cognitive-experiential model of dream formation and dream interpretation. She has approached her model researching both the client[151] and therapist[152] experiences using the model as well as the impact on the "we" of relationships related to dream work in the sessions.[153] Hill calls her theory the Cognitive-Experiential Model of Dream Formation and Interpretation. As seen here, in many ways Hill's model of dreams posits a self-system very similar to that of Loevinger and Cook-Greuter.

More than 20 studies use Hill's three-stage model. Hill sets forth an origin of dreams that is based on cognitive psychology. Cognitive researchers proposed that we create and maintain maps of the world that manifest as structures labeled *schemas* or *schemata*. Before going further, I offer some background on this idea of *schemas* or *schemata* (I use schemas for the plural). Schemas were described by Piaget as early as 1926 and referred to cognitive frameworks that govern the approach to problem solving and the way a person assimilates information.[154] Piaget's idea of assimilation is important in Hill's theory of dream work and will be important in the AQAL or Integral approach to dream work.

The neglected work of Edward Tolman in the first part of the 20th century was overshadowed by the behavioral psychologies that neither accounted for his findings nor ever led to anything resembling a theoretical approach. Tolman discovered that rats would learn a maze equally well whether they walked, swam, or were wheeled through it. This challenged the behavioral idea that behaviors had to be enacted and reinforced before learning could occur. Tolman concluded that the rats (and human beings) created cognitive maps of their environment and maneuvered it more by mentalist action than mere behavior.[155] In this sense, Tolman qualifies as a forerunner of what we now call *cognitive psychology*.

The anointed founder of cognitive psychology, Ulric Neisser, described schemas as internal structures that are specific to objects of perception.[156] In psychotherapy, we think of schemas as cognitive maps that point the direction of our thoughts (positive or negative).[157] Schemas have been described so variously that one doing a full literature review of the construct may wonder if there is any construct there at all. All existing definitions are very similar to the definitions of "faculties" offered by early psychologists like Thomas Reid. The best summary of a schema and its relation to self is by Daniel Robinson, who writes that schemas are cognitive in nature, not perceptual. In this sense, there has to be a sense of self to cogitate on perceptions for cognition to occur and influence schemas.[158]

Schemas and cognition (as noted earlier) are connotative and perception is denotative. For example, most adults recognize that a stop sign means something other than being a red octagon with the word "stop" on it. No one who understands a stop sign sits ad infinitum waiting for a "go" sign to appear. Mere perception is not the defining feature of a schema. It is in the cognitive meaning and understanding of certain laws of thought that schemas derive their power.

In Hill's theory of dream work, schemas comprise and generate themes or patterns to our experience and they are in essence cognitive, emotional, and behavioral. From her cognitive perspective, only details to which we attend in our waking lives are encoded as memories. Encoded events that are salient to us and thought about a great deal assume more importance in our schemas or maps of the world. The more a memory resurfaces and is thought about, the more resistant it is to fading away. Conversely, the less we recall a memory, the more likely it changes, distorts, or fades over time. The more erudite therapist will recognize here David Hume's notion that "every simple idea has a simple impression which resembles it and every simple impression, a correspondent idea."[159]

Schemas have individual elements called nodes or units. Elements are interconnected throughout a schema in a way that units that are closely related for a person are said to have an excitatory connection and those that are unrelated for a person are said to have inhibitory connections. Continual activation of a connection strengthens it and lack of use weakens it. In this way, people's reactions to waking events are thought by cognitive therapists to be based on what is stored in their schemata. Although little work has been done to explore this, it is reasonable to assume that one's ego identity is directly related to what is thus stored because ego or proximate self is how one defines what is self, what is other, and thus what is relevant to self. It equally stands to reason that as one's ego identity evolves, one's schemas evolve with it. In this case, schema theory gives us a metaphor that could be used to research the content of people's dreams at different levels of ego identity.

Getting back to Hill's model, based on the cognitive assumptions just discussed, she feels that our reactions to waking events can then trigger memories of similar reactions we had to similar events earlier in our lives. This of course is classic Freudian transference dressed in cognitive language. For Hill's purposes, she draws on evidence that dreams are often triggered by issues that are important to us in waking life. What happens in waking life can be congruent or discrepant with what is in our schemas. When what happens in waking life is congruent, we assimilate it in Piagetian fashion. When what happens in waking life is discrepant, it may cause distress. We can either accommodate it (find new ways of thinking about it) or deny/distort the event to fit our schema. Again, the relation to ego identity is clear as this notion of assimilation and accommodation is exactly what Loevinger detailed in her theory of the levels of ego identity.[160]

Hill believes that when we go to sleep, the schemas activated by the day's events may still be aroused and the ones that are likely to show up in dreams are the events we could not assimilate and had to deny or distort. Hill feels we think about these problems during non-rapid eye movement sleep and make stories about them (dream) in rapid eye movement (REM) sleep.

Thus, we dream about the issues that concerned us most, gave us the most pleasure, or stimulated us most during the day . . . our dreams thus appear to be a mechanism by which we try to process the salient information and emotions that have occurred to us and attempt to fit them into the appropriate schemata. . . . In this way, dreams seem to afford us the opportunity to work through emotions and problems that occur during waking life.[161]

Hill's three stages of dream work are exploration, insight, and action. In exploration the goals are to help the client become re-immersed in the dream, learn about the dream, and build/maintain the therapeutic alliance. The tasks are for the client to retell the dream in the present tense, explore emotions, associate with dream images, link images to waking life, and work with conflict. In the insight stage, the goals are to use the exploration material to facilitate understanding, try to determine the meaning of the dream for the client, and help the client accommodate the new information. The tasks of the insight stage are to introduce the stage by asking about the dream's meaning and restating the dream using associations from the exploration stage. The task of assisting the client with the meaning of the dream may come from four levels of interpretation: dream experience, relation to waking events, relation to past memories, or the dream as representing aspects of self. Finally, in the action stage data from the previous stages are used to facilitate change in the client's life and action is used to consolidate changes in schemata. The tasks at this stage are choosing the type of action (e.g., changing the dream in fantasy or while dreaming), continuing to work with the dream, behavioral or life changes, and having the client summarize what he or she has learned from the dream.

*Lucid Dreaming**

*Thanks to my colleague Alia Lawlor for her co-authorship of this section.

The phrase *lucid dreaming* is attributed to Dutch psychiatrist Frederick Van Eeden[162] and Hervey Saint-Denys who was introduced earlier in this chapter. Lucid dreaming is the experience of dreaming and being explicitly aware that we are dreaming.[163] As in defining all psychological constructs there are differences of opinion as to how lucid dreaming should be defined. Some insist that there should be control of the dream and recall of waking life.[164] For therapeutic purposes, simply being aware that one is dreaming is a more resourceful definition because there may be instances where witnessing or other less aware types of lucidity have therapeutic import. Other states that are similar to lucid dreaming include OBEs and near-death experiences, but these do not appear to be the same state.

Lucid dreams appear more likely to occur late in the sleep cycle and almost always during REM sleep.[165] This implies an activated brain and lucid dreams have been correlated with high levels of presleep activity, emotional arousal, meditation, and intensive psychotherapy.[166] Interrupting the sleep cycle with 30 to 60 minutes of wakefulness also has been shown to correlate with a higher probability of lucid dreaming.[167] Many people find themselves in the midst of a lucid dream after puzzling over oddities in content and then deciding "I must be dreaming." People who recall more dreams also are more likely to dream lucidly because they have spent time making dream content an object of awareness.[168]

The most active contemporary scholar in lucid dreaming is psychologist Stephen LaBerge who has demonstrated in studies that lucid dreaming is a skill that can be learned[169] and that has unique physiological correlates.[170] As with meditation, lucid dreaming should *not* be used by those clients (or therapists) who have trouble distinguishing waking reality and constructions of the imagination. Lucid dreaming will not cause the practitioner to lose contact with consensual reality—on the contrary, lucid dreaming is another technique we can use to help make aspects of ourselves and our lives objects of awareness.[171]

Like degrees of alterations in consciousness, there are degrees of lucidity in dreams. In the most lucid dreams, the dreamers claim to be fully in possession of their cognitive faculties, can remember the conditions of waking life, and can act voluntarily in dreamscapes while remaining asleep. In other types, the dreamers witness themselves in the dream pointing to an actor/observer differential in lucid dreams. When working with dreams in Integral Psychotherapy (discussed later), the lucid observer has a built-in subject–object dynamic where the lucid actor is more embedded in the subject. For the most part, all dreams seem to have a single-mindedness about them.[172] No one reports "Well I was dreaming I was a cat and at the same time thought about dreaming of being a jackal." The exception to this is of course the lucid dream where the ability to make the dream an object of awareness allows for meta-cognition about how the plot or scenes should unfold.

Psychologist Paul Tholey has summarized the advantages of lucid dreaming for therapeutic work. First, because of lucidity the dream ego may take more risks than it would in waking reality. Second, the lucid dreamer can use lucidity to get in touch with therapeutically relevant times, places, and people while dreaming. Third, using dialogue with dream figures, the dream ego can explore personality and interpersonal dynamics. Finally, the dreamer can change the set or structure of a dream to more directly address therapeutic goals.[173] With regard to the use of lucid dreaming for therapeutic purposes, LeBerge and Gackenbach note that clients should be guided to self-integration before self-transcendence. There are a variety of techniques for learning how to dream lucidly and, in the next section on AQAL dream work, I include some of LaBerge's techniques from his book *Lucid Dreaming.*[174]

An AQAL Approach to Dream Work

Having reviewed some of the history of dream work as well as current models, I know explore an AQAL approach to dreams that can be used by Integral psychotherapists and that has a solid foundation in the psychological and psychotherapeutic literature on dreams. From an Integral perspective, dreams can be understood in terms of the self-system and frequently as a "subject–other" dynamic that has as its goal the increased probability of the "other" being made an object of awareness and owned by the subject. As discussed in Chapter 1, the main activity of any psychotherapy is to help clients make aspects of themselves or their lives objects of awareness.

Although the next chapter covers the notion of psychological address, I introduce it briefly here. The psychological address of the client can be thought of as the client's issues in and balance across the quadrants, the client's level of ego identity, any traits or types that the client identifies with and/or consistently manifests, and the preponderance (or lack) of any particular states. Prior to dream work, I have a sense of how the client balances across the quadrants. If contemporary theories are correct, dreams may reflect interpersonal concerns in more concrete form and/or may address intrapsychic concerns. This depends on where the client's "hotspots" are across the quadrants. My experience has been that clients with hotspots in the lower-left quadrant will present dreams with interpersonal themes that reflect those hotspots. Clients struggling with issues in the upper-left quadrant present dreams that appear to have both manifest and latent layers, although not in the strict Freudian sense of wish fulfillment.

Also, I define to other terms I use: *dream ego* and *dreamscape*. Simply put the dream ego is the sense of self in the dream. My experience with clients is that the dream ego may mirror the waking ego identity but may be radically different in either level or type.[175] With regard to types in general, we need to realize that women appear to have more interest in dream work[176] and that the sex tendencies play out in dreams when the dream ego is congruent with the waking ego (e.g., men have more aggressive dreams and women have more communal dreams).[177] In Integral dream work, I refer to the structure of the dream (lower-right quadrant/perspective) as the dreamscape (from the 1984 movie of the same name). The dreamscape structure, like the lower-right in waking life, appears to be one of the dominant variables in the phenomenological experience (upper-left) of the nonlucid dreamer.

In dream work, we start with the first-person narrative as long as the client's ego strength is adequate. In symptom sets that cause the client to have trouble differentiating consensus reality from fantasy, I actively discourage dream work.[178] I encourage clients to record dreams in the first-person present tense and bring their logs to sessions. For many reasons, about 50% of clients do not record their dreams. In some cases, this appears to be resistance and in other cases, people just feel too busy. Either way, when the client comes in with a dream we follow the steps listed here:

1. Go through the narrative with the client speaking in first-person, present tense.

2. Lay out the dream in the quadrants and assess how the dream ego "balances" across the quadrants.

3. If we have not already done so, assess the client's ego identity and ego strength as well as his or her cognitive center of gravity.

4. Based on the data from Step 3, craft an intervention that may include reworking the dream in the session, analyzing the meanings for the client, and designing experiments for the client to follow up with.

Exploring the AQAL approach to dream work is easiest with a case example. The following is the case of Janine, a client suffering from recurrent nightmares. Janine was a 23-year-old client with a history of PTSD related to being date-raped at age 20. Although Janine functioned fairly well, she socialized rarely, and suffered migraines. She felt the rapist had not gotten the punishment he deserved (1 year in prison, probation, fine, and a restraining order) and that her work was beginning to suffer because she could not concentrate. Her family situation was complex in that her family was very religious and did not approve of premarital sex. Their reactions to Janine hinted that they felt this was some sort of divine punishment. Janine also had nightmares in which she was being chased by the rapist. The nightmares were part of what is called re-experiencing phenomena, which means the person has "flashbacks" to the traumatic episode. In her dreams, Janine said she always feels weak, terrified, and helpless—the way she felt during the rape. In the dreams, she tries to run and can't because her legs are too weak. If she tries to strike her attacker, he easily stops and restrains her. She would have these types of dreams about two to three times a week. Figure 6.1 illustrates Janine's "hotspot" sheet.

An important precondition for dream work is that the client is actually getting restful sleep (meaning going through the whole sleep cycle described above, several times a night). I referred Janine to a psychiatrist colleague who had experience with clients who suffered from PTSD. He prescribed her a "cocktail" of low doses of amitriptyline (Elavil, a tricyclic antidepressant), carisaprodal (Soma,a muscle relaxer), and extended-release alprazolam (Xanax, a benzodiazepine). This combination would make Janine sleepy and increase the probability of sleeping through the entire cycle without running the risk for disrupting the cycle or of tolerance or dependence to the medications. After Janine reported sleeping better for several weeks, we began her dream work regimen.

First we explored the general dream using the quadrant/perspectives of the integral model. In the upper-left, Janine reported consistent fear or terror in the dream and anger upon waking. Her dream ego is syntonic with her waking ego. In the upper-right, the dream ego tried to act against the attacker but was always neutralized in her efforts to do so. In the lower-left, there is an enmity with the rapist in the dream—sort of the antithesis of a "therapeutic we" aimed for in therapy. There is also the "shared belief" in the dream that the dream is real. In the lower-right we might say that there is the structure

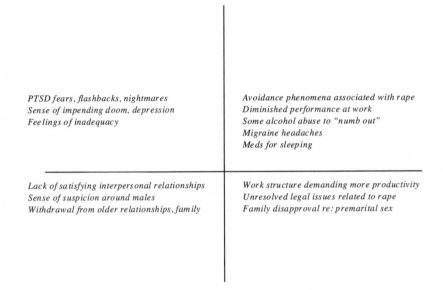

PTSD fears, flashbacks, nightmares
Sense of impending doom, depression
Feelings of inadequacy

Avoidance phenomena associated with rape
Diminished performance at work
Some alcohol abuse to "numb out"
Migraine headaches
Meds for sleeping

Lack of satisfying interpersonal relationships
Sense of suspicion around males
Withdrawal from older relationships, family

Work structure demanding more productivity
Unresolved legal issues related to rape
Family disapproval re: premarital sex

Figure 6.1. "Hotspot" sheet for Janine.

of the dreamscape itself or the "rules" for the dream state when the dream ego experiences itself as embedded in the dream. We refer to this simply as an "embedded" dreamscape (obviously dreamscapes can be lucid as well). In this case, the integral framework acts as a vehicle through which the client can distance herself from the dream and make aspects of it objects of awareness (without having to get too close).

As in all methods, Integral dream work includes a conscious recollection of the dream but in the integral method, after detailing the quadrants or perspectives with clients, I ask them to repeat the dream narrative, including the information delineated in the quadrants. Figure 6.2 (next page) illustrates how Janine laid out the nightmare using the perspectives of the quadrants. I also represent the self-system in the dream looking for whether the dream ego or proximate self is syntonic or dystonic, whether the shadow appears to be represented or embedded, and the quality of what is distal to the dream ego. Finally I note whether or not the antecedent self is experienced as subject, object, or embedded and not in any way an object of awareness.

When the client's ego is adequately boundaried, I ask him or her to describe the dream in the present tense. Typically, I then ask the client to comment on what comes to mind as he or she is describing the dream or immediately after finishing the description. In Janine's case she said "feeling stuck." As we

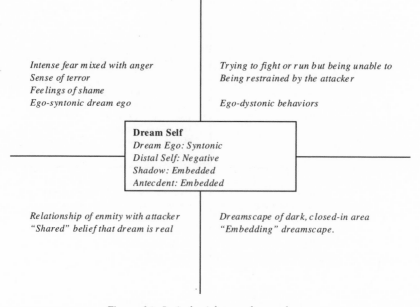

Intense fear mixed with anger
Sense of terror
Feelings of shame
Ego-syntonic dream ego

Trying to fight or run but being unable to
Being restrained by the attacker

Ego-dystonic behaviors

Dream Self
Dream Ego: Syntonic
Distal Self: Negative
Shadow: Embedded
Antecdent: Embedded

Relationship of enmity with attacker
"Shared" belief that dream is real

Dreamscape of dark, closed-in area
"Embedding" dreamscape.

Figure 6.2. Janine's nightmare by quadrant.

explored the "stuckness," it became more focused on feeling fearful and powerless in everyday life. Janine had come to an impasse. Further exploration confirmed the Jungian notion that she had come to therapy hoping the therapist (me in this case) knew the way out. As Jung also noted, if the therapist is honest he or she will admit not knowing the way but will employ his or her approach to help the client discover at least one way.[179]

Unlike Jungian therapy, in Integral psychotherapy, the self-system so succinctly outlined by Wilber can be used creatively in dream work. Janine had come to me because of a paper I had written on Integral Therapy and because I was generally familiar with Wilber's work. In light of this, I asked her if she would experiment with me on her dream and she readily agreed. In exploring her feelings of fear and weakness in the dream she indicated what she wanted to feel was strong. Although I had "prescribed" lucid dreaming exercises for Janine,[180] she had still not had lucidity in the repeating nightmare. We agreed that the fear and weakness, far from symbolizing anything esoteric, were direct correlations with how she felt while awake.

In contrast to Freud's theory, there is ample evidence that dreams are directly related to waking concerns.[181] Waking concerns, as noted by Loevinger, Cook-Greuter, and Wilber are filtered through the way a person differentiates self and other, which we call *ego* or *proximate self*. If we allow the assumption that our cognitive maps of the world (our schemas) are directly related to ego identity, we then have a starting point for working with clients' dreams in Integral Psychotherapy. Janine's ego identity tested out at late Achiever and it was this Achiever identity that was sorely tested in her dream ego. With regard to her dream, I asked Janine what would help her balance across the quadrants and she replied "strength and power in the upper-left [quadrant]." Hence, our next task was set for us.

Although researchers have demonstrated that dreams are far more directly related to waking concerns than Freud believed, the fact that the self-system is still authoring, producing, directing, and starring in the dreams helps explain why many dream images and experiences have highly symbolic and at times a hauntingly ineffable quality about them. From psychodynamic and cognitive perspectives aspects of self can be split off. These may be repressed memories (psychodynamic) or memories underlying a schema. Although Jung's theories about archetypes allowed for a far richer exploration of dreams than Freud's system, we need not revert to archetypes as long as we have shadow—golden or otherwise. From an Integral perspective, what is "other" in the dream may be part of self, including others that are threatening.

That said, an Integral therapeutic perspective does not insist that "others" are always a part of the self. Sometimes, dreams about co-workers are dreams about co-workers. From the perspective of contemporary research, real "others" who occupy a place in our waking concerns will show up in our dreams. We know that the self develops dialectically in the sense that we refine our sense of self based on feedback from others. There also is evidence that this process occurs in dreams dealing with interpersonal themes. As early as 1966, researchers confirmed that people dreamed about their views and feelings of other people.[182] Recent research confirms that dreams presented in therapy are frequently filled with interpersonal concerns.[183] Whether it is more resourceful to experience these as aspects of the self depends on both the client's psychological address, including level of ego identity, and presenting problem.

In Janine's case, it seemed most resourceful to allow the dream rapist to be "other." In exploring what Janine needed, we brainstormed a number of totem animals. The image that stood out for Janine was bees—thousands of bees stinging the attacker to death. This was a good image for several reasons. First, it arose spontaneously for Janine; second, it helped her metabolize some of the rage she still felt about the rape; and third, it satisfied a criteria of relentlessness that she wanted in her weapon against the attacker. We worked with the image in directed imagery and Janine finished the dream imaginatively with the bee scenario.

While practicing her lucidity exercise 2 weeks later, Janine realized she was actually dreaming. She reported feeling amazed and a sense of wonder seemed to override the nightmare for that night. Although the lucidity experience did not last long, it was an empowering experience for Janine as well as a nice break from the nightmares. Two nights later she had the nightmare with a small change—in the nightmare she was trying to run and found her legs weakening. This time, however, she found a car with keys in it and drove away. As she drove the rapist ran after her, keeping up with the car about 10 yards behind, but not gaining. She awoke from the dream at this point. The obvious difference here was the dream ego had some help. When describing the car, Janine said "it was old—I was afraid it would work because it hadn't been used for so long." At this point we reworked the dream in the quadrants adding the car as a structure in the lower-right quadrant. In this iteration, she added determination and concentration in the upper-left—these qualities emerging when she was using the car to get away. This is a good example of one relationship between the perspectives/quadrants that seems to hold in dream work. As noted in Chapter 1, the structures in the lower-right will have a major impact on the average mode of consciousness in the upper-left. This seemed to play out for Janine.

She continued to practice her lucidity exercise and reported two more brief, but powerful lucid dream experiences over the next week. We added a presleep suggestion that Janine wrote in her dream log: "Tonight I'll be able to call on the bees." After 10 days of using this suggestion, she found herself in the same dream and instead of running she tried to scream "Bees!" as loud as possible but found her voice no louder than a whisper. At this point she woke up, but this was another experience of some degree of control in the dreamscape. Although the dream ego continued to experience weakness and vulnerability, there was a conscious decision to bring in an element she had decided on during a waking state.

At this point, we were 9 months into treatment. In 1 week that month, Janine saw six bees (one at a time) in her house. Each one of them appeared at dusk and flew into the top of her halogen lamp, incinerating itself. She commented on this at a session, noting it sounded like what Carl Jung referred to as synchronicity or meaningful coincidence.[184] I agreed it certainly sounded like that and we continued with the session, spending most of it reviewing successes she had with other practices including accepting some social invitations. I had a message from her the next morning asking if she could schedule something as soon as possible. I arranged a session that evening and Janine came in quite energized holding her dream journal.

The journal held her dream recollections, sketches of the dream elements by quadrants, and other reflections. She held open a section and asked me to read it. The section is partially quoted here with her permission:

I am on the street running from him again but this time I seemed to have more energy. I happened to glance at my hands while running and suddenly stopped. As he gained on me I asked myself if I was awake or dreaming and I realized I was dreaming! At this point I turned and he was almost upon me. I screamed "BEES!" loudly and the scream turned into the buzzing of a swarm of thousands of bees. They had teeth rather than stingers and they devoured him. I was at first stunned as I watched these bees devour every inch of my attacker; then I felt ecstatic joy and strength. I thought I was going to pass out so much energy was surging through my body. At this point the swarm melded together into a golden light that pulsed with the beat of my heart. The glow became brighter and brighter embracing the scene, the street, and me. I felt a cool breeze and realized I was sitting on a beautiful rocky ledge high up in the mountains watching the sunrise. I woke up crying again but this time tears of joy, gratitude, and a sense of coming home.

Well. How can one use words to describe a breakthrough like this? Since the task here is predominantly instructive, I try to unpack this a bit using the Integral model. Like Jung, I don't come at a dream knowing anything other than tools to help the client metabolize it. Let's turn one more time to the AQAL analysis of this iteration of the nightmare.

If the dreamscape is structural it requires certain tools available to the proximate self in the self-system. Based on discussion with Janine it appeared that her lucidity practice and her enormous efforts in therapy laid the basis for this dreamscape—these provided the tools. Although this dream (like all dreams) could be interpreted in any number of ways, Janine and I agreed on the following:

1. She had laid the basis for it with her practices and work in therapy. This was perfectly syntonic with her achiever ego identity.

2. Her accomplishment with lucidity and therapy coincided with tools that may be interpreted as antecedent in nature (what Jung would likely have labeled related to the self archetype).

3. While the ego-dystonic sense of the attacker had to be dealt with, the antecedent bees ingested and transformed the attacker so as to be able to be integrated on some level in Janine.

Similar to the transformation of the dream ego, what was most noticeable was the transformation of Janine's waking ego. After this dream, she went from being a struggling achiever to a thriving achiever. The nightmares never recurred in the same sense (if they did recur she woke herself up or was able to exercise lucidity). Her overarching PTSD symptoms decreased to the point where it appeared that she had integrated the trauma and made meaning to the extent that it was able to become distal in her day-to-day awareness.

In reviewing this case we certainly could examine it from multiple theoretical frameworks. What I hope I have illustrated is that the Integral framework holds the interpretation lightly while allowing all useful tools from other frameworks to be used. It also supplies a straightforward set of tools in the self-system and its functions. The structure allows the dream states to be compared with waking states using the "hotspots" sheet and it includes in its assumptions a mechanism of transcendence that is developmental as well as state-related. In the final section, I examine psychedelics or entheogens in a similar manner to dreams.

Chemical Alterations of Consciousness: Chemically Induced States and Integral Psychotherapy

Chemically induced states and chemical alterations of consciousness are older than recorded history and paradoxically embedded in U.S. culture. They persist because the evidence suggests that a significant percentage of human beings like to change their state of consciousness. This is not limited to our species, but we limit discussion here to human beings. The evidence on human societies has led pharmacologist Ronald Seigel to postulate that the desire to change our state of consciousness is a fourth drive.[185] If this is true, there are certainly ways to induce alterations in consciousness with nonchemical techniques[186] but for many, the chemical techniques remain a mainstay because of their intensity and (allowing for set and setting) their consistency.

Although government agencies foolishly continue to disseminate misinformation on some drugs, government representatives depend on the lobbying money from pharmaceutical companies for their very livelihood. Many U.S. children walk into their school buildings under banners proclaiming "Drug Free School!" only to march straight to the nurse's office for their daily dose of some mind-altering medication. The United States and New Zealand are the only countries in the world where pharmaceutical companies can market prescription medications directly to consumers. This so-called direct-to-consumer marketing is responsible for exponential market shares for drugs so marketed. Currently, psychotropic prescriptions for children have more than tripled since the 1990s and currently 8% to 11% of all children in the United States receive prescriptions for psychotropic medication, despite the fact that there is a dearth of literature on the efficacy of these medications with children.[187] Additionally, the United States per capita has more of its citizens in prisons than any other industrial or postindustrial country. Almost 40% of prisoners in the United

States are in prison for nonviolent drug offenses.[188] I think it can be said that as far as beliefs about drugs go, the United States is as diseased a society as has ever existed on the planet. I like to think that we are at least beginning a move toward stabilizing the patient (our society), but we have a long way to go.

I have addressed prescription psychotropic medications[189] at length in other publications and focus here on those chemical compounds (mostly illicit) that users report to be associated with mystical states and states with great import for psychotherapy. Why include this information on a book in psychotherapy? Even psychiatrists are restricted from using most of these agents by federal law. There are three reasons I want to include this information. First, no literature on states and psychotherapy can even approach completion without including what we have learned from these compounds. Second, many clients presenting for psychotherapy have had a relevant experience (positive or negative) under the influence of one of these agents and may wish to discuss it. Finally, the turn toward a saner approach to illicit drugs has been heralded by a loosening of government restrictions on scientific studies using these agents. They have much to teach us. One example is the use of psychedelics in terminal cancer patients with results suggesting that these agents help patients prepare for and engage the dying process, as well as provide significant pain relief.[190]

This section of the chapter focuses on drugs that have variously been referred to as psychedelics, hallucinogens, psychointegrators, and entheogens. In 1957, Humphrey Osmond coined the term *psychedelic* these agents.[191] The Greek roots of psychedelic basically mean "mind-manifesting." Although the term is not without problems, it appears to be the broadest umbrella term for a range of more than 100 species of plants and dozens of chemical agents. *Hallucinogen* is a culturally loaded term implying that the experiences people have under the influence of a drug are not "real" in any sense.[192] Most people report illusions far more than hallucinations.[193] The term *entheogen* was coined by Richard Schultes and Albert Hoffmann in their book *Plants of the Gods*.[194] The word literally means "god-manifesting" and although a significant number of people use the compounds to have mystical experiences, a large number do not. Finally, the word *psychointegrator* was coined by anthropologist Michael Winkleman to reflect the neurological and experiential effects of these compounds. Winkleman stated that psychointegrators imply stimulation of the body, the mind, the emotions, the soul and the spirit toward integration.[195] Although this is perhaps the best operationalized term in the literature, I stay with the term *psychedelics* because of its prominence in the literature reviews in both psychology and medicine.

Some final caveats[196]: Because I do endorse an Integral approach as the most comprehensive map available for working with clients, I advocate abstinence from illicit substances. First and foremost, in the lower-right quadrant the black market is the most common way people obtain these substances and it cannot be trusted to deliver a product with safe and reliable ingredients, potency, and dosage. Second, from the upper-left perspective, psychedelics can open areas of the mind you are not equipped to deal with and most people don't take psychedelics in the presence of a trained therapist. Third, even a client who has a "bad trip" and goes to find a therapist will not likely find one who has the training to deal with it. Until recently, drug abuse training has been based in the counselor's previous experience as a drug user and the government propaganda about drugs. Neither is a useful therapeutic resource. In some states (e.g., Ohio), there are Chemical Dependency Professionals Boards that have educational requirements for therapists, but this movement is very new. Fourth, from the upper-right perspective, there can be serious side effects from psychedelic drugs like uterine contractions that may cause miscarriage in pregnant women. Finally, developmentally not everyone is able to benefit from a psychedelic drug experience. It requires a person with a high level of openness, adequate ego development (at least mid-conventional), and good ego strength (meaning healthy boundaries).

What have we learned about the mind and psychotherapy from psychedelics?

In 2006, Roland Griffiths and his colleagues published a definitive study confirming that psilocybin can induce experiences reported to be mystical in nature and have substantial and sustained personal/spiritual meaning.[197] This was a double-blind study with controls, 2-month follow-up, and included self-report and reports from others in the subjects' lives. In the study conducted at Johns Hopkins University, 30 "hallucinogen-naïve" volunteers received 30 mg of oral psilocybin and were monitored for 8 hours. They were encouraged to close their eyes and direct their attention inward. More than 67% of the subjects had a mystical experience that they rated as the most important spiritual experience of their lives or one of the top 5 most important.

In 2007, anthropologist Michael Winkelman and psychologist Thomas Roberts published a two-volume work on psychedelic medicine.[198] The work reviews numerous compounds including ayahuasca/ dimethyltryptamine, LSD, psilocybin, 3,4-methylenedioxy-N-methylamphetamine (MDMA; aka Ecstasy), ibogaine, ketamine, marijuana, and peyote. The contributors are some of the best minds in the field and include numerous scientists who have done or are doing government-approved work with these substances for psychotherapy, pain, so-called addictions, various types of headaches, and psycho-spiritual growth.

As with any psychological experience, there are multiple interpretations regarding the psychedelic experience. My aim here is to posit an Integral summary of the psychedelic experience that clinicians can use as a basis for working with clients who have had such an experience (the second aim with which I introduced this section). Drug states are like any other states in the sense that therapeutically we want to look at their fruits while not entirely ignoring the roots. It is difficult to give a summary of a "typical" psychedelic experience because the experience differs with the psychedelic used, the mindset of the user, and the setting in which use takes place. The first AQAL element in understanding a psychedelic is the four quadrants or perspectives. Clinicians who are working with clients who use psychedelics, are contemplating their use, or have used them in the past should go over the psychedelic of choice quadrant-by-quadrant just like in the dream work described in the previous section.

Therapeutically, I recommend starting with the upper-left quadrant and exploring with the client the experience he or she had or the experience he or she expects. In many cases, the basis of the "good trip" is the experience of getting outside of what Alan Watts called "the skin-encapsulated ego."[199] This experience can allow one's sense of self to transcend bodily form and the identity of the proximate self and meld with others (both those suffering and those in ecstasy) or with other creatures (e.g., totem animals) or with various plants or minerals or the earth itself.[200] These are classed as experiences in types of empathy by some researchers and although the empathy in question is quite different than what we might recognize as such in waking consciousness, the term seems accurate.[201] Perhaps one of the classic descriptions of such experiences (without the imposition of a theoretical framework) is in a book by natural foods advocate Adelle Davis (written under the name Jane Dunlap.[202] Davis (aka "Dunlap") describes a session where she identified with creatures from our long lineage going through billions of years of evolution. For her, this was a breathtaking experience that added to her sense of the sanctity of life.

If the client had a "bad trip" or negative experience it is equally important to run the experience quadrant by quadrant. Stanislav Grof made a compelling case for the idea that "bad trips" are the result of complexes that he calls systems of condensed experience (COEX systems). COEX systems function like transference reactions where something that is similar to a trauma triggers these repressed memories and as they come to the fore of consciousness symptoms appear. In the case of a "bad trip," the psyche's defenses are chemically dismantled and the person's unconscious contents come spilling out (what Grof refers to as the effects of psychedelics being nonspecific amplifiers of consciousness). If a well-meaning but ignorant medical or psychological professional tries to stop the trip experience, it essentially freezes the person in the bad trip with negative, previously repressed materials frozen as objects of awareness. In such a case, the symptoms persist or return in a form of rebound, which is mistakenly attributed to the chemical rather than the psyche (e.g., the "flashback" phenomenon). Grof's clinical approach is to support the client through the symptoms (or flashbacks as the case may be) and allow the organism to heal itself through metabolizing these intrapsychic elements.[203] From an Integral point of view, Grof's work is enabling one of the functions of a healthy self-system—that of metabolism. Repression of trauma or fixation on trauma via an interrupted "bad trip" in this case intensifies symptoms. Accessing what we are calling an altered state (what Grof calls a nonordinary state) allows for the completion of the metabolic process.

From the upper-right quadrant you include any behavioral or physiological sequelae from whatever psychedelic was ingested, but it also is important to do some client education around the pharmacodynamics and pharmacokinetics of the psychedelic. Pharmacodynamics are the mechanisms of drug action in the body and pharmacokinetics are how the body reacts to and on the drug eventually eliminating it from the system. In most cases, we don't know the full picture in either case (and this goes for prescription psychotropic drugs as well). However this is also a good point to address *how* the client knows what the drug he or she took was.

One client (Ethan) enjoyed taking Ecstasy (MDMA) at raves. MDMA is a chemical cousin of the amphetamine but in this molecular version it produces profound experiences of empathy. It is sometimes referred to as an empathogen or an enactogen[204] which, in the right conditions, "reduces or somehow eliminates the neurophysiological fear response to a perceived threat to one's emotional integrity . . . with this experience of fear eliminated, a loving and forgiving awareness seems to occur quite naturally and spontaneously."[205] Ethan had four such experiences but during the fifth he felt anxious and somewhat paranoid. He spent the evening trying to calm down. The bottom line was that it appears Ethan did not take MDMA the fifth time but instead ingested an amphetamine. He did not recall the exact marking on the pill but he was surprised that it had a pharmaceutical imprint on it. Through researching the description in the Physician's Desk Reference we concluded he was given a moderate dose of methylphenidate (Ritalin—a stimulant used to treat narcolepsy and attention-deficit hyperactivity disorder). Although Ethan was lucky not to suffer any long-lasting side effects, he finally understood that even if he trusted his friends, he could in no way trust the people who supplied the drug to his friends without knowing how, when, where, and who made it.

This brings us to the lower quadrants. With clients I try to explore the shared beliefs about the use of psychedelics (or any drugs) and whether there is a system of shared beliefs in the people with whom the client identifies and spends time. Again, the beliefs that can be made objects of awareness by exploring this quadrant are quite various ranging from healthy community (beliefs associated with rituals involving peyote, ibogaine, and ayahuasca) to the unhealthy and fragmented beliefs of those who use drugs to numb themselves from awareness of waking reality. In the lower-right quadrant certainly the laws and the black market have to be addressed. Here I have seen a profound contradiction in many clients who want to pursue expanded consciousness but are supporting a criminal black market and placing themselves (and possibly their families) at risk for prosecution under the existing laws which, although unreasonable, are still the laws. Exploring the contradiction here can reveal what Wilber calls a pre-/transfallacy. In some instances clients who are supposedly concerned with saving the world have, at least, a preconventional shadow that responds to any limits with a "fuck you" attitude. This can be a valuable area to explore in therapy and the help the client make safe choices.

Finally, it is important to understand the relationship of psychedelics to developmental concerns and state stages in general. First, we know that in order to transcend the ego, there must be an ego to start with.[206] Second, that ego must be part of a functioning self-system that can metabolize what life feeds it or translate in a healthy manner regardless of the level it inhabits. We hear a lot of government rhetoric about keeping kids off drugs but of course one of the most important reasons to do this is never mentioned—in most cases, the self-system of children and adolescents is too labile and not stable enough to survive a chemically induced hyper-drive out of the world of the familiar and into the essence or structure of consciousness itself. This is not emphasized because the next logical conclusion is that of course there are adults who do have the self-system stability to benefit from such a journey. In the current climate the only people allowed to speak about their drug experiences are those who were not prepared for them. Developmentally, it seems that a client should be at least at mid-conventional (Expert) in terms of ego identity and ideally at least post-formal operational in cognitive ability.

With a new era of psychedelic study beginning, we can only hope that the scientific spirit will prevail and substances that consistently prove to have therapeutic value will eventually be moved to Schedule II allowing supervised medical use. Until that time we have much to learn in from the research that is ongoing with psychedelics and what we learn should enhance how states can be used in Integral Psychotherapy.

Conclusion

We have covered a lot of ground in this chapter and have only skimmed the surface. Whole volumes can and have been written about the various states discussed here and their use in psychotherapy. Although states are only one component of Integral Psychotherapy, I hope I have given readers a sense of the breadth and depth of states, some of the rules that apply to states, and their application in psychotherapy. This is the last AQAL element that we cover in isolation from the others. Now we move on to pulling it all together in the final two chapters, which cover the client's psychological address and the place of spirituality in Integral Psychotherapy.

7

Psychological Address

R. ELLIOTT INGERSOLL

In his 2006 book *Integral Spirituality*, Wilber set forth the metaphor of *Kosmic address* that referred to altitude plus perspective.[1] The basic idea was to offer a metaphor that, like the metaphor *center of gravity*, helped us understand how a person (ourselves or others) was translating his or her life experience. The idea was that things may exist that may not register in human consciousness (or a particular human's conscious experience) because that consciousness has not evolved the tools to apprehend the thing that exists. At the same time, some things must be co-constructed with consciousness to actually exist in some form (e.g., linguistic representations of complex systems). Wilber noted that he uses the metaphor of ladder, climber, and view to describe development. The climber is the self-system described in Chapter 3. Wilber's use of "altitude" can be thought of as rungs on a ladder. The more rungs you climb, the higher your altitude and the better your view. At the psychological level, the metaphor of psychological address includes a client's perspective-taking ability (generally referred to as cognitive ability), the client's ego identity (or level of ego development), typological or stylistic variables important to the client, states impinging on the client, and relevant elements from the four quadrants that the self is nested in. That in a nutshell is what I mean by psychological address. This is a metaphor I find helpful when working with clients. The goal of the psychological address is to simplify to a "snapshot" the complex Integral view of a client (or therapist) in psychotherapy. If clinicians find this useful I encourage them to decide whether or not the particular constructs I am wed to work for them. If not, they should construct their own version of psychological address. As long as clinicians address cognition, self, types, states, and the four quadrants the psychological address will be more or less complete. The next part of this chapter discusses the basic elements in the psychological address and how clinicians (or the interested lay reader) can create their own version.

The Basic Elements of the Psychological Address

Perspective-Taking or Cognition

As noted in Chapter 2, if cognition can be defined as what you are aware of (or can be aware of), then ego identity can be defined as of the things you are aware of, what do you identify with or consider "I?" Perspective-taking ability or cognition in this sense is necessary but not sufficient for ego development. Both Loevinger and Wilber have asserted this point. An example may be helpful. When I was in elementary school, we had large maps of the world in each classroom that depicted the United Soviet Socialist Republic (USSR). On the maps as I recall them, the USSR was proportionately much larger than the United States. At the time, Communism was presented as embodied in the USSR and believed by many to be the greatest threat to our society. As a child barely out of preoperational thinking, I remember looking at the map, seeing how much bigger the USSR was on the map than the United States and thinking "we're in trouble." My cognition at that time did not include awareness of cartography, the debates on how to create a map legend let alone the distortions that occur in Mercator projections.[2] My concrete interpretation certainly increased my fear of the USSR and strengthened my identity as "American."

As I developed I learned that in fact what I see on a map may be a more or less accurate depiction of what the map is supposed to convey. I know that there are multiple ways to create a map, that the process is very political and that it is important to know the politics behind the map. My identity is much more fluid now and more dependent on my firsthand experience of the context rather than secondhand information given to me by others. This gives my sense of self more fluidity than I had back in first or second grade and that fluidity rests on perspective-taking or cognitive abilities.

Some sense of cognition is always the first aspect of psychological address. If we carry the metaphor of address to its logical end, we might say that cognition gives us a sense of what is possible in a given neighborhood. Urban neighborhoods, for example, usually are well placed near cities in order to allow occupants access to the cultural riches that cities possess. They are not, however, good sites for amateur astronomers because the artificial lighting will obscure the view of the night sky. So what is possible based on a client's cognition? That is an answer clinicians should be able to get from the client's psychological address.

Having said that, however, most therapists I know do not do a formal cognitive assessment unless there is a specific reason to. Such assessments can be costly but for the most part, therapists rely on their general understanding of cognition and perspective-taking when making decisions about a client's cognitive abilities. There is evidence that intelligence testing can be useful but can also be easily misused even by well-intentioned clinicians.[3] Yale psychologist Robert Sternberg noted that states of mind (the topic of the last chapter) can play an enormous role in testing intelligence. Sternberg has proposed a construct called successful intelligence that is supposedly broader than general intelligence and defined as the ability to achieve success in life in terms of your personal standards within your sociocultural context.[4] By emphasizing cognitive ability I am not necessarily limiting myself to the elusive construct of intelligence. Although intelligence tests can be helpful in determining a client's level of cognitive ability (ala Piaget) they are only one of several options.[5]

Most frequently it appears that clinicians rely on their own sense of the client's cognitive abilities based on therapeutic dialogue. By way of example, let me share some case excerpts. One client, Isaiah, was ordered in to treatment by the courts as part of his early release from prison following conviction on a drug trafficking charge. Isaiah presented in the manner attributed to opportunists, as described in Chapter 3. He was quiet, watchful, and appeared impatient with my silences. At one point in the session, he noted that being out of prison and assigned to a job solved two problems for him. I commented somewhat absent-mindedly "Yeah, that killed two birds with one stone" and he said "What' you talking about birds for? I wanna know what to do next?" Here was a clue that Isaiah's cognitive skills seemed to lean more toward the concrete rather than the abstract.

Another client, Jackson, presented in a totally different manner. When I asked him about his goals, he chuckled then said, "You know, stay clean, come clean, keep my nose clean—all that saintly cleanliness that our society seems to love so much." In contrast to Isaiah, Jackson seemed to have quite a store of abstract cognitive ability and further exploration bore that out. In this sense, Jackson's cognitive neighborhood gave him access to more opportunities than Isaiah's cognitive neighborhood. In subsequent ego development testing, Jackson tested out at the pluralistic level, which was unusual for the population of inmates with whom I had been working.

The clinical question remains as to the ethics and wisdom of "guesstimating" cognitive ability in this manner. Although I never use such "guesstimates" in reports to the court, I do find them helpful particularly in dialogue with clients. With clients like Isaiah, I avoid metaphors, allegories, similes, and language that require abstract thinking ability. Part of meeting clients where they are is, to some extent, mirroring their language to some extent. In some cases, a client like Isaiah will share more as time goes on and reveal that what seemed like concrete thinking was really caution about me and the therapeutic relationship. If this is the case, I can adjust accordingly. Clinicians who are curious about this notion of psychological address need only decide what they base their sense of the client's cognitive ability on. Some will only feel comfortable with formal tests and if they are a routine part of those clinicians work so much the better.

Others will want to reflect on how they make sense of how the client sees the world and that includes cognition. Many will find that they have never really thought about *how* they do it—they just do it.

Ego Development

The next component in the psychological address is how the client thinks about her or himself. I have found the SCTi to be an excellent tool in giving me a glimpse of how the client sees the self and reacts to life. Because the test has acceptable degrees of validity and reliability, I invested in learning how to administer and score the SCTi through Cook-Greuter & Associates. Another question that remains, however, is the extent to which a formal assessment of ego identity is necessary to, again, "guesstimate" generally whether the client has a preconventional, conventional, or postconventional sense of self.

We are currently (at the time of this writing) conducting a study on this at Cleveland State University. Study subjects agree to take the SCTi and then do a 30- to 40-minute recorded counseling session with me. We score the SCTi and then send the recorded counseling session to others trained in the use of the SCTi. We are asking these experts what they guess the client's level of ego identity is based on the 30 to 40 minutes of counseling. The theory behind this is that the client's ego identity may be conveyed to the trained listener in the way the client uses language. As Cook-Greuter wrote, "language not only 'reflects' human experience, but it also organizes and filters it . . . the premise that language is constitutive of experience is a cornerstone of ego-development theory."[6] People trained in ego development and administering/scoring the SCTi should, theoretically, be able to discern a client's general level if, all things being equal, the client feels comfortable and feels he could "be himself" with me in the session (this is checked by a post-session questionnaire). The outcome of this study will lend validity to the idea that simply studying ego development may help a clinician become more accurate in assessing the client through therapeutic dialogue.

I am well aware that different therapists have different concepts of how to describe the self. My point here is not to debate the merits of one over another but to assert it is an essential part of this overarching idea of psychological address. I prefer ego development for many reasons, but there may be others who prefer to conceptualize self based on what we call a *self-related line*. As discussed in Chapter 4, these may be labels that come from Kegan's orders of consciousness, Kohlberg's theory of moral development, Lectical Assessment,[7] or even Clare Graves' metaphor of spiral dynamics. As noted throughout the book, however, a therapist is bound to practice using constructs that have been subjected to study and operationalized based on research. Spiral dynamics is not such a construct and, although it could function as a useful metaphor, therapists are advised to rely on constructs with research that supports their validity (recall that validity is the extent to which a construct describes what it claims to describe).

What about broader philosophical constructs like Wilber's levels of consciousness? Although I respect these as philosophical works based on Wilber's encyclopedic understanding of psychological and spiritual traditions, I do not believe he ever intended them to be used as psychological constructs proper. His work is groundbreaking in that he is using language to point to the evolution of consciousness and in this respect he has been quite successful. In psychotherapy, however, we are in a different game and the game rules require that, to the extent possible, we work with constructs we can test.

This does not mean we cannot address concepts like "spirituality" in psychotherapy. We can, but we must remain open or undecided on the ontological status of such concepts beyond the reality of our own experiences or as psychological facts of existence. This is discussed in greater depth in Chapter 8, but this notion of something that is potentially trans-psychological being a psychological fact of existence goes back to Carl Jung in his Terry Lectures at Yale University. Jung noted that psychological facts were those that pointed to the existence of concepts or ideas that people claimed had an impact on their lives. Jung used the idea of the motif of the virgin birth as an example. To speak of the fact that there is such an idea rather than trying to prove or disprove its historicity is to speak of the psychological fact of existence. Similarly, what Jung called the *numinosum*[8] was a dynamic agency that seized control of its subject who is more its victim than creator.[9] As noted, this comprises the topic of the next chapter.

Types or Styles

Another component of psychological address is type or style, to the extent that the client identifies with it. Client identification with a concept seems the best way to proceed where the type or style is ego syntonic. As noted in Chapter 5, if a client comes to me saying "I'm an ENFJ," I will want to know what that means to her, the history of that idea for her, and the way she sees it as relevant to the aims she sets for therapy. Here again we can work with ego-syntonic type as an aspect of the client's style. One client (Alicia) shared that she had powerful insights from taking the Enneagram. Her results indicated a strong preference for Type 5, the "observer" or "thinker." As we talked about the relationship of this to her life, it was clear that her parents had always pushed her to be outgoing and to help others (more what could be described in Enneagram language as the "giver"). Here of course I had to keep open to her identification with the "observer" as a reaction formation[10] to the direction her parents wanted her personality style to take. Over the course of a couple

Integral Psychotherapy

sessions I could comfortably rule that out, as Alicia seemed to have made her parents' expectations an object of awareness and made her peace with them. At this point, her resonance with the type of the "observer" was helpful in challenging her and helping her benefit from therapy.

What about styles that are ego syntonic like the so-called personality disorders?[11] Here the first goal is to establish a therapeutic alliance with the client. In object-relations theory, the ideal for such clients is to be a stable object for them. This means conveying that within the parameters of therapy giving them the sense that you will be available and present to them. Clients meeting the criteria for disorders like BPD usually show up in therapy for other issues (e.g., mood, anxiety, or substance abuse problems). I have found in most cases clients have worked with me for anywhere from 3 to 8 months on symptoms related to depression, substance abuse, or anxiety before we got to the personality variables. Then it was usually a "bumpy ride" during which the client was deciding whether and how much to trust me. If the trust was adequate (it comes and goes) and the style is causing sufficient pain, the client often will work directly on the problematic style.

One such client was Dana, who initially came to see me for cocaine dependence. She was on probation for cocaine possession, having served 3 months in jail. Her family was supportive and able to provide her some money for living expenses and treatment. After 90 days in an intensive residential facility, Dana came out sober and we began treating her depression (much of which seemed related to her body "clearing" the drug),[12] as well as her relationships, which had always been stormy. After working with me for 3 months, Dana violated the terms of her probation and was facing more jail time or extended probation and counseling. She chose the latter and we continued.

We had been using dialectical behavior therapy in an Integral manner (complemented with exercise and some relaxation using a binaural beat technology). She was alternately fighting with or pleading with her family and finally hit a "bottom" emotionally, not so much around her drug use but her personality style. Growing up without a father, Dana had always had conflicted relationships with men. Her mother was so busy working she did not have a lot of time for Dana. When her mother remarried a relatively wealthy man, Dana simmered with anger and jealousy. It wasn't until she was able to talk about all this that she could start articulating what she really wanted from her family.

Dana will likely always be "intense" to say the least, but she didn't have to be a slave to her personality style. She completed 5 years of therapy and, at follow-up last year, was living what she considered to be a good life. She is still sober and has meaningful work and good relationships with her family. She still struggles with romantic relationships, but at least now feels she has the tools to deal with issues when they arise. A couple times a year we do a "booster" session, but for the most part Dana is able to negotiate life with her style. For

Dana, there was no getting around her style but it took a good deal of time before we could work with it directly. The tragedy is that in an era of scarce mental health resources, clients like Dana frequently don't have the support or money for such extensive therapy.

States

In thinking about states and their relation to the psychological address, we might draw the analogy that states are like the weather in the cognitive neighborhood inhabited by the client. There are regular patterns of weather in most neighborhoods but at times unexpected fronts move in that can disrupt the whole area. As far as states go, as noted in Chapter 6, I want to know of states related to symptoms and states that potentially may be part of the treatment. In Dana's case anxiety was a common state that was like a front that usually heralded a period of stormy weather. In teaching her how to use brief witnessing (the "wise-self" in dialectical behavior therapy), she learned that she was not her anxiety and had the choice as to whether or not she wanted to gain some distance from the anxiety. Here we see a trained state (witnessing) used to treat a symptomatic state. In our analogy of weather, if there was anything capable of changing the weather that would be trained states like witnessing, concentration meditation, or awareness meditation.

States in the psychological address also include what Wilber has referred to as subpersonalities. As noted in Chapter 3, this is a construct used by many therapists. For the purposes of psychological address the therapist must decide how she is going to think about or represent subpersonalities. Will she use Grof's COEX systems? Assagiloli's version of subpersonalities? Jung or Adler's complexes? Once the decision is made then the subpersonality is linked to the emotional state most correlated to its emergence. Recall in Chapter 3, Tasha's experience of humiliation waiting for her father to meet her in the restaurant after she got her driver's license. She pushed the experience out of awareness (and similar experiences over the years) to the point where the thing being pushed out of awareness took on a life of its own (a COEX system or subpersonality). From that point on, whenever this subpersonality emerged she would seek to protect herself from disappointment in relationships by seeking unavailable men. The underlying fear of disappointment was one of the primary emotional states driving this thus that state is included in the psychological address in the upper-left quadrant.

States may also be thought of as "coloring" the picture we paint of the client. In a manner akin to the portrait of Dorian Gray, the picture we paint of the client in different states changes tone and color. During a state of depression, the portrait may have a heavy, dark use of colors associated with it. During a state of mania, the portrait may be painfully bright. Teaching clients how to

mix and apply the paint to the portrait could be a metaphor for teaching them
states that they can use to decrease symptoms. Types persist and states arise and
fall away relative to the upper-left quadrant of the Integral quadrants. It is to
those quadrants that we now turn in our discussion of psychological address.

Psychological Address and the Four Quadrants

Bearing in mind all the information about the quadrants from the first three
chapters, I noted previously that in terms of psychological address the self-system
is nested in the four quadrants. In my notes I use a graph similar to that shown
in Fig. 7.1, which illustrates some of the "hotspots" in Dana's case.

I share these figures with clients when I feel it is resourceful to do so. In
Dana's case, the "painful emotions" in the upper-left quadrant and the reference to the "style not working" in the self-system oval represent the criteria
BPD that Dana did meet. I have found describing the aspects of the emotional
style that aren't working or are causing pain is a more effective way to start the
dialogue rather than retreating to the clinical labels, which where personality
are concerned, don't help the therapeutic relationship (e.g., "Your problem is

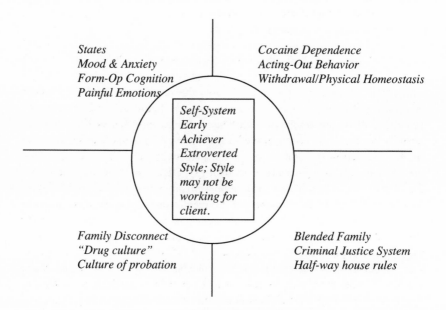

Figure 7.1. Dana's Integral psychological address.

that your whole personality is disordered"). At one time, Dana asked me "Do you think I'm a borderline?" I said "No, I think you suffer from a lot of the emotional pain described in that category but you are not your pain anymore than you are the category. That is why I won't refer to a client as a diagnostic label. Do you meet the criteria for what is called Borderline Personality Disorder? Yes but that is not who you are." After that she said, "PhD must mean pile it higher and deeper." We had a laugh about it, but continued to work with the distinction between labels and people.[13] For Dana, who was more than adequate in formal operational thinking and in many ways saw the world as achievers do, this work was fruitful. For clients like Isaiah (who think in more concrete terms), such dialogue would not likely be helpful (although where diagnosis is concerned I still insist that clients are not labels and try to convey that in developmentally appropriate ways).

In any psychological address, things like cognitive ability, ego identity, and personality style will remain more or less consistent. Elements that appear in the quadrants and things like states may come and go and change many times over the course of therapy. In Dana's case, her involvement with the criminal justice system diminished until she was off probation. She graduated from a half-way house that was highly structured, including regular drug testing to a three-quarter house and then to living independently with a sober roommate. In this sense, the illustrations of her psychological address shifted and changed as her life continued and her choices improved.

Psychological Address and the Spectrum of Pathology

As I noted early on, Wilber exhaustively researched the theories of psychogenic pathology and created a spectrum of psychopathology based on this research. Again, I want to emphasize that I believe it was never Wilber's intent to account for all psychological suffering through psychogenic etiology. Rather, he has consistently stated that psychopathology is always an AQAL affair and may have determinants that are primarily biological, psychological, familial, or in some cases social. By way of example, consider some of the current thinking around the etiology of schizophrenia. For several years from the mid-1950s onward, clients with schizophrenia were given medications that blocked dopamine receptors called dopamine antagonists (DA).

These medications helped some but not all clients suffering from symptoms of schizophrenia. In those cases where such medications helped it was hypothesized that because blocking DA receptors and thus diminishing the activity of DA in the central nervous system seemed to decrease symptoms, then perhaps the symptoms were the result of some sort of DA over activity or imbalance. This was called the dopamine theory of Schizophrenia. We know it is not accurate

today particularly because the latest antipsychotic medications block some DA
receptors but mostly serotonin (5-HT) receptors. If schizophrenia were a disorder
caused by over activity of DA why would blocking 5-HT receptors help just
as much (in a few cases more than) blocking DA receptors? In both cases (DA
and 5-HT) it seems we may be asking the wrong question.

Evidence is accumulating supporting the hypothesis that in many cases
schizophrenia results from poorly constructed brain circuits. During gestation
and early infancy, neurons (brain cells) are formed in central growth plates and
must migrate into position in the growing brain where they then branch out
to form synapses (make connections) with other neurons. These processes are
referred to as neuronal migration and synaptogenesis. This theory posits migration may be more or less normal. Normal migration leads to easier connections
with other neurons. Less normal or abnormal migration is hypothesized to make
synaptogenesis difficult and to cause problems with the resulting brain circuit.
The hypothesis is that these problems (as yet unspecified) are what lead to the
symptoms of schizophrenia. The abnormal neuronal migration and resulting
problems may be caused by a number of things from gene–gene interactions
to viral infection of the mother during pregnancy.[14,15]

So here is another theory that posits the root of disorders like schizophrenia in physiological processes. This is not to say that all the other AQAL
elements aren't important—even if schizophrenia turns out to have a primarily
physiological etiology, therapists will still have to work with clients suffering
from the symptoms and help them create as much quality of life as possible. In
this sense, AQAL still offers a promising approach. As psychiatrist Stephen Stahl
summarizes "some of the problems of gene function can arise from the person's
experiences, from stressors arising in the environment, and from chemicals and
toxins outside the brain."[16] Here we see where an AQAL understanding of this
situation is critical. If we can determine whether a person is genetically vulnerable
to disorders like schizophrenia, we can at the very least provide early interventions
regarding what those children are exposed to and how they handle stressors.
This is in fact the latest approach to early childhood mental health.[17]

In this manner, an AQAL approach to psychopathology would be similar
to Wilber's spectrum of pathology but actually be a pathology spectrum that
included important variables from each quadrant at each developmental window.
Thus, rather than a purely psychogenic spectrum, a complete AQAL spectrum
will be three- or even four-dimensional akin to a spectrum of Rubik's Cubes[18]
where there is a cube at each level of development (however those are parsed
out). The four sides of the cube could house important variables (Zones 1 and
2 from Chapter 3) from the four quadrants. Physiological variables from genome
to gene expression to behavior would comprise one side. Psychological variables
including ego-identity, states, and type or style would comprise the second side.
The third side would include family and cultural norms as well as other shared

signifieds related to language. The fourth side would map environment and particularly those environmental stressors thought to be related to negative gene expression or thought to exacerbate existing vulnerabilities. The top of the cube could reflect ego identity and the bottom of the cube cognitive ability.

Although this is a complex scheme it will be a more complete map than the psychogenic spectrum and, with some computer technology to enhance it, could be elegant to use. Now recall that this image is a Rubik's Cube and in such a cube each section of each of the six faces can pivot independent of the others. I feel that this begins to approach representing the complexity of how variables in one's psychological address interact. Unlike a Rubik's Cube, the goal of the psychological address is not to get all the faces in uniform alignment but to appreciate the complex manner in which each variable in the address interacts with others.

In this sense there is as much art as science to understanding how to identify a variable that has become a "hotspot" in the case or a variable that represents a vulnerability that could be exacerbated by other aspects of the psychological address. If this seems complex it is because it is. I do not find there are many shortcuts to dealing with complexity of a human life and I am a bit suspicious of those "one-size-fits-all" theorists who, I suspect, are more theorists than clinicians.

Benefits and Drawbacks of the Psychological Address

The primary benefit of using this model of psychological address is that it provides a heuristic for the therapist who is integrally informed that is succinct and complements existing tools like Andre Marquis' Integral intake.[19] The flexibility of the psychological address emphasizes the Integral map, which as I wrote in Chapter 1, is one of the more comprehensive integrative maps we can use. This emphasis does not dictate, however, how clinicians operationalize the variables. As I noted, one clinician may prefer to "guesstimate" cognitive ability, whereas another would prefer to administer the Kaufman Brief Intelligence Test. One clinician may prefer to conceptualize self as ego as per Loevinger and Cook-Greuter, whereas another may find Lectical Assessment more to his or her liking. Without further research, which is complex, expensive, and unlikely to happen any time soon, we must simply emphasize using reliable, valid constructs to operationalize the variables in the psychological address. But I believe that using the model in a manner that suits one's clinical wisdom and training is still better than relying on a two-dimensional model like a symptom checklist.

Another benefit to the model of psychological address is that, in the Integral spirit, it honors the truths each aspect contributes to understanding the client without a flatland reduction to just one or two variables. We know now that no one inherits a mental illness. Mental and emotional disorders, unlike cystic fibrosis or muscular dystrophy, are not single-gene illnesses. The most we can say is that genetics may make someone vulnerable to a disorder or set of symptoms. That vulnerability in turn may be triggered or buffered by the client's environment and his or her psychological reaction to the environment. Rather than trying to identify the "gene" for alcoholism, current research tries to look at the genetic configurations correlated with vulnerability and then predict what variables in the environment are more or less likely to trigger that vulnerability. This may in fact finally move us toward a true wellness model where wellness is defined by the types of factors that buffer someone with vulnerability as opposed to triggering that vulnerability. The Integral Model and this version of the psychological address can easily accommodate such research and make it clinically relevant more efficiently. If a clinician is in general agreement with the model, accommodating research that deals with interactions between things like genes and environment is an easy step to take.

The biggest drawback to this approach is that in fact it has not been empirically tested. It is one thing to say that integrally informed therapy is likely to be better but is it really? That is the question that only research will answer and frankly there are not a lot of incentives to conduct this type of expensive outcomes-based research. One study is being done (at the time of this writing) by Andre Marquis at the University of Rochester. It is designed have trained raters view videorecordings of integrally informed therapists, then code for Integral variables that occur in the sessions. There are outcome measures that will be compared to supposed "non-Integral" therapists. Given that the common factors most associated with therapeutic change are client variables (like resilience and support systems) and the relationship itself, it is hard to make definitive statements about improved efficacy with the Integral model.[20]

Another potential drawback to this notion of psychological address is that it can be easy to lose sight of the trees when you are enamored of the forest. Integrative models in general call on clinicians to work harder by considering more variables in treating their clients. I can speak from experience that it takes me about three times as long to do an Integral case note than the old standard case notes I used to do at agencies. Most clinicians are not going to undertake using the Integral model unless they are already fans of the model. This sets up a potential problem in that there is a chance that the clinician is so focused on Integral Theory that they miss something more obvious and directly related to a single variable.

As I stated in the prologue, what I think is "dead" in psychotherapy is how we view the mind and the work of therapy. This calls for a new approach to therapy that is only going to be undertaken by enthusiasts. If a clinician specializes in dialectical behavior therapy, limits her work to clients suffering from substance abuse and problems in personality style, there is little motivation for her to adopt this more complex model other than to satisfy her own curiosity about whether it will give her a more well-rounded approach to therapy. As I stated several times the beauty of Integral thinking is its ability to embrace complexity and see complexity in clients. One of the potential drawbacks is becoming enamored of complexity to the point of theoretical obsession. If this occurs, the theory becomes more interesting than the client and the clinician is closer to a philosopher than a therapist.

Communicating Integral Psychotherapy Ideas to Clients

At some point, you may find it helpful to teach your client a little bit about Integral Theory. There are few good "soapbox speeches" for Integral Theory. However, at this point you likely have some grasp of the ideas in this book and clients with different "tools" and "rules" will likely "get" these ideas if you choose your words carefully. The stage from which our translations come will vary according to the complexity of the subject–object boundary (deciding what is "I" vs. "me"). Likewise, the translation of our meaning constructions is shaped by the stage, but is not dictated by it. Some clients may appreciate being able to see a model of their complexity-in-action, a snapshot of which can be shown on the Integral Psychotherapy cube as follows:

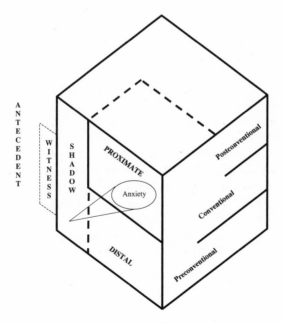

Figure 7.2. Integral Psychotherapy cube.

Using Fig. 7.2, therapist and client could "rough out" the client's (and therapist's) psychological address. You might think of cognition as being the size of the cube proper designating the space the client "can" be aware of. The ego identity (or proximate self) can be written in on the left-facing side of the cube. I noted three different general levels of ego identity using Loevinger/Cook-Greuter's version of ego development. Those are represented as three levels by stepwise lines with the middle level (conventional) possessing most of the space. The content of the ego/proximate self will to some degree give a rough estimate of what is in the shadow. Through the course of therapy you can mark in self-related contents from the proximate self and the shadow that have been made distal for the client (again, and the therapist because this could easily be adapted for supervision). The type or style might be thought of as the color of the cube. The client could color it in any way that seems apt. For some clients, this might be one color for some clients multiple colors. So how would states figure in? One way to represent them is as appearing/disappearing ovals in the ego or proximate self. In this example, the client suffers from anxiety that arises in psychodynamic fashion. This means that emerges from the shadow or unconscious to emerge in awareness. Probably the most realistic way to do this is with an actual Rubik's Cube. After using a marker to label the various components, have the client then start rotating parts of the cube and mixing them up. This would represent how each aspect of the self affects all the others and how, in reality, we cannot demarcate one "aspect" of self from another.

What Next?

We have come through a vast and rich model exploring its application to psychotherapy. In the previous chapters I hope I have conveyed not only how I use the model in psychotherapy but also how to use the variables of the model in the least speculative fashion. In a way, our journey has taken the form of an ever-widening ellipse. We are orbiting an approach to therapy that honors the complexity of a human life and provides a map that has a good probability of reflecting at least some of that complexity. Our initial orbit flew close to a good deal of the mainstream literature on psychotherapy. With our ever-widening elliptical journey, our coverage of the psychological address leaves us more at the outer limits where mainstream literature is scarce. The final chapter continues this journey in an integral exploration of the role of spirituality in psychotherapy.

8

Spirituality and Integral Psychotherapy

DAVID M. ZEITLER AND R. ELLIOTT INGERSOLL

> Psychology is a very old science; we have a complete treatise from the hand of Aristotle (384–322 B.C.). But the experimental method has only recently been adopted by psychologists.
>
> —Daniel Robinson[1]

> You have to be somebody before you can be nobody.
>
> —Jack Engler[2]

> To fashion an integral pattern is the task of a lifetime—and more.
>
> —Gordon Allport[3]

If you thought the concept of psychological address was speculative, hold on to your hat as we now explore what is historically one of the most contentious issues in psychology and psychotherapy. Spirituality has consistently been a thorn in the side of some psychologists and way out of psychological dead ends for others. Despite this bifurcation, it is increasingly becoming "respectable" in mainstream psychology as evidenced by the number of books and scholarly articles published in the last 10 years alone (the number of books approaches 20, many of which are published by the American Psychological Association). In this chapter we provide an overview of the concept of spirituality in psychology and psychotherapy proper and then move into a more integral discussion of the concept.

The history of psychology is largely a story of psychologists seeking to shun being labeled as "philosophers" and aspiring to title of "scientists." According to the American Psychological Association, the ideal of the clinical or counseling psychologist is that of the scientist-practitioner who can study research in the lab or in journals and apply that research in work with clients. This scientist-practitioner model is called the Boulder model.[4] It is fair to say that despite the efforts of training models like the Boulder model there appear to be very few scientist-practitioners and most psychologists identify as either scientist or practitioner. There are those rare psychologists like Donald Micenbaum[5] who succeed as scientists and practitioners, however, a preference for one over the other seems the norm.[6] We anticipate that if Integral Theory continues to make inroads into mainstream psychology and psychotherapy, the ideal of the scientist-practitioner may not only be resuscitated but evolve into an more integral scientist-practitioner who cannot only apply the findings of psychological research but have a good understanding of other psychology specializations and perhaps other disciplines. Experimentalism is only one of the partial truths an Integral psychotherapist needs to understand.

Anyone familiar with the history of psychology knows that mainstream psychologists champion Wilhelm Wundt as the first experimental psychologist. He developed the first German psychology laboratory in Leipzig between 1876 and 1879. Until that time the ship of psychology "rocked" between the Scylla and Charybdis of philosophy and physiology. Rightly it was Wundt's research methods that are credited with freeing the ship and setting it to sail its own course with a domain and methodology all its own. Wundt's methods were unique to psychology and not just an offshoot of physiology.

Wundt's approached developed into a movement called Structuralism because he and his students were trying to discern the structures of the consciousness. In many ways this is not so different than Integral Theory's exploration of levels of consciousness. The Structuralists' hope was that Structuralism would be to psychology what Anatomy was to the biological sciences. In 1876 Wundt published *Principles of Physiological Psychology* and this book went through six editions between 1876 and 1911. *Principles* is thought of as the book that laid the basis for psychology as an independent science. A little-known development, however, is that toward the end of his career Wundt became convinced that not all psychological questions could be answered by experimental investigations. Despite training subjects in how to introspect (look within at the products of consciousness), Wundt was never able to get subjects to introspect identically on separate occasions. One of the partial truths he discovered was that the contents of consciousness are infinitely idiosyncratic and to force the introspector into a fixed system pulled their attention away from the thing the Structuralists were studying.

In his book *Integral Psychology*,[7] Wilber makes a good case that there is no single founder of psychology proper particularly to the extent that *psyche* is defined as an animating force or spirit in the body. In that sense, *psychology* can be thought of as "the study of the soul or spirit as it appears in humans."[8] Wilber in particular champions the efforts of Gustav Fechner who was a professor of physics at Leipzig but who at heart was much more of a philosopher, poet, and satirist. His famous contribution to the history of psychology is in

psychophysics, which Fechner intended not as a sole discipline but as a complement to philosophy. With this ambition, Fechner certainly appears Integral in
his interest in both physics and the philosophy of the psyche, soul, or internal
world. One of Fechner's contributions is the Weber–Fechner law, which posits
a connection between the external world and one's experience of that world via
the senses. The law attempts to describe the relationship between the physical
magnitude of a stimulus and the perceived intensity of it. Although it is an
important part of the history of psychology, the Weber–Fechner Law is too
inflexible to actually describe the relationship between multiple senses and
incoming stimuli.[9]

Much of psychology and psychotherapy as we know them today arose
in the period dominated by what has been described in Integral books as
"the modern mind." The modern mind is not an end point but a phase in
the development of human consciousness where the self is experienced as a
separate subject that can study objects in a world of the given. This world of
the given has been somewhat successfully contested by postmodernists but the
experience of the modern mind, of consciousness that can seemingly study an
external world, persists. To the extent that experimental psychology adopts the
scientific method with underlying modernist ontological assumptions, we may
say it is limited in what it can tell us about the human condition. But to this
extent it is fair to say that the first laboratories were developed by Wundt in
Germany, James Baldwin in Canada, and William James and G. Stanley Hall
in the United States. However, Wundt's was clearly the most populated and
popular lab receiving students from various countries (including a younger
William James who recoiled in boredom).

To be fair, Fechner was certainly Integral in his approach to writing,
life, and his philosophy about life after death.[10] Fechner published *Elements of
Psychophysics* in 1860 and referred to it as an exact science of the functional
relations between body and mind. It was this work on psychophysics that was
to inspire Wundt in establishing his new psychology on the basis of Fechner's
psychophysics.[11] In this sense, Wundt was certainly inspired directly by Fechner
but Wundt went further in establishing the experimental methods that were
to put psychology on the map as a science (his student, Englishman Edward
Titchener, continued this Structuralist crusade in the United States). Historian
of psychology Daniel Robinson wrote, "Notwithstanding the painfully apparent liabilities of the Wundtian–Titchenerian studies, the experimental method
remained at the core of psychology and still does. In a way, it is a method in
search of a subject."[12]

Unlike Wundt, Fechner had no interest in training disciples to carry on
his views thus his fall into relative obscurity. This is of course the politics of
academia in general. If you do not nurture followers of a theory or approach,
that approach is likely to slip into obscurity unless it has a profound effect

within its discipline. In fairness, it should be noted that Wundt, like Fechner, also had what could be interpreted as integral leanings. From his earliest days as a student at Heidelberg he believed there to be many types of psychology. *Naturwissenschaft* or psychology as a natural science that was experimental, *Geisteswissenschaft* or social psychology that was empirical but not experimental, and *Volkerpsychologie*, literally a "psychology of the people" that dealt with cultural developments and was to be studied with the methods of history. Some of this reflects the quality of higher education in Germany in the 19th century and the German ideal of what an educated person should know.

Wundt came to believe that the most important psychological questions derived from the relationship between the individual and society (upper vs. lower quadrants in the integral model). He wrote a scholarly volume on folk psychology wherein he posited a psychological history of the development of humankind similar to James Baldwin's "genetic psychology."[13] This led to an interest in what Wundt called "ethnic psychology"—the study of the mental products that are created by a community of human beings (lower-left quadrant) and inexplicable in terms of individual consciousness. Wundt also studied linguistics concluding that cultural psychology is rooted in the signifieds and signifiers of language.[14]

In his later years, Wundt himself admitted that mental events cannot be reduced to physiological events although there are physiological correlates to mental experience. This is very important because in essence this is an integral statement. It is the same as saying that even though we have sophisticated brain imaging technologies we have not yet any clue as to whether or how a physical operation (like a neuron firing) "causes" a mental event.[15] Wundt was far closer to an Integral thinker than many history of psychology professors give him credit for. There are currently at least 57 areas of specialization if one surveys various psychological associations.[16] The scientific or experimental approach to psychology is only one subtype, despite being touted by many as the core discipline

Thinking back to Chapter 2 (we know it's been a while), the emphasis on a scientific approach to psychology reflects the modern mindset through which much of psychology was developed. As Wilber noted on numerous occasions, the distinction between art, morals, and science is a huge achievement of the modern mind. This achievement can be a pitfall if these three areas are not also integrated.[17] In this case, a species (like a client) must first have a center of gravity where certain things are made objects of awareness and differentiated from one another. At some point, however, ownership must occur that allows integration of those things differentiated, otherwise dissociation will be the result.

The modern, scientific approach to psychology will likely resonate with those psychologists who identify at the Expert or Achiever levels of ego development. A case can be made that the founding of Humanistic and Transpersonal

psychology movements were, in some instances, efforts to represent the experiences of psychologists with postconventional ego identities. If we look at the
variance of ego identity in Western countries, we see that the modal identity is
Expert followed by Achievers and Diplomats. If this distribution is reflective of
psychologists in general, it is easy to see why there is still such an emphasis on
scientific psychology. But is this really representative of psychology as a discipline?
The point of this historical digression is that claiming psychology to be *only* a
science in the experimental sense linked solely to Wundt's experimental work is
really an incomplete bias fueled by underlying metaphysical assumptions.

So what are psychology's metaphysical assumptions? We really need to
address this before discussing spirituality in psychotherapy proper. Metaphysical
assumptions are ontological and epistemological in nature. It is important to
point out that neither ontological or epistemological assumptions can be scientific—they are metaphysical or, more generally, philosophical. Robinson noted
that psychology is cut from the larger fabric of intellectual history.[18] In our case,
that history includes philosophy and theology. The first stage in the development of a discipline is what he calls "ontological legislation." This is deciding
what items, events, entities, or processes are to be included in the discipline.
"We'll include these but not those items, events, entities, and processes, etc."
Ontological claims are claims as to what is "real" and should be the object of
study for the discipline in question. These are not to be confused with epistemological claims, which deal with the process, acts, and methods of knowing.
Although ontology addresses what is real and *can* be studied, epistemology
addresses *how* we should study that which we have agreed is real[19] Do you see
the connection? This is an important part of every discipline but, ironically,
this foundational process is rarely made explicit in teaching newcomers to the
profession (at least in the case of psychology). Very few psychology professors
spend time discussing the ontological assumptions of psychology before teaching the subject. The reasons for this vary, but the omission is something that,
from an Integral perspective, has to be corrected.

So if the ontological assumptions of a discipline are the legislating of "what
is real," the epistemological methods of a discipline are all the things you can
do to study what has been agreed on as "real." As philosopher Bertrand Russell
pointed out, epistemology itself does not point toward a single method. There
are things we may know directly or by acquaintance and things we may know
only by description, and each of these may require different epistemological
methods.[20] Enter here so-called spiritual experiences.

When I (Ingersoll) was 15 I almost drowned. We had a creek (frequently
pronounced "crick" in Ohio) near our residence that would flood to river status
regularly every spring and summer. One summer my friends and I decided it
would be a good idea to tie several inner tubes together and "shoot the rapids"
in the flooded creek. Needless to say, we hadn't gotten far when a fallen tree

intersected with our tubes and flipped us all into the water. For a period of time, I was trapped underwater as the tangle of tubes above me and the water crushing me against the fallen tree prevented me from surfacing. I recall feeling very calm and at one point my consciousness seemed to explode as if detonated. There was a distinctly different sense of self at this point and I recall wondering "will they write an article about that boy who drowned in the creek?" At about this point the water pushed me under the fallen tree and I surfaced on the other side (literally and figuratively) gasping for breath and clawing my way toward the shoreline. I didn't recollect the experience until I was safely ashore but it presented me with a dilemma. Who was I when I was wondering about the boy that I had mistakenly thought to be me? Here is a good illustration of knowledge by acquaintance or experience. Now the question, is this experience within the domain of psychology and psychotherapy? For psychologists or therapists whose ontological claims allow for such experiences the answer is "yes." The epistemological questions include how do we go about exploring the experience and how do we know if we have learned anything? For psychologists whose ontological assumptions are materialist (the mind is a side effect of the brain) this experience is merely a psychological anomaly likely brought on by oxygen deprivation.

Epistemological questions bring us back to Wundt's interest in the relationship between the individual and the group (which as you recall from the discussions of the quadrants is of interest in Integral Theory as well). What happens if a group politically appointed to be the guardians of a discipline set forth ontological legislation that limits its members from exploring certain events or phenomena? What happens is you end with splinter groups or, in the case of psychology, 57 specializations. Given the heterogeneity of individuals within any discipline it seems safe to say that although guidelines can be set forth, it falls to those populating a discipline's specializations to decide under what ontological and epistemological claims they will labor.

Even in psychology's 57 specializations, there always will be individuals who want to push the edge of whatever ontology or epistemology is approved by even the smaller group of specialists. This really is in many ways the function of a specialization. The professionals can offer guidance based on similar interests, experiences, or needs. They also can use the three steps outlined in Chapter 1 that reflect Wilber's three injunctions:

1. Define what you want to know.

2. Take up a practice that is supposed to provide an experience that addresses what you want to know.

3. Compare your results with a community of like-minded/hearted practitioners.

The specializations in psychology provide these communities. They also can provide ethical guidelines while at the same time providing more leeway to explore areas that the larger group may consider off limits. The bottom line, however, is that all disciplines and specializations make these ontological claims and none of them (including the most scientific) can pretend to be derived from science.

Here is how the matter stands with professional organizations. In the American Counseling Association there is a subdivision called the Association for Spiritual, Ethical, Religious, and Value Issues in Counseling (ASERVIC). ASERVIC has its own bylaws and its own implied ontological and epistemological claims. It was the latter claims that led to a special issue of the division's journal (*Counseling and Values*) to be dedicated to Integral approaches to counseling. The counselors who are drawn to ASERVIC usually have different interests than those drawn to the Association for Evaluation and Measurement in Counseling (AEMC). As the editor of that special issue I (Ingersoll) received many e-mails from ASERVIC members but none from AEMC members.

It is important to understand this much of the politics and history related to psychology and the other helping professions where spirituality is concerned. In mainstream practice this is how new areas of research and human experience come to be embraced by a broader group of professionals. If you are following the argument you are likely aware that this is by necessity a slow process. One of the truths about human beings (a truth that keeps psychotherapists in business) is that changes of heart and mind come about slowly in the individuals and even slower where groups are concerned. Wilber quoted physicist Max Planck once noting that "knowledge proceeds funeral by funeral," the idea being that new ideas can be embraced more easily when the holders of power who believe older ideas die off.[21] It may be that as the bastions of behaviorism gave way to cognitive science and humanistic psychotherapies, we had reached a critical mass that allowed spirituality to be explored by psychology and psychotherapists.

It also should be noted that spirituality and religion have historically been topics of interest in American psychology, particularly when compared with European psychology around the time Wundt was most active. Despite this, those (like Behaviorists) seeking to dominate the field frequently have driven them to the periphery of psychology. Even the more philosophically inclined psychodynamic forces being marshaled by Freud were distinctively anti-religious/spiritual until dissenters like Jung struck out on their own. The contrast between William James Functionalist approach to exploring religion (which asks "what is the function of religion?" without committing to religious experience as ontologically different than psychological experience) and Freud's dismissal of religion as an infantile yearning for a parent figure is quite stark. Despite the politics, American psychologists have been studying religion and spiritual from the inception of psychology.

In American psychology, the first full-length work on the psychology of religion was written by Edward Starbuck in 1899.[22] Starbuck took a developmental approach that tried to outline differences in religious consciousness across the life span. This was quickly followed (and obscured by) James' *Varieties of Religious Experience* in 1902. In contrast to the German efforts to measure or observe psychological variables (which James had little patience for), James felt that only a limited range of human experience could be directly observed and that phenomenological reports added to the psychology of religion *and* the richness of psychology in general. Eight years later, Edward Ames published *The Psychology of Religious Experience*[23] wherein he used anthropological sources to confirm that religion historically had been the holding tank to affirm humankind's most important social values.

David Arnold summarizes these historical works as bringing psychometric, personalistic, and comparative methods to the psychology of religion.[24] He also notes that criticism of these approaches began as early as 1898 by Hugo Munsterberg and James Mark Baldwin (who ironically was doing a similar thing though with an obtuse and still hard-to-read style). The critics were taking the perspective of experimental psychology when in fact many of the early pioneers were laboring more in what Eugene Taylor calls a folk psychology of interest in the spiritual, which can be traced back to the founding of the American colonies.[25] For the experimentally minded psychologists, the primary problem of phenomenological methods (particularly the personalistic and comparative methods) seemed to be that they were too philosophical. So here again is the European tension between psychology and philosophy but with an American twist. The "twist" is basically an epistemological disagreement. This disagreement has never been resolved and this has resulted in a wasteland of descriptions and definitions of what exactly "spiritual" and "religious" mean. It is into that wasteland that we wade with our Integral framework.

What Do We Mean by "Spiritual" and "Religious"?

Like the notion of psychological address in the last chapter, there are many ways clinicians and researchers can describe spirituality. In a scholarly approach to topics we have to *operationalize* terms. Operationalizing means that we describe what we mean when we use a particular term and in psychotherapy that usually is through references to what clients are experiencing. For example, anxiety is defined as a negative mood state that can be characterized by somatic symptoms, cognitive apprehension about the future, unpleasant affect or a set of behaviors (fidgeting, looking worried). Many studies of anxiety only look at one of these or some combination of two out of three and researchers admit that in humans anxiety is very hard to measure.[26] The same can be said of spirituality and probably the best descriptions of it in relation to psychotherapy state that it is frankly hard to define.[27]

There have been many ways that spirituality is operationalized in the psychological literature. In the mid- to late-20th century, psychologists and therapists were just beginning to offer general descriptions of what spirituality meant. Here is a sampling: Spirituality has been described as the ultimate or deepest needs of the self that when met, move the individual toward meaning and purpose[28] and as one's journey toward union with God.[29] Counselor Mel Witmer described spirituality as a belief in a force or thing great than oneself.[30] Psychiatrist Gerald May noted that spirituality has an elusive nature in that it seemed paradoxically indwelling yet rooting in something eternal.[31] Counselor Howard Clinebell described spirituality as living in meanings, hopes, and beliefs about what is ultimately important.[32]

You'll note in all these samples, a dearth of reference to religion and religiosity. That is likely because James set the tone of investigation into the healthy aspects of religion in his famous Gifford Lectures[33] and Gordon Allport followed this lead in his book *The Individual and his Religion.*[34] Psychologists from James to Allport thus birthed the construct of religiosity and the construct is pedagogically set apart from constructs like "spirituality" or "spiritual wellness." Psychologist Carl Thoresen addressed the complexity of teasing apart religiosity and spirituality. He noted:

> both concepts are complex with several facets or features, some
> of which are latent, that is, not directly observable but are
> inferable. . . . Very important concepts remain difficult to articulate
> and lack complete agreement about how best to define them . . . given
> this complexity there is no clear consensus on how to best describe,
> define, or measure spirituality and religion. Both concepts are clearly
> related to each other and both contain a connection to what is
> perceived as sacred in life.[35]

In an effort to more clearly specify what is meant by spirituality, many researchers beginning with sociologist David Moberg,[36] who began looking more at constructs that implied spiritual health or wellness. These included spiritual well-being, spiritual wellness, and spiritual health. As I summarized these efforts in 1994,[37] the idea was that spirituality was described in so many different ways; perhaps focusing on measurable aspects of people who had a spiritual practice would clarify what healthy spirituality meant for clients (and clinicians). These efforts were more precise and led to the development of some scales to measure spiritual wellness[38] but diverged sharply from the manner in which clients described their spirituality. Clients rarely come in, sit down, and say, "I had a spiritual experience that is best operationalized by Ellison's subscale on existential well-being."

Since the late 1990s, it seems a second round of efforts has been made to more clearly operationalize both religiosity and spirituality. The gap between spirituality and religion continues as psychologist David Wulff explained:

> sensing that the words *religious* and *religion* fail today to denote certain positive inward qualities and perceptions but, to the contrary, seem increasingly to be associated with prejudicial attitudes, violence, and narrow social agendas, people in various walks of life are choosing to use the terms *spiritual* and *spirituality* instead.[39]

Psychologists Scott Richards and Allan Bergin noted the following:

> by spiritual, we also mean those experiences, beliefs, and phenomena that pertain to the transcendent and existential aspects of life . . . the transcendental relationship between the person and a Higher Being, a quality that goes beyond a specific religious affiliation, that strives for reverence, awe, and inspiration, and that gives answers about the infinte."[40]

These same two authors, 3 years later, owned the Western biases in the previous description and added a full-page table of the differences between Western and Eastern worldviews.[41]

Bruce Scotton differentiated spiritual and religious writing:

> *Religious* refers to the belief system of a specific group, whose members usually gather around specific contents and contexts that contain some transpersonal elements. *Spiritual* refers to the realm of the human spirit, that part of humanity that is not limited to bodily experience. *Transpersonal experience* in addressing all human experience beyond the ego level includes spiritual experience but also includes embodied human experience of higher levels.[42]

Again, we would caution here that the idea of levels being "higher" or "lower" is not the best use of language. Perhaps calling such levels "broader and deeper" is more resourceful.

Most recently, authors have focused on the difficulty of defining words like spirituality and religion with some authors devoting entire chapters to the problem.[43] Psychologists Brian Zinnbauer, Kenneth Pargament, and Allie Scott conducted an analysis of the panoply of definitions and asserted that contemporary theorists have polarized spirituality and religiousness in three ways. The first was the polarization between organized religion versus personal spirituality. The second was substantive religion versus functional spirituality. The third was negative religiousness versus positive spirituality. The authors then integrated these constructs concluding that the polarizations unnecessarily constricted the definitions.

Their solution is twofold. First, they noted there is a need to resolve the tension between remaining pluralistic enough to include the varieties of spiritual and religious experiences while also allowing researchers to be specific enough to carry out a coherent research program. Second, they felt there had to be a way to distinguish between "spirituality" and "religion" without polarizing them. To accomplish these aims, they endorsed Kenneth Pargament's description of spirituality as "a search for the sacred" and his definition of religion as "a search for significance in ways related to the sacred."[44] In these definitions, spirituality is central to religion and religion can be the culturally shaped vessel that ideally nurtures the search for the sacred.

Although these definitions do not solve all the problems, they give us a starting point for entering into an Integral discussion of the issue. We may start with Pargament's definitions and view them through the integral quadrants shown in Fig. 8.1.

Probably the most important point to be drawn from Fig. 8.1 is that the person (client or therapist) represented in the "self-system" will, to a large extent,

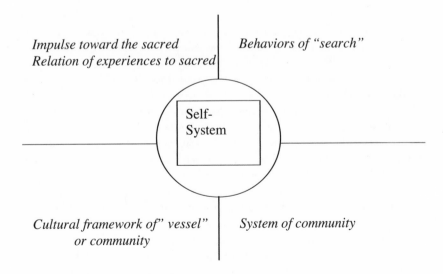

Impulse toward the sacred
Relation of experiences to sacred

Behaviors of "search"

Self-System

Cultural framework of" vessel"
or community

System of community

Figure 8.1. AQAL basics of spirituality and religion

filter the experiences of his or her search for the sacred through the psychological address (if we are accurate in the way we defined psychological address). This developmental piece is one of the unique contributions of Integral Theory and including it forges a new way to "draw the line" between psychotherapy and spirituality. It is to that "line" that we now turn.

The "Line" Between Psychotherapy and Spirituality

Psychologist Len Sperry wrote that spirituality is a direct experience of the sacred unmediated by particular belief systems.[45] This belies a common misconception. From a developmental and Integral perspective, experience seems *very* mediated by the structures of the mind (or consciousness if you will) and those structures may in fact include belief systems. Can there be unmediated experience and if so, how common is it?

To answer that it may help to review Wilber's notion of states and stages of development. The idea is straightforward. Structure stages are stages of development that allow access to particular states on a more or less consistent basis. Consider the Magician stage (also called ego aware or construct aware) in Cook-Greuter's later stages of ego identity. She called this stage the gateway to transcendence or the transpersonal.[46] Here a person can access perspectives that appear to transcend (and include) the ego but they can do so consistently. If we risk using the metaphor of directionality we would say structure stages can be thought of as *vertical* in nature. If you don't like directional metaphors then think of structure stages as moving stepwise from "earlier" to "later." Each earlier stage is transcended and included by later stages. Structure stages allow the self to stand on a higher rung of the ladder of development and thus to have a broader, deeper view. This is not to say the self experiences this view constantly but consistently can access it (sometimes the self is more focused on the rung in front, the next rung above or something off to the side). The idea of structure stages has powerful implications for psychotherapy. If structure stages exist wherein the ego consistently becomes an object of awareness (e.g, the Magician) then is "therapy" with a client at such structure stages really *psy-cho*-therapy? Is it something else? We don't have an answer to these questions. There is no psychotherapy outcome research that we know of that focuses on therapy process with people who have postconventional ego identities. Our aim here is to raise the question because it may be a boundary that our discipline of psychotherapy has yet to see let alone reach.

Now let's turn from structure stages and consider state stages. Consider someone who perhaps identifies at the ego level of Expert and who has also practiced meditation for 9 years. This person has access to states wherein she experiences perspectives that appear to transcend and include her ego but these experiences are more frequent and fleeting during meditation practice. The experiences themselves bear some resemblance to what the Magician has consistent access to but after the experience, the Expert interprets or metabolizes them with "tools" common to Experts. These are what we call state stages and, again risking orientation via directionality, might be thought of as horizontal in nature. Again, if you prefer nondirectional metaphors, think of state stages as a field. Everyone, regardless of where they are in terms of structure stages, has access to the entire field but may interpret the experience of different field areas in different ways. State stages help the self make the most of the rung it is on and whatever tools, rules, or views come with that rung.

Wilber emphasized that this difference between structure stages (e.g., the Magician developing and seeing life through the lens of a trans-ego perspective) and state stages (e.g., the Expert experiencing a transcendent state after years of practice but not living through or seeing through that lens in areas of life outside of her meditation practice). To be sure, the Expert in this example may grow into later ego identities more quickly because of her practice and this may turn out to be a side effect of practice itself.

So given this difference between state and structure stages, is there a line between psychotherapy and spirituality? Like most things, it depends on the perspectives that you use from the perspectives that are available to you. The perspectives *available* to you depend on your growth and development, whereas the perspectives that you *use* are a mosaic of your life conditions, your personality type, and your state experiences. Growth and development are both vertical (structure stages) and horizontal (state stages) in nature, whereas life conditions, typologies, and state experiences (phenomenal or general) are translative in nature. Life conditions are best mapped on the quadrants, whereas typologies can be mapped in a number of ways (see Chapter 5), and state experiences (Chapter 6) can be contractive or expansive.

There also are general states that we all have access to whether we have a spiritual practice or not (waking, dreaming, deep sleep, and supposedly nondual states). These four are supposedly linked to corresponding realms and even bodies coextensive with those realms. This was not discussed in Chapter 6 because, by its very nature, it is more speculative than the psychological literature on states proper. It is important to be clear when we are going beyond the mainstream metaphysical assumptions. All of the preceding states however are germane to a discussion of Integral spirituality in a psychotherapeutic context.

So rather than a line between psychotherapy and spirituality we think of a boundary. Like all boundaries, it must be generated successfully before it can be transcended and included in one's perspective. This is what we meant by stating that structure stages consistently give the self a particular view. This also is the essence of becoming somebody before becoming nobody—transformation (somebody) and transcendence (nobody). We can think of our growth (and our clients' growth) as occurring within the forces of eros and agape *without*; and translation, differentiation, and reintegration *within*. Eros seems best described as a force of self-transcendence and agape as the force that helps the self integrate the view Eros has made available. Just as the physical world has strong/weak, electromagnetic, and gravitational forces, sentience seems to have agapic and erotic forces. Every outside has an inside. In an Integral treatment of spirituality, the integrity of the self-system can be thought of as a measure of the balance of these forces. Just as physicists are searching for a theory to unite the four known physical forces, we use Integral Theory to unite the disparate forces of consciousness.

What About Transpersonal Psychology? Transpersonal Problems From an Integral Theory Perspective

In the *Textbook of Transpersonal Psychiatry and Psychology*, Bruce Scotton gives an overview of transpersonal themes, particularly in Western contexts.[47] In addition to the standard differentiation between "religion" and "spiritual" (explored at the beginning of the chapter), Scotton lists the key players in the transpersonal field: James (first to use the word *transpersonal*, as redress for science's false dichotomy between subject and object); Jung (analytic psychology); Roberto Assagioli (psychosynthesis); Abraham Maslow (humanistic and transpersonal self-actualization); Stanislav Grof (perinatal COEX); Shamanism; yoga; psychedelics, Buddhism; Kabbalah; Christian mysticism; meditation; and quantum physics.

Owing to the eclectic nature of transpersonal psychology and psychotherapy, each of those main topics is addressed in a separate chapter in this edited volume. In this way, the *Textbook of Transpersonal Psychiatry and Psychology* follows a pattern similar to the *DSM*—take phenomena as they come, and do not get overly concerned with theoretical/etiological interpretations. Nevertheless, the editors call their approach a "multifaceted approach to spirituality and psychiatry. Taken together, these interdisciplinary perspectives provide an understanding of the human psyche that is more comprehensive than current psychiatric and psychological approaches . . . honoring the biopsychosociospiritual continuum that is the human condition."[48] Not wanting to reduce a client to his or her symptoms—or worse, to the reductionistic interpretations of perspectives that rule out spiritual phenomena—transpersonal practitioners find it helpful to use multiple interpretations of theory. However, not wanting to evaluate theories—or worse, plot them along a hierarchy—transpersonal authors are involved in a defacto truce (not better or worse, just different!). In this way the field—despite such excellent work as the *Textbook of Transpersonal Psychiatry and Psychology*—remains stuck in a bit of a quagmire. This quagmire may be why a recent meta-analysis of meditation practices and health made the following conclusion:

Many uncertainties surround the practice of meditation. Scientific research on meditation practices does not appear to have a common theoretical perspective and is characterized by poor methodological quality. Firm conclusions on the effects of meditation practices in healthcare cannot be drawn based on the available evidence. Future research on meditation practices must be more rigorous in the design and execution of studies and in the analysis and reporting of results.[49]

It seems fair to say that the field of transpersonal psychology exhibits a sin of omission in that it is unwilling or unable to systematize itself about a core in which less-complex individuals can recognize themselves reflected in the metaphysical assumptions of the field. By focusing on the unconscious (psychoanalysis), behavior (cognitive-behavioral psychology), or universal principles of actualization (humanistic), the other forces of psychology dovetail with human life at many levels of complexity. This allows people to see themselves reflected in the patterns those theories highlight, despite the fact that their meaning-constructions may contain less depth (or in the language of Chapter 3, more rules and fewer tools). Transpersonal psychology, by intentionally eschewing "religion" for state experiences of "spirituality," essentially cut itself off from mundane connection to the majority of people presenting as psychotherapy clients. Recall that the modal level of ego identity in the United States and United Kingdom is hypothesized to be Expert. In the words of Robert Kegan, the field of transpersonal psychology seems to be "over the heads" of most people. In the absence of state or state stage issues, most people will gravitate away from transpersonal and toward those forms of psychotherapy that they resonate with and in which they can recognize at least *most of who they are* or *some of who they are becoming*. A psychology and psychotherapy that attempts to connect with people by reflecting *mostly who they are becoming* is placing clients in over their heads. As a field, then, transpersonal psychology may be guilty of spiritual bypassing, reflected in the fact that it remains a fringe enterprise.

Integral psychotherapists literally integrate the structure stages, states, and state stages in a way that breathes life into the religious and spiritual experiences of people without a loss in the authenticity of their less-complex meaning constructions. By concerning ourselves with the overall health of where someone's psychological and Kosmic addresses locate them, Integral psychotherapists seek to stabilize, enrich, and then (if necessary) frustrate the meaning constructions of their client. The power and problems of most forms of psychotherapy lie in the particular theoretical linkages that generate acceptance and repudiation of the patient's phenomenal experiences. This happens consciously or unconsciously by psychotherapists, including transpersonalists, which makes the aforementioned tension between symptoms and theory that much more troubling.

Taking a stand as to what is mirrored and what is actively repudiated in your client reflects your understanding of your discipline's ontology and epistemology (as discussed in the first part of this chapter). Transpersonal psychology offered its own understanding in this sense as Scotton wrote, "the crucial question here is not whether a claim made by a particular discipline is true or false but in what sense it is true and how it helps transpersonal psychiatry alleviate human suffering."[50] This assertion leaves ontological "wiggle room." In Integral Psychotherapy we try to understand what is true as well as what is *false* for clients. We meet them on the playing field of what is true for them and if that field lacks the tools they need or is inundated with rules that hamper their performance, we help them broaden the field.

An Integral Psychospiritual Map

So how does all this relate to the self-system of Chapter 3 and the dynamics of development in Chapter 4? We've reviewed the self-system as a psychological construct. Does it have actual substance? Is it a *chimera*—a mythic beast with a lion's head, a goat's body and a serpent's tail (or in a genetic sense an organism composed of two or more genetically distinct tissues)? Along these same lines we may ask, is the self at once mundane and transcendent, beastly and godly, bound and free? If so, that is where spirituality and psychotherapy (or psychology for that matter) can never have a distinct line drawn between them. We are back to a permeable boundary and the definition of psyche covered at the beginning of this chapter. If psyche is an animating force inextricably woven through the body and mind, then treatment of any one element implies treatment of the others. Similar to our Integral Psychotherapy cube, the Integral Theory elements mixing in each client have no clear dividing lines but are like ingredients in a recipe uniquely mixed in each client.

From a spiritual perspective we might describe development in the following way. An erotic, transcendent impulse urges us onward, whereas an agapic mystery helps us integrate and metabolize what Eros has given. We may stumble in this process through our own fault or that of others and we may be injured in ways that derail the process for the mind while the body and spirit continue on to some degree. And so as we stumble forward we add dimensions to our various knowledge quests, our awareness, our aspirations for practice and we evolve from fusion to dualism to multiperspectival systems of making sense out of our favorite topic: ourselves.

These chimaerac characteristics of the self-system are more than merely polarized forces. When Allan Combs and Wilber introduced the *Wilber–Combs matrix*,[51] an integral union of psychology and spirituality (psychospirituality) began to realize its full potential. Figure 8.2 offers a modified variation of the matrix using Loevinger and Cook-Greuter's levels of ego identity on the ordi-nate or *y-axis* and the four general states of waking, dreaming, deep sleep, and nondual on the abscissa or *x*-axis.

In the modified Wilber–Combs matrix we see that there are nine levels of ego identity represented and four possible states accessible to all the levels of ego identity. According to the theory of ego identity, each identity comes with a set of tools (and rules) unique to its own level as well as tools brought from earlier levels. If we equate the levels of ego identity to rungs on a ladder, wherever the self-system is when experiencing one of the four states, it will have tools appropriate to its rung but not necessarily the state. Thus, states are interpreted with the rules and tools the person has based on the rung or structure stage they occupy.

As far as spiritual experiences we can use this modified Wilber–Combs matrix to find what Wilber calls the Kosmic address of the experience. Similar to psychological address, the Kosmic address of the experience in this example would be ego stage plus state. For example a Diplomat who had a waking experience of the Divine might interpret that as a vision of Christ. Another, depending on the context of the AQAL quadrants she is nested in may inter-pret it as a connection with a totem animal. An Achiever having a dream that includes Divine imagery may interpret guides in the dream as angels or perhaps Jungian archetypes. Another way to conceptualize the Wilber–Combs matrix

States →	Waking	Dreaming	Deep Sleep	Non Dual
Unitive	*	*	*	*
Magician	*	*	*	*
Strategist	*	*	*	*
Pluralist	*	*	*	*
Achiever	*	*	*	*
Expert	*	*	*	*
Diplomat	*	*	*	*
Opportunist	*	*	*	*
Impulsive	*	*	*	*

Ego Identity

Figure 8.2. Modified Wilber–Combs matrix.

is using the Integral Psychotherapy cube introduced in Chapter 7. Figure 8.3 shows how the matrix, now presented in the cube format, may play out for a client or therapist.

Now this latter use of the matrix assumes a stable self-system but the self-system itself (in Integral spirituality) is the result of the forces of eros and agape. One could think of these forces as plotted along x, y axes, respectively, to illustrate how spirituality plays a role in the practice of psychotherapy.[52] If eros is the impulse to growth and transcendence that coaxes one through ego identity (ordinate or y-axis) then agape is the stabilizing force that helps the self metabolize whatever identity it has (abscissa or x-axis). Now let's add a "z"-axis to the Wilber–Combs matrix to represent the self-system's placement with regard to a continuum that runs from health to pathology. To do this, look at Fig. 8.3, which presents the Wilber–Combs matrix as a three-dimensional Integral Psychotherapy cube. Think of the z-axis cutting through at an angle to mark the level of ego identity and type of state being experienced. On this z-axis, the self-system can slide between healthy and unhealthy. If you imagine this axis in the three-dimensional cube with the Wilber–Combs matrix on the front face, imagine that the closer the z-axis is to the front face the healthier it is functioning. The farther away it is from the front face (and closer it is toward the rear

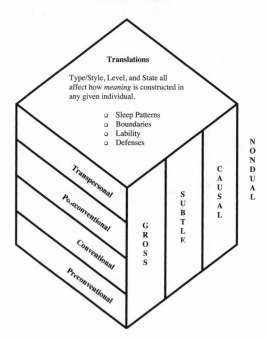

Figure 8.3. The Wilber–Combs matrix in the Integral Psychotherapy cube.

face of the cube) the less healthy is the system. Taking all this into account, the Integral psychotherapist seeks to guide the self-system toward the healthy end of the z-axis so it can make where it is in the matrix an object of awareness.

Conceptualizing the z-axis this way is suggesting sets of polarities that the self must maneuver. We may find that these are precisely the common polarities that have plagued transpersonal psychology and psychotherapy. Table 8.1 illustrates some of these polarities.

This is not an exhaustive list, but it highlights issues that transpersonal psychotherapists have been facing for the last 30 years. The right-hand column in Table 8.1 describes pathologies that are emphasized in most schools of psychotherapy. The left-hand column describes antidotes frequently emphasized in schools of transpersonal psychology. Sadly, transpersonal psychology and psychotherapy continue to be overly permissive about validating spiritual experiences as authentic without understanding that sometimes, spiritual experiences can be pathologically metabolized on the z-axis. Also, because state experiences (stable or otherwise) are the guiding professional indicators, transpersonal psychology and psychotherapy seem to valuable to a limited subset of individuals seeking therapy.[53] Despite this, transpersonal psychology did achieve the monumental task set before it: to legitimize the reckoning of mind and spirit implicit in the word *psyche*. From this perspective, transpersonal psychology reflects the natural, Kosmic processes of evolution, whereby the *negation* of previous limitations leads to a period of opening, precipitating a phase of *reintegration*.

Symptoms and Diagnoses Related to Integral Spirituality

For the Integral psychotherapist, it is important to know that 4.5% of all clients bring mystical experiences into treatment and 30% to 40% of the general

Table 8.1. Polarities that Limit Transpersonal Psychotherapies

For boundaries:	Self-Contraction	...or Self-Distraction?
For leadership:	Surrender	...or Submission?
For state seeking:	Release	...or Escape?
For detachment:	Non-Attachment	...or Indifference?
For joy:	Bliss	...or Ego Inflation?
For melancholy:	Emptiness	...or Depression?
For psychic issues:	Paranormal	...or Primary Process Projection?
For shaking up ego:	Crazy Wisdom	...or Personality Disorder?
For the occult:	Mystical	...or Delusional?
For integrity:	Autonomy	...or Ego Defense?
For connection:	Communion	...or Disintegrated Social-Holon?

population has had what they consider a mystical experience.[54] Despite this, the ontological and epistemological structures with the most influence in mainstream psychotherapy damn mystical experiences with the faint praise of "psychological well-being" or "meaning and purpose to life."

Robert Turner and David Lukoff have been pioneers in advancing the need for the *DSM-IV* to integrate religious and spiritual issues in ways that do not necessarily pathologize them. The coding for "Religious or Spiritual Problem" that was accepted into *DSM-IV*, includes issues like questioning or losing faith, conversion, intensification of beliefs or practices, new religions, cults, and mystical experience. The fact that these are listed under what is called a "V code" means that the experiences themselves are not pathological but may be related to psychological distress.[55]

This V code is an excellent first step at dovetailing issues germane to Integral Psychotherapy with current nosology. However, it continues a trend in transpersonal psychotherapy of focusing on states without allowing for the possibility of state stages or structure stages. The problem here is that there are states but also structure stages and state stages that may lie at the source of these state experiences. For example if we accept the ontological assumptions of the modified Wilber–Combs matrix in Fig. 8.3, we accept that no matter what one's ego identity one has access to at least four states of consciousness and those states will be interpreted differently depending on the tools and rules accompanying each ego level. Furthermore, differentiating and reintegrating phenomenal states and general states (loosely, inside vs. outside the self-system) assists the Integral psychotherapist who is dealing with clients that exhibit issues across the x-axis, y-axis, and z-axis. Co-constructions between therapist and client can thereupon generate more specific meaning for healing purposes.

Spirituality, Psychotherapy, and Integral Post-Metaphysics

As Wilber wrote:

> It's astonishing that I can deny I. That I can take parts of my self, my I-ness, and push them on the other side of the self-boundary, attempting to deny ownership of those aspects of my self that are perhaps too negative, or perhaps too positive, to accept. Yet pushing them away does not actually get rid of them, but simply converts them into painful neurotic symptoms, shadows of a disowned self come back to haunt me, as I look in the mirror of that which most disturbs me about the world out there, and see only the shadow of my disowned self.[56]

We have already equated the self-system with a chimera. Specifically, we mean that the vertical and horizontal manifestations of growth and development representing structure stages and bodies (what Wilber might call *Kosmic habits*) impact the self-system in specific ways. This is more than another transpersonal polarity. By way of analogy, consider the makeup of DNA. This highlights the complexities of translation: the order of four chemical bases (guanine, adenine, thymine, and cytosine) in humans results, among other things, in unique fingerprints for all 6 billion of us. *Four base pairs, about 30,000 genes producing 50,000 proteins resulting in 6-billion unique fingerprints.* Now suspend disbelief long enough to consider that the self-system in this book represents at least the basic elements of who we are. Just as with the path from DNA to your fingerprint, the path of the self-system through the Wilber–Combs matrix to your unique self-system is a complex one. Unlike DNA, which is rarely a chimera,[57] if the definition of psyche includes mind, soul, and spirit then the self-system is always a chimera—a beast of forces that quilts together the Kosmic habits and life conditions that generate each of us. And as with the move from genotype (code) to phenotype (expression), variation, mutation, and disease enter into the picture. From the stable Kosmic habits to their expression through your self-system, joy, and pain flow.

One of the most common "mutations" that occurs in the self-system is depression. One of the many ways that Integral spirituality affects Integral Psychotherapy is through *Integral Post-Metaphysics*. Integral Post-Metaphysics is supposed to be a multiperspectival system that provides explanatory power without any of the baggage of modern or postmodern views. Although Wilber is still developing this area, that is, in a nutshell, the general direction in which he is aiming. Integral Post-Metaphysics is basically ontology for the post-post-modern period. Understanding depression via this ontology will provide the next example.

Modern-era psychotherapy allows that depression is overdetermined in etiology, meaning that it may have multiple variables underlying it. Even the bastion of modern-era diagnosing, the *DSM-V* taskforce, admits there are no consistent physiological correlates underlying any mental or emotional disorder. This means that unlike a single-gene disorder like cystic fibrosis or muscular dystrophy, disorders like MDD have only physiological correlates that occur in some but not all clients in any given study (the same applies to the more chronic disorders like Schizophrenia and Bipolar I Disorder).[58]

There are theories of depression that are physiological,[59] psychodynamic,[60] and even interpersonal in nature.[61] These derive from modern and postmodern ontological assumptions. An Integral Post-Metaphysics would allow all these possibilities and add dimensions that include the spiritual. Specifically, given the depth and breadth of possibilities for the self-system in the Wilber–Combs matrix, depression could also be related to vertical and horizontal "Kosmic habits" referred to as structure and state stages, respectively. Depression is one of the most common symptoms reported by clients seeking psychotherapy. It can align with disruptions of states (states of depression), state stages (a dark night of the senses in meditation practice that mimics the vegetative symptom of anhedonia)[62] and structure stages (transitions from particularly conventional senses of self to postconventional senses of self).

Depression, as Kegan pointed out, is not only the group of symptoms it appears to be in the *DSM*, but could be intimately involved with disruptions along the vertical structure stages of identification.[63] Depression could be understood as being symptoms that we would plot along the z-axis (self-system health), which essentially is an axis of translation. But what is even more fascinating, and more important for the Integral psychotherapist, is the fact that by differentiating vertical and horizontal growth, Integral Theory allows us to not only differentiate depression, but also to also reintegrate what may be causing the depression. A good example of how differentiation and reintegration help us understand spirituality and its impact for the Integral psychotherapist is in depression and suicide.

Suicide can be experienced and interpreted as a reversal of the self-system (i.e., toward dissolution rather than greater complexity) and a failure to maintain *any* meaning constructions. This disrupts all state *experiences* and *state-stage* developments (horizontal), which are interpreted as meaningless because of a lack of eros. Eros is the energy of transcendence and integration—the self-system with suicidal ideation does not have an appetite for transcendence and integration ("I just can't seem to get moving, I can't pull it together"), nor can the individual make sense of what is happening with the available rules and tools ("I am falling apart, doc"). This second piece sounds like what happens when agape (differentiation and embrace) lacks a connection to its complementary force, eros. This leads to dissolution, a dissolving of the self-system, which is exactly what suicide is. No erotic drive, and agape becomes *thanatos*, a pathological regression in to the ultimate return, dissolution of the self. Integral psychotherapists who understand that these forces can be in and out of balance can provide better treatment plans. Recall the case of Mel White, whose lost connection to eros (literally, erotic love for White), led directly to suicidal ideation. It is hard to embrace life (agape) when we feel our connection with our own larger life force (eros) is lost.

In the case of depression, as the result of structure-stage transition problems between, for example Strategist and Magician, the depression may be a result of overwhelming disruptions to the individual's life conditions. Perhaps the client is depressed because he is losing his "culture of embeddedness."[64] In a client like this, we may posit that there is more going on than the self-system nested in the four Integral quadrants. From the perspective of Integral

Post-Metaphysics, this client may in fact be isolated from eros itself. As seen with Mel White, connection with eros may be the general issue, manifesting in several different symptoms (e.g., lost motivation; lost connection to activities that once brought joy; lack of desire to rise from bed). Connection with eros may be lacking in someone who is depressed. In this case, meditation would be of little help because all states—phenomenal and general—must be *interpreted* according to structure stage. But in this example, the structure stage is in transition and lacks integration or may be heading toward dissolution (suicidal). In the latter case, on the z-axis, all of the client's interpretations are *disintegrative*. On the z-axis, therapeutic efforts include increasing positive phenomenal states (happiness) and using cognition (the leading line for integration is cognition) to track emotion.[65]

As you can see, Integral Post-Metaphysics allows us to take the notion of differential diagnosis further than modern or postmodern metaphysical frameworks do. The addition of a z-axis allows psychotherapists to honor the complexity of the self-system. If we can allow for depression to be understood in this way, the impact of depressive symptoms begins to make a different, fuller, richer sense

A Case Example

Janine is a 34-year-old female of mixed ethnicity/race. She presented for therapy noting that depression was her primary symptom. Using the Integral intake and the Integral Post-Metaphysical assumptions it allowed for, the story of her depression turned out to be rich, painful, and complex. She had good relationships with both her parents, although her father had suffered from depression off and on since age 42. Janine's family identified as Roman Catholic, although they were on the liberal end of the spectrum. Janine was always described as precocious and graduated from high school as a National Merit Scholar. She attended Columbia University and graduated magna cum laude in psychology. She completed her combined master's and doctorate at Princeton University in clinical psychology and, once licensed, began seeing clients part time and teaching full time at a prestigious midwestern university. Her symptoms began when she was 22 years old and at that time she believed them to be the stress of graduate school combined with a genetic vulnerability to depression.

At age 28, she had what she described as a spiritual experience. She was lecturing on Maslow's hierarchy of needs and felt an "at-one-ment" with the students in her class. In thinking about it later she laughed at the obviousness of the connection. She declined to share this with her colleagues, most of whom were very materialist and modern in their attitudes toward mind and brain. Although trained in the rigors of the Boulder model in clinical psychology,

Janine always read spiritual literature and was fascinated by the works of Wilber, Grof, and Roger Walsh. Her "at-one-ment" experience was a trigger to return to the Catholic Church. Although fairly well versed in the Christian mystics, Janine felt she could not be spiritually fed in the church, although she met an Anglican spiritual director and began a practice of contemplation.

Throughout this time, Janine experienced an increased severity in her depressive symptoms. The symptoms most prominent were a pronounced sadness, despair, and deep emotional pain related to what she perceived as the suffering of humanity. From a diagnostic perspective, Janine met the criteria for MDD, Recurrent Episodes. This was clear enough even to her but none of the modern or postmodern metaphysical assumptions fit her case very well. From a modern perspective, she had few vegetative signs of depression so was not a good candidate for an antidepressant medication (not that she would have taken one anyway). One of her colleagues framed her depression as rooted in the competitive and sexist environment at the university. Despite decades of political correctness, the department was mostly made up of males who were trained in cognitive psychology and they let Janine know in subtle ways that they may make her journey toward tenure difficult.

In terms of ego development, Janine tested out validly at the Magician level. Recall that this level has been referred to by Cook-Greuter as a gateway to the transcendent. Janine struggled mightily with increased experience where her ego was actually an object of awareness. Her contemplation had evolved to the point where she identified more with the witness of all her thoughts and feelings than with the thoughts and feeling themselves. At several points she felt what she described as the experience that "God and I are one." She qualified this extensively as a source of confusion because, as she stated, "I am an individual and God and I are one. I am a creation rooted in the eternal."

During the course of her therapy, Janine was going through the end of a 3-year relationship that she had hoped would lead to marriage. Her companion in the relationship admitted to having affairs for the past year while lying about his monogamous commitment. Janine experienced confusion, anger, detachment, and at times dissociation throughout this period. At the same time, her spiritual director died of problems related to multiple sclerosis. Janine's worst depressive episode was a suicidal period lasting about 4 days following the funeral of her spiritual director. During this time, she underwent what she described as a "dark night" where she felt totally separate from people and God. She was still able to practice witnessing but wondered if it wasn't just a "trick" of the brain after all. She agreed to a 3-day stay at a mental health facility that she paid for out of pocket because she didn't want her insurance company to know what her symptoms were. The doctors there honored her insistence that she simply wanted structure, not medication. At the end of the 3-day period the suicidal crisis passed but the depression remained.

If we allow for the Integral Post-Metaphysical assumptions discussed earlier in the chapter, we have a framework capable of embracing the breadth and depth of Janine's symptoms and person. In large part, her psychotherapy was existential although her spiritual practice played a large role. As noted earlier in this chapter and in Chapter 3, people at the Magician stage frequently feel alienated from others as there simply are not that many people who can share their perspective. For Janine, this isolation became unbearable and was a key ingredient in her suicidal phase. To try to explain this away as a "chemical imbalance" or even a psychobiologic reaction to the breakup of her relationship would not do justice her. Janine's nested self-system when she was going through her suicidal period is represented in Fig. 8.4.

Now add to this the third dimension of the z-axis (the health and functioning of the self-system) and we would see that Janine's self-system moved toward the pathological end of the axis as her depression increased culminating in the extreme of suicidal ideation. At this point she was cut off from her own experience of eros or the urge to grow as well as all the tools and rules that she had access to from her "rung on the ladder" of self-development. Shadow aspects for Janine included both modern and postmodern elements like family pressure to have a family and integrating radical postmodern deconstructivism, which gave her permission to not have a family despite her desire to have one.

Fortunately for Janine, she could rely on her knowledge of psychology to guide her in her consistent opposition to antidepressant medications. As noted,

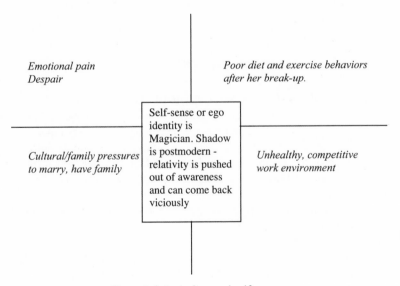

Figure 8.4. Janine's nested self-system.

clients whose symptoms are primarily vegetative are the best candidates for these medications.[66] In some cases, taking medication can merely mask symptoms and distract attention from the underlying problem. This may have been the case had Janine tried antidepressants. Working through her psychological pain and asking for structure when she needed it seemed to be the things that helped Janine the most. In therapy she metabolized many memories of feeling emotionally cut off from her father when he was depressed and how these shadows lingered and colored her experience with men and even, sometimes, her thoughts about God. At last follow-up, Janine had been symptom-free for 3 years, the longest period since the onset of her symptoms. There is no miracle cure here—just a complete framework that allowed us to fully embrace the depth and breadth of Janine's symptoms and person and how these were really just two sides of the same coin.

Now for some readers Janine may seem like an exceptional client, but the point is that the same framework can be used with a client who identifies at the Diplomat or Expert level of ego, has had a subtle-level spiritual experience and whose self-system is suffering symptoms of depression. One such client was Al, a cleric of the Methodist denomination in Christianity. Al tested at the Expert level on ego identity and suffered from depression following the pedophilia scandal in the Roman Catholic Church. For Al, this felt like overwhelming evidence that there was no personal God. At the same time, he had a lucid dream where he met St. Peter who spoke to him about human suffering and the need to be able to face it in order to heal it. Integrating this dream (which could be interpreted as a subtle spiritual experience) into therapy was a critical turning point for Al.

Concluding Thoughts

Writing about spirituality is fraught with pitfalls and this chapter is no different from other efforts. Particularly in the context of psychotherapy, it is hard to tease out just what is spiritual and what is psychological. The etymology of the word *psyche* likely is what it is because of this difficulty. The aim in this chapter has been to take the psychological address of Chapter 7 one step further. By covering some of the history of spirituality in psychology and psychotherapy we hope the reader understands the context for this discussion a bit better. Even if this goal has been attained, there is no doubt that we all must come to our own conclusions about the metaphysical assumptions of our psychotherapy discipline. In so doing, we continue to craft our own metaphysical assumptions. To what extent belief and experience play a role in this crafting is also something we have to decide and not something to be taken lightly. If we have succeeded in conveying the complexity of structure stages, you are aware that you are seeing these words through structures that affect how you interpret the words and how we put them down in the first place.

We need to proceed mindfully; not fearfully, but mindfully. When thinking about psychotherapy and spirituality, two common risks are related to ontological assumptions. If our ontological assumptions that consciousness can exist without a body (the dual-substance solution to the mind–body problem in Chapter 1), then we need to redefine psyche in the psychotherapy mainstream and consider that, after certain postconventional stages of development have been reached by a client, work with that client is a different kind of psychotherapy. Similarly, if our ontological assumptions about spirit are mistaken or misguided, we may be missing more subtle causes of symptoms entirely by looking in the wrong area (in this case a spiritual area that does not exist). Psychotherapy and spirituality is truly a razor's edge of sorts where Occam's razor may or may not apply.

Hopefully this book has helped you gain an appreciation of what the Integral Model offers psychotherapists, the practice of psychotherapy and clients. The Integral framework is a rich map of the human experience and provides tools that help therapists make their assumptions (and those of their discipline) objects of awareness. In the beginning of the book we noted that in essence, psychotherapy is helping clients make aspects of themselves and their lives objects of awareness. To the extent that therapists can align themselves with the erotic force pulsing within, they can make aspects of themselves objects of awareness. Ideally, this facilitates growth as a therapist and contributes to what they can offer clients.

We have aimed to ground Integral Psychotherapy in the literature of mainstream psychotherapy and viewed it as an integrative framework. Much research needs to be done to streamline and validate this framework. Integral psychotherapists face many of the same obstacles to such research as other psychotherapists. Our focus is usually more on therapy and less on research. Such research is expensive and time consuming and it is hard to find foundations that want to invest in research that is so exploratory in nature. Despite this, we are confident that more projects will be undertaken to explore the validity of our assumptions and the "replicability" of our model.

We began and remain open to the possibilities that Integral Theory holds for psychotherapy, but without losing sight of the firm foundations that have come before us. This is what "transcend and include" means to us, and it is—part and parcel—the force of eros. We are all in the same boat and that boat is riding an erotic current. In our own way, each of us must decide how we are going to engage the journey. We find that Integral framework is a mighty vessel for the challenging currents of the therapeutic journey. Perhaps our decisions are the agapic force that helps eros stabilize; perhaps our decisions, after all, are decisions of Kosmic proportion. We shall see . . .

A Case Study of Short-Term Psychotherapy and Transformation

David M. Zeitler

Integral Psychotherapist:
Analysis of Self-as-Instrument and Relevant Experience

This case study begins, as all Integral case studies should, with a brief analysis of the Integral psychotherapist. The relevant experiences, Integral life practices, quadratic mapping of life conditions, clinical assessment of level/line combinations, states, and type/style all are explored. I refer to the psychotherapist as "Mark."

Immediately before and throughout the course of the therapy discussed herein, Mark was living on the East Coast of the United States. He received his undergraduate degree from a traditional East Coast institution of higher learning, and attended a nontraditional West Coast institution of higher learning for his graduate degree. Mark had been a psychotherapist in two psychiatric wards for 2 years prior to the case described here. Of all of the possible relevant experiences for Mark in terms of this case, one stands out more than any other: Mark had gone through a similar existential malaise after graduating with an undergraduate degree in the sciences. The experience shifted his attention from medical school and toward nontraditional psychology.

Integral Psychotherapist: Integral Life Practice

Shadow Module

Mark was engaged in psychotherapy on a weekly basis. During the time of this case study, he was working on relationship issues. His typical pattern was being attracted to women with poor boundaries, with whom he would emotionally fuse, and subsequently enact what were often emotionally violent breakups. He was making great strides, and had begun dating a woman who had more mature boundaries than the women he had been attracted to in the past. Mark had also recently engaged in a deep regression process due to acute family of origin issues.[1]

Body Module–

Mark was engaged in a traditional and physically demanding martial arts practice three times a week. He also engaged in mountain biking once a week, and aerobic exercise on a gym machine twice a week. Mark's physical practices gave him an opportunity to form a specific rapport with Cheryl, the client in this case study. Cheryl was physically active and quite fit. Cheryl respected Mark's discipline, which likely went a long way in fostering therapeutic resonance. As we see here, each time Cheryl was "seen" for who she felt she was, many opportunities for healing and transformation followed.

Mind Module–

Mark was writing several academic papers before, during, and after the course of therapy. These papers were on Integral Psychology and Integral Psychotherapy. Mark also was part of a weekly discussion group that would read graduate-level texts and engage in graduate-level discourse around the themes in those texts. Frankly, Cheryl could be dismissive of people whom she did not think were intelligent. This can be used as a defense mechanism, but once again, Mark's continual honing of his mind via his mind module lent him the credibility he needed for connecting with Cheryl. Like many people who have both a psychiatrist and a psychologist, Cheryl viewed her psychiatrist as a medicine-giver, but not as someone with whom she might dialogue.

Spirit Module–

Mark had two spiritual practices before, during, and after therapy. One was Tai Chi, which can be studied as either a martial art, a healing art, or a *moving meditation*. Mark practiced Tai Chi as a moving meditation. The other was Ch'an mindfulness meditation, which is similar to Zazen meditation. Cheryl was suspicious of organized religion in general (despite her connection to an organized religion). However, Mark's spirit module included two practices that are becoming mainstream: Tai Chi and mindfulness. Cheryl enjoyed doing Tai Chi with Mark, and although she was skeptical of mindfulness, the secular literature on mindfulness and its anxiolytic properties was intriguing to her.

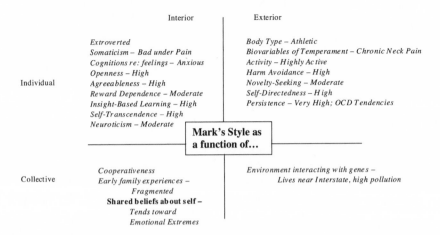

Figure A.1. Quadratic heuristic of Mark's style.

Integral Psychotherapist: Quadratic Mapping

Mark's quadratic mapping is represented in Fig. A.1

UPPER-RIGHT QUADRANT MAPPING

Mark was generally in good health in terms of his upper-right quadrant. His most recent medical issue was a knee injury that required arthroscopic surgery, from which he had fully recovered. Mark's behavioral routine was another issue——he had two jobs that required different hours. Because of this, Mark claimed that he was often tired in the morning, and cites this time period as when he first began drinking coffee. Although Mark's work ethic was never an object of therapy, Cheryl knew how to spot a hard worker when she saw one. She would openly comment on the group therapy projects and how well thought out they were.

UPPER-LEFT QUADRANT MAPPING

Mark's personality style leans toward extroversion, high openness, high agreeability, moderate reward dependence, high insight, high self-transcendence, and moderate neuroticism. Mark's openness and agreeability are sometimes linked to expected rewards. He is aware of this, and has been using cognitive-behavioral techniques (e.g., reframing scripts) to attenuate the neurotic symptoms that can result when expectations and reality do not in fact line up. When stressed, he tends toward anger and seclusion, or sarcasm. According to Mark, this can lead to low self-directedness at times and high avoidance. For Mark, this showed up in particular with his family of origin. Mark would be considered an "epicurean" in Helen Palmer's use of the Enneagram system of typology.[2]

LOWER-LEFT QUADRANT MAPPING

As mentioned, Mark had recently had an issue with his family of origin. There was a rift with his mother, for which he had also engaged in a deep regression process (see *Shadow* section). Mark came from a somewhat fragmented family of origin in terms of shared values. Christianity, Judaism, atheism, agnosticism, and secular materialism were separately and deeply held by several influential family members. This made Thanksgiving dinner particularly interesting, but day-to-day relationships were somewhat strained. Despite this, Mark shared many values with his "adoptive" family), which according to him is a nourishing and mutually beneficial arrangement. Mark was welcomed into the family of his best friend during college, which was almost the opposite of his family of origin. The parents were still together; shared values (as opposed to eclectic and idiosyncratic values) were openly discussed; and merit-based discussions were augmented (not *replaced*) by self-esteem dialogues. At first blush, Cheryl's family reminded Mark of his adoptive family, and Mark was careful to attenuate any counter-transference. Of importance was not constructing Cheryl as an "adopted mother-figure."

LOWER-RIGHT QUADRANT MAPPING

Mark lived in an East Coast city before, during, and after the therapy from this case. He held two jobs with different schedules, both of which actually reduced his commute stress because they were a reverse commute. He lived in an apartment with a cat, and was a short distance from his gym and martial arts school.

Integral Psychotherapist: Clinical Assessment of Level/Line Development

Mark had yet to take an *empirical* assessment of his stage of identification, but had worked with several developmentalists, including developmental psycho-therapists and developmental psychometricians. His main source of developmental-level/line clinical reflections came from his relationship with his mentor, a clinical psychologist who also is a leader in the field of Integral Theory. Another important source for Mark came from his longtime friend and confidante, who is known by all of his friends for cutting through the bullshit. Based on several courses of intense dialogue and discussion, the following *clinical* assessment of Mark's level/lines is made.

At the time of treatment, Mark appeared to cognitively and interpersonally be in the reintegration subphase of the strategist. Emotionally and morally, Mark appeared to be in the early repudiation subphase of the pluralist. There were indications that Mark's moral line of development was shifting out of pluralist meaning constructions. For example, Mark was given a dilemma on torture by his mentor, and was able (according to his mentor) to readily differentiate the endless relativity of pluralism from the context-based inclusion of relativity within an overall balance of justice and care.[3]

This information is relevant because Mark was treating a woman who was herself going through a developmental transformation from achiever to pluralist. Mark's own repudiation of pluralist-stage translations may have led to a mild mismatch. As I show, this seems to have showed up mostly in the form of Mark's focus on music as a point of departure for the therapeutic relationship.

Case Study: Integral Psychotherapy in Context

The purpose of the remainder of the case study is to flesh out and illustrate the benefits of using Integral Theory in a short-term psychotherapeutic care environment. Considerations on the Integral sychotherapist will continue to be peppered throughout. The case study itself follows a template that was created by R. Elliott Ingersoll and& the Integral Institute Psychotherapy Seminar Team.[4] First, a traditional *DSM-IV-TR* diagnosis is presented. This is followed by a summary of the case when looked at using the lens of quadrants, levels, lines, states, and types. A four-quadrant analysis is used to assess the client in terms of biology, psychology, social matrix, and cultural matrix. Levels and lines are given in parallel; for clinical purposes (and perhaps psychometrically as well), the tools and rules of a level occur in specific lines of development. As such, seven lines of development are looked at cognitive, self-identity, interpersonal, moral, emotional, bodily kinesthetic, and musical. Specific attention is paid to the self-related lines of development, as these are particularly useful for clinical assessment of stage-related thoughts and behaviors. The case study proceeds from the level/line discussion to a presentation of types—the "horizontal style" of a client. Next, the case study looks at states of consciousness, particularly in terms of the intersubjective matrix of the therapeutic relationship and of self-as-instrument. Finally, the original, traditional *DSM-IV-TR* diagnosis is augmented using Integral Theory, to create an Integral diagnosis and treatment. Although not a typical case, these situations often serve as important lessons for therapists.

Traditional Diagnosis and Evaluation

From Sunday, October 12 to Saturday, October 25, 2003, Mark was given an extremely rare opportunity as a therapist to help midwife someone who was in the throes of developmental stage transformation. As a group psychotherapist in two separate, locked psychiatric wards, Mark's role has generally been to patch people up and send them on their way. The populations to whom Mark offered therapy have already had their defenses broken down. Rather than probing and working with defense mechanisms, Mark mainly attempt to bolster those that exist, and offer coping skills that may help the patient live another day, week, or month without acting on suicidal or homicidal ideation. In many ways, Mark felt like the field medic in an army, administering acute care to folks who are, clinically speaking, "in combat."

CASE OVERVIEW

Upon admission, Cheryl was put on two combination therapies based on her history and symptoms: in the upper-right, a regimen of olanzapine (Zyprexa) and fluoxetine (Prozac)[5]; and in the upper-left and lower-left, individual and group therapy, respectively. During initial sessions, Mark noted that Cheryl was both sad *and* strong. Cheryl had a strong presence wherever she was, in every way. At first impression, she struck Mark as a natural "alpha" role, particularly because she consistently became the de facto leader of group therapy, although she was never dominating or inappropriate in any way. While consistently gloomy, Cheryl also maintained a highly developed sense of humor. Normally, when someone presents the amount of intelligence and depression that Cheryl had, Mark would look for the biting, sarcastic humor typical of a defensive posturing. Yet Cheryl had none of that. Interestingly, her humor was only evident during group therapy.

Mark was intrigued by the constellation of Cheryl's issues and symptoms. Cheryl would eventually divulge a miscarriage that had occurred several months before, but did not think that it played a role in her depression. She had allegedly processed throughout that painful period, and was able to be emotional about it without falling apart. It was not until they had gone through several therapy sessions that Mark was able to determine the kind of effect that the miscarriage had on her situation. It was not what he had expected.

Cheryl is extremely intelligent. She was valedictorian in high school, college, and upon graduating from the Wharton School of Business at the University of Pennsylvania. During the course of therapy, it became evident that Cheryl was questioning the drive to be *the best* at everything she set her mind to, a drive that had shadowed her for years. This questioning emerged in therapy after her spontaneous construction of her life's narrative as a series of "wins." With minimal probing from Mark, Cheryl framed her life in terms of challenges that were overcome, wins over losses, and the creation of business structures that she had single-handedly accomplished. This same construction colored her presentation of her family, her successful marriage, and her skill at raising two healthy, happy, and intelligent children. Her latest and most successful venture was in founding, owning, and operating a business that caters to the educational needs of children from wealthy families in the Philadelphia and New York metropolitan areas. She personally coaches these children for success during the major academic milestones of yearly standardized tests, the PSAT, the SAT, and eventually the GRE.

Cheryl is also a well-respected member of her community, a character trait that was readily apparent in group therapy. She presented strong boundaries to fellow patients—sometimes too strong for the other patients to cope with—but she did not isolate herself. There was, however, a growing recognition within Cheryl that the respect she commanded and the strong boundaries that she continually renegotiated were beginning to wear on her. A constellation of responses led Mark to this conclusion, and they did not appear to be the fatigue of medication nor the remaining depression from her miscarriage.[6] To gain the respect of others seemed to be a need that was waning for her; this process of *needing respect* appeared to be an achievement that she no longer wanted to continually declare. Although she never isolated herself, Cheryl did spend much time in introspection. Mark had at first neglected these moments as sedation from the side effects of medication or recovery from mental and physical exhaustion. But on reflection, he believed that something else was happening. He felt that Cheryl was literally creating the intrapsychic space necessary to form a new self-identity with new values and a new worldview.

Cheryl seemed to be creating a new self out of new needs. At the pluralist stage of self-identity, the need to open up emotionally, the need to connect, and the need for group activity or togetherness all become part of the new "rules." Themes about the meaning of life started to crop up as early as the second day of her stay in the psychiatric ward. It was during this day that Mark began to "hear" the distinct sound of two separate voices within Cheryl. Her depression started to make much more sense when Mark began to understand that her struggle revolved around a shift in values, and the excitement and guilt that usually accompany such a transition. Her examples from the lower-right and lower-left quadrants reflected her old self-identity bristling against her emerging self-identity.

For example, Cheryl would vacillate between expressing themes of respect (achiever self-identity), and themes of openness (pluralist self-identity). She began to juxtapose themes of success with themes of existential malaise in the face of such success ("What does it mean, ultimately, to have this success?"). It was not the expression of respect or openness itself that led Mark to consider possible developmental stage transformation. Rather, it was the way in which those themes were juxtaposed in Cheryl's meaning constructions. Cheryl was reframing the drive for success and respect within a larger context of the meaning of life itself. The fact that she could no longer see financial and personal success as an end in and of itself led Mark to the conclusion that she was in the middle of a developmental transformation from achiever to pluralist. This particular transformation often will have the existential themes that Cheryl certainly was reflecting on.

ADMITTANCE AND FIRST IMPRESSIONS

Mark felt a mixture of joy and anxiety when Cheryl presented several signs of transformation during the first session together. At the time, Cheryl was a 44-year-old married woman who was athletic, driven, and extremely successful. Two of the most important guides for gauging someone's level of psychological development are *spontaneous constructions* (often reveals "rules") and the ways in which *objects of consciousness are held* (often reveals the "tools"). Spontaneous constructions includes but is not limited to the ways in which people place value, accountability, and emotional resonance. It also can show up as the way they appear to be intentionally leaving out seemingly important information, and whether that information is simply outside of their awareness (i.e., they might simply be repressing thoughts/feelings). The other piece, holding objects, refers to the ways in people report on their inner-selves. The more developed a person is, the more the person is able to "hold" several thoughts/feelings/ considerations at once. The simplest example in emotional development is the development of the emotion known as "bittersweet." This emotion refers to something that is at once appealing and understood as necessary, yet somehow painful at the same time. Increased stage development leads to greater insight because the capacity to hold more "objects" simultaneously increases (whether or not someone actually engages such holding is a matter of style, pathology, and the extent to which they are asynchronously developed across their lines of development).

Cheryl presented with *good insight* about her situation. She was admitted to the psychiatric ward of the hospital where Mark worked after an intervention from family members and friends due to depression. As she herself put it, "I know that things are 'off.' " She did not protest, and was under a voluntary 72-hour watch. Her emotional state was one of exhaustion. She was emotionally spent. She appeared distraught, with hunched shoulders that gave her body the reflection of the internal load she was carrying. She was pleasant but extremely sad—this is Mark's clearest image of her. She knew that she looked "worn out," and her major concern on admittance was the possible permanent disruption that this hospital visit would have on her life. Despite this anxiety, Cheryl decided after 72 hours that she would stay a full 2 weeks. Neither Cheryl nor Mark realized at the time that she would look back on those concerns with a bittersweet smile from the perspective of a budding self-identity.

Summary of Diagnostics and Clinical Impressions

In the following sections, I flesh out Mark's four-quadrant analysis with several examples from his time with Cheryl. This case study presents traditional perspectives on psychotherapy in a short-term environment, augmented with insights using a four-quadrant analysis. The five major aspects of Integral Theory are addressed. Cheryl's traditional *DSM-IV-TR* diagnosis (Fig. A.2) at admittance to the psychiatric ward, which is revisited later, is presented in Fig. A.2.

Before diving into an Integral analysis, let me summarize where the meeting point between Cheryl and Mark takes place, clinically speaking. At first, Mark witnessed someone who seemed tired and depressed, so his assumption was that she suffered from depression, bipolar disorder, or cyclothymia. Her intelligence was immediately apparent, and she did not isolate herself, despite the fact that she seemed to enjoy being alone. Mark was intrigued by her emotional stability in light of her history and diagnosis. There were some things that seemed "off" to Mark about her diagnosis. For example, she seemed quite emotionally bal-

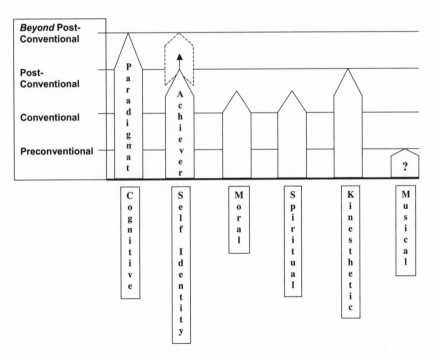

Figure A.2. Cheryl's *DSM* diagnosis.

anced. Mark doubted that her medication had taken effect, yet she was able to be tearful without falling apart while discussing painful issues during his assessment of her. Her thoughts were not scattered, she appeared to take relatively good care of herself, and she did not isolate. Finally, Mark resonated with something about Cheryl, that he could not define. His clinical intuition was on high alert. Although he did not understand what he was feeling, he kept an open mind about this resonance, and did not attempt to explain it away as counter-transference on his part. Although it is rare, he slowly began to disagree with the diagnosis and course of treatment being given to Cheryl. Her symptoms seemed to be "outside" of the purview of traditional psychiatry/psychotherapy.

These first impressions and the traditional medical-model diagnosis are revisited during the discussion. Of particular importance is the criteria by which Cheryl's depressive episode (suicidal ideation), and the psychotic features of her manic episode (disorganized speech and delusions of reference), were diagnosed. What follows here is an analysis of Cheryl's issues as viewed through the lenses of Integral Theory.

QUADRANTS

The quadrants provide clinicians a scanning tool of the life conditions of their clients, both when first assessing them, and throughout the course of treatment. These are the dimensions that, when explored with a clinician, can help differentiate between significant areas of expertise/mastery, and neglect/omission. The following is a four-quadrant analysis of the phenomena impacting Cheryl.

Upper-Left Quadrant Analysis: "Why I Do." Cheryl presented with moderate-to-severe acute depression, and mild-to-moderate chronic depression.[7] Cheryl had experienced only one episode of manic cycling, with racing thoughts, increased goal directedness, decreased sleep, and increased talkativeness. It was not severe, but it lasted for almost 2 weeks. Furthermore, her speech had become disorganized, and she was making associations between seemingly incongruent occurrences. A problem with self-report among clients with bipolar disorderis that they will often *not* report hypomanic (or even manic) symptoms, because they do not see these "symptoms" as problematic.[8] Cheryl never displayed this tendency. She seemed to be genuinely disturbed by it.

The "why" of Cheryl's activities revolve around her personality style and her stage of development. Cheryl displayed the kind of self-assured approach to life typical of an ambitious extrovert. Furthermore, her self-identity (i.e., her spontaneous constructions of value, worldview, and ego perspective) was consistent with the achiever stage of development. This particular level/type combination works extremely well together. Cheryl consistently presented themes of self-sufficiency, respect, and success. These attitudes are the cornerstones of the translations typical of someone who has this personality type at this stage of self-identity.

Upper-Right Quadrant Analysis: "What I Do." Cheryl is a 44-year-old White woman. She is 5'5" tall, of athletic build, with brown hair and brown eyes. Her bipolar diagnosis stems from several factors. Cheryl had, in the weeks previous to her admittance, a mixed depressed and manic episode. This manic episode had psychotic features to it, according to the admitting psychiatrist (more on this later). Cheryl's depression was severe, differentiating her diagnosis from cyclothymia, which would be more appropriate for someone with a mood cycle that shifts between mild depression and hypomania. She had brief suicidal ideation. Other important upper-right factors that were ruled out are hyperthyroidism, drug intoxication (acute and chronic), as well as brain injury. In any case of adult-onset bipolar disorder, the later the onset, the less typical it will be. (I revisit this important point in my evaluation of using Integral Theory to augment traditional psychotherapy.)

Polypharmacy often is necessary with for individuals with bipolar disorder.[9] Cheryl was no exception and she was placed on Zyprexa and Prozac for her acute depression.[10] Careful monitoring is required with any medication, and particularly with this type of combination pharmacotherapy. As noted earlier, the use of SSRIs may induce mania. Paying careful attention to the possible disconnects between upper-left self-reports and upper-right behavior that you see using your *self-as-instrument* is extremely important for tracking this side effect. Mark paid close attention to body language, tone of voice, and any speech that might be construed as disorganized. He contrasted this with Cheryl's self-reported moods. Cheryl never appeared manic, nor even under distress.

Also important in the upper-right analysis was Cheryl's routine. She jogged and lifted weights every day. She also worked every day, including at least 1 day on most weekends.

(I also add Cheryl's miscarriage to the upper-right analysis. At the time, Mark was not aware of Cheryl's miscarriage, but it seems appropriate to add it in here. What is important in this quadrant is the actual *behavior* that brings someone into the care of a psychotherapist of any variety. Something is going wrong, which creates behavior patterns that the self-system, friends, family, or larger social networks begin to select *against*. They may then seek therapy on their own, or from outside pressure. In Cheryl's case, her depression and disorganized thinking led to time off work, and eventual submission into hospital care.)

Lower-Right Quadrant Analysis: "What We Do." This quadrant represents the clinician's most immediate access to information about the client. Aside from the obvious location in a locked psychiatric ward, Cheryl hailed from a high socioeconomic status (wealthy upper-class). She was a proud business executive, and the owner/operator of a successful company. She attended business meetings

Why I do | What I do

Why We do | What We do

in her clients' homes, and paid weekly visits to her temple. Finally, according to her self-report, Cheryl ran an impeccable home.

Mark's only lower-right-quadrant interaction with Cheryl was in the psychiatric ward, which is a strange mixture of privacy without "real" privacy (doors with no locks that must be kept ajar unless it is time for bed). This balance between privacy and forced interaction actually helped Cheryl because it challenged her emerging self-identity to engage the group. It selects against isolation, which can masquerade as an achiever self-need to be autonomous.[11]

Lower-Left Quadrant Analysis: "Why We Do." Cheryl engages in two "cultures," both of which are influencing the expression of the emerging "rules" gained in the transformation of her self-identity. The first is her Reformed Jewish community. She attended temple weekly. In other contexts, she purportedly displayed the sort of extreme hyperindividuality that is often associated with achiever-stage consciousness in Western cultures. Cheryl both presented and expected industriousness, accountability, and a consistency of excellence.

Cheryl was active in her temple. It is in fact the only other group activity in which she engaged apart from spending time with family. Her moral reasoning was hard to gauge, other than her ability to frame her miscarriage in purely biological terms. She did not "blame God," nor did she feel the need to make sense out of "God's will." Her lower-left quadrant cultural rules were generated in familial and temple environments, and only minimally in work-related contexts, as she was a solo operator.

Mark had difficulty in assessing how Cheryl's Jewish community affected her lower-left quadrant. This is despite the fact that he was semi-adopted into a Reformed Jewish community through his stepfather.[12] What was apparent to Mark were the ways in which Cheryl's culturally derived meanings impacted her in the form of achiever-stage forms of business networking and operations, and her family, where she most certainly occupied the role of *chief executive officer*.

Levels and Lines of Development

Cheryl's Trajectory of Self-Identity in Terms of Levels. During one individual therapy session, Cheryl was speaking from the self she was "leaving," her achiever self-identity. She was spontaneously constructing her perspective from this identity. In speaking to her "leading edge" of consciousness, Mark attempted to bring up classic existential themes, hoping to see if his intuition that she was shifting identities was correct. He began by re-contextualizing her themes of respect, industriousness, and stability as possible routes to (respectively) alienation, workaholism, and rigidity.[13] Her eyes shone with the kind of mixed hope and fear that is readily available to anyone undergoing a developmental shift. Indeed, Mark's goal was to help Cheryl realize that it was okay to feel as if her "old self" was no longer adequate. Yet he was treading lightly, for the very *essence* of the achiever self-identity is the drive to be *more than adequate*.

This is an integral way of using the clinical/existential tool known as "selective frustration." Mark was selectively choosing points of contact with Cheryl whereby he could invite her to disidentify with her old self, and begin to objectify the meanings that she held from the perspective of that old self. He wanted to give her *new rules* for turning her *old rules* into *new tools*. He was also trying to elicit more selective translations. He juxtaposed her achiever stage translations with pluralist stage translations (or, more precisely, he was framing the terms that he used with intentionally pluralist overtures and tones). He was holding her, and he was pushing her—gently. This process resonates with *where* someone in transition finds themselves—stuck between a rock and a hard place. The key is to have compassion for the death of an outlived self-identity—and to allow the client such compassion as well. This was extremely difficult for Cheryl because of her well-honed skills as someone identified at the achiever stage.

People whose personality type or style and life conditions sync up well at the achiever stage seem to excel at creating stable and lucrative systems. It is therefore no easy task to present the contradictory theme of *inadequacy* to them as a means for disidentification. Achievement itself resonates with someone developing out of such an identity, as both heaven and hell. The hell of the constant managing; the heaven of stability. The risk was that her leading edge would thirst for a *better* understanding as to why she felt so fatigued. The hope was that a larger pluralist stage view would offer that understanding. Cheryl was the quintessential example of achiever-stage success. Mark imagined that her perception of the "destruction" of that identity must be particularly poignant for someone who has nearly perfected the meaning-making activity of the achiever stage, which is nearly synonymous with the ability to be successful. Mark understood that Cheryl's fear was that the "world" *as she knew it* would no longer be there when she returned with a new and more adequate self-identity.

In one of the group sessions, Cheryl was describing a particular time earlier that year, discussing her familial woes (which are few) and professional hopes (which are many). Mark felt that she was being overly protective, his instincts told me she was defending against the higher stage, and was not speaking from her emerging self-identity in any way. Mark noted aloud that her words were "pregnant with meaning." She was visibly shaken by Mark's use of this often used phrase, which seemed to jolt her out of her well-built emotional stability. At the time, he had not known of the miscarriage that she had suffered a year earlier (again, it was neither in her history nor in her *DSM-IV-TR* diagnosis). She became tearful, and began an emotionally charged dialogue centering on the miscarriage that had taken place during that time period.

Cheryl had not discussed the miscarriage with anyone but her husband, and the couple had determined that they had processed their way through this terrible experience.[14] Cheryl had been unsure about having a new baby in her life. She worried about her age, and she worried that a baby would not "fit" with the lifestyle that she and her husband enjoyed, with their other children rapidly approaching college age. Although seen as a blessing, the developing baby also was ultimately seen as a disruption to daily life. Cheryl was being open and honest, but there remained a guilty ambiguity that surrounded the miscarriage and her recall of it. Although she mourned the loss of her fetus, she clearly had residual emotions, but went back to work believing that the miscarriage did not affect her current life situation. Note the spontaneous framing that Cheryl made of the situation: the baby "fitting" into a system of her lifestyle; a possible "disruption"; her presentation was closest to a systemic, rational-mind analysis than any other, again indicative of the achiever stage of self-identity. Clinically speaking, her framing of the miscarriage in this way only added to her guilt-ridden ambiguity. Cheryl was a person "in-between" value perspectives.

This miscarriage, Mark later concluded, became the central feature of Cheryl's disrupted psyche. Her feelings of relief over the miscarriage were an invitation for primary-process or preoperational meanings. These primal ways of feeling into the world are driven by impulse and fantasy. Not being able to tell the difference between fantasy and reality, Cheryl had a break from herself and reality. This happened to occur at the same time that she was beginning a transformation to the next level of development. She was repressing her guilt, but she was also repressing her emerging identity.[15]

There was *clearly* a repression going on with Cheryl. It was a repression in which her husband was willing to join her (he was present during the intake). Although Cheryl had processed throughout this terrible period, it seemed cavalier to not give this information to the attending psychiatrist during her initial intake/history. At the same time, Cheryl *did* appear to Mark that she was able to handle complex emotions and thoughts without the type of disorganization that he usually experienced with client's who suffer from bipolar disorder. Mark was perplexed but he noted that there must be at least one variety of repression occurring. He discovered that there were *two* repressions occurring, and that the key to unlocking the repression of the lower feelings and higher transformations would be the same event—the miscarriage.

It wasn't until Cheryl heard the words "pregnant with meaning" within the context of an existential shift that she was able to link many of her thoughts and feelings surrounding her miscarriage. After group therapy, Mark went to her to discuss synchronicity in the patient–therapist relationship.[16] He pointed out that it seemed peculiar that he should choose such language when Cheryl was discussing an unrelated event that nevertheless occurred concomitant to the miscarriage. He talked about how her emotional sensibility had seemed to change, thus prompting him to question her guardedness in a roundabout way, describing her language as "pregnant." As an Integral psychotherapist, it was important for Mark to be able to differentiate synchronicity from delusions of reference. Synchronicity can mean the simultaneous awareness of multiple systems of meaning, their differences, and their interconnectedness. It can also be used to support romantic and/or new-age narcissism—the interconnectedness where *I* occupy the center, and everything is connected to *me*.

Cheryl seemed intrigued that Mark openly discussed this with her, given her diagnosis. He asked her about her "disorganized speech" and "delusions of reference" on her admittance. As it turned out, Cheryl was "babbling" [her words] about the process we had briefly discussed after the group therapy session—synchronicity.[17] She was making many associations between life and death, with an obsessive type of pattern that she had thought would "reveal" *why she should live*. In fact, it turned out that her "suicidal ideation" label came from the honest question that she posed to her attending psychiatrist as to "why I should live . . . if our lives amount to work, sprinkled with small bits of illusory happiness." Notice that there are primal as well as sublime forces at work here. This is to be expected when the self-system is "open" (e.g., when fractured because of dissociation caused by trauma, or because of normal disidentification from transformation; *both* were occurring with Cheryl). This conversation was riddled with existential themes, and it further convinced Mark that Cheryl was in the midst of transformation.

Both preconventional and postconventional meaning-making was present in the way Cheryl discussed her issues. The transrational perspective, stimulated by the opening of her self-system during her transformation from achiever to pluralist, would of course be collapsed by the attending psychiatrist. Furthermore, both the repressed-submergent-unconscious and the repressed-emergent-unconscious were actively protecting Cheryl from the chaos of life.[18] Being aware of this allowed Mark to begin to differentiate and support authentic transrational insights from prerational delusions. It was extremely difficult to help someone with this double repression of the less- and more-developed levels navigate such treacherous waters of development. Some of Cheryl's thinking was not under her control—she was "had by" these thoughts and feelings (hence her acute psychotic symptoms). There were some delusions of reference, with obsessive features. However, there were plenty of genuine insights, and many times Cheryl was able to differentiate them, both with and without Mark's help (particularly as the neuroleptic effects of the medication began to work).

How do you speak to the many sides of someone with acute pathology who *also* is in the process of transformation (which may itself have influenced or even been the primary cause of the acute pathology)?[19] In Cheryl's case, Mark selectively supported the openness and bonding of the pluralist stage while

Mari = magical =
self-protective
mythic → metaphor

through
Art the
by support of
their visual
representation
of each
stage

challenging the fantasy and primary process of the impulsive stage. Clinicians also can speak to these many sides by selectively supporting and challenging the dynamics of the transformation from achiever to pluralist. The process of repression is similar whether it is directed toward earlier or forthcoming stages of identity, because the *goal of defense mechanisms is protecting the integrity of the self-system.* Of all the important points of agreement between Wilber and Kegan, this is perhaps the most valuable for Integral psychotherapists. Defense is simply an integrity that has outstayed its welcome.

Mark made a conscious effort to help Cheryl open up and talk more about the experience of her miscarriage; but something else also was happening. He intentionally framed the experience in a way that he thought her leading edge of consciousness would appreciate. If there were two repressions occurring, he felt that they might be colluding with one another to keep Cheryl "where she was," developmentally speaking. Mark's suggestion to her that things are interrelated in ways that we often cannot understand was a powerful way for her to affirm that she was perhaps not going crazy. Rather, they might be the intimations of a *new need* for connectedness, which she expressed in rare and timid moments. This was risky because Mark could have further stimulated her primary process, her impulsive stage expression that she wasn't only affected by her miscarriage, but that she actually *caused* the miscarriage. A part of Cheryl felt guilty of infanticide. Mark pointed out that we don't always understand our interconnectedness because of our perspective, and that looking at things in new ways can be helpful. Another risk that Mark was taking was in validating nonachiever stage thinking and feeling. It must have been frightening to have such *intrusive* thoughts validated. At the same time, he had to invalidate irrational beliefs that she had caused her miscarriage.

Cheryl was beginning to open up as we worked on holding some things close, and letting other things go. That is the correct emotional space for psychotherapy with someone who is in transformation. Mark expressed to Cheryl that perhaps there was some validity to seeing patterns in the universe. Perhaps we are *not* merely disconnected from one another in our skin-encapsulated egos. At one key moment Mark was standing in the doorway to Cheryl's room and she opened up and cathected [20] onto him because he normalized her struggle with dying to an old self-identity that no longer made sense.[21] Mark connected with Cheryl by "seeing" both sides of her transforming self-system—this gave him the "credit" to challenge and differentiate her impulsive fantasies from authentic insights about pluralist stage holism.

Cheryl's Trajectory of Identity in Terms of Lines. The next few examples cover the interplay between the cognitive, spiritual, and bodily kinesthetic lines of development. It was during Mark's prescription of an *ILP* for Cheryl where he focused on lines as ways of helping her *stabilize her transformation.*

Cheryl seemed well "put together." After spending time in therapy with her, it seemed likely to Mark that most of her developmental lines reflected an achiever stage of self-identification. Exceptions were her cognitive line, which appeared to be at the *paradigmatic* stage of development[22]; and her spiritual line, which seemed to be at the *conventional* stage of development.[23]

Cheryl engaged in many solitary activities. She ran her own business, where she worked alone; she was a jogger; she liked to spend her evenings home alone, reading; and she encouraged her family to be independent and successful. Cheryl's sole group activity was attending her synagogue. Mark's goal was to be an ally to her emerging self-identification. As such, he used his knowledge of developmental lines to stabilize the growth that was naturally occurring. One way of looking at Integral Psychotherapy is that you are an ally to evolutionary motion. But this is where unconditional positive regard, particularly listening with an open heart, is so important. *Listen Without Theory.* Mark suggested Cheryl use yoga as a replacement for jogging for two reasons.[24] First, he wanted Cheryl to engage in a *group* exercise program that would stimulate her bodily kinesthetic line to grow. He thought that yoga would be satisfying because it is a group activity that allows people to express themselves individually, while simultaneously providing group participation and interaction. Furthermore, yoga can be extremely challenging, which naturally "speaks" to her old self.[25]

Second, Mark thought yoga could be a safe way for Cheryl to explore the philosophical questions she had about spirituality in general. Her spiritual line seemed as if it was still rooted in a quasi-ethnocentric Judaism.[26] Far from wanting to replace her spiritual practice, he wanted to augment it with one that would allow her to accept *or* reject the philosophical and spiritual components as she saw fit. Mark explained that yoga might be able to help her frame her spiritual and philosophical questions in a larger context within a practice that was thousands of years old.

Something that Mark found slightly troublesome was Cheryl's utter lack of interest in or knowledge of music. He often ran a "music" group therapy (one of the most popular), where he will play an eclectic mix of songs, and have the client's express their reactions to the words, melodies, and flow of the music in both pictures and words. He was always careful to include songs from a wide variety of genres, and until Cheryl, there was always at least *one* song that each client would resonate with. Cheryl couldn't have cared less about this group, nor about music in general, according to her. At first glance, there does not appear to be any therapeutic value in making an issue of this with a client. Mark included this in the "Other" category of Cheryl's psychograph because it is an anomaly that he thought might be worth pursuing.[27]

Types and States of Development

Cheryl's Translations in Terms of Her Style or Type. Mark attempted to glean a little bit about Cheryl's type by noting her initial presentation to others, as well as her "posture" in group therapy. Cheryl seemed to be quite sanguine, to use Wundt's original differentiation of the four main types—low emotional-ity (again, the medications had not taken when Mark first saw Cheryl), and extroverted. As with levels and lines of development, it is impossible to get an empirically accurate picture of someone's stable, continuous type in a short-term situation. However, as with levels and lines, it is nevertheless clinically valuable to make such an attempt using your self-as-instrument

Cheryl seemed to be masculine, type A, and "the performer," to use Palmer's Enneagram label.[28] The performer type is self-assured, driven, image conscious, and competitive. Putting this into the more general "style" terms: Cheryl exhibited low emotional reflection; high openness; high agreeability; was quite conscientious; had high reward dependency; low insight (despite her rather high cognitive development); a *shifting* low to high self-transcendence (an artifact of stage transformation?); and low neuroticism.

She exhibited a tremendous drive to succeed, and claimed that she has always "excelled at whatever she set her mind to." She is direct, linear, and logi-cal. She presented as an approachable Mr. Spock from *Star Trek*. She may not have had tremendous warmth, but her warm humor connects her with others. While on the unit, she put her best foot forward, even under such stressful conditions. Differentiating this type and her overall style from an identifica-tion with the achiever stage can be daunting. Yet this was not so with Cheryl. Long before she stabilized an achiever self-identity (which rarely happens before the age of 20),[29] Cheryl was *valedictorian from middle school through graduate school*. Every time!

The downside of the performer personality style is the possibility that the person will blindly pursue success and status as a means in and of itself. This posed yet another challenge for Cheryl, in the same way that speaking to her about *relative competence* at the same time that she is emerging out of a level identity that centers around competence, can be daunting. In other words, for the performer, the achiever self-identity can often be translated to a much greater degree than for other personality styles.[30] The pursuit of success and status is often associated with translation at the achiever stage of self-identifica-tion. Cheryl's difficulty with disidentifying from the pursuit of success/status as having *essential* value was palpable. This was one of the reasons that Mark came to the working conclusion that Cheryl carried the aforementioned styles and began clinically operating under the assumption of a "performer" type.

Cheryl's Translations in Terms of Her States of Consciousness. First and foremost, it is imperative that Integral psychotherapists differentiate a client or patient's state in terms of upper-left and upper-right phenomena. For example, Mark knew that one of the side effects of Zyprexa is sedation. In someone who is experiencing acute depression, it is difficult to assess whether or not the sleepiness, hunched shoulders, and drowsy-looking eyes are more the product of phenomena in the upper-left or upper-right. Mark knew that both would be present. But Mark also asked himself, "is the client's 'poor eye contact' a means to avoid emotional connection, or is it the Zyprexa working its magic?" In other words, one must not only be aware of immediately available symptoms, but also the complex range of interaction among symptoms.[31]

The client's state of consciousness helps therapists to answer the question of "why now?" What makes a person seek out therapy? *Dysphoric states of consciousness caused by imbalance(s) across the stages and quadrants* is the simplest and most general explanation for why people seek therapy. Cheryl's depression was not only part of her diagnosis, but also was part of her state of consciousness at admission. She also had been experiencing what we referred to in Chapter 7 as a "nonordinary" states, which turned out to be experiences of synchronicity. Cheryl exhibited both the primal, loose associations of the preconventional stages, and the sublime insights of the postconventional stages.

She felt that her consciousness was "altered," and dialoguing about synchronicity in the psychiatric ward was both a challenge and a blessing for her. She still "felt crazy" for even considering that something like "holism or spiritual interconnectedness" has *value*, let alone having *validity* as an actual phenomenon. But, she also understood that her current ways of looking at her life were inadequate. Cheryl was at the end of her rope, and felt like she was being torn apart.

There is an almost palpable energy that surrounds someone who is in the state of transformation that Cheryl was in when she arrived on the psychiatric ward. After all of the clinical tools and therapy sessions that Mark had with Cheryl, he realized that from the beginning, it was her openness, her raw experiences of fear, tinged with bliss over the new possibilities of a wider perspective, that drove him to look for signs of developmental transformation. It was the original resonance about which Mark also had kept an open mind. This is how the *self-as-instrument* operates. It is the Integral Psychotherapy use of clinical judgment.

Summary of Integral Psychotherapy Analysis

So far, I have summarized how Cheryl presented from the differentiated perspectives of quadrants, level/lines, states, and types/styles. Mark mostly understood where Cheryl was in terms of her environment, her culture, her behavior, her medications, and her *likely* stage of self-identification. He hypothesized, based on several sessions of individual and group therapy (as well as observing her on the unit during each of his 9-hour shifts), that Cheryl was going through a developmental transformation.

I have also attempted to show the traditional medical-model approach to Cheryl's condition. I revisit several key points of connection and departure between traditional medicine/therapy and Integral Psychotherapy later.[32] Finally, before leading into the actual course of Integral Psychotherapy, allow me to reiterate the importance of self-generation. Being a good Integral psychotherapist is *more* about listening correctly than about helping someone to evolve. People who are in the Integral community-at-large often are blindsided by a love of transformation. Dare I say a *fetish*? Yet 99.99% of the time, your job will be to help someone who needs to *retranslate* their meaning constructions in a *more healthy* fashion. Listening to the ways that people spontaneously construct their values and perspectives will go a long way to helping you form an integral diagnosis and therapy goals. However, this requires that you have first already achieved an ability to map those spontaneous constructions; that is, you must have a large enough embrace wherein you can then "hang" the experiences your client brings up, and the *ways* in which they bring them up. Then you can take a step back and look at the connections between them, which surfaces the systems that are in operation. The AQAL model will help you in this process.

The Benefits of Integral Psychotherapy

By acknowledging her fears and stimulating her leading edge, Mark invited Cheryl into a truce with her fears and depression. He invited her to see her current situation as completely normal, even though she may have never experienced anything like it. Being a part of her transformation was fascinating, and he cherished the opportunity. Without Integral Theory, he relayed that he might have treated her like several other healing professionals had—molecules running through arteries.

The communal nature of the pluralist felt like a form of dependency to the part of Cheryl that was still identified with her achiever self. This *perceived* dependency was confused with the dependency that she *actually* needed, both medically for her miscarriage and psychologically from her family and from myself. Mark gently encouraged Cheryl to recognize what her fear and depression were feeding on—the fear of losing her "self." She was terrified of dying to her old self. It was a terror that seemed justified by the actual death of her unborn baby, which the powerful episode during group therapy made clear.

The benefit of using the AQAL model with Cheryl was the ability to view her symptoms from several perspectives at once. Cheryl was indeed repressing residual yet powerful emotions surrounding her miscarriage (repressed-*submergent*-unconscious). Top among them were the *anguish* of the event itself, the *relief* of not having what she framed as a disruption, and the *guilt* over feeling such relief. Confusing these issues was her unconscious belief that she may have in fact been the cause of the miscarriage. But she was *also* repressing the drive of eros—the drive to grow (repressed-*emergent*-unconscious). Her repression barrier was in full response to her transformation, and her threat zone limited her in her move beyond an achiever self-identity. This is despite the fact that she was already "seeing" certain things from a more developed pluralist set of perspectives. In other words, part of Cheryl was repressing the next wave of her development, and part of her was repressing her feelings surrounding her miscarriage.

Any number of therapies would be able to reveal the relationship between Cheryl's depression and her miscarriage. However, the Integral Psychotherapy lens allowed Mark to quickly see that the *actual* miscarriage mirrored and energized Cheryl's miscarriage of her birth into a pluralist stage of self-identity. There were two repressions occurring, and they were feeding into one another *in the name of integrity*. Cheryl's repression of her emotions surrounding her miscarriage was an attempt to avoid pain, for sure. But it was also serving to inhibit her own evolution. Every stage identification maintains its integrity until the bitter end, until the emerging self-identity can stably view and reframe experiences according to a more adequate perspective. fusion, differentiation, integration

Cheryl's "developmental miscarriage" into a pluralist self-identity was supported by a phenomenon Integral Theory sheds much light on: stage-specific translation. Cheryl translated an identity from the achiever stage unlike anyone Mark had ever met or even read about. She was so skilled at this level that it must have been extremely difficult for her to give up such an identity. My hope is that Integral psychotherapists will be able to tease apart the dynamics of types/styles and states that seem to play a large role in *how* we translate our experiences at particular level/line combinations. Mark seemed able to do this. To someone who is highly skilled at translating an achiever self-identity, any hint at transformation *beyond* this way of seeing the world must feel like sheer madness![33] Wherever she turned, the reflections of her successful rational ego stared back at her. By recontextualizing these successes as "failures" from the perspective of her emerging pluralist self-identity, Mark was able to speak to *both* Cheryls at once. Her achiever self-identity, responding immediately to the notion of failure itself was able to relax into the possibility that "success" may in fact be a relative term. Exhausted from years of maintaining rigid systems and being overworked, it is likely that this part of her identity was ready to relax. To her emerging pluralist self-identity Mark sought to quench the thirst for openhearted dialogue and holistic patterns of human connection.[34]

I mentioned earlier that Cheryl's humor most often emerged during group therapy. The isolation often felt by individuals who are burdened with a now limiting achiever self-identity often is coupled with a joy for the celebration of human bonding.[35] Cheryl's new need for group connection was reflected in her bright and warm humor with others during group.

I'd like to finish this part of the case study with a final note about Mark's therapeutic occasions with Cheryl. Cheryl was bright enough to understand developmental psychology and Integral Theory. Mark wanted to give her something to satisfy her formidable mind. He already had experienced a synchronicity with

her, which spoke volumes to her heart and to her emerging self. But he wanted
to give to her mind the food of patterns that are revealed to anyone who uses
the Integral Theory. In their last session together, Mark brought in the larger
pattern of developmental death and birth. There are many ways to frame developmental growth, and he chose the labels of "death" and "birth" because these
labels are particularly poignant to someone who is engaging in the decidedly
existential shift between the achiever and pluralist stages of self-identification.
Mark helped her see that her own experiences are part of a larger pattern that
we all go through, but that few recognize. He trusted that Cheryl had enough
of her "rules" from her emerging self, and wanted to give her some "tools" that
would allow more healthy translations after leaving his care. He showed her
that we are constantly dying and being re-born, and that this pattern is based
on our actual existential dilemma of physical birth and death.[36]

Cheryl took her first steps at reframing her miscarriage during that session,
heaving a sigh of relief that she had been holding inside for a year. Her relief
even washed over *Mark*, and something seemed to "click" inside of her. It does
not happen often in a psychiatric ward in terms of psychological development,
but she was a different person right then and there. After a year of anguished
developmental arrest, and 2 weeks of pharmacotherapy and Integral Psychotherapy, Cheryl changed right before Mark's eyes. But this is the sort of shift
that happens subtly, yet is profound. The "evidence" for such a shift is in the
new translations that people make, and is nothing so drastic as the formation
of wings. Nevertheless, his suspicion was that Cheryl had taken another half
step, but that this particular half step left her on the *other* side of the fulcrum
between achiever and pluralist.

The ability to "hold" several pieces of someone else's life simultaneously
and in relation to one another is an important task in therapy—but it is absolutely vital for anyone who is engaged in Integral Psychotherapy. Using the
AQAL model, we must be willing and able to "hold" not only the pieces of
someone else's life across one level or one line (i.e., the emotional fallout from a
miscarriage), but we also must hold those pieces together across their constantly
shifting perspectives during translation (the norm) and transformation (rare).
Diagnosis and treatment are moving targets. But they move in the patterned
way that chaos theory so elegantly covers in the study of weather patterns.

There is another important benefit in using integral psychotherapy—*you*
will be transformed. One of the major components that I have attempted to
point to is the *self-as-instrument*. The ability to objectify your self-as-instrument
while engaged in psychotherapy is itself a practice of transformation. Think of
developmental psychology—it is by objectifying our previous identities that we
begin to transform our consciousness to higher levels. Turning rules into tools.
Objectifying our own self-as-instrument calls us into this realm of transforma-

tion. You are not only objectifying yourself, but the *ways in which you use your "self."* You will be called to see the system of "you" as a tool in order to run a systems-of-systems analysis. You will be the witness of these interrelating systems. Informing these decisions during therapy will be the systems of quadrants, levels/lines, states, and types/styles, all running through and around the points of contact between you and your client. This is what *hypertransference* means—the *viewing and using* of these simultaneous interactions, and the *heart and mind considerations* that we take for our client's contexts of work and love.

Integral Life Practice

It bears repeating that 99.9% of the time, our work as therapists is to be a coach for healthy translation and retranslation of stage-relevant meanings. But keeping an open mind to other possibilities proved valuable. Furthermore, Mark's knowledge of developmental lines strongly influenced his suggestions to Cheryl. Yoga has become an important part of her life, and she has not abandoned her Judaism. Her spiritual life and physical exercise program have worked in concert to stimulate growth. Mark encouraged her to continue her weight training—and discussed with her the connections that such exercise would have with her metabolism, energy, growth, and yoga. This was another both/and combination that Cheryl liked: the building of muscle combined with the stretching of her body, mind, and spirit.

Mark suggested that Cheryl spend more time with her family. It was easy for her old identity to see happy, healthy family members as a reason to *not* spend time with them. The old Cheryl valued independence in herself and those around her above most things. And a happy, healthy family can mean "the system is running perfectly!" But she also needed to see that soon, her relationship with her children would be reorganized with or without her. They would be at college, and she would be at home. "Why wait?" Mark asked her. He suggested that she begin this process by reconnecting to her family in new ways. Mark's hope was to let her see that *passively* spending time with family (i.e., without a goal, lesson, or highly structured activity) can *itself be a goal.* It is important that she present a solid and warm holding environment during the time that her children leave for college. He explained to her that this is a vital aspect of growth—that the symbols or representatives of the previous "nest" should remain in place while they are being disidentified with, lest you risk a developmental fixation. By discussing the human bonding with her family in the context of developmental dynamics, Mark invited Cheryl to mirror her own needs for keeping stable representations of an achiever form in place (such as her career) even as they are being reorganized in terms of their ultimate meaning for her (such as family and religion).

Mark also suggested several books to Cheryl, paying particular attention to her state of consciousness near the end of her stay. I will list a few of them here, only to highlight the intention of informing her ILP. He suggested *Zen and the Art of Motorcycle Maintenance* by Robert M. Pirsig because it is a book about a highly intelligent and developed person whose search for meaning and value from an existential perspective lands him in a psychiatric ward. He also suggested *No Boundary* as an introduction to Wilber's work. Mark's hope was that reading about boundaries in general would help Cheryl objectify her own strong tendency toward boundary formation.

He also let Cheryl know that there are groups of people who are dedicated to reading books of this nature in a community. He shared with her that he had once been a part of such a community, and that there are several places on the Internet where these groups can be found. He suggested this because Cheryl enjoyed reading alone, yet she was attempting to seek validation for her emerging needs for group connection. A reading group dedicated to dialoguing about books with existential and integral themes seemed appropriate.

Finally, Mark also suggested that Cheryl listen to music. He wanted her to go back to a time when she did listen to music, in her childhood, and pick up from that place. As a child, she had listened to pop music in the 1960s. There did not seem to be any active repression of the aesthetic dimensions in general, just a disinterest (arrest?) for music in particular. It seemed like the right time for her to revisit this line of development.[37]

Upon her arrival, Cheryl had seemed to be reaching for a reflection to her intuition that there is depth and value apart from the achiever values that she was so good at upholding. Often with sadness, Cheryl would openly ponder this possibility. Yet her identity was not strong enough to provide her with an answer. Children eventually are able to soothe themselves after they reach the diplomat stage of self-identity. But until that time, such soothing must come from without. It is a process that moves outside-in during the development of that self-identity. It would not be misleading to say that during her stay at the psychiatric ward, Cheryl's new self-identity was looking for ways to move the process of "existential soothing" outside-in. In this way, there are rare moments that Integral psychotherapists can become both crucible and catalyst: crucible in the sense that you are a holding container (Kegan's "culture of embedded-ness"); catalyst in the sense that you can help stimulate healthy translations or even the rare stage transformation in others. You will not always go through your own developmental transformation (after all, a "catalyst" is a chemical substance that stimulates a change while itself remaining unchanged). However, by witnessing the hypertransference across your self-as-instrument in relationship with the constellation of AQAL issues in your client, you will make the objectification of rules-to-tools a part of your being. This process, insofar as it mimics transformation, can certainly stimulate growth.

Conclusion

Cheryl's 2-week hospital visit is certainly atypical. According to Mark, he is usually in full agreement with the *DSM-IV-TR* diagnosis of the client's personal or attending psychiatrist. Nevertheless, developmental patterns will be evident and useful as a tool for engaging a client. There are also many cases where someone will temporarily regress and act out from lower perspectives. But, as Kegan is so fond of saying, we live much of our lives *out of balance*.[38] For this reason alone, knowledge of the development of consciousness and its effect upon people is extremely valuable for the integral psychotherapist.

This is true despite the fact that we don't normally deal with individuals who are in the midst of a transformation. From the perspective of Integral Theory, Cheryl's *DSM-IV-TR* diagnosis seems limiting for two important reasons. First of all, the failure to take into account the fact that people are continually evolving places a large blind spot in terms of diagnosis. Perhaps this is why it is the *symptom* rather than the *source* of the disorder that is so often treated. This is not to say that we know the source of any disorder—only that there are perhaps new ways that we can look at disorders that might help us understand what is actually happening, and therefore how best to treat people who are suffering.

Cheryl's case illustrates this well. According to the *DSM-IV-TR*, adult-onset bipolar symptoms usually indicate medical issues or illicit drug abuse as a causative factor. Yet it is equally likely that a transformation of self-identity to a higher level can bring about *any* of the symptoms listed for bipolar.[39] The self-system is inundated with lower impulses and higher state experiences during the delicate developmental shifts across the fulcrum of self-identity. We are literally "energized" during such shifts. Like heat added to any system, whatever had been occurring will continue to occur, and much more chaotically. Furthermore, these "symptoms" would be particularly present in someone with a performer personality type or the style of openness and goal-directed activity that Cheryl has always had, who is also transforming out of the achiever stage. Even so, the inability to handle love and work at the same time is the Western culture's definition of insanity. For someone experiencing transformation, a shift *out of* the achiever stage will undoubtedly create an inability to deal with both love and work.

This is why it is vitally important that should you experience someone who is transforming or even retranslating in a manner that is consistent with what we know to be an aspect of the evolution of the individual, you normalize that experience for them. Another part of the traditional *DSM-IV-TR* diagnosis that piqued Mark's interest was the bipolar-mixed aspect. This diagnosis often is not used, to put it mildly. Drawing a circle around a constellation of symptoms can be helpful for our clinical work. But we can never let the labels become the people. This is not only good moral advice, but good clinical advice as well, as I have attempted to show here.

Cheryl's disorganized speech turned out to be mostly normal from the perspective of someone leaving an achiever level of self-identification, which also means leaving most of Western culture in general. Furthermore, her suicidal ideation also turned out to be the normal existential malaise that accompanies such a developmental transformation. This is not to say that people cannot or will not commit suicide while going through this particular shift of consciousness. It does, however, recontextualize our approach to clinical criteria: Not *all* thoughts about the meaninglessness of existence stem from the hopeless emptiness that is a clinical feature of deep depression. Sometimes these thoughts are a normal part of growth and evolution. It also is important here to note that Mark's first impressions of Cheryl did not seem to fit her diagnosis, nor with his experiences of other client's diagnosed with bipolar disorder. She seemed too well put together, too functional, and had too much insight (low insight in general insofar as her style, but too much to qualify for bipolar disorder). The attending psychiatrist simply did not have a large enough frame of reference. Since dealing with Cheryl, Mark more fully understood why many critics claim that bipolar disorderis too often used as a diagnosis.

As for Cheryl, there was marked improvement in her mood, not to mention Mark's sense that there was a definitive shift of gravity in terms of her overall stage of identification. Like most therapists, Mark unfortunately lacked the metrics or time to *empirically* verify this. He was not attempting to say that she was whole and stable. She still faced a fear of moving between selves. The difference was that it would now be the fear of sliding *back into old* patterns rather than the fear of *transcending* (*phobos*). Cheryl will still be dealing with the possibility that manic and depressive symptoms may return, or that coming off the regimen of drugs may cause some delusions to recur. But it seems that these were acute symptoms of a trauma tangled with a developmental transformation.

Cheryl's breakthrough was that she was able to let go of an *exclusive* identification with the achiever stage of development. She left the hospital in mourning–both for her miscarried fetus and for her old self-identity. She had begun to metabolize some of the pain surrounding her miscarriage, instead of letting the pain "have her." Her Achiever self-identification was ill equipped to metabolize the feelings and contradictions associated with her two miscarriages, yet novel perspectives and meaning-making systems seemed to be moving outside-in. She was becoming familiar with the new rules, and had begun using the new tools. Her prototype was ready to roll.

The transformation from achiever to pluralist is nearly synonymous with existential malaise. By stepping briefly into the wave of her own evolution, Cheryl was able to make most of the necessary connections across the fragmented parts of her life. By being allowed to plausibly explore these connections, instead of simply pathologizing them as psychoses, Cheryl was able to integrate *healing* with *transformation*. At least, she was invited to do so.

Final Thoughts

Looking back over this experience, it seems like the attempt to write about one client's extremely rare and powerful transformation is a lot like attempting to describe a piece of visual art that moves you with mere words. It seems artificial, and it is certainly cumbersome to describe in linear fashion something that is so powerful and obvious when witnessed firsthand.

Cheryl's case contains the kind of dynamics that can help integral psychotherapists learn about turning theory into practice. Mark learned that his suspicions about the limitations of the medical model made sense. He also learned that for the most part, the *DSM-IV-TR* is accurate in describing and collating symptoms into workable categories of psychopathology. Cheryl appears to have been a brilliant example of the reality of ontogenesis, of human evolution and transformation. She was evolving beyond the current mainstay of sociocultural development (i.e., the achiever stage values that dominate the Western mindscape). For this reason, the tools created from those rules are bound to miss most of the subtle differences between pathology and transcendence. After all, people identified at any stage will often interpret more developed meaning constructions as developmental arrest. This is part of the process of integrity. Admitting stages beyond our own is difficult if not impossible.[40] Cheryl is a living, breathing example of many aspects of Integral Theory, and I hope that this case study has illustrated this. Furthermore, I hope that it may also reinforce the idea of trusting our *self-as-instrument* in using the principles of Integral Theory during psychotherapy.

Mark had only brief contact with Cheryl beyond his intense 2 weeks with her at the psychiatric ward. He cherished the opportunity that he had, knowing full well that he might never again get such a vibrant, textbook example of many important elements from Integral Psychotherapy. My hope is that by telling her story of transformation, the small but important percentage of clients who *are* in developmental need may in synchronous fashion find their way to you, and we can all learn how to better midwife these tremendous births of consciousness.

Notes

Notes to Prologue

1. Nietzsche, F. (1954). *Thus spoke Zarathurstra* (W. Kaufmann, Trans.). New York: Penguin.

2. Kojeve, A. (1980). *Introduction to the reading of Hegel: Lectures on the phenomenology of spirit.* Ithaca, NY: Cornell University Press.

3. Quoted in Macey, D. (1993). *The lives of Michel Foucault.* New York: Vintage, p. 89.

4. Barthes, R. (1978). *Image–music–text* (S. Heath, Trans.). New York: Hill & Wang.

5. See Moursund, J. P., & Erskine, R. G. (2004). *Integrative psychotherapy: The art and science of relationship.* Pacific Grove, CA: Brooks/Cole and Prochaska, J. O., & Norcross, J. C. (2003). *Systems of psychotherapy: A transtheoretical analysis* (5th ed). New York: Thomson.

6. See, for example, Slife, B. D., Reber, J. S., & Richardson, F. C. (Eds.). (2005). *Critical thinking about psychology: Hidden assumptions and plausible alternatives.* Washington, DC: American Psychological Association.

7. For example, the circular relationship between psychotropic medications, diagnostic categories, and instruments derived from cognitive researchers (e.g., the Beck Depression Inventory) guarantees "job security" for all three. No psychotropic medication can be approved unless shown to treat a "disorder" (thus *DSM-IV-TR*). No "disorder" can be conceptualized without a list of symptoms (thus the Beck Depression Inventory). And nothing is better for selling your inventory than linking it to existing diagnostic nosologies.

8. See, for example, Seligman, M. E. P. (1995). The effectiveness of psychotherapy. *American Psychologist, 50,* 965–974.

9. For our purposes, gene expression is the ability of a gene to make a biologically active protein. In July 2007, the U.S. National Human Genome Research Institute announced that it now appears very likely that genes express in networks based on interaction with the environment. This announcement is a radically more complex understanding of gene expression that outdates most of what we thought we knew about genetic influence on psychological disorders. See Bankura, S. (2007). *Human genome: Need to start afresh?* Retrieved August 21, 2007 from http://www.scienceahead. com/entry/human-genome-need-to-start-afresh/.

10. This clumsy label for what comes after a postmodern age is for me transitional. As I point out later if we can engage what is opening to us we may in fact create, together, an Integral period. The post-postmodern was described by Tom Turner in *City as Landscape: APost-Postmodern View of Design and Planning*. He noted that modernity was typified by reason but reason has limits. Postmodernity degenerated into "anything goes." which doesn't work. He said "let us embrace post-postmodernism and pray for a better name." One suggestion from Raoul Eshelman was performatism, described as a period where subject, sign, and thing come together in a way that is transcendent (see http://www.artmargins.com/content/feature/eshelman.html)

11. Wilber, K., Patten, T., Leonard, A., & Morelli, M. (2008). *Integral life practice: A 21st-century blueprint for physical health, emotional balance, mental clarity, and spiritual awakening*. Boston: Integral Books.

Notes to Chapter 1

1. As shown in Chapter 7, the psychological address of the client gives us a clue as to how a person co-constructs the universe.

2. As noted in the prologue, I hold this concept lightly and we explore it more fully in Chapter 8.

3. Zeig, J. K. (1990). What is psychotherapy? In J. K. Zeig & W. M. Munion (Eds.), *What is psychotherapy? Contemporary perspectives*. San Francisco: Jossey-Bass., pp. 1–14.

4. This description was crafted by Wilber in multiple conferences with the Integral Psychotherapy team of myself, Dr. Jeff Soulen, Dr. Bert Parlee, Willow Pearson, and David M. Zeitler.

5. Throughout this book I follow Wilber in using the Greek word *Kosmos* to describe not just the exterior universe (cosmos) but the interior universe as well——what Joseph Campbell referred to as "the inner reaches of outer space."

6. Integral Psychotherapy may be thought of as an integrative framework. These have increased in popularity and utility over the past 20 years as more and more therapists draw from multiple approaches in treating clients. More therapists prefer to label what they do as "integrative" rather than "eclectic." See Norcross, J. C., Karpiak, C. P., & Lister, J. M. (2005). What's an integrationist? A study of self-identified integrative and (occasionally) eclectic psychologists. *Journal of Clinical Psychology, 61,* 1587–1594.

7. William James had a similar idea he referred to as one's center of personal energy which is the center in one's mind that houses and/or gives birth to those things that are of most importance or even of ultimate importance. He also discusses one's "center of interest" which includes one's conscience, sense of helplessness and incompleteness. See James, W. (1902). *The varieties of religious experience: A study in human nature.* New Hyde Park, NY: University Books, pp. 196 and 36, respectively.

8. Psychological address is discussed as including "developmental altitude" in all lines of development, how one is nested in an AQAL matrix, as well as relevant types and states, and how all of these make up the psychological address that is described in Chapter 7.

9. The *pooka* (also *phouka* and *puca)* is a mythic creature that likely evolved in Scandinavian cultures and has a rich history in County Down, Ireland. In one version

of its history, it is a deformed goblin that demands a share of the harvest every year and if no share is forthcoming it tears down fences, scatters livestock, and creates all manner of havoc. In tamer versions of the story, the pooka is a 6-foot white rabbit that delights in scaring pub-crawlers heading home after a night of reverie. Here again the pooka may not share ontological status with a Volkswagon microbus but can provide a rich metaphor for some aspects of our own personality.

10. Rogers, C. R. (1951). *Client centered therapy.* Boston: Houghton Mifflin. Rogers only had two defense mechanisms in his theory of psychotherapy: denial and distortion. He felt that generally speaking these were the most common ways we caused ourselves suffering.

11. Alloy, L. B., & Abramson, L. Y. (1988). Depressive realism: Four theoretical perspectives. In L. B. Alloy (Ed.). *Cognitive processes in depression* (pp. 223–265). New York: Guilford.

12. Allan, L. G., Siegel, S., & Hannah, S. (2007). The sad truth about depressive realism. *The Quarterly Journal of Experimental Psychology, 60,* 482–495.

13. Moore, M. T., & Fresco, D. M. (2007). Depressive realism and attributional style: Implications for individuals at risk for depression. *Behavior Therapy, 38,* 144–154.

14. Douglas Adams (1952–2001) was an English author famous for his trilogy *The Hitchhikers Guide to the Galaxy.* He was also known for environmentalism and radical atheism. *Life, the Universe and Everything* is the title of the third book in his "five-book trilogy."

15. If this seems a little confusing, hang in there. As noted I unpack these ideas chapter by chapter.

16. Tarnus, R. (1991). *The passion of the Western mind: Understanding the ideas that have shaped our world view.* New York: Ballentine.

17. Freud of course emphasized sublimation——or taking raw primal desires and channeling them into things like art, sports, or one's vocation.

18. Or in a more Freudian sense, you keep the feelings about the relationship safely unconscious but the threat of them erupting into awareness results in another symptom like anxiety.

19. In his book *Dark Night Early Dawn: Steps to a Deep Ecology of Mind,* philosopher Chris Bache carries this idea to an extreme positing a framework where the individual is a microcosm of the universe and vice-versa. Although there may be limitations to Bache's model, he beautifully articulates the relationship between the individual and the Kosmos and the possibility of impacting the Kosmos if we choose to deal with our own unconscious. This, of course, can lead to what Wilber has called "psychic inflation," where one mistakes the transitory aspects of one's being for timeless truths.

20. These three perspectives in no way exhaust the possibilities. Physician Jan Gullberg has documented that many Austronesian languages have two to five forms of pronouns. See Gullberg, J. (1997). *Mathematics from the birth of numbers.* New York: Norton.

21. Dialectic is a form of argument that shows up in both Western and Eastern philosophy and psychology. It is rooted in the dialogue between two people having different views. The dialectical methods seek to resolve the difference in points of view through various means. For example, in Greek philosophy the thesis and antithesis (two points of view) may be resolved when one point of view follows logically to a

contradiction followed by the holder of that point of view surrendering it. Probably the best-known Western dialectical model in philosophy is that of Georg Wilhem Frederich Hegel, which posits that an antithesis negates or contradicts a thesis and resulting tension is resolved by a synthesis. This model was actually a popularization of Hegel by Johann Gottlieb Fichte.

22. For more on this simile, see Walsh, R. (2007). *The world of shamanism: New views of an ancient tradition.* Woodbury, MN: Llewellyn.

23. This metaphor of self as story was initially derived from McAdams, D. P. (1996). Personality, modernity, and the storied self: A contemporary framework for studying persons. *Psychological Inquiry, 7,* 295–321.

24. Many writers in psychology from Bruno Bettleheim to Jane Loevinger remind us of the problems of translating Freud's work. In an early essay on psychological growth, Wilber reminds us that Freud used the words "I," "it," and "over-I" rather than "ego," "id," and "superego." The original words make much more sense in the context of psychotherapy. See Wilber, K. (1983). Where it was, there I shall become: Human potential and the boundaries of the soul. In R. Walsh & D. H. Shapiro (Eds.), *Beyond health and normality* (pp. 67–151). New York: Van Nostrand. Also see Loevinger, J., & Wessler, R. (1978). *Measuring ego development 1: Construction and use of a sentence completion test.* San Francisco: Jossey-Bass, pp. 1–2. See also Ornston, D. G. (Ed.). (1992). *Translating Freud.* New Haven, CT: Yale University Press. The usage by Freud is in Freud, S. (1928). *The problem of lay-analyses.* London: Brentano LTD., p. 55.

25. Richard Dawkins, Daniel Dennett, and Sam Harris have very clearly described this dynamic regarding taboos in their description of the taboo on questioning religion. They maintain that the taboo dynamic is that your best course of defense is to consider any questioning an offense thus putting the questioner on the defensive. See their modernist critiques of premodern versions of religion in Dawkins, R. (2006). *The God delusion.* Boston: Houghton Mifflin; Dennet, D. C. (2006). *Breaking the spell: Religion as a natural phenomenon.* New York: Penguin; Harris, S. (2004). *The end of faith: Religion, terror, and the future of reason.* New York: Norton

26. Think of "introjected" as the equivalent of swallowing a food without chewing, digesting, or metabolizing any of it. It is in the system but not really integrated into the system.

27. Some of the best work on emotional intelligence is in Salovey, P., Brackett, M. A., & Mayer, J. D. (Eds.). (2004). *Emotional intelligence: Key readings on the Mayer and Salovey model.* New York: Dude Publishing.

28. Watts, A. W. (1966). *The book: On the taboo against knowing who you are.* New York: Vintage.

29. Hoffer, E. (1951). *The true believer.* New York: Harper & Row.

30. The author thanks Bianca Clemmons for this quote—a healer in her own right, a nurse who became a therapist to heal more deeply.

31. The manner in which a client responds to me is always a function of their "psychological address" as I explain in Chapter 7. In Chapter 5, I summarize the way that ego identification impacts a person's psychological address and how that impacts how the person relates to his or her own accomplishments (e.g., "you really got me through that crisis"). It is important to recognize that there are some clients who construct the world in mainly a relational fashion. I go into this in further detail in the chapter on ego development. For now, it is enough to know that these clients may feel abandoned if you *always*

put the ball back in their court. This is why I say things like, "I wonder if it was not also you that played a part in your healing?" Such a phrase invites clients to consider their own expertise and self-authoring without abandoning any need they might have for emotional security in the presence of the "expert" that they have likely made you out to be.

32. These dynamics are nicely summarized by psychiatrist Arthur Deikman. See Deikman, A. (1990). *The wrong way home: Uncovering the patterns of cult behavior in American society.* Boston: Beacon and Hassan, S. (1988). *Combatting cult mind control.* Rochester, VT: Park Street Press.

33. Wilber, K. (1996). *Eye to eye: The quest for the new paradigm.* Boston: Shambhala.

34. Hubble, M. A., Duncan, B. L., & Miller, S. D. (Eds.). (1999). *The heart and soul of change: What works in psychotherapy.* Washington, DC: American Psychological Association.

35. Note that this is more generic than Carl Jung's notion of shadow as an archetype. To a large extent, Integral follows Occam's Razor in that it includes only those things necessary to account for human experience—nothing in addition is necessary including the concept of archetypes.

36. This is a variation of an old philosophical problem gone into in exquisite detail in Irwin, W. (Ed.). (2002). *The matrix and philosophy: Welcome to the desert of the real.* Chicago: Open Court.

37. Psychologist Martin Seligman initially proposed a behavioral theory of depression called learned helplessness based on an experimental model with dogs. He soon came to see that human sentience made human depression unique across mammals. His initial and revised theories are summarized in Abramson, L. Y., Seligman, M. E. P., & Teasdale, J. D. (1978). Learned helplessness in humans: Critique and reformulation. *Journal of Abnormal Psychology, 87,* 49–74.

38. Abramson, Seligman, & Teasdale (1978).

39. Young, J. E., Klosko, J. S., & Weishaar, M. E. (2003). *Schema therapy: A practitioner's guide.* New York: Guilford.

40. Freud described one aspect of our psychological life as preconscious. Preconscious elements are things we have access to even though they may not be in our awareness 24 hours a day. Take for example your best friend's phone number. Reading this footnote you can likely recall it but it was not on your mind until you read this prompt. In successful therapy, things like shame, anger, and personal weaknesses can be characteristics we have access to. Once this is the case we are able to preclude self-sabotage because we have a good idea of what parts of our selves are likely to cause problems.

41. As you can imagine, energy fields are not a dominant concept in mainstream psychology or psychotherapy. There is a movement called "energy psychology" that is only just now being discussed in peer-reviewed literature. The energy psychology systems may hold promise as narratives that help shift client focus, but to date we do not possess ways to test the primary assumption that the bodymind contain/emit energy fields different from the electromagnetic, strong/weak nuclear, and gravitational forces. See Feinstein, D. (2008). Energy psychology: A review of the preliminary evidence. *Psychotherapy Theory, Research, Practice, Training, 45,* 199–213.

42. Generally speaking, gene expression is the ability of a gene to create a biologically active protein. It is estimated that the average human has 30,000 genes that direct the production of 50,000 proteins. Although we are learning more about this

process, we are nowhere near being able to link gene expression to particular mood states like depression or anxiety. For an introduction to genetics see Smith, G. (2005). *The genomics age: How DNA technology is transforming the way we live and who we are.* New York: Amacom.

43. If most mental/emotional disorders are "caused by" chemical imbalances why are there no peer-reviewed papers on these so-called imbalances. At the time of this writing a search of the research databases MedLine and PsychInfo turned up fewer than 20 papers spanning a 50-year period. One of the problems is the difficulty of measuring the ratios of chemicals in the brain. See interview with psychologist James Pennebaker in Paul, A. M. (2004). *The cult of personality: How personality tests are leading us to miseducate our children, mismanage our companies and misunderstand ourselves.* New York: Free Press, p. 204 "levels of neurotransmitters in living humans, for example, can only be estimated from the quantity of by-products (produced when they are broken down) found in blood, urine, or cerebrospinal fluid." See also Baughman, F. (2006). There is no such thing as a psychiatric disorder/disease/chemical imbalance. *PLoS Medicine, 3,* 317; France, C. M., Lysaker, P. H., & Robinson, R. P. (2007). The "chemical imbalance" explanation for depression: Origins, lay endorsement and clinical implications. *Professional Psychology: Research and Practice, 38,* 411–420; Lachter, B. (2001). "Chemical imbalance": A clinical non sequitur. *Australasian Psychiatry, 9,* 311–315.

44. Epiphenomenon: The prefix from the Greek is "Epi" meaning around or secondary. So an epiphenomenon is considered causally secondary to a primary phenomenon.

45. Damasio, A. (2006). *DesCartes' erro: Emotion, reason and the human brain.* New York: Vintage.

46. Churchland, P. S. (1995). *Neurophilosophy: Toward a unified science of the mind/brain.* Cambridge, MA: MIT Press. Churchland, P. M. (1995). *The engine of reason, the seat of the soul.* Cambridge, MA: MIT Press.

47. Houshmand, Z., Livingston, R. B., & Wallace, B. A. (1999). *Consciousness at the crossroads: Conversations with the Dalai Lama on brain science and Buddhism.* Ithaca, NY: Snow Lion.

48. Gabbard, G. O. (2001). *Treatments of psychiatric disorders: Vol. 1.* Washington, DC: American Psychiatric Association.

American Psychiatric Association. (2000). *Practice guidelines for the treatment of psychiatric disorders: Compendium 2000.* Washington, DC: Author.

49. A detailed description of the issues of discussing mind and brain is Chalmers, D. (1995). Facing up to the problem of consciousness. *Journal of Consciousness Studies, 2,* 200–219.

50. Kandel, E. (2007). *In search of memory: The emergence of a new science of mind.* New York: Norton; Kandel, E. (2005). *Psychiatry, psychoanalysis, and the new biology of mind.* Washington, DC: American Psychiatric Assocation.

51. Khan, A., Leventhal, R. M., Khan, S. R., & Brown, W. A. (2002). Severity of depression and response to antidepressants and placebo: An analysis of the Food and Drug Administration database. *Journal of Clinical Psychopharmacology, 22,* 40–45.

52. Salmon, P. (2001). Effects of physical exercise on anxiety, depression and sensitivity to stress: A unifying theory. *Clinical Psychology Review, 21,* 33–61.

53. Brody, A. L., et al. (2001). Regional brain metabolic changes in patients with major depression treated with either paroxetine or interpersonal therapy: Preliminary findings. *Archives of General Psychiatry, 58,* 631–640.

54. For an excellent summary of how language shapes our awareness see Cook-Greuter, S. R. (1995). *Comprehensive language awareness: A definition of the phenomenon and a review of its treatment in the postformal adult development literature.* Wayland, MA: Cook-Greuter & Associates

55. Schoen, S. (1991). Psychotherapy as sacred ground. *Journal of Humanistic Psychology, 31,* 70–75.

56. Joiner, T., & Coyne, J. C. (1999). *The interactional nature of depression: Advances in interpersonal approaches.* Washington, DC: American Psychological Association.

57. Blatt, S. J. (2004). *Experiences of depression: Theoretical, research and clinical perspectives.* Washington, DC: American Psychological Association.

58. Licinio, J., & Wong, M, L. (2002). Brain-derived neurotrophic factor in stress and affective disorders. *Molecular Psychiatry, 7,* 519.

59. Fromm, E. (1973). *The anatomy of human destructiveness.* New York: Holt, Rinehart, & Winston.

60. George Engel developed this approach. See Engel, G. (1992). The need for a new medical model: The challenge for biomedicine. *Family Systems Medicine, 10,* 317–331.

61. MacCluskie, K. M., & Ingersoll, R. E. (2001). *Becoming a 21st-century agency counselor.* Pacific Grove, CA: Brooks Cole.

62. Zachar, P, & Leone, F. T. L. (2000). A ten-year longitudinal study of scientist and practitioner interests in psychology: Assessing the Boulder model. *Professional Psychology: Research and Practice, 31,* 575–580. Frank, G. (1984). Boulder model: History, rationale, and critique. *Professional Psychology: Research and Practice, 15,* 417–435.

63. Bjork, D. W. (1983). *The compromised scientist: William James in the development of American psychology.* New York: Columbia University Press.

64. Penis envy was originally said by Freud to be the reaction of a girl who realizes she does not have a penis. It also has been used metaphorically to refer to anxiety men have about the size of their genitals or, in this case, the size of their datum.

65. Wilber documented this crime against Fechner in *Integral Psychology* and dedicated the book to him.

66. Sprinthall, N. A. (1990). Counseling psychology from Greystone to Atlanta: The road to Armageddon? *The Counseling Psychologist, 18,* 455–463.

67. See, for example, PDM Task Force. (2006). *Psychodynamic diagnostic manual (PDM).* Silver Spring, MD: Alliance of Psychoanalytic Organizations.

68. Rogers, C. (1957). The necessary and sufficient conditions of therapeutic personality change. *Journal of Consulting Psychology, 21,* 95–103. Freud also noted the potency and value of the intersubjective. What you may not know is the level of care and sensitivity that he brought to this understanding. He stated that "Essentially . . . the cure is effected by love . . ." See Freud/Jung Letters. (1974). *The correspondence between Sigmund Freud and C. G. Jung.* W. Mcguire (Ed.). Princeton, NJ: Princeton University Press, p. 68.

69. Peck, M. S. (1978). *The road less traveled: A new psychology of love, traditional values, and spiritual growth.* New York: Simon & Schuster, p. 81.

70. Garbarino, J. (2000). *Lost boys: Why our sons turn violent and how we can save them.* New York: Anchor

71. Eron, L. D., Gentry, J. H., & Schlegel, P. (1996). *A reason to hope: A psychosocial perspective on violence and youth.* Washington, DC: American Psychological Association.

72. Wilson, R. A. (1994). *Prometheus rising.* Tempe, AZ: New Falcon Publications.

73. All references to interviews with Wilber are from the archive at www.integralnaked.org.

74. Pinchbeck, D. (2002). *Breaking open the head: A psychedelic journey into the heart of contemporary shamanism.* New York: Broadway Books. Pinchbeck, D. (2006). *2012: The return of Quetzalcoatl.* New York: Tarcher.

75. See also Walsh, R., & Grob, C. S. (Eds.). (2005). *Higher wisdom: Eminent elders explore the continuing impact of psychedelics.* Albany: State University of New York Press; Strassman, R. (2001). *DMT: The spirit molecule.* Rochester, VT: Park Street Press; Jansen, K. (2000). *Ketamine: Dreams and realities.* Sarasota, FL: MAPS and Eisner, B. (1994). *Ecstasy: The MDMA story.* Berkley, CA: Ronin.

76. Pinchbeck, D. (2006). *2012: The return of Quetzalcoatl.* New York: Tarcher, p. 392.

77. See also Esborn-Hargens, S., & Zimmerman, M. E. (2009). *Integral ecology: Uniting multiple perspectives on the natural world.* Boston: Shambhala.

78. Ego syntonic simply means consonant with who the person feels him or herself to be. For example, in personality disorders, when the personality style of the person is described as problematic, the person with that style will likely respond "that's just how I am." This is quite different from Axis I disorders like depression or schizophrenia where the client would very much like to be rid of the symptoms and sees them interfering with who he or she is.

79. Engel, G. (1992). The need for a new medical model: The challenge for biomedicine. *Family Systems Medicine, 10,* 317-331.

80. Helzer, J. E., & Hudziak, J. J (2002). *Defining psychopathology in the 21st century: DSM-V and beyond.* Washington, DC: American Psychiatric Association.

81. Charney, D. S., et al. (2002). Neuroscience research agenda to guide development of a pathophysiologically based classification system. In D. J. Kupfer, M. B. First, & D. A. Regier (Eds.), *A research agenda for DSM-V* (pp. 31–84). Washington, DC: American Psychiatric Association.

82. Kupfer, D. J., First, M. B., & Regier, D. A. (Eds.). (2002). *A research agenda for DSM-V.* Washinton, DC: American Psychiatric Association.

83. Beach, S. R., et al. (Eds.). (2006). *Relational processes and DSM-V: Neuroscience, assessment, prevention, and treatment.* Washington, DC: American Psychiatric Association.

84. Saunders, J. B., Schuckit, M. A., Sirovatka, P. J., & Regier, D. A. (Eds.). (2007). *Diagnostic issues in substance use disorders: Refining the research agenda for DSM-V.* Washington, DC: American Psychiatric Association.

Notes to Chapter 2

1. Perspectivism was a powerful part of Nietzsche's philosophy emphasizing that knowledge is always constrained by one's perspective. Nietzsche was in part refuting Kant's notion of a world that existed totally separate from our knowledge of it—a "thing in itself." As noted in Chapter 2, Wilber refers to this Kantian doctrine as the "myth of the given." Michel Foucault's structuralism generally is agreed to be influenced by Nietzsche's perspectivism. Rather than thinking of perspectives as constraining, Integral Theory recognizes the gifts and limits of single perspectives *and* celebrates the ability to take multiple perspectives as the way we participate in the co-construction of experience, evolve as individuals, and take steps closer to understanding perspectives as the play of Spirit.

2. General Semantics is a discipline pioneered by Alfred Korzybski in the early part of the 20th century. Among other things, it aims to make an object of awareness the whole human reaction to words as symbols to facilitate clarity of thinking. It has been drawn on extensively by cognitive therapists.

3. Cushman, P. (1995). *Constructing the self, constructing America: A cultural history of psychotherapy.* Reading, MA: Addison-Wesley.

4. Moll, H., & Tomasello, M. (2006). Level I perspective-taking at 24 months of age. *British Journal of Developmental Psychology, 24,* 603–613.

5. Decety, J. (2005). Perspective taking as the royal avenue to empathy. In B. F. Maeel (Ed.), *Other minds: How humans bridge the divide between self and others* (pp. 143–157). New York: Guilford

6. Burack, J. A., et al. (2006). Social perspective-taking skills in maltreated children and adolescents. *Developmental Psychology, 42,* 207–217.

7. Vescio, T. K., Sechrist, G. B., & Paolucci, M. P. (2003). Perspective taking and prejudice reduction: The meditational role of empathy arousal and situational attributions. *European Journal of Social Psychology, 33,* 455–472.

8. Flavell, J. H., Miller, P. H., & Miller, S. A. (2001). *Cognitive development* (4th ed.). Upper Saddle River, NJ: Prentice-Hall.

9. Abrahams, B. A. (1980). *An integrative approach to the study of the development of perspective-taking abilities.* Unpublished doctoral dissertation, Stanford University, Stanford, CA.

10. Nangle, D. W., Hecker, J. E., Grover, R. L., & Smith, M. G. (2003). Perspective taking and adolescent sex offenders: From developmental theory to clinical practice. *Cognitive and Behavioral Practice, 10,* 73–84.

11. Parker, S. K., & Axtell, C. M. (2001). Seeing another viewpoint: Antecedents and outcomes of employee perspective taking. *Academy of Management Journal, 44,* 1085–1100.

12. Block-Lerner, J., Adair, C., Plumb, J. C., Rhatigan, D. L., & Orsillo, S. M. (2007). The case for mindfulness-based approaches in the cultivation of empathy: Does nonjudgmental, present-moment awareness increase capacity for perspective-taking and empathic concern? *Journal of Marital and Family Therapy, 33,* 501–516.

13. Cook-Greuter, S. (2006). Ego development: Nine levels of increasing embrace. p. 15. www.Cook-Greuter.com.

14. Burack, J. A., et al. (2006). Social perspective-taking skills in maltreated children and adolescents. *Developmental Psychology, 42,* 207–217.

15. In Chapter 3 we cover the self-system in Integral Psychotherapy. In the parlance of the self-system, the therapist working through her childhood traumas, keeping the objects of awareness and owning them is facilitating the movement of these things from proximate self (and shadow) to distal self where that which was subject, becomes object for a more complex subject.

16. We come back to this dynamic later in the discussion of how first-, second-, and third-person perspectives expressed in language may indicate that an aspect of the client's life is not "owned" and is in fact being pushed out of awareness by defenses and made "other."

17. Lamm, C., Bateson, C. D., & Decety, J. (2007). The neural substrate of human empathy: Effects of perspective-taking and cognitive appraisal. *Journal of Cognitive Neuroscience, 19,* 42–58.

18. Perrine, R., & Decety, J. (2003). What you believe versus what you think they believe: A neuroimaging study of conceptual perspective-taking. *European Journal of Neurosciences, 17,* 2475–2480. It is important, however, not to confuse technology like brain scans with understanding the brain. As Jerome Kegan pointed out, just because a part of the brain "lights up," reflecting oxygen usage during a mental task, we have no clue what percentage of the neurons in the "lit up" area are excitatory or inhibitory. In this case, "lighting up" may mean "shutting down" certain functions. This seems to be a case where our technology is way ahead of our understanding of what it reflects. See Kagan, J. (2009). *The three cultures: Natural sciences, social sciences and the humanities in the 21st century.* New York: Cambridge University Press.

19. Walsh, R. (2007). *The world of shamanism: New views on an ancient tradition.* Woodbury, MN: Llewellyn, p. 196.

20. We also know that schizophrenia usually has negative symptoms——symptoms that are deficits meaning functions that should be there but aren't. Memory is one of these and memory deficits associated with schizophrenia may be one of the biological correlates of the disorder. See Kandel, E. R. (1991). Disorders of thought in schizophrenia. In E. R. Kandel, J. H. Schwartz, & T. M. Jessell (Eds.), *Principles of neural science* (3rd ed., pp. 853–868). New York: Elsevier.

21. There is strong evidence that severe mental and emotional disorders impair a person's perspective-taking ability. See Langdon, R., Coltheart, M., & Ward, P. B. (2006). Empathetic perspective-taking is impaired in schizophrenia: Evidence from a study of emotion attribution and theory of mind. *Cognitive Neuropsychiatry, 11,* 133–155; Schiffman, J., et al. (2004). Perspective-taking deficits in people with schizophrenia spectrum disorders: A prospective investigation. *Psychological Medicine, 34,* 1581–1586; Langon, R., Coltheart, M., Ward, P. B., & Stanley, V. (2001). Visual and cognitive perspective-taking impairments in schizophrenia: A failure of allocentric simulation? *Cognitive Neuropsychiatry, 6,* 241–269.

22. Most therapist training programs from psychology to counseling to social work prescreen candidates on a cognitive measure like the Graduate Record Exam (GRE) or the Millers Analogy Test. The cutoffs used do not guarantee that the person will be a good therapist but at least that the person has the cognitive ability that is necessary (but not sufficient) to take a third-person perspective.

23. Genograms are like emotional family trees. They map out not only who "begat" whom but the types of relationships (close, volatile) as well as triumphs and tragedies that are part of every family. This is all done with a series of diagrams that can encompass two to three generations.

24. This idea of a dominant monad is critical particularly in distinguishing a group from an organism. The dominant monad is a "governing capacity that all of its subcomponents follow." Wilber, K. (2006). *Integral spirituality: A starting new role for spirituality and religion in the postmodern world.* Boston: Shambhala, p. 145. Put simply, when you get up to get a beer, all your cells and organs follow——the whole "shebang" goes to the bar or fridge as the case may be. This is not the case in groups, cultures, flocks, etc. and understanding this precludes the error of assuming groups are somehow "organisms" composed of cells that happen to be individuals. This is not the case nor will it ever be. Even the "sci-fi" Borg of *Star Trek* proved fallible in terms of the dominant monad.

25. Ingersoll, R. E., & Rak, C. F. (2006). *Psychopharmacology for helping professionals: An integral exploration.* Pacific Grove, CA: Brooks Cole.

26. Marquis, A. (2008). *The integral intake: A guide to comprehensive idiographic assessment in integral psychotherapy.* New York: Routledge.

27. Brown, G. S. (1973). *Laws of form.* New York: Bantam.

28. Wilber has described a holon drawing from Arthur Koestler as something that is both a whole and a part. See Koestler, A. (1967). *The ghost in the machine.* New York: MacMillan, p. 58.

29. "Hermeneutics" is basically the practice of making something clear through interpretation. Interpretation in this case requires dialogue with the person or group that is the focus of the interpretation. It is one thing for you to tell me your dream and have me offer an interpretation; quite another for me to then be open to feedback from you as to *your* reaction of *my* interpretation. Through this therapeutic process, the therapist and client come to form an understanding that will be discussed as the basic structure of the "magic we" of the therapeutic alliance.

30. The "signifieds" of language can be most simply thought of as what comes to your mind when you encounter words. As any therapist knows this can vary tremendously across different cultures using the same language, in the same culture across time, and across people with different developmental altitudes. For example, consider Friedrich Nietzsche's book *The Gay Science.* Many 21st-century undergraduates see the title and think it is about the study of sexual orientation. Nietzsche was trying to convey his lighthearted and at times irreverent treatment of philosophy by choosing the German word *"frohliche,"* which is best translated as "gay." Another example is the current colloquialism "disrespected" as expressed in "he disrespected me" or "he dissed me." English-language experts of 30 years ago would likely not know what to make of the latter sentence but many English-speakers today immediately understand what is being signified by these phrases.

31. Signifiers in language are the aural-material symbols (words) used to communicate an idea or evoke a signified in the listener. They appear as the printed or recorded word and thus are "material" or "measurable." As alluded to in Note 11, the same signifier can evoke a variety of signifieds.

32. Biological psychiatry can be summarized as a subdiscipline within psychiatry that seeks to correlate the relief of mental or emotional symptoms with psychotropic

medication and other allopathic interventions. From studying these interventions then, biological psychiatry explores hypotheses about the role of physiological variables like brain chemistry in the genesis of symptoms and disorders.

33. Wilber (2006) labels these zones consecutively 1 to 8. For ease of introduction, I used two labels (Zone 1 and Zone 2) for each quadrant. Students in my graduate courses seemed to have an easier time with this approach thus my use of it in this book.

34. Wilber, K. (2006). *The 1-2-3 of God* (audio recording with Tami Simon) Boulder, CO: Sounds True.

35. I use the word *tragedy* in its fullest sense here. A recent exploration of survey courses in human development at a midwestern university showed that the norm in these courses was to focus on cognitive development and discuss development from infancy to early adulthood and then throw in a few modules on aging—that's it and that is not even the proverbial "tip of the iceberg."

36. As noted earlier, a summary of this theory and how it is used in Integral Psychotherapy is the focus of Chapter 4.

37. Robert DeRopp advanced the view in the early 1960s that *all* psychological symptoms would likely be discovered to be biochemical in nature given enough time. Early experts in pharmacology like Nathan Kline echoed this sentiment. See DeRopp, R. S. (1961). *Drugs and the mind.* New York: Grove Press.

38. Staats, A. (1999). Unifying psychology requires new infrastructure, theory, method,

and a research agenda. *Review of General Psychology, 3,* 3–13.

39. I use the phrase "style of learning" loosely because it is far more related to the political correctness movement in education and higher education than it is to any reproducible research. See Robert Brown's critique of the construct in Brown, R. D. (2001). Learning styles inventory. In J. C. Impara & B. S. Plake (Eds.), *Fourteenth mental measurements yearbook.* Omaha, NE: Buros Institute of Mental Measurements, p. 679.

40. Burns, L. C. (2006). *Influence of patient perception of depression on antidepressant medication beliefs and adherence.* Unpublished doctoral dissertation, Cleveland State University.

41. Epley, N., Caruso, E., & Bazerman, M. H. (2006). When perspective taking increases taking: Reactive egoism in social interaction. *Journal of Personality and Social Psychology, 91,* 872–889.

42. I use the phrase "word magic" to refer to creating an illusion of certainty with words where in fact no certainty exists. I developed this idea in Ingersoll, R. E., & Rak, C. F. (2006). *Psychotropic medication for helping professionals: An integral approach.* Pacific Grove, CA: Brooks/Cole.

43. Hubble, M. A., Duncan, B. L., & Miller, S. D. (1999). *The heart and soul of change: What works in therapy.* Washington DC: American Psychological Association.

44. There is a readiness to change approach and scale that can give clinicians a "ballpark figure" of how ready the client is to engage therapy and change. See Prochaska, J. O., & DiClemente, C. C. (1982). Transteoretical therapy: Toward a more integrative model of change. *Psychotherapy: Theory, research, & practice, 19,* 276–288 and Fosberg, L., Halldin, J., & Wennberg, P. (2003). Psychometric properties and factor structure of the readiness to change questionnaire. *Alcohol and Alcoholism, 38,* 276–280.

45. Rogers, C. R. (1957). The necessary and sufficient conditions for therapeutic personality change. *Journal of Consulting Psychology, 21,* 95–103.

46. Rogers (1957).

47. Wilber, K. (2006). *Integral spirituality: A startling new role for religion in the modern and postmodern world.* Boston: Shambhala, p. 156.

48. Ingersoll, R. E., & Cook-Greuter, S. (2007). The self-system in Integral counseling. *Counseling & Values, 51,* 193–208.

49. But just as there are no little *homunculi* labeled "id," "ego," and "superego" running around inside your skull, there are no file cabinets behind your frontal lobes labeled "proximate" and "distal."

50. This observation was made by both Wilber *(The Atman Project)* and Kegan *(The Evolving Self).* I further elaborate on it in the next chapter.

51. Breuer, J., & Freud, S. (2006). *Studies on hysteria* (J. Strachey, Trans.). New York: Basic Books.

52. Parlee, B. (2005). Integral psychotherapy: An introduction. *AQAL: Journal of Integral Theory and Practice, 1,* 3.

Notes to Chapter 3

1. From Nietzsche, F. (1954). *Thus spoke Zarathustra.* New York: Bantam, p. 55.

2. Self-esteem can be thought of as self-liking or self-attractiveness and may be conscious or unconscious see Sakellaropoulo, M., & Baldwin, M. W. (2007). The hidden sides of self-esteem: Two dimensions of implicit self-esteem and their relations to narcissistic reactions. *Journal of Experimental Social Psychology, 43,* 995–1001.

3. Self-efficacy is defined as people's beliefs about their ability to produce levels of performance that exercise influence over events that affect their lives. See Bandura, A. (1994). Self-efficacy. In V. S. Ramachaudran (Ed.), *Encyclopedia of human behavior* (Vol. 4, pp. 71–81). New York: Academic Press.

4. This can refer to physical injury or psychological injury generated by the individual.

5. Perls, F. (1973). *The gestalt approach & eyewitness to therapy.* New York: Bantam.

6. Wilber, K. (2000). *Integral psychology: Consciousness, spirit, psychology, therapy.* Boston: Shambhala.

7. Wilber, K. (1986). The spectrum of psychopathology. In K. Wilber, J. Engler, & D. P. Brown (Eds.), *Transformations of consciousness: Conventional and contemplative perspectives on development* (pp. 107–159). Boston: Shambhala.

8. Sullivan, H. S. (1953). *The interpersonal theory of psychiatry.* New York: Norton, p. 373.

9. Loevinger, J. (1998). Completing a life sentence. In P. M Westenberg, A. Blasi, & L. D. Cohn (Eds.), *Personality development: Theoretical, empirical, and clinical investigations of Loevinger's conception of ego development* (pp. 347–354). Mahwah, NJ: Erlbaum.

10. Categorical psychiatry uses lists of symptoms statistically determined to co-occur and then groups them into categories. This approach was first used in *DSM-III* in 1980 and replaced the model of the first two manuals that was primarily based in psychodynamic thinking. What was gained is scientific and descriptive rigor. What was lost is the idiosyncrasies of the individual client. Many psychiatrists are lobbying for a more dimensional approach that would be more able to embrace the complexity of the individual. See Helzer, J. E., & Hudziak, J. J. (2001)2). *Defining psychopathology in the 21st century: DSM-V and beyond.* Washington, DC: American Psychiatric Association; Dilts, S. L. (2001). *Models of the mind: A framework for biopsychosocial psychiatry.* Philadelphia, PA: Brunner/Routledge; O'Donohue, W., Fowler, K. A., & Lilienfeld, S. O. (Eds.). (2007). *Personality disorders: Toward the DSM-V.* New York: Sage; Stein, D. B., & Baldwin, S. (2000). Toward an operational definition of disease in psychiatry and psychology: Implications for diagnosis and treatment. *International Journal of Risk & Safety in Medicine, 13,* 29–46.

11. Charney, D. S., et al. (2002). Neuroscience research agenda to guide development of a pathophysiologically based classification system. In D. J. Kupfer, M. B. First, & D. A. Regier (Eds.), *A research agenda for DSM-V* (pp. 31–84). Washington, DC: American Psychiatric Association.

12. Kandel, E. (2006). *In search of memory: The emergence of a new science of mind.* New York: Norton.

13. See Foreman, M. (2010). *A guide to integral psychotherapy: Complexity, integration and spirituality in practice.* Albany: State University of New York Press.

14. This is similar to Freud's revised sense of the "over-I" (mistranslated as "super-ego"), which is repressing but not itself repressed. Rather the person is embedded in the "over-I" components of introjected authority figures and the ideal image of self.

15. Cook-Greuter and I designed this figure. I gratefully acknowledge her permission to use it here.

16. Again see Ingersoll, R. E., & Cook-Greuter, S. (2007). The self system in Integral counseling. *Counseling & Values, 51* 193–208, for the elaboration of how the dynamics manifest in counseling. These dynamics were pioneered and developed by both Wilber and later Kegan. See Wilber, K. (1980). *The Atman project: A transpersonal view of human development.* Wheaton, IL: Quest and Kegan, R. (1982). *The evolving self: Problem and process in human development.* Cambridge, MA: Harvard University Press.

17. Wilber, K. (2006). *Integral spirituality: A startling new role for religion in the modern and postmodern world.* Boston: Shambhala.

18. Wilber, K. (1980). *The Atman project: A transpersonal view of human development.* Wheaton, IL: Quest, p. 81.

19. Wilber, K. (2006). *Integral spirituality: A startling new role for religion in the modern and postmodern world.* Boston: Shambhala.

20. Kegan, R. (1982). *The evolving self: Problem and process in human development.* Cambridge, MA: Harvard University Press, p. 77.

21. The word *abreaction* derives from psychoanalytic psychotherapy and refers to the reliving of an experience to purge it of emotional energy that has been repressed or, as we say in Integral Psychotherapy, pushed out of awareness.

22. Freud, S. (1928). *The problem of lay-analyses.* London: Brentano's LTD., pp. 38–39.

23. Although archetypes have been debated throughout the history of Western philosophy and psychology, no one can really state with certainty what they are. This is a problem. Richard Tarnus summarized descriptions of archetypes from Aristotle to Wittgenstein and illustrated the lack of consensus on the construct. To use Occam's Razor, the construct is unnecessary to the reality that we can push things out of awareness and they can gather psychic energy that erupts into conscious. See Tarnas, R. (2006). *Cosmos and Psyche: Intimations of a new worldview.* New York: Viking.

24. Carl Jung and Alfred Adler described this entity, which could increase in psychic energy, as a complex; Stanislav Grof described it as a system of condensed experience (COEX system). See Grof, S. (1975). *Realms of the human unconscious: Observations from LSD research.* New York: Viking.

25. Rowan, J. (1990). *Subpersonalities: The people inside us.* London: Routledge.

26. Assoagioli, R. (1965). *Psychosynthesis: A manual of principles and techniques.* New York: Hobbs, Doorman.

27. Ferrucci, P. (1982). *What we may be: Techniques for psychological and spiritual growth through psychosynthesis.* New York: Tarcher.

28. Whitmore, D. (1991). *Psychosynthesis counselling in action.* London: Sage, pp. 78–79.

29. A good example of this is the constant "reinventing" of stages of ego identity—another topic of this chapter. Loevinger and Cook-Greuter have been the primary researchers in this area, but that doesn't stop others from taking the fruits of their work, relabeling it, and presenting it as part of their "new" framework.

30. Rowan, J. (1990). *Subpersonalities: The people inside us.* London: Routledge, pp. 7–8.

31. Dekel, R., & Hobfoll, S. E. (2007). The impact of resource loss on holocaust survivors facing war and terrorism in Israel. *Aging and Mental Health, 11,* 159–167.

32. Wilber, K. (2000). *Integral psychology: Consciousness, spirit, psychology, therapy.* Boston: Shambhala.

33. Ferrucci, P. (1982). *What we may be: Techniques for psychological and spiritual growth through psychosynthesis.* New York: Tarcher, p. 48.

34. Ellis, A. (1994). *Reason and emotion in psychotherapy: A comprehensive method for treating human disturbances: Revised and updated.* New York: Birch Lane Press.

35. Whitmore, D. (1991). *Psychosynthesis counselling in action.* London: Sage.

36. Grof. S. (1975). *Realms of the human unconscious: Observations from LSD research.* Albany: State University of New York Press, p. 46.

37. Whitmore, D. (1991). *Psychosynthesis counselling in action.* London: Sage.

38. Wilber has written a wonderful early essay on this statement quoted from Freud, S. (1964). *Introductory lectures on psychoanalysis* (Vol. 1). London: Hogarth Press, p. 80. Wilber's essay is Wilber, K. (1983). Human potential and the boundaries of the soul. In R. Walsh & D. H. Shapiro (Eds.), *Beyond health and normality: Explorations of exceptional psychological well-being,* pp. 67–119.

39. Loevinger, whose work on ego development is the topic of the next section of this chapter, also used this language. For Piaget, assimilation was trying to adapt incoming stimuli to an existing set of tools and rules. Accommodation was changing the tools and rules one is using to deal with incoming stimuli in new, novel ways. The relation of these constructs to personality is nicely outlined in Loevinger's discussion

of cognitive developmentalism in Loevinger, J. (1987). *Paradigms of personality.* New York: Freeman.

40. I am indebted to Dr. Mark Foreman for his input on this matter. He has shared this idea with me during panels we were on at a conference on Integral Theory. He also writes about it in his aforementioned book on Integral Psychotherapy (see Note 14 in this chapter). The idea he imparted to me was that we sometimes devalue the "mini-transformations" that occur in clients. Large-scale, full-stage ego transformation is rare, but Foreman's view is that seeing someone make small but profound changes and feel better as a result is no less magical and can be a very rewarding part of the therapy process.

41. Wilber, in discussion with the Integral Psychotherapy team, developed this dynamic of quasi-transformation in 2005.

42. Fichte, J. G., & Breazeale, D. (1988). *Fichte: Early philosophical writings.* Princeton, NJ: Cornell University Press.

43. James, W. (1890). *The principles of psychology.* New York: Henry Holt.

44. Deikman, A. (1983). *The observing self: Mysticism and psychotherapy.* Boston: Beacon Press.

45. These stages are outlined later in the chapter. See also Cook-Greuter, S. (2003). *Postautonomous ego development: A study of its nature and measurement.* Wayland, MA: Cook-Greuter & Associates.

46. Maharshi, R. (2000). *Talks with Ramana Maharshi: On realizing abiding peace and happiness.* Carlsbad, CA: Inner Directions.

47. Linehan, M. M. (1993). *Skills training manual for treating borderline personality disorder.* New York: Guilford and Dimeff, L. A., & Koerner, K. (Eds.). (2007). *Dialectical behavior therapy in clinical practice: Applications across disorders and settings.* New York: Guilford.

48. See, for example, Williams, M. Teasdale, J., Segal, Z., & Kabat-Zinn, J. (2007). *The mindful way through depression: Freeing yourself from chronic unhappiness.* New York: Guilford.

49. Kingston, T., Dooley, B., Bates, A., Lawlor, E., & Malone, K. (2007). Mindfulness-based cognitive therapy for residual depressive symptoms. *Psychology and Psychotherapy: Theory, Research, & Practice, 80,* 193–203.

50. Freud, A. (1967). *Ego and the mechanisms of defense.* New York: International Universities.

51. Vaillant, G. E. (1992). *Ego mechanisms of defense: A guide for clinicians and researchers.* Washington, DC: American Psychological Association.

52. There are several therapeutic approaches to such impasses but a good summary is Zola, M. F. (2007). Beyond infidelity-related impasse: An integrative, systemic approach to couples therapy. *Journal of Systemic Therapies, 26,* 25–41.

53. Pearson, W. (2007). Integral counseling and a three-factor model of defenses. *Counseling & Values, 51,* 215.

54. Pearson (2007). p.216.

55. Marquis, A. (2007). What is integral theory? *Counseling & Values, 51,* 164–179.

56. Harris, S. (2004). *The end of faith: Religion, terror, and the future of reason.* New York: Norton.

57. Dawkins, R. (2006). *The God delusion.* Boston: Houghton Mifflin.

58. Templeton, C. (1996). *Farewell to God: My reasons for rejecting the Christian Faith.* Toronto: McClelland & Stewart.

59. Hitchens, C. (2007). *God is not great: How religion poisons everything.* New York: p. 12.

60. Loevinger, J. (1987). *Paradigms of personality.* New York: Freeman, p. viii.

61. Dr. Martin Greenman taught and was chair of philosophy at Youngstown State University during this period. He was compassionate with colleagues, generous with students, and perhaps the funniest "stand-up philosopher" I have ever encountered.

62. Loevinger (1976), p. 57.

63. For an up-to-date discussion of the evolution of the sentence completion test see Loevinger, J. (1998). *Technical foundations for measuring ego development: The Washington University Sentence Completion Test.* Mahwah, NJ: Erlbaum and Cook-Greuter, S. R. (2003). *Post-autonomous ego development: A study of its nature and measurement.* Wayland, MA: Cook-Greuter & Associates.

64. Principle of Cook-Greuter and Associates, http://www.cook-greuter.com/

65. See Cook-Greuter, S. (2000). Mature ego development: A gateway to ego transcendence? *Journal of Adult Development, 7,* 227–240.

66. As noted, Loevinger has written on several occasions that, in retrospect, she prefers the word "self" more closely following Harry Stack Sullivan's "self-system."

67. Noam, G. G. (1992). Development as the aim of clinical intervention. *Development and Psychopathology, 4,* 679–696.

68. Cohn, L. D., & Westenberg, P. M. (2004). Intelligence and maturity: Meta-analytic evidence for the incremental and discriminant validity of Loevinger's measure of ego development. *Journal of Personality and Social Psychology, 86,* 760–772

69. This plays a role in the study of evolution where some aspects of an organism evolve or change at different rates due to multiple factors like environment and the organism in question. The term can be used to think of differential change in developmental lines or domains. For a discussion of this see Dawkins, R. (2009). *The greatest show on earth: The evidence for evolution.* New York: Free Press, p. 207.

70. We note exceptions to this in adult life later. Adults at very early stages of ego identity referred to as preconventional usually do not fare well in society.

71. Loevinger, J. (1968). The relation of adjustment to ego development. In S. B. Sells (Ed.), *The definition and measurement of mental health,* Washington, DC: U.S. Department of Health Education & Welfare, p. 70.

72. Loevinger, J. (1976). *Ego development.* San Francisco: Jossey-Bass, p. 427.

73. Gast, H. L. (1984). The relationship between stages of ego development and developmental stages of health self care operations. *Dissertation Abstracts International,* 44, 3039B.

74. Biekle, P. A. W. (1979). The relationship of maternal ego development to parenting behavior and attitudes. *Dissertation Abstracts International,* 40 4519B.

75. Zilberman, K. L. (1984). Ego development and patterns of family interaction. *Dissertation Abstracts International,* 45, 1929B.

76. Bushe, G. R., & Gibbs, B. W. (1990). Predicting organization development consulting competence from the Myers-Briggs type indicator and stage of ego development. *The Journal of Applied and Behavioral Science, 26,* 337–357.

77. Noam, G. G. (1998). Solving the ego development-mental health riddle. In P. M. Westenberg, A. Blasi, & L. D. Cohn (Eds.), *Personality development: Theoreti-*

cal, empirical and clinical investigations of Loevinger's conception of ego development (pp. 271–296). Hillsdale, NJ: Erlbaum.

78. Callanan, R. A. E. (1986). Moral reasoning and ego development as factors in counseling. *Dissertation Abstracts International, 47,* 2455A.

79. Blatt, S. J., & Shahar, G. (2005). A dialectic model of personality development and psychopathology: Recent contributions to understanding and treating depression. In J. Corveleyn, P. Luyten, & S. J. Blatt (Eds.), *The theory and treatment of depression: Towards a dynamic interactionism model* (pp. 137–162). Mahwah, NJ: Erlbaum.

80. Blatt & Shahar (2005).Erlbaum.

81. Adler, A. (1956). *The individual psychology of Alfred Adler* (H. L. Ansbacher & R. R. Ansbacher, Eds.). New York: Basic Books.

82. Sullivan, H. S., Grant, M. W., & Grant, J. D. (1957). The development of interpersonal maturity: Applications to delinquency. *Psychiatry, 20,* 373–385.

83. Mischel, W. (1996). *Personality and assessment* (re-released ed.). Mahwah, NJ: Erlbaum.

84. Paul, A. M. (2004). *The cult of personality: How personality tests are leading us to miseducate our children, mismanage our companies, and misunderstand ourselves.* New York: Free Press.

85. Loevinger, J. (1976). *Ego development.* San Francisco: Jossey Bass, p. 311.

86. Reference to Dr. Cook-Greuter's statements are from video clips posted on www.integralnaked.org.

87. The labels used to name these stages are drawn from Bill Torbert and Cook-Greuter. They differ from most of Loevinger's original labels in that they are supposed to be more semantically neutral. Labels like "conformist" are experienced by many people pejoratively, thus the desire to move toward more neutral words to label stages. This effort also is important because, with the exception of the impulsive stage, people can function or translate reality in a healthy manner at almost any stage.

88. The labels of these stages come from Torbert, B., et al. (2004). *Action inquiry: The secret of timely and transforming leadership.* San Francisco: Berrett-Kohler. The labels differ from those used by Loevinger and were chosen as they were thought to be more neutral and less likely to be construed as pejorative.

89. The phrase "toxic environment" comes from psychologist James Garbarino. He uses it to describe environments that are chronically unsafe, neglectful, and do not provide for children's other basic needs.

90. Examples of responses in this section come from Hy, L. X., & Loevinger, J. (1998). *Measuring ego development* (2nd ed.). Mahwah, NJ: Erlbaum.

91. Cook-Greuter, C. G. (2007). *Ego development: Nine levels of increasing embrace.* Wayland, MA: Cook-Greuter & Associates, p. 9.

92. Cook-Greuter (2007), p. 10.

93. Cook-Greuter (2007), p. 10.

94. Cook-Greuter (2007), p. 11.

95. Rogers, C. (1957). The necessary and sufficient conditions of therapeutic personality change. *Journal of Consulting Psychology, 21,* 95–103. The six conditions are two people in psychological contact, a client who is incongruent, a therapist who is congruent, the therapist expressing unconditional positive regard for the client, the therapist experiencing empathy for the client, and the client experiencing the therapist

as having unconditional positive regard and empathy. All six are important and it is amazing how many textbooks only site Conditions 2, 3, and 4.

96. Torbert, B. et al. (2004). *Action Inquiry: The secret of timely and transforming leadership.* San Franscisco: Berrett-Kohler.

97. Much of this research is summarized in Westenberg, P. M., Blasi, A., & Cohn, L. D. (Eds.), *Personality development: Theoretical, empirical and clinical investigations of Loevinger's conception of ego development.* Hillsdale, NJ: Erlbaum

98. Cook-Greuter (2007). *Ego development: Nine levels of increasing embrace.* Wayland, MA: Cook-Greuter & Associates.

99. Vonnegut, K. (1992). *Fates worse than death.* New York: Berkely Trade.

100. See Wilber, K. (2006). *Integral spirituality: A startling new role for religion in the modern and postmodern world.* Boston: Shambhala and Harris, S. (2006). *The end of faith: Religion, terror and the end of reason.* New York: Norton.

101. Loevinger, J., & Wessler, R. (1978). *Measuring ego development 1: Construction and use of a sentence completion test.* San Francisco: Jossey Bass. In this first manual the authors note that the transition between the diplomat and achiever "is marked by heightened consciousness of self and of inner feelings. This transition appears modal for students during the first two years of college" (p. 5).

102. Holt, R. R. (1980). Loevinger's measure of ego development: Reliability and national norms for male and female short forms. *Journal of Personality and Social Psychology, 39,* 909–920

103. Cook-Greuter, S. R. (2007). *Ego development: Nine levels of increasing embrace.* Wayland, MA: Cook-Greuter & Associates, p.

104. Torbert, B., et al. (2004). *Action inquiry: The secret of timely and transforming leadership.* San Francisco: Berrett-Koehler.

105. Cook-Greuter, S. R. (2007). *Ego development: Nine levels of increasing embrace.* Wayland, MA: Cook-Greuter & Associates, p. 17

106. Cook-Greuter (2007), p. 18

107. This label was developed by Cook-Greuter in 2005.

108. Torbert, B., et al. (2004). *Action inquiry: The secret of timely and transforming leadership.* San Francisco: Berrett-Koehler, p. 93.

109. Cook-Greuter, S. R. (2007). *Ego development: Nine levels of increasing embrace.* Wayland, MA: Cook-Greuter & Associates, p. 22.

110. Some of these controversies are discussed in Horowitz, D. (2006). *The professors: The 101 most dangerous academics in America.* Washington, DC: Regnery.

111. Cook-Greuter (2007), p. 22.

112. Cook-Greuter (2007), p. 23.

113. Cook-Greuter (2007), p. 24.

114. Torbert et al. (2004), p. 110.

115. Torbert et al. (2004).

116. Torbert et al. (2004), p. 106.

117. Cook-Greuter (2007), p. 25.

118. Hy, L. X., & Loevinger, J. (1998). *Measuring ego development* (2nd ed.). Mahwah, NJ: Erlbaum.

119. Hy & Loevinger (1998).Erlbaum

120. Cook-Greuter (2007), p. 26.

121. Cook-Greuter (2007), p. 26.
122. Cook-Greuter (2007), p. 26.
123. Cook-Greuter (2007)
124. Cook-Greuter (2007), p. 28.
125. Torbert et al., (2004), p. 179.
126. Torbert et al. (2004)., p. 182
127. Cook-Greuter, S. (1995). *Comprehensive language awareness*. Unpublished document from www.cookgreuter.com.
128. The examples are taken from Cook-Greuter (2005).
129. Loevinger (1976), p. 423.
130. Loevinger (1976), p. 430.
131. Cook-Greuter (2007), p. 30
132. Cook-Greuter (2007), p. 30.
133. Cook-Greuter (2007), p. 30.
134. Cook-Greuter (2007), p. 31.
135. Cook-Greuter (2007), p. 32.
136. Cook-Greuter (2007), p. 32.
137. Maslow, A. H. (1971). *The farther reaches of human nature*. New York: Penguin, p. 111.

Notes to Chapter 4

1. Loevinger, J. (1976). *Ego development: Conceptions and theories*. San Francisco: Jossey-Bass, p. 176.
2. Wilber, K. (1997). *The eye of spirit: An integral vision for a world gone slightly mad*. Boston: Shambhala, p. 228.
3. The psychograph or psychography dates back to the early 20th century when German psychologist William Stern proposed it as a way to measure individual differences. Psychography and the idea of psychographs was further developed by American psychologist Gordon Allport. See Stern, W. (1910). Abstracts of lectures on the psychology of testimony and on the study of individuality. *American Journal of Psychology*, 2, 270-282 and Allport, G. (1937). Common traits: Psychography. In Allport, G. W. *Personality: A psychological interpretation*, pp. 400–434. New York: Holt. The *Lectical Assessment System* (LAS) claims the ability to generate psychographs——I briefly go into the specific points of connection and departure with respect to empirical versus clinical issues in psychometrics later in this chapter.
4. Freud, A. (1981). The concept of developmental lines: Their diagnostic significance. *The Psychoanalytic Study of the Child, 36*, 129–136.
5. Freud, A. (1981). *The writings of Anna Freud: Volume VIII: 1970–1980*. New York: International Universities Press, p. 7.
6. Neubauer, P. (1984). Anna Freud's concept of developmental lines. *The Psychoanalytic Study of the Child, 39*, 5–27.
7. Freud, A. (1981). *Psychoanalytic psychology of normal development. The writings of Anna Freud* (Vol. 8). Boston: International Universities Press.
8. Müller-Brettel, M., & Dixon, R. (1990). Johann Nicolas Tetens: A forgotten father of developmental psychology? *International Journal of Behavioral Development, 13*, 215–230.

9. Brett, G. S. (1921). The beginning of German psychology. In G. S. Brett (Ed.), *A history of psychology: Vol. II: Mediaeval & early modern period* (pp. 328–336). London: George Allen & Unwin–.

10. Charlesworth, W. R. (1994). Charles Darwin and developmental psychology: Past and present. In R. D. Parke, P. A. Ornstein, J. J. Rieser, & C. Zahn-Waxler (Eds.), *A century of developmental psychology* (pp. 77–102). Washington, DC: American Psychological Association.

11. Schultz, D. P., & Schultz, S. E. (2008). *A history of modern psychology* (9th ed.). Belmont, CA: Thomson.

12. Schultz & Schultz (2008), p. 409.

13. Wilber, K. (1995) *Sex, ecology, spirituality: The spirit of evolution.* Boston: Shambhala, p. 153.

14. White, S. H. (1994). G. Stanley Hall: From philosophy to developmental psychology. In R. D. Parke, P. A. Ornstein, J. J. Rieser, & C. Zahn-Waxler (Eds.), *A century of developmental psychology* (pp. 103–125). Washington, DC: American Psychological Association.

15. It is important to note most contemporary readers have not found James Mark Baldwin to be an accessible writer about psychology. He uses words idiosyncratically in a manner that is not accepted in contemporary parlance. We translate these words as they come up throughout the chapter. This seems to be one of the reasons his contributions are not better understood and appreciated. See Cairn, R. B. (1992). The making of a developmental science: The contributions and intellectual heritage of James Mark Baldwin. *Developmental Psychology, 28,* 17–24.

16. It is important that the reader understand that by "genetic" Baldwin meant different things at different times. Generally by "genetic logic" it seems he meant in some writings the social and mental development of children and in other writings the "knower's logic" that dealt with the elaboration of natural thought processes. Again, however, what this exactly means is unclear. See Cahan, E. D. (1984). The genetic psychologies of James Mark Baldwin and Jean Piaget. *Developmental Psychology, 20,* 128–135. Currently, "genetic psychology" deals with the influence of actual genetics on one's psychological development. This is quite far from Baldwin's use of the phrase and illustrates one of many of the problems with his writing.

17. Broughton, J. M. (1981). The genetic psychology of James Mark Baldwin. *American Psychologist, 36,* 402.

18. Baldwin, J. M. (2000). *Thought and things,* Vol. II. [Facsimile] Chestnut Hill, MA: Adamant Media Corporation. (Original work published 1908), p. 5.

19. Niaz, M. (1998). The epistemological significance of Piaget's developmental stages: A Lakatosian interpretation. *New Ideas in Psychology, 16,* 47–59.

20. Gruber, H. E., & Vonèche, J. J. (Eds.). (1995). *The essential Piaget: An interpretive reference and guide.* New York: Aronson, p. 155.

21. See Kohlberg, L. (1971). From is to ought: How to commit the naturalistic fallacy and get away with it in the study of moral development. In T. Mischel (Ed.), *Cognitive development and epistemology.* New York: Academic Press.

22. Wilber, K. (2000). *Integral psychology: Consciousness, spirit, psychology, therapy.* Shambhala: Boston, pp. 35–36.

23. Recall that Wilber has delineated two types of stages; those that arise in a developmental line as levels called structure stages and those that fall out in an unvarying

sequence during training-specific states called state stages. State stages are addressed more in Chapters 7 and 9.

24. Callaway, W. R. (2001). *Jean Piaget: A most outrageous deception.* New York: Nova.

25. Freud, 1965, p. 64.

26. Freud, A. (1965). *Normality and pathology in childhood: Assessments of development.* New York: International Universities Press, pp. 84–87.

27. Freeman, A., & DeWolf, R. (1993). *The 10 dumbest mistakes smart people make and how to avoid them: Simple and sure techniques for gaining greater control of your life.* New York: Harper Paperbacks. The mathematical genius Kurt Goedel is said to have suffered paranoid delusions and would not eat any food unless his wife tasted it first. This says a lot about how someone can be brilliant in mathematical intelligence yet profoundly disturbed in terms of emotional or interpersonal dynamics. Imagine being his wife!

28. Not all developmental psychometrics show this scattering; for example, Kegan's *Subject/Object Interview* is designed to hone in on extremely specific substage dynamics——to the point where researchers using this tool can detect subtle transitions between core meaning-making dynamics. In fact, it is consistent to say that the *Subject/Object Interview* uses "Emotional Stems" in the same way that the *Sentence Completion Test* uses "Sentence Stems." It may in fact be that because of this metric design, Kegan's model is more a model of emotional development than any of the other lines of development, including his three other cited lines cognitive, interpersonal, and intrapersonal. See Lahey, L., Souvaine, E., Kegan, R., Goodman, R., & Felix, S. (1988). *A guide to the subject-object interview: Its administration and interpretation.* Self-published manuscript, Harvard Graduate School of Education, Boston, MA.

29. Wilber, K. (2000). *Integral psychology: Consciousness, spirit, psychology, therapy.* Boston: Shambhala, p. 35

30. Kegan, R. (1982). *The evolving self: Problem and process in human development.* Cambridge, MA: Harvard University Press, p. 276.

31. Wilber, K. (1996). *Eye to eye: The quest for the new paradigm* (3rd ed.). Boston: Shambhala.

32. I am using the term *Level/Line Fallacy* a little differently than Wilber does in *Integral Spirituality.* I am using it to explain specific issues in developmental research, particularly the interpretation of data, the data analysis phase of research. Nevertheless, my specific usage is consistent with his general idea. Here, I mean the tendency for previous developmentalists to confuse issues of content (i.e., disparate development in lines) for context (i.e., that regression of the self-system to a previous view explains the discrepancies of disparate development——this is the issue that Kegan deals with in the notes to *In Over Our Heads,* pp. 370–373). The other way that this happens is that context (the 25–50–25 Rule) becomes confused for content (e.g., that the psychometric does not differentiate between capacities, which is why the content of the answers appear disparate when correlated with other models or in correspondence with our actual lived experience——this is the issue that Kohlberg and Loevinger were dealing with in analysis of their own psychometrics).

33. Wilber, 2006, p.184.

34. Eddington, A. S. (1926/1927). "The Nature of the Physical World," University of Edinburgh Gifford Lecture Series. London: Kessinger Publishing, 2005, p. 201.

35. Kagan, J. (2007). *An argument for mind.* New Haven, CT: Yale University Press, p. 234.

36. Loevinger, 1976, p. 188, p. 441.

37. Gardner, H. (1993). *Multiple intelligences: The theory into practice, a reader.* New York: Basic Books, p. 42.

38. Gardner (1993), p. 37.

39. Gardner (1993), p. 37.

40. Gardner (1993), pp. 26–28; 38–39; 33–37; 169.

41. Gardner (1993), p. 33.

42. Gardner (1993), p. 41.

43. Gardner (1983), p. 61.

44. Gardner (1993), p. 43.

45. Chalmers (1996).

46. Gardner (1993), p. 27.

47. Gardner has made a case against the construct of spiritual intelligence. See Gardner, H. (2000). A case against spiritual intelligence. *International Journal for the Psychology of Religion, 10,* 27–34.

48. Gardner (1993), p. 46.

49. Gardner (1993), pp. 17–25; [Postulated]–1999, pp. 48–64.

50. Gardner (1983), p. 322.

51. State stages are addressed more in Chapters 6 and 8. It is interesting to note that this is one of the more revolutionary ideas from Integral Theory that apply to Integral Psychotherapy. Akin to physicists search for a physical "theory of everything" when you start teasing apart aspects of the psyche you find surprises that initially don't make sense until on further reflection we find that we are looking at two separate phenomena. Michio Kaku tells the story of how, in searching for a way to unite the four physical forces, physicists have re-written Einstein's equations adding dimensions. When a fifth dimension was added by Theodr Kaluza, a new quality arose reflecting James Maxwell's theory of electromagnetism. Similarly, when we think in terms of structures *and* stages, we find structure stages and state stages. Wilber's pioneering insight was that these were truly two separate phenomena. Of course Kaluza's "discovery" was later found to be inadequate but he offered a new way of understanding physical phenomena that is still being experimented with in string theory to create a Grand Unified Theory. See Kaku, M. (2005). *Parallel worlds: A journey through creation, higher dimensions, and the future of the cosmos.* New York: Anchor, p. 199.

52. Gardner has addressed some of these issues in his more recent work. See Gardner, H. (2008). *5 minds for the future.* Boston: Harvard Business Press.

53. For Fischer, domains can develop in a disparate fashion, but individual aspects of one's consciousness *do not* develop beyond the overall altitude of the self-system: "Within a task domain, the *sequence of development* for a given assessment context can be predicted and explained in detail. Across domains, there is an upper limit on the complexity of skills that a person can show at any one time, the person's *optimal*

level. This limit constitutes the highest developmental level that a person can produce consistently, and it is hypothesized to reflect a central information-processing limit. People commonly function below optimum, with optimal-level performance occurring primarily when the environment provides support for complex behavior." Fischer & Farrar, 1987, p. 647.

54. Kegan, R. (1994). *In over our heads: The mental demands of modern life.* Cambridge, MA: Harvard University Press. pp. 372–373, n. 26.

55. Dawson, T. L. (2004). Assessing intellectual development: Three approaches, one sequence. *Journal of Adult Development, 11*(2), 71–85.

56. Christopher, J. C., Manaster, G. J., Campbell, R. L., & Weinfield, M. B. (2002). Peak experiences, social interest, and moral reasoning: An exploratory study. *The Journal of Individual Psychology, 58*(1), 35–51.

57. See Snarey, J. R. (1985). Cross-cultural universality of social-moral development: A critical review of Kohlbergian research. *Psychological Bulletin, 97*(2), 202–232.; Jaffee, S., & Hyde, J. S. (2000). Gender differences in moral orientation: A meta-analysis. *Psychological Bulletin, 126*(5), 703–726; Walker, L. J. (1984). Sex differences in the development of moral reasoning: A critical review. *Child Development, 55*(3), 677–691; and Woods, C. J. P. (1996). Gender differences in moral development and acquisition: A review of Kohlberg's and Gilligan's models of justice and care. *Social Behavior and Personality, 24*(4), 375–384.

58. See Wilber, K. (1986). *Transformations of consciousness: Conventional and contemplative perspectives on development.* Boston: Shambhala, p. 80 and Wilber (2000), pp. 91–92.

59. Kegan (1982), p. 265.

60. For a look at the uses of cognition, basic structures (basic features), transitional structures (surface features), and self-system in Wilber's work, see Wilber (1996), pp. 264–280; (1997), pp. 228–229; (2000), pp. 123–125; (2007), p. 113.

61. Rowan, J. (1990). *Subpersonalities: The people that live inside us.* New York: Routledge, pp. 8–10.

62. Wilber (1997), p. 146.

63. Kegan (1982), p. 276.

64. Kegan (1994), p. 371, n. 26.

65. Kegan (1982), pp. 74, 81, 95; (1994), pp. 94–94, 363, n. 12.

66. Kegan (1994), p. 363, n. 12.

67. Kegan (1994), pp. 372–373, n. 26.

68. Kegan (1994), p. 373, n. 26.

69. Loevinger (1976), p. 441.

70. Dawson, T. L., & Wilson, M. (2003/2004). The LAS: A computerized scoring system for small- and large-scale developmental assessments. *Educational Assessment, 9*(3/4), 154.

71. Dawson, T. L. (2004). Assessing intellectual development: Three approaches, one sequence. *Journal of Adult Development, 11*(2), 72–74.

72. See Gardner (1983, 1993), and Gardner, H. (1999). *Intelligence reframed: Multiple intelligences for the 21st century.* New York: Basic Books.

73. These examples of exceptional people are not meant to be coextensive with lines, but are rather examples of the one line that likely had the *most influence* in overall development of their self-system. Otherwise, what good does it do us as researchers and

theoreticians to look at the disparate development of lines in the first place? I submit that from such a perspective, it would be useless. Pathologies and excellence have been helping to define "normal" in the field of psychology for centuries; savants, occupying both categories, may become a rich source of information, as well as a litmus test of our collective development along our ethical line.

74. Vygotsky, L. S. (1978). *Mind in society: The development of higher psychological processes.* Cambridge, MA: Harvard University Press.

75. Chomsky, N. (2006). *Language and mind.* New York: Cambridge University Press.

Like Gardner, Chomsky grounds his theory of linguistic acquisition in biology—specifically in cognitive science's connectionist models. Nevertheless, the "Chomsky Hierarchy" is a clear example of just how innate the rules of linguistic acquisition are for humans across the globe, speaking a multitude of languages.

76. Selman, R. L. (1977). A structural-developmental model of social cognition: Implications for intervention research. *Counseling Psychologist, 6*(4), 3–6.

See also Domino, G., & Affonso, D. D. (1990). A personality measure of Erikson's life stages: The inventory of psychosocial balance. *Journal of Personality Assessment, 54*(3/4), 576–588; and Jenkins, S. M., Buboltz W. C. Jr., Schwartz, J. P. & Johnson, P. (2005). Differentiation of self and psychosocial environment. *Contemporary Family Therapy, 27*(2), 251–261.

77. Goleman, D. (1995). *Emotional intelligence: Why it can matter more than I.Q.* New York: Bantam Books. For a good review of the current state of construct psychometrics for this proposed line of development, see Van Rooy, D. L., Viswesvaran, C., & Pluta, P. (2005). An evaluation of construct validity: What is this thing called emotional intelligence? *Human Performance, 18*(4), 445–462.

78. Fowler, J. W. (1981). *Stages of faith: The psychology of human development and the quest for meaning.* San Francisco: Harper San Francisco.

79. This is the way I discuss it with my students: The "necessary-but-insufficient" clause refers the fact that developmental balance across all lines takes time, and ultimately never happens. It is similar to the drive toward homeostasis within the human body—if the body ever actually achieved its long-sought battle for homeostasis, it would perish. It appears that there is a similar drive in the upper-left quadrant, and it may turn out that it is in fact our disparate developments across lines that compel us to grow, which furthers the disparity of development across lines, beginning the process anew. This is for future researchers to figure out, but the fact that one must *know* how to take a perspective before *deciding* to take a better perspective, and one must *decide* to take a better perspective before *acting* on that better perspective, is why cognition is necessary but insufficient for morality, and morality is necessary but insufficient for ethics. Logic, then, seems to dictate the plausibility of the *necessary-but-insufficient* clause, but future research will be needed to verify and then map these relationships out.

80. Gardner (1983), p. x.

81. I imagine a set of experiments where a participant enters a room with several objects, whose relationship with one another remains unclear. The objects can be created and situated in such a way that they relate to one another with increasing levels of complexity. The participant will naturally self-generate the coordination of objects according to his or her own level of development. This may be one way to create a nonlinguistically derived metric. Again, it even might be useful to include a linguistic

component, as a corollary; but linguistics need not be the primary or only mode of study. Early in the creation of these nonlinguistic psychometrics, it would be useful to correlate them with existing linguistically derived measures. I believe that Kegan's Subject/Object Interview would be ideal for such a task, for even though it uses language, more than any other psychometric it is concerned with the self-generated constructions of meaning that give rise to language, behavior, emotions, and cognition. Furthermore, it attempts to get at the very subject–object dynamics that—by all accounts—seem primary to development across *all* lines.

82. (1995). p. 132. Later in that same passage, Piaget warns future psychotherapists: "there is never complete objectivity: at every stage there remains in the conception of nature [i.e., the self-identity] what we might call 'adherences,' fragments of internal experience which still cling to the external world."

83. Spelke, E. (1995). Initial knowledge: Six suggestions. In J. Mehler & S. Franck (Eds.), *Cognition on cognition*. Cambridge, MA: The MIT Press.

84. Wynn, K. (1992). Addition and subtraction by human infants. *Nature*, *358*(6389),
749–750.

85. One of the few involutionary givens that Wilber posits is mathematical principles. I take the research of Wynn and Spelke as tacit recognition that we surely come "preloaded" with an intuitive understanding of rudimentary math. It seems literally to be an *instinct*, although whether or not it is a *reflex* remains to be seen. And, as with all other developments, we grow into it with each passing year.

86. For an example of some of the creative ways that nonlinguistically mediated developmental research can occur, see Cheries, E. W., Wynn, K., & Scholl, B. J. (2006). Interrupting infants' persisting object representations: An object-based limit? *Developmental Science*, *9*(5), F50–F58.

No matter which level the self-system is at, or which line groupings the self-system has an affinity for, it seems that subject–object dynamics are *always* involved in such differentiations. Taking subject–object differentiations as the basis for observation and testing may be the future of research into this exciting new territory.

87. That the "role" consciousness of concrete operations *automatically* becomes socialization at full formal operational cognition, or that "reciprocal" consciousness *automatically* becomes systems maintenance at the full formal operations seems far fetched to me. It strikes of adding epicycles to explain what is more simply and readily explained by a discreet, qualitatively differentiated overall level or altitude.

88. Grof, S. (1998). *Holotropic breathwork: Moving towards wholeness*. California Institute of Integral Studies, Course Lecture.

89. An exhaustive scope of this phenomenon is beyond this book, but interested readers should check out the excerpts from Wilber's *Kosmos Trilogy* that are available on at www.shambhala.com.

90. Wigglesworth, C. (2006). Why spiritual intelligence is essential to mature leadership. *Integral Leadership Review*, *6*(3), 5.

91. In 1998, Paul van Geert wrote an outstanding dynamic-systems analysis of Piaget and Vygotsky, covering almost everything discussed herein, including domain specificity versus generalizability. See van Geert, P. (1998a). A dynamic systems model of basic developmental mechanisms: Piaget, Vygotsky, and beyond. *Psychological Review*, *105*(4), 634–677. From an entirely different discipline, he comes to a similar under-

standing of that proposed here, that asynchronous development across lines (domains) shows greater quasi-dependence than quasi-independence. Quasi-independence seems favored during developmental transition, whereas quasi-dependence seems favored during developmental stability or homeostasis. This makes intuitive sense to me, and the evidence appears to support this:

Piaget used the concept of horizontal décalage to refer to the fact that a stage shift eventually takes place within a limited range and is completed only later. For instance, children apply concrete operational thinking . . . years before they are able to apply it to conservation of volume. Put differently, there exist two levels of functioning at the same time whose expressions depend on the kind of problems the child is confronted with [i.e., the context]. [This] could be an illustration of the fact that development is domain specific and that the model of the development in a single individual is in fact a concatenation of several independent developmental trajectories . . . [or] could imply that, within a domain, some contents are assimilated earlier to a new stage than others, thus implying the simultaneous existence of different levels, or multimodality . . . [T]he present model produces such *temporary bimodality* in the vicinity of a sudden jump as a natural outcome of the stage shifts. (van Geert, 1998, pp. 656–657)

Furthermore, his research on a number of different researchers (including Fischer) supports Kegan and Fischer, in that in toto but temporary regressions are the *norm*, and not representative of pathology (pp. 655–666). Despite the fact that different domains were discussed, van Geert's work is a meta-analysis of many studies, most of which use cognitive line measures. Therefore, it provides granularity mainly to levels, but little to lines. Nevertheless, using dynamic systems modeling is another potentially useful tool for helping developmentalists create better tools of observation.

Finally, van Geert correctly laments, in his cleverly titled "We Almost Had a Great Future Behind Us," that developmental psychologists have not seriously taken dynamic systems modeling into their studies. I agree—as we begin to truly grapple with the notions of relative independence of lines, it becomes more clear that a *new level* of thinking-feeling-being is *required* for the studies that we are called to perform. It would be a cruel irony if developmental studies were to remain arrested.

92. See especially Kegan's (1982) chapter on *Natural Therapy*. In summation, the levels of depression seem to always be the in toto loss of the self, caught between demands. During psychopathology, according to Kegan, we do not necessarily feel the other naturally occurring sensation that of feeling beside ourselves, outside of our own skin. I take that "feeling besides myself" as a tacit acknowledgment that development is occurring, which means asynchronous line development is happening, and is pulling the self-system upward.

Notes to Chapter 5

1. Pound, E. (1934). *A B C of reading.* New York: New Directions, p. 35.

2. O'Donohue, W., Fowler, K. A., & Lilienfeld, S. O. (Eds.). (2007). *Personality disorders: Toward the DSM-V.* Thousand Oaks, CA: Sage.

3. Sperry, L. (1995). *Handbook of diagnosis and treatment of the DSM-IV personality disorders.* New York: Brunner/Mazel.

4. For examples and discussion of the development of the integral intake see Marquis, A. (2008). *The integral intake: A guide to comprehensive idiographic assessment in integral psychotherapy.* New York: Routledge.

5. Dialectical Behavior Therapy was developed by psychologist Marsha Linehan initially for suicidal clients. Because most people suffering from BPD become suicidal, Linehan found herself becoming an expert in working with such people. Her therapy is outlined in Linehan, M. (1993). *Cognitive-behavioral treatment of borderline personality disorder.* New York: Guilford.

6. Lilienfeld, S. O., Fowler, K. A., Lohr, J. M., & Lynn, S. J. (2005). Pseudoscience, nonscience, and nonsense in clinical psychology: Dangers and remedies. In R. H. Wright & N. A. Cummings (Eds.), *Destructive trends in mental health: The well-intentioned path to harm.* New York: Routledge, p. 190.

7. Hillman, J. (2007). Egalitarian typologies versus the perception of the unique. Retrieved from http://members.shaw.ca/competitivenessofnations/Anno%20Hillman%202.htm on December 28, 2007.

8. Coon, D. (2004). *Introduction to psychology: Gateways to mind and behavior* (10th Ed.). Belmont, CA: Thomson.

9. Wilber, K. (2000). *Integral psychology: Consciousness, spirit, psychology, therapy.* Boston: Shambhala, p. 53.

10. Hicks, L. E. (1984). Conceptual and empirical analysis of some assumptions of an explicitly typological theory. *Journal of Personality and Social Psychology, 46,* 1118–1131.

11. Potkay, C. R., & Allen, B. P. (1986). *Personality theory, research, and applications.* Monterey, CA: Brooks/Cole.

12. This dichotomy was also presented by Nietzsche in *The Birth of Tragedy* as a delicate balance of artistic impulses required for dramatic art that he felt had not been equaled since ancient Greek tragedy.

13. These Jung adopted as the extravert and introvert respectively.

14. Schiller, F. (1795). *Uber die asthetische ezsiehung des menschen.* Cited by C. G. Jung (1923). *Psychological types or the psychology of individuation* (H. G. Baynes, Trans.). London: Kegan Paul.

15. Sandys, J. E. (1909). *The characters of Theophrastus: An English translation from a revised text with introduction and notes by R.C. Jebb.* London: Macmillan.

16. Mischel, W. (1968). *Personality and assessment.* Mahwah, NJ: Erlbaum.

17. This was the case until the agreement that personality was an interaction between the person and the environment. This led to the introduction of the Five-Factor Model discussed later in this chapter. For an excellent summary of the impact of Mischel's work on the psychology community, see Paul, A. M. (2004). *The cult of personality: How personality tests are leading us to miseducate our children, mismanage our companies, and misunderstand ourselves.* New York: Free Press.

18. This is a situation that is leading to legislation to license or certify coaches in the United States. Justman, S. (2005). *Fool's paradise: The unreal world of pop psychology.* Chicago: Ivan Dee and Ehrenreich, B. (2009). *Bright-sided: How the relentless promotion of positive thinking has undermined America.* New York: Metropolitan.

19. Lanyon, R., & Goodstein, L. (1971). *Personality assessment.* New York: Wiley.

20. As noted in Chapter 1, there has been no documentation of a chemical imbalance proper that leads to psychiatric illness. Rather, we have seen that chemical intervention can be useful in decreasing the symptoms a person is suffering from. This in no way implies there was an imbalance to begin with.

21. Gregory, R. L. (Ed.). (1987). *The Oxford companion to the mind.* Oxford: Oxford University Press.

22. Kretschmer, E. (1925). *Physique and character: An investigation of the nature of constitution and of the theory of temperament.* New York: Harcourt.

23. Sheldon, W. H., & Stevens, S. S. (1942). *The varieties of temperament: A psychology of constitutional differences.* New York: Harper & Row; Sheldon, W. H. (1954). *Atlas of men: A guide for somatotyping the adult male at all ages.* New York: Gramercy;

24. Robinson, D. N. (1995). *An intellectual history of psychology* (3rd Ed.). Madison: University of Wisconsin Press.

25. This parallel was drawn by Annie Murphy Paul. I recommend her book Paul, A. M. (2004). *The cult of personality: How personality tests are leading us to miseducate our children, mismanage our companies, and misunderstand ourselves.* New York: Free Press.

26. Here it is well to note the Webster unabridged dictionary definition of *temperament.* "1. The combination of mental, physical and emotional traits of a person; natural predisposition. 2. unusual personal attitude or nature as manifested by peculiarities of feeling, temper, action, etc., often with a disinclination to submit to conventional rules or restraints. 3. (old physiology) the combination of the four cardinal humors, the relative proportions of which were supposed to determine physical and mental constitution." The word stems from a Latin root meaning "due mixture." So it seems fair to assume that all these meanings of temperament have a theme of "mixture" regarding physical, psychological, and emotional traits. Perhaps like recipes for making certain food dishes, this recipe in toto is what makes each of us unique. The problem of course is that we don't understand the ingredients.

27. Cloninger, C. R. (1987). A systematic method for clinical description and classification of personality variables: A proposal. *Archives of General Psychiatry, 44,* 573–588 and Cloninger, R. C., Svarakic, D., & Przybeck, R. (1993). A psychobiological model of temperament and character. *Archives of General Psychiatry, 50,* 975–990. We can see here that the 20th-century description of temperament is not all that different from the definitions in the last note that date to antiquity. The variables are a little more specific but still the construct is more speculative than instructive.

28. McDougall, W. (1908). *Introduction to social psychology.* New York: Scribners.

29. Meumann, E. (1910). *Intelligenz und wille.* Leipzig: Barth.

30. Kollarits, J. (1912). *Charakter und nervositat.* Budapest: Knoedler.

31. See summary in Millon, T. (1981). *Disorders of personality: DSM-III: Axis II.* New York: Wiley and Maddi, S. R. (1968). *Personality theories: A comparative analysis.* Homewood: Dorsey.

32. Ribot, T. (1890). *Psychologie des sentiments.* Paris: Delahaye and Lecrosnier.

33. Queyrat, F. (1896). *Les caracteres et l'education morale.* Paris: Alcan.

34. Kendler, H. H. (1987). *Historical foundations of modern psychology.* Pacific Grove, CA: Brooks/Cole.

35. Although in Chapter 1 I noted that archetype is poorly operationalized, for this section I rely on archetype as a permanent deposit in the mind of an experience

that has been repeated for generations. It is a universal thought form (idea) that is charged with a large element of emotion. Although even this description has residues of Lamarkian heritability it is still in use. See Hall, C. S., & Lindzey, G. (1978). *Theories of personality* (3rd ed.). New York: Wiley, pp. 120–121.

36. This was Jung's preferred spelling of the term rather than the Americanized "extrovert."

37. Jung, C. G. (1971). A psychological theory of types. In *Collected works* (Vol. 6). Princeton, NJ: Princeton University Press.

38. Object relations theory was pioneered in the 1940s and 1950s by British psychologists Ronald Fairbairn, Harry Guntrip, and Donald Winnicott. It is basically a psychodynamic theory that posits that the ego (what we are calling the proximate self) exists in relation to others (called "objects") that are external and internal. The primary "others" are parents and children who can have three emotional experiences with regard to them: attachment, rejection, or frustration. These emotional states and early experiences are then seen as the basis of one's personality. One can only wonder at the incredible lack of imagination that went in to the name "object relations."

39. Jung, C. G. (1923). *Psychological types or the psychology of individuation.* London: Kegan Paul, p. 414.

40. Blatt, J. S., & Shahar, G. (2005). A dialectic model of personality development and psychopathology: Recent contributions to understanding and treating depression. In Corveleyn, J., Luyten, P., & Blatt, S. J. (Eds.), (2005). *The theory and treatment of depression: Towards a dynamic interactionism model* (pp. 137–162). Mahwah, NJ: Erlbaum.

41. McGuire, W., & Hull, R. F. C. (Eds.). (1977). *C. G. Jung speaking.* Princeton, NJ: Princeton University Press.

42. Jung, C. G. (1923). *Psychological types or the psychology of individuation.* London: Kegan Paul, p. 423.

43. By individuation, Jung meant "to denote the process by which a person becomes a psychological 'in-dividual,' that is, a separate, indivisible unity or 'whole.'" From Jung, C. G. (1959). *The archetypes and the collective unconscious* (R. F. C. Hull, Trans.). Princeton, NJ: Bollingen, p. 275.

44. A history of the development of the test as well as the relationship between mother and daughter is presented in Saunders, F. W. (1991). *Katherine and Isabel: Mother's light, daughter's journey.* Palo Alto, CA: Consulting Psychologists Press. It also should be noted that the Army Research Institute concluded that the instrument should not be used for career planning as the types are more like stereotypes. See McCrae, R. R., & Costa, P. T. (1985). Reinterpreting the Myers-Briggs type indicator. *Educational and Psychological Measurement, 2,* 2–31.

45. Comment made by Robert Clifton, PhD October 2007.

46. Thompson, B., & Ackerman, C. M. (1994). Review of the Myers-Briggs type indicator. In J. T. Kapes, M. M. Mastie, & E. A. Whitfield (Eds.), *A counselor's guide to career assessment inventories* (pp. 283–289) Alexandria, VA: National Career Development Association.

47. David Kiersey has developed a shorter version called The Keirsey Temperament Sorter. See Keirsey, D. (1998). *Please understand me II: Temperament, character, intelligence.* Del Mar, CA: Prometheus Nemesis.

48. Barbuto, J. (1997). A critique of the Myers-Briggs type indicator and its operationalization of Carl Jung's psychological types. *Psychological Reports, 80,* 611–625.

49. For example, see Carlson, J. G. (1989). Affirmative: In support of research-ing the Myers-Briggs type indicator. *Journal of Counseling & Development, 67,* 484–486.

50. Thompson, B., & Ackerman, C. M. (1994). Review of the Myers-Briggs type indicator. In J. T. Kapes, M. M. Mastie, & E. A. Whitfield (Eds.), *A counselor's guide to career assessment inventories* (pp. 283–289) Alexandria, VA: National Career Development Association.

51. Wiggins, J. S. (1989). Review of the Myers-Briggs type indicator. In J. C. Conoley & J. J. Kramer (Eds.) *Tenth mental measurements yearbook* (pp. 537–538). Lincoln, NE: Buros Institute.

52. Howes, R. J., & Carskadon, T. G. (1979). Test–retest reliabilities of the Myers-Briggs type indicator as a function of mood changes. *Research in Psychological Type, 2,* 67–72.

53. Matthews, P. (2004). The MBTI is a flawed measure of personality. Bmj. com Rapid Responses

54. Smith, G. T. (2005). On construct validity: Issues of method and measure-ment. *Psychological Assessment, 17,* 396–408.

55. McCrae, R. R., & Costa, P. T. (1989). Reinterpreting the Myers-Briggs type indicator from the perspective of the five-factor model of personality. *Journal of Personality, 57,* 17–40.

56. Arnau, R. C., Bradley, A. G., Rosen, D. H., Gleaves, D. H., & Melancon, J. G. (2003). Are Jungian preferences really categorical? An empirical investigation using taxometric analysis. *Personality and Individual Differences, 34,* 233–251.

57. See Hicks, L. E. (1984). Conceptual and empirical analysis of some assump-tions of an explicitly typological test. *Journal of Personality and Social Psychology, 46,* 1118–1131.

58. Stricker, L. J., & Ross, J. (1964). An assessment of some structural proper-ties of the Jungian personality typology. *Journal of Abnormal and Social Psychology, 68,* 162–71.

59. Stricker & Ross (1964). See also Arnau et al. (2003) in Note 18.

60. Jung, C. G. (1971). Psychological types. In W. McGuire (Ed.), *The collected works of C. G. Jung* (Vol. 6, Bollinger Series XX). Princeton, NJ: Princeton University Press, pp. 515–516.

61. Jung wrote "there are exactly four psychological functions, no more and no fewer." In Jung, C. G. (1971). A psychological theory of types. In In W. McGuire (Ed.), *The collected works of C. G. Jung* (Vol. 6, Bollinger Series XX). Princeton, NJ: Princeton University Press, p. 540.

62. Johnson, W. L., Johnson, A. M., Murphy, S. D., Weiss, A., & Zimmerman, K. J. (1998). A third-order component analysis of the Myers-Briggs type indicator. *Educational and Psychological Measurement, 58,* 820–831.

63. The theory of humors (humorism) held that the balance of four humors (black bile, yellow bile, phlegm, and blood) resulted in health. Disease was mistakenly believed to be an imbalance among these humors. The humors also provided a primitive theory of types where in characteristics resulted from excesses or deficits of humors.

64. Eyesenck, H. J. (1953). *The structure of personality.* London: Merthuen.

65. Merenda, P. F. (1991). Additional comments regarding the Myers-Briggs type indicator. *Measurement and Evaluation in Counseling & Development, 23,* 179.

66. Coffield, F., Moseley, D., Hall, E., & Ecclestone, K. (2004). *Learning styles and pedagogy in post-16 learning: A systematic and critical review.* Learning and Skills Research Center.

67. See Norcross, J. C., Koocher, G. P., & Garofalo, A. (2006). Decredited psychological treatments and tests: A Delphi poll. *Professional Psychology: Research and Practice, 37,* 515–522. In this survey the MBTI was rated as falling somewhere between *unlikely discredited* and *possibly discredited.* The Enneagram was closer to *probably discredited.*

68. Beebe, J. (2004). Can there be a science of the symbolic? *Journal of Analytical Psychology, 49,* 177–191.

69. Paul, A. M. (2004). *The cult of personality: How personality tests are leading us to miseducate our children, mismanage our companies, and misunderstand ourselves.* New York: Free Press, p. 128.

70. Paul (2004), pp. 129–130.

71. Druckman, D., & Bjork, R. A. (1991). *In the mind's eye: Enhancing human performance.* Washington, DC: National Academy Press.

72. Nugent, R. A., Parr, P. E., Newman, I, & Higgins, K. K. (2004). The Riso Hudson enneagram type indicator: Estimates of reliability and validity. *Measurement and Evaluation in Counseling & Development, 36,* 226–237; Wagner, J., & Walker, R. (1983). Reliability and validity study of a Sufi personality typology: The enneagram. *Journal of Clinical Psychology, 39,* 712–717.

73. Kolasinski, P. A. (1997). *Leading with skill and soul: Using the enneagram and the Brent personality assessment system.* Unpublished doctoral dissertation, Seattle University, Seattle.

74. Luckcock, T. (2007). The soul of teaching and professional learning: An appreciative inquiry into the Enneagram of reflective practice. *Educational Action Research, 15,* 127–145; Matise, M. (2007). The Enneagram: An innovative approach. *Journal of Professional Counseling: Practice, Theory, and Research, 35,* 38–69.

75. Gamard, W. S. (1987). *Inter-rater reliability and validity judgments of Enneagram personality types.* Unpublished doctoral dissertation, California Institute of Integral Studies, San Francisco; Wagner, J. P. (1981). *A descriptive reliability and validity study of the Enneagram personality typology.* Unpublished doctoral dissertation, Loyola University, Chicago; Randall, S. (1981). *The development of an inventory to assess Enneagram personality type.* Unpublished doctoral dissertation, California Institute of Asian Studies, University of California, Berkeley.

76. Naranjo, C. (1995). *Enneatypes in psychotherapy: Slected transcripts of the first international symposium on personality enneagrams.* Prescott, AZ: Hohm Press.

77. Riso, D., & Hudson, R. (2000). *Understanding the enneagram: The practical guide to personality types* (rev. ed.) Boston: Houghton Mifflin.

78. Riso, D., & Hudson, R. (1999). *The wisdom of the Enneagram: The complete guide to psychological and spiritual growth for the nine personality types.* New York: Bantam.

79. Washington, P. (1995). *Madam Blavatsky's baboon: A history of mystics, mediums, and misfits who brought spiritualism to America.* New York: Schoken Books.

80. Riso, D. *Romancing the Enneagram* retrieved at http://www.enneagraminstitute.com/articles/NArtRomE.asp.

81. Matise, M. (2007). The Enneagram: An innovative approach. *Journal of Professional Counseling: Practice, Theory, and Research, 35,* 38–69.

82. Nugent, R. (2001). *An investigation of the reliability and validity of the Riso-Hudson enneagram type indicator.* Unpublished doctoral dissertation. University of Akron, Akron, OH.

83. Ichazo named his school for the coastal city in Chile where he founded it.

84. Palmer, H. (1991). *The Enneagram: Understanding yourself and others in your life.* New York: HarperOne.

85. Ouspensky, P. (1971). *The fourth way.* New York: Vintage.

86. Retrieved from Robert Todd Carroll, The Skeptics Dictionary at http://skepdic.com/enneagr.html.

87. Retrieved from http://www.natcath.com/NCR_Online/documents/ennea2.htm#TOP.

88. Zinkle, T. (1974). *A pilot study toward the validation of the Sufi personality typology.* Unpublished doctoral dissertation, United States International University, Nairobi, Kenya.

89. Palmer (1991).

90. Wagner, J. P. (1981). *A descriptive, reliability and validity study of the Enneagram personality typology.* Unpublished doctoral dissertation, Loyola University, Chicago.

91. Daniels, D., & Price, V. (2009). *Essential Enneagram: The definitive personality test and self-discovery guide.* New York: HarperOne.

92. http://www.enneagraminstitute.com/validated.asp

93. Nugent (2001), p. 98.

94. Thurstone, L. L. (1934). The vectors of the mind. *Psychological Review, 41,* 1–33.

95. Ewen, R. B. (1998). *Personality: A topical approach.* Mahwah, NJ: Erlbaum.

96. Kenrick, D. T., & Funder, D. C. (1988). Profiting from controversy: Lessons from the person–situation debate. *American Psychologist, 43,* 23–34.

97. Allport, G. W., & Odbert, H. (1936). Trait-names: A psycho-lexical study. *Psychological Review Monographs, 211.*

98. Eyesenck, H. J., & Eyesenck, M. W. (1985). *Personality and individual differences.* New York: Plenum.

99. Fehriinger, H. M. (2005). Contributions and limitations of Cattell's Sixteen Personality Factor Model. Retrieved at http://www.personalityresearch.org/papers/fehringer.html.

100. McCrae, R. R., & Costa, P.T. (1980). Openness to experience and ego level in Loevinger's Sentence Completion Test: Dispositional contributions to developmental models of personality. *Journal of Personality and Social Psychology, 39,* 1179–1190.

101. Manners, J., & Durkin, K. (2000). Processes involved in adult ego development: A conceptual framework. *Developmental Review, 20,* 475–513.

102. Loevinger, J. (1994). Has psychology lost its conscience? *Journal of Personality Assessment, 62,* 2–8.

103. Horney, K. (1945). *Our inner conflicts.* New York: Norton.

104. This point will come up again at the end of the chapter in Loevinger's criticism of types and traits in general.

105. The scale is named after its creator, Rensis Likert who first published it in Likert, R. (1932). A technique for the measurement of attitudes. *Archives of Psychology, 140,* 1–55.

106. Soldz, S., & Vaillant, G. E., (1999). The big five personality traits and the life course: A 45-year longitudinal study. *Journal of Research in Personality, 33,* 208–232.

107. It is critical to remember, however, that almost all genetic research related to mental health shows that gene expression is always a function of the genes themselves and the environment—nature via nurture. For a layperson's introduction to this see the popular books of Matt Ridley.

108. Jang, K. L., McCrae, R. R., Angleitner, A., Riemann, R., & Livesley, W. J. (1998). Heritability of facet-level traits in cross-cultural twin sample: Support for a hierarchical model of personality. *Journal of Personality and Social Psychology, 74,* 1556–1565; Loehlin, J. C., McCrae, R. R., Costa, P.T., & John, O. P. (1998). Heritabilities of common and measure-specific components of the Big Five personality factors. *Journal of Research in Personality, 32,* 431–453.

109. Costa, P. T., & McCrae, R. R. (1992). Normal personality assessment in clinical practice: The NEO Personality Inventory. *Psychological Assessment, 4,* 5–13.

110. Block, J. (1995). A contrarian view of the Five-Factor approach to personality description. *Psychological Bulletin, 117,* 187–215.

111. Block, J. (2001). Millennial contrarianism: The Five-Factor approach to personality description 5 years later. *Journal of Research in Personality, 35,* 98–107.

112. Saucier, G., & Goldberg, L. R. (1998). What is beyond the big five? *Journal of Personality, 66,* 495–524.

113. Paunonen, S. V., & Jackson, D. N. (2000). What is beyond the big five? Plenty! *Journal of Personality, 68,* 821–835

114. For a complete bibliography of reviews and research using the NEO-PI-R and NEO-FFI see Costa, P. T., & McCrae, R. R. (2003). *Bibliography for the revised NEO Personality Inventory (NEO-PI-R) and the NEO Five-Factor Inventory (NEO-FFI).* Lutz, FL: Psychological Assessment Resources. Available online at http://www3.parinc.com/uploads/pdfs/NEO_bib.pdf.

115. Again see Paul (2004).

116. Block, J. (1995). A contrarian view of the Five-Factor approach to personality description. *Psychological Bulletin, 117,* 187–215.

117. Bagby, R. M., & Marshall, M. B. (2003). Positive impression management and its influence on the revised NEO personality inventory: A comparison of analog and differential prevalence group designs. *Psychological Assessment, 15,* 333–339.

118. McCrae, R. R. (2000). Trait psychology and the revival of personality and culture studies. *The American Behavioral Scientist, 44,* 10–31.

119. McAdams, D. P. (1992). The Five-Factor model in personality: A critical appraisal. *Journal of Personality, 60,* 329–361. McAdams and colleague Jennifer Pals have more recently advocated for a new five-factor model. Their new five factors are broad and hold promise for uniting many divisions of psychology. The new factors are 1) Evolution and human nature; 2) The Dispositional Signature; 3) Characteristic Adaptations; 4) Life Narratives; and 5) The Differential Role of Culture. See McAdams, D. S. & Pals, J. L. (2006). A new big five: Fundamental principles for an integrative science of personality. *American Psychologist, 61,* 204–217.

120. McAdams (1992, p. 329).

121. Lynam, D. R., & Widiger, T. A. (2001). Using the Five-Factor model to represent the DSM-IV personality disorders: An expert consensus approach. *Journal of Abnormal Psychology, 110,* 401–412.

122. Malouff, J. M., Thorsteinsson, E. B., & Schutte, N. S. (2005). The relationship between the Five-Factor model of personality and symptoms of clinical disorders: A meta-analysis. *Journal or Psychopathology and Behavioral Assessment, 27,* 101–114.

123. Costa, P. T., & McCrae, R. R. (1992). Normal personality assessment in clinical practice: The NEO personality inventory. *Psychological Assessment, 4,* 5–13; Miller, T. R. (1991). The psychotherapeutic utility of the Five-Factor model of personality: A clinician's experience. *Journal of Personality Assessment, 57,* 415–433.

124. Loevinger, J. (1994). Has psychology lost its conscience? *Journal of Personality Assessment, 62,* 2–8.

125. Loevinger (1994), p. 3

126. Loevinger (1994), p. 6

127. Tomita, T. et al. (2000). Factor structure of psychobiological seven-factor model of personality: a model-revision. *Personality and Individual Differences, 29,* 709–727.

128. Hansenne, M., Delhez, M., & Cloninger, R. C. (2005). Psychometric properties of the Temperament and Character Inventory-Revised (TCI-R) in a Belgian sample. *Journal of Personality Assessment, 85,* 40–49.

129. American Psychiatric Association. (2000). *Diagnostic and statistical manual of mental disorders* (4th ed., text revised). Washington, DC: Author.

130. For a summary of character diagnosis see McWilliams, N. (1994). *Psychoanalytic diagnosis: Understanding personality structure in the clinical process.* New York: Guilford.

131. Freud, S. (1932). Libidinal types. In *Collected papers* (English translation, Vol. 5, 1950). London: Hogarth.

132. Reich, W. (1949). *Character analysis* (3rd ed.) New York: Farrar, Straus, & Giroux.

133. See in particular Fenichel, O. (1945). *The psychoanalytic theory of neurosis.* New York: Norton.

134. Spitzer, R., Endicott, J., & Robins, E. (1978). Research diagnostic criteria: Rationale and reliability. *Archives of General Psychiatry, 35,* 773–782.

135. Schneider referred to these as first- and second-rank symptoms building on the work of John Hughlings Jackson. This was then elaborated into positive symptoms (things that are there but shouldn't be, like hallucinations) and negative symptoms (things that should be present but aren't, like a range of affect).

136. Schneider, K. (1950). *Psychopathic personalities* (9th ed., English translation). London: Cassell.

137. Sullivan, H. S. (1947). *Conceptions of modern psychiatry.* New York: Norton.

138. Horney, K. (1945). *Our inner conflicts.* New York: Norton.

139. Freud, S. (1991). Some character-types met with in psycho-analytic work. In M. F. R. Kets de Vries & S. M. Perzow (Eds.), *Handbook of character studies: Psychoanalytic explorations.* (pp. 27–50). Madison, CT: International Universities Press. (Original work published 1916)

140. Horney, K. (1939). What is a neurosis? *American Journal of Sociology, 45,* 426–432.

141. Rosse, E. C. (1890). Clinical evidences of borderland insanity. *Journal of Nervous and Mental Diseases, 17,* 669–683.

142. Kernberg, O. (1967). Borderline personality organization. *Journal of the American Psychoanalytic Association, 15,* 641–686.

143. Bradley, R., Conklin, C. Z., & Westen, D. (2007). Borderline personality disorder. In W. O'Donohue, K. A. Fowler, & S. O. Lilienfeld (Eds.), *Personality disorders: Toward the DSM-V* (pp. 167–202) New York: Sage.

144. McWilliams, N. (1994). *Psychoanalytic diagnosis: Understanding personality structure in the clinical process.* New York: Guilford.

145. McWilliams, N. (1994). *Psychoanalytic diagnosis: Understanding personality structure in the clinical process.* New York: Guilford, p. 63.

146. Allport, G. (1937). *Personality: A psychological interpretation.* New York: Holt, p. 24.

147. Lilienfeld, S. O. (1995). Is borderline personality disorder a diagnosis of questionable validity? In S. O. Lilienfeld (Ed.), *Seeing both sides: Classic controversies in abnormal psychology.* Pacific Grove, CA: Brooks/Cole., pp. 198–199.

148. Fiester, S. J., Ellison, J. M., Docherty, J. P., & Shea, T. (1990). Comorbidity of personality disorders: Two for the price of three. *New Directions in Mental Health Services, 47,* 103–114.

149. First, M. B., Spitzer, R. L, Gibbon, M., & Williams, J. B. W. (1997). *Structured clinical interview for DSM-IV personality disorders.* Washington, DC: American Psychiatric Association Press.

150. Jameson, J., & Strauss, N. (2004). *How to make love like a porn star: A cautionary tale.* New York: HarperCollins, p. 7.

151. Dimorphism is the phenomenon in which female and male forms of an organism display distinctly male and female characteristics of biological form.

152. Greenwood, N. A., & Cassidy, M. L. (1990). A critical review of family sociology textbooks. *Teaching Sociology, 18,* 541–549.

153. Spence, J., & Helmreich, R., (1978). *Masculinity and femininity.* Austin: University of Texas Press.

154. Laner, M. R. (2000). "Sex" versus "gender": A renewed plea. *Sociological Inquiry, 70,* 462–474.

155. Bem, S. L. (1981). The BSRI and gender schema theory: A reply to Spence and Helmreich. *Psychological Review, 88,* 369–371.

156. Bem, S. L. (1985). Androgyny and gender-schema theory: A conceptual and empirical integration. In T. B. Sonderegger (Ed.), *Nebraska symposium on motivation: Psychology of gender* (pp. 179–226). Lincoln: University of Nebraska Press.

157. Bem, S. (1993). Dismantling gender polarization and compulsory heterosexuality: Should we turn the volume up or down? *The Journal of Sex Research, 32,* 329–334.

158. Bem, S. (1974). The measurement of psychological androgyny. *Journal of Clinical and Counseling Psychology, 42,* 155–162.

159. Hoffman, R. M., & Borders, L. D. (2001). Twenty-five years after the Bem sex-role inventory: A reassessment and new issues regarding classification variability. *Measurement and Evaluation in Counseling and Development, 34,* 39–55.

160. O'Keefe, J. O., & Dostrovsky, J. (1971). The hippocampus as a spatial map: Preliminary evidence from unit cell activity in the freely moving rat. *Brain Research, 34,* 171–175.

161. Maguire, E. A., Burgess, N., & O'Keefe, J. (1999). Human spatial navigation: Cognitive maps, sexual dimorphism and neural substrates. *Current Opinion in Neurobiology, 9,* 171–177.

162. Kandel, E. R. (2006). *In search of memory: The emergence of a new science of mind.* New York: Norton, p. 316.

163. Hoffman, R. M., & Borders, L. D. (2001). Twenty-five years after the Bem sex-role inventory: A reassessment and new issues regarding classification variability. *Measurement and Evaluation in Counseling and Development, 34,* 39–55.

164. Hoffman & Borders (2001).

165. Spence, J. T., Helmreich, R. L., & Stapp, J. (1975). Ratings of self and peers on sex-role attributes and their relation to self-esteem and conceptions of masculinity and femininity. *Journal of Personality and Social Psychology,32,* 29–39.

166. Bem (1981).

167. Blanchard-Fields, F., Suhrer-Roussel, L., & Herzog, C. (1994). A confirmatory factor analysis of the Bem Sex-Role Inventory: Old questions, new answers. *Sex Roles, 30,* 423–457.

168. Bem, S. L. (1995). Working on gender as a gender-noncomformist. *Women and Therapy, 17,* 43–53, pp. 44 & 46.

169. Bem (1995), p. 46.

170. To be clear, as of the date of this writing, there is no evidence that any therapies (psychological or physiological) can "change" ego-syntonic sexual identity. See Segraeves, R. T., & Levine, S. B. (2001). Sexual and gender identity disorders. In G. O Gabbard (Ed.), *Treatments of psychiatric disorders* (3rd ed., pp. 1843–2069). Washington, DC: American Psychiatric Association.

171. White, M. (1994). *Stranger at the gate: To be gay and Christian in America.* New York: Plume.

172. See http://www.soulforce.org/ as well as White, M. (2006). *Religion gone bad: The hidden dangers of the Christian right.* New York: Tarcher.

173. Segraves & Levine (2001). 174 Ellis, L., & Ames, M. A. (1987). Neurohormonal functioning and sexual orientation: a theory of homosexuality–heterosexuality. *Psychological Bulletin, 101* 233–258 and Kimble, J. (2007). The mysteries of sexual identity: The germ cell's perspective. *Science, 316,* 400–401.

Notes to Chapter 6

1. Smith, H. (2000). *Cleansing the doors of perception: The religious significance of entheogenic plants and chemicals.* New York: Tarcher, p. 3.

2. Harris, S. (2004). *The end of faith: Religion, terror, and the future of reason.* New York: Norton, p. 208.

3. Huxley, A. (1925). *Those barren leaves.* London: Chatto & Windus/Doran.

4. From Carl Rogers onward, research has supported the existence and therapeutic utility of this "we" in psychotherapy. We are also starting to trace this "dyadic expansion of consciousness" back to infant–adult interactions. See Tronick, E. Z. (1998). Dyadically expanded states of consciousness and the process of therapeutic change. *Infant Mental Health Journal, 19,* 290–299.

5. The idea is that on the path of spiritual practice, what I call states training (or state stages), practitioners are usually advised to allow phenomena to arise and fall away even if they are unusually appealing.

6. Robbins, T. (2006). *The edge: The power to change your life now, volume 1.* Audio CD: San Diego, CA: Anthony Robbins Companies.

7. Shorter, E. (1998). *A history of psychiatry: From the era of the asylum to the age of Prozac.* New York: Wiley.

8. Shorter, E., & Healy, D. (2007). *Shock therapy: A history of electroconvulsive treatment in mental illness.* New Brunswick, NJ: Rutgers University Press.

9. Griffiths, R. R., Richards, W. A., McCann, U., & Jesse, R. (2006). Psilocybin can occasion mystical-type experiences having substantial and sustained personal meaning and spiritual significance. *Psychopharmacology, 187,* 268–283. See also the two-volume set by Winkelman, M. J., & Roberts, T. B. (Eds.). (2007). *Psychedelic medicine: New evidence for hallucinogenic substances as treatments.* Westport, CT: Praeger.

10. Grob, C. S. (2007). The use of psilocybin in patients with advanced cancer and existential anxiety. In M. J. Winkleman and T. J. Roberts (Eds.), *Psychedelic medicine: New evidence for hallucinogenic substances as treatments* (pp. 206–216).Westport, CT: Praeger.

11. See Kirsch, I., & Lynn, S. J. (1995). Altered state of hypnosis: Changes in theoretical landscape. *American Psychologist, 50,* 846–858 and Nash, M. R., & Benham, G. (2005). The truth and the hype of hypnosis. *Scientific American Mind, 16,* 46–53.

12. Jamieson, G. A. (Ed.). (2007). *Hypnosis and conscious states: The cognitive neuroscience perspective.* Oxford: Oxford University Press.

13. Wilber, K. (2006). *The 1-2-3 of God.* Boulder, CO: Sounds True Recording.

14. In psychotherapy, anxiety is more worry based in fears of what may occur in the future, whereas panic is a present-centered experience of fear where no apparent threat has occurred and that is crippling in its intensity. Thus in treatment, anxiety is generally more future-oriented worry whereas panic is fear in the present.

15. Bensen, H., Beary, J. F., & Carol, M. P. (1974). The relaxation response. *Psychiatry: Journal for the Study of Interpersonal Processes, 37,* 37–46.

16. Tyson, P. D. (1998). Physiological arousal, reactive aggression, and the induction of an incompatible relaxation response. *Aggression and Violent Behavior, 3,* 143–158.

17. Greenwood, M. M., & Bensen, H. (1977). The efficacy of progressive relaxation in systematic desensitization and a proposal for an alternative competitive response: The relaxation response. *Behaviour Research & Therapy, 15,* 337–343.

18. Baruss, I. (2003). *Alterations of consciousness: An empirical analysis for social scientists.* Washington, DC: American Psychological Association, p. 9.

19. As with all states-related treatment, there is evidence to support sleeping as a way to temporarily decrease depression and evidence that deprivation of REM sleep also alleviates depression. Either way, both are temporary strategies.

20. In psychotherapy, tolerance and dependence are preferable to the word *addiction*, which carries so much emotional baggage in our society that it has become clinically meaningless. Specifically, a person can develop psychological or physiological dependence. Physiological dependence is characterized by withdrawal when a person stops taking the drug on which he or she is dependent. Psychological dependence is the

person believing he or she can't get through the day without the drug. Probably the best general definition of addiction comes from psychiatrist Roger Walsh who described it as unhealthy attachment. See Walsh, R. (1999). *Essential spirituality: The 7 central practices to awaken heart and mind.* New York: Wiley.

21. Wilber, K., Engler, J., & Brown, D. P. (1986). *Transformations of consciousness: Conventional and contemplative perspectives on development.* Boston: Shambhala.

22. As noted in previous chapters, dialectical behavior therapy is well-suited to teaching state-stage methods to people suffering from severe psychopathology due to structural problems in the personality.

23. Harris, B. (2002). *Thresholds of the mind: Your personal roadmap to success, happiness, and contentment.* Beaverton, OR: Centerpointe Press.

24. Monroe's books are well worth reading and include the following: Monroe, R. A. (1971). *Journeys out of body.* Garden City, NY: Anchor; Monroe, R. A. (1985). *Far journeys.* New York: Doubleday; Monroe, R. A. (1994). *Ultimate journey.* New York: Doubleday.

25. See Lilly, J.C. (1977). *The deep self: Profound relaxation and the tank isolation technique.* New York: Warner; Lilly, J. C. (1978). *Communication between man and dolphin: The possibilities of talking with other species.* New York: Julian.

26. For example, see Lilly, J. C. & Miller, A. M. (1961). Vocal exchanges between dolphins. *Science, 134,* 1873–1876; Lilly, J. C., Truby, H. M., Miller, A. M., & Grissman, F. (1967). Acoustic implications of interspecies communication. *Journal of the Acoustics Society of America, 42,* 1164.

27. Monroe, R. A. (1985). *Far journey.* New York: Doubleday, p. 50.

28. Lilly, J C. (1997). *The scientist: A metaphysical autobiography.* Berkely, CA: Ronin.

29. Csikszentmihalyi, M. (1990). *Flow: The psychology of optimal experience.* New York: Harper & Row.

30. Thompson, K. F. (1988). Motivation and the multiple states of trance. In J. K. Zeig & S. R. Lankton (Eds.), *Developing Ericksonian therapy: State of the art.* New York: Brunner/Mazel, pp. 149–163.

31. Grof, S. (1980). *LSD psychotherapy: Exploring the frontiers of the mind.* Alameda, CA: Hunter House.

32. Trevarthen, C., & Reddy, V. (2007). Consciousness in infants. In M. Velmans & S Schneider (Eds.), *The Blackwell companion to consciousness.* Oxford, UK: Oxford University Press, pp. 41–57.

33. Winkelman, M. (1986). Trance states: A theoretical model and cross-cultural analysis. *Ethos, 14,* 174–203, p. 174.

34. Winkelman, M. (2007). Therapeutic bases of psychedelic medicines: Psychointegrative effects. In M. J. Winkelman & T. B. Roberts (Eds.), *Psychedelic medicine: New evidence for hallucinogenic substances as treatments* (pp. 1–20). Westport, CT: Praeger.

35. Robinson, D. N. (1979). *Systems of modern psychology: A critical sketch.* New York: Columbia University Press, p. 144.

36. Griffiths, R. R., Richards, W. A., McCann, U., & Jesse, R. (2006). Psilocybin can occasion mystical-type experiences having substantial and sustained personal meaning and spiritual significance. *Psychopharmacology, 187,* 268–283.

37. For example, see Kalat, J. (2001). *Biological psychology* (7th ed.). Stamford, CT: Thomson Learning.

38. Pinker, S. (1997). *How the mind works*. New York: Norton.

39. Ausubel, D. P., & Kirk, D. (1977). *Ego psychology and mental disorder: A developmental approach to psychopathology*. New York: Grune & Stratton.

40. Grof, S. (1985). *Beyond the brain: Birth, death and transcendence in psychotherapy*. Albany: State University of New York.

41. The ethical guidelines for the International Coach Federation can be found at http://www.coachfederation.org/ICF/For+Current+Members/Ethical+Guidelines/. Also, a number of states are now considering the licensing of coaches. I expect that in 10 years most states will have such licenses.

42. Wilson, R. A. (2004). *Maybe logic: The lives of Robert Anton Wilson*. Berkeley, CA: Deepleaf Productions DVD.

43. Walsh, R. (2007). *The world of shamanism: New views of an ancient tradition*. Woodbury, MN: Llewellyn, p. 185.

44. Walsh, R. (2007). *The world of shamanism: New views of an ancient tradition*. Woodbury, MN: Llewellyn, p. 186.

45. Thompson, H. S. (2003). *Kingdom of fear: Loathsome secrets of a star-crossed child in the final days of the American century*. New York: Simon & Schuster.

46. Streatfield, D. (2007). *Brainwash: The secret history of mind control*. New York: St. Martin's Press.

47. In working with veterans, I have learned secondhand how the military uses states in every aspect of boot camp where the aim is to build a coherent machine responsive to orders. One client, an ex-Army Airborne Ranger, remembers how he could whip up controlled rage in combat for the identified enemy while feeling the love of brotherhood for a fellow soldier who, in civilian life, he found quite distasteful.

48. We also know that the phrase "gene expression" is inaccurate. Genes are simply blueprints for making proteins. Chromosomes are approximately 50% DNA and 50% protein sheath covering the DNA. When the sheath is temporarily removed in response to some event external to the cell, the mRNA can read the blueprint and begin the process of protein synthesis. Thus, gene expression is really more akin to a temporary unveiling of the blueprint and enactment of its instructions.

49. Rossi's work is detailed in Rossi, E. (2002). *The psychobiology of gene expression: Neuroscience and neurogenesis in hypnosis and the healing arts*. New York: Norton.

50. Bruce Lipton has made an attempt to explain this but, although his biological knowledge appears superb, he misses many vital psychological points along the way.

51. For one example of Wilber's many discussions of these see Wilber, K. (2006). *Integral spirituality: A startling new role for religion in the modern and postmodern world*. Boston: Shambhala. The fourth and fifth states Wilber refers to with the Sanskrit labels "turiya" and "turiya-tita."

52. Because of the emotionality, misunderstanding, and in many cases superstitious hysteria surrounding the word *drugs*, I will, when possible, use a less-emotionally loaded word or phrase.

53. I know, I know—"healthy" is in the eye of the beholder but I think we can make some orienting generalizations here. First, things that promote and maintain the functioning of one's body are healthy. As a nonpracticing smoker I certainly enjoyed

the effects of inhaling tobacco, but wasn't willing to trade the health of my pulmonary system for those effects.

54. If you're curious about your own standing on this, try the following: Keep a calendar next to your bed. Every morning upon rising, rate your feeling about facing the day from −10 ("I'm going to get a bottle of vodka and drink it beneath the covers for the rest of the day") to +10 ("I love my life so much I am thrilled to be awake and getting to it"). Over the course of a week or a month take stock of your ratings.

55. Recall one of the older "laws" of psychology–the Yerkes-Dodson law, which in essence states that arousal in moderation is optimal. Too little produces lethargy and stagnation, whereas too much causes paralyzing vigilance which is counter-productive to accomplishing goals. See Yerkes, R. M., & Dodson, J. D. (1908). The relation of strength of stimulus to rapidity of habit formation. *Journal of Comparative Neurology and Psychology, 18*, 459–482.

56. *Normal* and *altered* are the words Wilber has used for the most part. Clinicians like Stanislav Grof prefer *ordinary* and *nonordinary* because they are clinically useful and offer nonjudgmental labels that may encourage dispassionate clinical and research applications. For the sake of consistency, I retain Wilber's words.

57. The term *entheogen* is a fairly recent term applied to a drug that has the capacity to elicit a spiritual experience; Walsh, R., & Grob, C. S. (2005). *Higher wisdom: Eminent elders explore the continuing impact of psychedelics*. Albany: State University of New York Press, p. 242.

58. Huxley, T. H. (1866). *Lessons in elementary physiology*. London: MacMillan.

59. Wundt, W. (1894). *Lectures on human and animal psychology* (J. E. Creighton & E. B. Titchner, Trans.). London: Swan Sonnenschein, p. 7.

60. Robinson, D. N. (2008). *Consciousness and mental life*. New York: Columbia University Press, pp. 201–202.

61. Robinson (2008), p. 204.

62. Baruss, I. (2003). *Alterations of consciousness: An empirical analysis for social scientists*. Washington, DC: American Psychological Association, pp. 6–7.

63. James, W. (1950). *Principles of psychology* (Vols. I & II). New York: Holt, p. 225.

64. See also Tassi, P., & Muzet, A. (2001). Defining states of consciousness. *Neuroscience and Biobehavioral Reviews, 25*, 175–191 and Churchland, P. S. (2002). *Brain-wise: Studies in neurophilosophy*. Cambridge, MA: MIT Press.

65. Baars, B. J. (1998). Metaphors of consciousness and attention in the brain. *Trends in Neuroscience, 21*, 58–62.

66. Newberg, A., & d'Aquili, E. G. (2000). The neuropsychology of religious and spiritual experience. *Journal of Consciousness Studies, 7*, 251–266.

67. Horgan, J. (1999). *The undiscovered mind: How the human brain defies replication, medication, and explanation*. New York: Free Press, p. 23.

68. Niedermeyer, E. (1994). Consciousness: Function and definition. *Clinical Electroencephalography, 25*, 86–93. Neurologist Antonio Damasio has noted that this is not always an appropriate synonym because some languages (like English) make a distinction between consciousness and awareness, whereas others (French, Italian, and Spanish) do not. See Damasio, A. R. (1999). *The feeling of what happens: Body and emotion in the making of consciousness*. New York: Harcourt Brace.

69. These are adapted from Walsh, R. (2007). *The world of shamanism: New views of an ancient tradition.* Woodbury, MN: Llewellyn, pp. 238–239.

70. Walsh, R., & Shapiro, S. L. (2006). The meeting of meditative disciplines in Western psychology: A mutual enriching dialogue. *American Psychologist, 61,* 227–239.

71. See Brown, D. P. (1977). A model for the levels of concentrative meditation. *International Journal of Clinical and Experimental Hypnosis, 25,* 236–273 and Anderson, J. (2000). Meditation meets behavioural medicine: The story of experimental research on meditation. *Journal of Consciousness Studies, 7,* 17–73.

72. Walsh, R., & Roche, L. (1979). Precipitation of acute psychotic episodes by intensive meditation in individuals with a history of schizophrenia. *American Journal of Psychiatry, 136,* 1085–1086.

73. Otis, L. S. (1984). Adverse effects of transcendental meditation. In R. Walsh & D. H. Shapiro (Eds.), *Meditation: Classic and contemporary perspectives,* 201–208.

74. Strupp, H. H., Hadley, S. W., & Gomez-Schwartz, B. (1978). *Psychotherapy for better or worse: The problem of negative effects.* New York: Wiley.

75. American Psychiatric Association. (2000). *Diagnostic and statistical manual of mental disorders* (4th ed., text rev.). Washington, DC: Author, p. xxxi.

76. Smith, H. (2000). *Cleansing the doors of perception: The religious significance of entheogenic plants and chemicals.* New York: Tarcher/Putnam, p. 153. In the context of the quote, Smith attributes it to psychologist Robert Ornstein.

77. Wilber, K. (2006). *Integral spirituality: A starting new role for religion and spirituality in the postmodern world.* Boston: Shambhala.

78. Walsh, R. (2007). *The world of shamanism: New views of an ancient tradition.* Wodbury, MN: Llewellyn.

79. Csikszentmihalyi, M., & Csikszentmihalyi, I. (Eds.). (1988). *Optimal experience: Psychological studies of flow in consciousness.* New York: Cambridge University Press.

80. Tart, C. (Ed.). (1969). *Altered states of consciousness: A book of readings.* New York: Wiley, pp. 1–2.

81. Baruss, I. (2003). *Alterations of consciousness: An empirical analysis for social scientists.* Washington, DC: American Psychological Association, p. 8.

82. Tassi, P., & Muzet, A. (2001). Defining states of consciousness. *Neuroscience and Biobehavioral Reviews, 25,* 175–191.

83. Had Sami met the criteria for panic disorder his "states" or "attacks" would be considered "cued." meaning he knew what would trigger them. As it was, he simply suffered from situational anxiety that was not unreasonable but still began interfering with his life, causing distress and impairment.

84. Anxiety symptoms may manifest as predominantly physiologically, cognitively, emotionally, or behaviorally (or some combination of the four). Many people "lead with" a style of anxiety that is primarily physiological (sweating, headaches, racing heart), cognitive (racing thoughts), emotional (feeling frightened and out of control), or behavioral (fleeing or avoiding situations that trigger anxiety). To some extent, these three styles characterize anxiety disorders. For example, in panic disorder physiological symptoms predominate, whereas in generalized anxiety disorder cognitive symptoms predominate. From an AQAL perspective, we seek to understand the client's hotspots and how these relate to states and symptoms of anxiety.

85. Many clinicians believe that panic disorder is a malfunction of the nervous system areas related to signaling potential threat. Neuropsychologist Jeffrey Gray

identified a brain circuit that appears to be relevant to human anxiety. Dubbed the behavioral inhibition system (BIS), it is activated by signals from the brain stem and amygdala and is thought to trigger our fight–flight–freeze response. This alarm and escape (or freeze) response in animals looks very similar to panic in human beings. See McNaughton, N., & Gray, J. H. (2000). Anxiolytic action on the behavioral inhibition system implies multiple types of arousal contribute to anxiety. *Journal of Affective Disorders, 61,* 161–175.

86. See Coelho, H. F., Canter, P. H., & Edzard, E. (2007). Mindfulness-based cognitive therapy: Evaluating current evidence and informing future research. *Journal of Consulting and Clinical Psychology, 75,* 1000–1005.

87. Gaudino, B. A. (2006). The "third wave" behavior therapies in context: Review of Hayes et al.'s (2004) *Mindfulness and acceptance: Expanding the cognitive-behavioral tradition* and Hayes S. C., & Strosahl, K. D. (2004) *A practical guide to acceptance and commitment therapy. Journal of Cognitive Therapy, 6,* 101–104.

88. Bishop, S. R et al. (2004). Mindfulness: A proposed operational definition. *Clinical Psychology: Science and practice, 11,* 230–241.

89. See also Germer, C. K., Siegel, R. D., & Fulton, P. R. (Eds.). (2005). *Mindfulness and psychotherapy.* New York: Guilford.

90. Hammond, C. (1992). *Hypnotic induction & suggestion: An introductory manual.* Des Plains, IL: The American Society of Hypnosis, p. 3.

91. This description comes from Dr. Chris Faiver, professor and chair of counseling at John Carroll University. Dr. Faiver is a fully certified Ericksonian hypnotherapist.

92. Schmidt, D. (2005). Revisioning antebellum American psychology: A new on-line resource for the history of psychology. *History of Psychology, 8,* 403–434.

93. Tart, C. (Ed.). (1969) *Altered states of consciousness: A book of readings.* New York: Wiley.

94. Hammond (1992).

95. Hilgard, E. R. (1987). *Psychology in America: A historical survey.* San Diego, CA: Harcourt Brace Jovanovich.

96. Quoted material in this paragraph from Robinson, D. (1997). *The great ideas of psychology: Part 3.* Chantilly, VA: The Teaching Company, pp 157–159.

97. Ellenberger, H. F. (1970). *The discovery of the unconscious: They history and evolution of dynamic psychiatry.* New York: Basic Books.

98. See Gruzelier, J. (2005). Altered states of consciousness and hypnosis in the twenty-first century. *Contemporary Hypnosis, 22,* 1–7.

99. Spanos, N. P., Menary, E., Gabora, N. J., DuBreuil, S. C., & Dewhirst, B. (1991). Secondary identity enactments during hypnotic past-life regression: A sociocognitive perspective. *Journal of Personality and Social Psychology, 61,* 308–320.

100. Wade, J. (1998). The phenomenology of near-death consciousness in past-life regression therapy: A pilot study. *Journal of Near-Death Studies, 17,* 31–53.

101. Ruzek, N. (2007). Transpersonal psychology in context: Perspectives from its founders and historians of American psychology. *Journal of Transpersonal Psychology, 39,* 153–174.

102. See Hoyt, I. P. et al. (1989). Daydreaming, absorption and hypnotizability. *International Journal of Clinical and Experimental Hypnosis, 37,* 332–342; Kuzendorf, R., Brown, C., & McGee, D. (1983). Hypnotizability: Correlations with daydreaming and sleeping. *Psychological Reports, 53,* 406; Singer, J. L., & Pope, K. S. (1981). Daydreaming

and imagery skills as predisposing capacities for self-hypnosis. *International Journal of Clinical and Experimental Hypnosis, 29,* 271–281.

103. Klinger, E. (1990). *Daydreaming: Using waking fantasy and imagery for self-knowledge and creativity.* Los Angeles: Tarcher, p. 9.

104. Baruss, I. (2003). *Alterations of consciousness: An empirical analysis for social scientists.* Washington, DC: American Psychological Association.

105. Singer, J. L., & Antrobus, J. S. (1972). Daydreaming, imaginal processes, and personality: A normative study. In P. W. Sheehan (Ed.), *The function and nature of imagery* (pp. 175–202). New York: Academic Press.

106. Baruss (2003), p. 38

107. Recall that a reaction formation is a defense whereby what is expressed is the opposite of the urge being repressed. In one instance of a client who constantly fantasizes about heroic deeds, exploration of shadow material unearthed a great deal of repressed aggression and urges to harm (rather than rescue) other people.

108. Rothbaum, B. O., Marshall, R. D., Lindy, J., & Mellman, L. (2001). Posttraumatic stress disorder. In G. O. Gabbard (Ed.) *Treatments of psychiatric disorders* (Vol. 2, 3rd ed., pp. 1539–1566). Washington, DC: American Psychiatric Association.

109. Samuels, M., & Samuels, N. (1975). *Seeing with the mind's eye: The history, techniques and uses of visualization.* New York: Random House.

110. Irwin, M. R. (2008). Human psychoneuroimmunology: 20 years of discovery. *Brain, Behavior, and Immunity, 22,* 129–139; Gruzelier, J. H. (2002). A review of the impact of hypnosis, relaxation, guided imagery and individual differences on aspects of immunity and health. *Stress: The International Journal on the Biology of Stress, 5,* 147–163.

111. For a summary of Jung's active imagination technique see Cwik, A. J. (1995). Active imagination: Synthesis in analysis. In M. Stein (Ed.), *Jungian analysis* (2nd ed., pp. 137–169).

112. Hardy, J. (1987). *A psychology with soul: Psychosynthesis in evolutionary context.* London: Arkana; Gerard, R. (1967). Symbolic visualization in interpersonal psychosynthesis. *Psychotherapy and Psychosomatics, 15,* 24.

113. Cardin, L. (2005). Dying well: The Bonny method of guided imagery and music at the end of life. *Journal of the Association for Music and Imagery, 10,* 1–25.

114. Scherwitz, L. W., McHenry, P., & Herrero, R. (2005). Interactive guided imagery-super (sm) therapy with medical patients: Predictors of health outcomes. *Journal of Alternative and Complementary Medicine, 11,* 69–83.

115. Roffe, L., Schmidt, K., & Ernst, E. (2005). A systematic review of guided imagery as an adjunct cancer therapy. *Psycho-Oncology, 14,* 607–617.

116. Crow, S., & Banks, D. (2004). Guided imagery: A tool to guide the way for the nursing home patient. *Advances in Mind–Body Medicine, 20,* 4–7.

117. A good summary of the areas of agreement on recovered memories is Knapp, S. & VandeCreek, L. (2000). Recovered memories of childhood abuse: Is there an underlying professional consensus? *Professional Psychology: Research and Practice, 31,* 365–371.

118. American Psychiatric Association. (2000). *Diagnostic and statistical manual of mental disorders, fourth edition, text-revised.* Washington, DC: Author.

119. James, W. (1950). *The principles of psychology* (Vols. I & II). New York: Dover, p. 294. (Original work published 1890)

120. Robinson, D. (1999). *Aristotle's psychology.* New York: Columbia University Press, p. 68.

121. In biological psychology, dreaming is viewed as the brain's effort to make sense of distorted information perceived but never organized during the day. The activation-synthesis hypothesis asserts that dreams begin with bursts of activity called PGO waves as they begin in the pons, move to the lateral geniculate, and then the occipital cortex. Each PGO wave is synchronized with an eye movement in REM sleep. These waves activate many but not all parts of the cortex. The cortex then combines this input with whatever other activity is already occurring and tries to synthesize a story that makes sense of it all. Needless to say, this is really anthropomorphizing the brain. See Hobson, J. A. (2001). *The dream drugstore: Chemically altered states of consciousness.* Cambridge, MA: The MIT Press.

122. Jastrow, J. (1888). Dreams of the blind. *New Princeton Review, 5,* 18–34.

123. Foulkes, D. (1999). *Children's dreaming and the development of consciousness.* Cambridge, MA: Harvard University Press.

124. Kerr, N. H., & Domhoff, G. W. (2004). Do the blind literally "see" in their dreams? A critique of a recent claim that they do. *Dreaming, 14,* 230–233.

125. Gilliland, J., & Stone, M. (2007). Color and communication in the dreams of hearing and deaf persons. *Dreaming, 17,* 48–56.

126. Freud, S. (1953). *The interpretation of dreams* (J. Strachey, Trans.). New York: Hogarth. (Original work published 1900)

127. This summary is drawn primarily from Freud's *Interpretation of Dreams,* Henri Ellenberger's *History of the Unconcscious* and Vande Kamp, H. (2006). The dream in periodical literature: 1860–1910. *Journal of the History of the Behavioral Sciences, 17,* 88–113. The books mentioned in the summary are, sadly, difficult to find.

128. Displacement is when an emotionally evocative image in a dream is devoid of emotion that is "displaced" to allow the image to emerge. In condensation, multiple figures from waking life are condensed into one dream figure. Both of these are thought to be the psyche's way of getting us closer to those things repressed but requiring expression or to be made objects of awareness. So the one interpretation of this is that the dream "tricks" us into getting close to things that we need to make objects of awareness of to free up psychic energy. This is of course a psychodynamic interpretation and, as in all things phenomenological, there is always room for multiple interpretations. The psychodynamic one is, however, congruent with what I've said is the primary aim of Integral Psychotherapy: helping clients make aspects of themselves or their lives objects of awareness.

129. Schwartz, W. (1990). A psychoanalytic approach to dreamwork. In S. Krippner (Ed.), *Dreamtime and dreamwork: Decoding the language of the night.* (pp. 49–58). New York: Tarcher/Putnam.

130. Gutheil, E. A. (1951). *The handbook of dream analysis.* New York: Liveright, p. 92.

131. See Jung, C. G. (1984). *Dream analysis: Notes of the seminar given in 1928–1930* (W. McGuire, Ed.). Princeton, NJ: Bollingen; Singer, J. (1990). A Jungian approach to dreamwork. In S. Krippner (Ed.), *Dreamtime and dreamwork: Decoding the language of the night.* (pp. 59–68). New York: Tarcher/Putnam; Mattoon, M. A. (1984). *Understanding dreams.* Dallas, TX: Spring.

132. This summary is drawn from Hill, C. E. (1996). *Working with dreams in psychotherapy.* New York: Guilford; Johnson, R. (1986). *Inner work.* San Francisco: Harper & Row.

133. Adler, A. (1963). *Individual psychology.* Paterson, NJ: Littlefield, Adams, p. 214.

134. Adler (1963), p. 215.

135. Oberst, U. (2002). An Adlerian-constructivist approach to dreams. *The Journal of Individual Psychology, 58,* 122–131.

136. Bird, B. E. I. (2005). Understanding dreams and dreamers: An Adlerian perspective. *The Journal of Individual Psychology, 61,* 200–216.

137. Hill, C. E. (1996). *Working with dreams in psychotherapy.* New York: Guilford.

138. Clark, P. (1989). *Gestalt counselling in action.* London: Sage, p. 107.

139. This summary is drawn from Polster, E., & Polster, M. (1973). *Gestalt therapy integrated: Contours of theory and practice.* New York: Vintage, pp. 265–278.

140. Cartwright, R. D. (1993). Who needs their dreams? The usefulness of dreams in psychotherapy. *Journal of the American Academy of Psychoanalysis, 21,* 539–547.

141. For example, see Glucksman, M. L., & Warner, S. L. (Eds.). (1987). *Dreams in a new perspective: The royal road revisited.* New York: Human Sciences Press and Schwartz, W. (1990). A psychoanalytic approach to dreamwork. In S. Krippner (Ed.), *Dreamtime and dreamwork: Decoding the language of the night* (pp. 49–58). Los Angeles: Tarcher.

142. Hill, C. E. (1996). *Working with dreams in psychotherapy.* New York: Guilford, p. 35.

143. Hill (1996). 144 Craig, P. E., & Walsh, S. J. (1993). Phenomenological challenges for the clinical use of dreams. *New directions in dream interpretation.* Albany: State University of New York Press, pp. 103–154.

145. Rogers, C. (1980). *A way of being.* Boston: Houghton Mifflin, p. 106.

146. Meador, B., & Rogers, C. (1973). Client-centered therapy. In R. Corsini (Ed.), *Current psychotherapies* (119–166). Itasca, IL: F. E. Peacock.

147. Barrineau, P. (1992). Person-centered dream work. *Journal of Humanistic Psychology, 32,* 90–105, p. 96.

148. Kan, K., Miner-Holden, J., & Marquis, A. (2001). Effects of experiential focusing-oriented dream interpretation. *Journal of Humanistic Psychology, 41,* 105–123.

149. Gendlin, E. (1981). *Focusing.* New York: Bantam.

150. See Cartwright, R. D., & Lamberg, L. (1992). *Crisis dreaming: Using your dreams to solve your problems.* New York: HarperCollins.

151. Crook, R. E., & Hill, C. E. (2004). Client reactions to working with dreams in psychotherapy. *Dreaming, 14,* 207–219.

152. Crook, R. E., & Hill, C. E. (2003). Working with dreams in psychotherapy: The therapists' perspective. *Dreaming, 13,* 83–93.

153. Kolchakian, M. R., & Hill, C. E. (2002). Dream interpretation with heterosexual dating couples. *Dreaming, 12,* 1–16.

154. Piaget, J. & Inhelder, B. (1969). *The psychology of the child.* New York: Basic Books.

155. See Tolman, E. C. (1948). Cognitive maps for rats and men. *The Psychological Review, 55,* 189–208.

156. Neisser, U. (1976). *Cognition and reality: Principles and implications of cognitive psychology.* New York: Holt.

157. Beck, A. T. (1963). Thinking and depression: I: Idiosyncratic content and cognitive distortions. *Archives of General Psychiatry, 10,* 561–571.

158. See Robinson, D. N. (1987). *Systems of psychology: A critical sketch.* New York: Columbia University Press, chapter 4.

159. Hume, D. (1965). *A treatise of human nature* (L. A. Selby-Bigge, Ed.). New York: Dover, p. 162.

160. For a detailed discussion of this see Loevinger, J. (1987). Cognitive developmentalism. In *Paradigms of personality* (pp. 175–246). New York: W.W. Freeman.

161. Hill, C. E. (1996). *Working with dreams in psychotherapy.* New York: Guilford, pp 52–53.

162. Van Eeden, F. (1913). A study of dreams. *Proceedings of the society for psychical research, 26,* 431–461.

163. LaBerge, S., & Gackenbach, J. (2000). Lucid dreaming. In E. Cardena, S. J. Lynn, & S. Krippner (Eds.) *Varieties of anomalous experience: Examining the scientific evidence.* (pp. 151–183). Washington, DC: American Psychological Association.

164. Tart, C. (1988). From spontaneous even to lucidity: A review of attempts to consciously control nocturnal dreaming. In J. Gackenbach, & S. LaBerge (Eds.), *Conscious mind, dreaming brain* (pp. 67–103). New York: Plenum.

165. For those unfamiliar with the standard human sleep cycle it begins in stage 1 sleep, which lasts between 1 and 10 minutes. Stage 2 sleep is initiated by a "K complex" or a "sleep spindle." Sleep spindles are bursts of fast (13–15 Hz) electroencephalogram (EEG) activity lasting about 2 seconds. K complexes are phasic events where there is a sudden increase in negativity on the scalp followed by a positive wave that lasts between 0.5 and 2 seconds. In stage 2 sleep, larger, slower waves appear in the EEG less than 2 Hz. When these take up 20% of the sleep record, the criteria are met for stage 3 sleep. A typical adult reaches this within 20 minutes. Stage 3 sleep comprises 20% to 50% of the sleep record dominated by slow, deep waves. Stage 4 sleep comprises more than 50% of the slow-wave record. Most people do not have any REM sleep for at least 45 minutes and then there is an alteration between slow-wave and REM sleep with REM recurring about every 90 minutes. REM is associated (but not exclusively) with dreaming and is characterized by saccadic (tracking) eye movements and loss of neck muscle tone. See Empson, J. (1989). *Sleep and dreaming.* London: Faber & Faber

166. Rossi, E. (1985). *Dreams and the growth of personality: Expanding awareness in psychotherapy.* New York: Brunner/Mazel. (Original work published 1972)

167. LaBerge, S., Phillips, L., & Levitan, L. (1994). An hour of wakefulness before morning naps makes lucidity more likely. *NightLight, 6,* 1–5.

168. Snyder, T. J., & Gackenbach, J. (1988). Individual differences associated with lucid dreaming. In J. Gackenbach & A. A. Sheikh (Eds.), *Dream images: A call to mental arms* (pp. 55–78). Amityville, NY: Baywood.

169. LaBerge, S. (1980). Lucid dreaming as a learnable skill: A case study. *Perceptual and Motor Skills, 51,* 1039–1042.

170. LaBerge, S., Levitan, H., & Dement, W. C. (1986). Lucid dreaming: Physiological correlates of consciousness during REM sleep. *Journal of Mind & Behavior, 7,* 251–258.

171. LaBerge, S. (2004). *Lucid dreaming: A concise guide to awakening in your dreams and in your life.* Boulder, CO: Sounds True.

172. Rechtschaffen, A. (1978). The singlemindedness and isolation of dreams. *Sleep, 1,* 97–109.

173. Tholey, P. (1988). A model for lucidity training as a means of self-healing and psychological growth. In J. Gackenbach & S. LaBerge (Eds.), *Conscious mind, sleeping brain* (pp. 263–287). New York: Plenum.

174. LaBerge (2004).

175. It is important to note that we now know people sleep in REM and slow-wave sleep (stages 3 and 4). More importantly, the representations of self are more congruent with the waking self in REM dreams and more widely divergent in slow-wave sleep dreams. Psychologically, both are of interest regardless of the meaning in the correlates with stages of sleep. See Occhionero, M., Cicogna, P., Natale, V., Esposito, M. J., & Bosinelli, M. (2005). Representation of self in SWS and REM dreams. *Sleep and Hypnosis, 7,* 77–83. There also appear to be developmental differences in self-representations–see McNamara, P., McLaren, D., & Durso, K. (2007). Representation of the self in REM and NREM sleep. *Dreaming, 17,* 113–126.

176. Schredl, M., & Piel, E. (2008). Interest in dream interpretation: A gender difference. *Dreaming, 18,* 11–15.

177. Schredl, M., Ciric, P., Gotz, S., & Wittmann, L. (2004). Typical dreams: Stability and gender differences. *The Journal of Psychology, 138,* 485–494.

178. Although this is not a book on psychopathology, we are ethically bound to meet the client where he or she is. If the client's symptoms make his or her sense of self fragile, our first order of business is stabilization.

179. This is the essence of the both the therapy relationship and therapeutic dream work. See Jung, C. G. (1984). *Dream analysis: Notes of the seminar given in 1928–1930.* Princeton, NJ: Bollingen.

180. The exercise Janine was working with was looking at her hands once an hour and asking herself if she was awake or dreaming. This technique is described in LaBerge (2004).

181. See Cartwright, R., Agargun, M. Y., Kirkby, J., & Friedman, J. K. (2006). Relation of dreams to waking concerns. *Psychiatry Research, 141,* 261–270; Jennings, J. L. (2007). Dreams without disguise: The self-evident nature of dreams. *The Humanistic Psychologist, 35,* 253–274.

182. Hall, C. S., & Van de Castle, R. L. (1966). *The content analysis of dreams.* New York: Appleton-Century-Crofts.

183. Hill, C. E., Spangler, P., Sim, W., & Baumann, E. (2007). Interpersonal content of dreams in relation to the process and outcome of single sessions using the Hill dream model. *Dreaming, 17,* 1–19.

184. Jung, C. G. (1960). On synchronicity. In C. G. Jung/R.F.C. Hull (Trans.) *The collected works of C.G. Jung, Volume 8: The structure and dynamics of the psyche* (pp. 417–520). Princeton, NJ: Bollingen.

185. Siegel, R. K. (1989). *Intoxication.* New York: Pocket Books.

186. See Wells, P., & Rushkoff, D. (1995). *Stoned free: How to get high without drugs.* Port Townsend, WA: Loompanics Unlimited; Masters, T., & Houston, J. (1972). *Mind games: The guide to inner space.* New York: Delta/Viking.

187. Medco Health Solutions. (2006). *2006 Drug Trend Report.* Retrieved from http://medco.mediaroom.com/index.php?s=64&cat=5

188. Wistosky, S. (1990). *Beyond the war on drugs: Overcoming a failed public policy.* Buffalo, NY: Prometheus Books; Duke, S. B., & Gross, A. C. (2004). *America's longest war: Rethinking our tragic crusade against drugs.* New York: eReads.

189. Ingersoll, R. E., & Rak, C. F. (2006). *Psychotropic medication for helping professionals: An integral approach.* Pacific Grove, CA: Brooks/Cole; Ingersoll, R. E. (2005). Herbaceuticals: An overview for counselors. *Journal of Counseling & Development, 83,* 434–444; Ingersoll, R. E., Bauer, A. L., Burns, L. (2004). Children and psychotropic medication: What role should advocacy counseling play? *Journal of Counseling and Development, 82, 337–343;* Ingersoll, R. E., Bauer, A. L., & Burns, L. (2004). National school counselor survey on psychotropic medication: Assessing the need for additional training. *The Professional School Counselor, 1,* 13–27.

190. Grof, S., Soskin, R. A., Richards, W. A., & Kurland, A. A. (1973). LSD-assisted psychotherapy in patients with terminal cancer. *International Pharmaco-psychiatry, 8,* 104–115; Kast, E., & Collins, V. (1964). Lysergic acid diethylamide as an analgesic agent. *Anesthesia and Analgesia, 43,* 285–291; Kurland, A. (1985). LSD in the supportive care of the terminally ill cancer patient. *Journal of Psychoactive Drugs, 17,* 279–290.

191. Osmond, H. (1957). A review of the clinical effects of psychotomimetic agents. *Annals of the New York Academy of Science, 66,* 418–434.

192. Winkleman, M. J. (2007). Therapeutic bases of psychedelic medicines: Psychointegrative effects. In M. J. Winkleman & T. B. Roberts (Eds.), *Psychedelic medicine: New evidence for hallucinogenic substances as treatments.* (pp 1–19). Westport, CT: Praeger.

193. In mental health parlance, an *illusion* is a distortion of a stimulus that exists, whereas an *hallucination* is a perception of a stimulus that does not exist.

194. Schultes, R. E., Hoffmann, A., & Ratsch, C. (1979). *Plants of the gods: Their sacred healing and hallucinogenic powers.* New York: Healing Arts Press.

195. Winkleman, M. J. (1996). Neurophenomenology and genetic epistemology as a basis for the study of consciousness. *Journal of Social and Evolutionary Systems, 19,* 217–236.

196. These are based in the caveats written by Thomas Roberts from the syllabus for his course *Social Foundations of Psychedelic Studies* and reproduced in Winkelman, M. J., & Roberts T. B. (Eds.). (2007). *Psychedelic medicine: New evidence for hallucinogenic substances as treatments.* Westport, CT: Praeger.

197. Griffiths, R. R., Richards, W. A., McCann, U., & Jesse, R. (2006). Psilocybin can occasion mystical-type experiences having substantial and sustained personal meaning and spiritual significance. *Psychopharmacology, 187,* 268–283.

198. Winkleman, M. J., & Roberts T. B. (Eds.). (2007). *Psychedelic medicine: New evidence for hallucinogenic substances as treatments.* Westport, CT: Praeger

199. Watts., A. W. (1972). *The book: On the taboo against knowing who you are.* New York: Vintage.

200. Psychiatrist Stanislav Grof has probably the most extensive record of such experiences in sessions. See his books Grof, S. (1975). *Realms of the human unconscious: Observations from LSD research.* New York: Viking; Grof, S. (1980). *LSD psychotherapy.* New York: Hunter House; Grof, S. (1985). *Beyond the brain: Birth, death and transcendence in psychotherapy.* Albany: State University of New York State University of New York Press.

201. This term was tentatively coined in Masters, R. E. L., & Houston, J. (1966). *The varieties of psychedelic experience.* New York: Delta, p. 108.

202. Dunlap, J. (1961). *Exploring inner space: Personal experiences under LSD–25.* New York: Harcourt, Brace & World Inc.

203. For Grof's work in this area see the references in Note 197. Also, Sounds True in Boulder, Colorado has an excellent 8–hour lecture series by Grof titled *The Transpersonal Vision*

204. Eisner, B. (1989). *Ecstasy: The MDMA story.* Berkeley, CA: Ronin.

205. Greer, G., & Tolbert, R. (2007). Therapeutic uses of MDMA. In M. J. Winkelman & T. B. Roberts. (Eds.), *Psychedelic medicine: New evidence for hallucinogenic substances as treatments* (pp. 141–153). Westport, CT: Praeger

206. Wilber, K., Engler, J., & Brown, D. P. (1986). *Transformations of consciousness: Conventional and contemplative perspectives on development.* Boston: Shambhala.

Notes to Chapter 7

1. Wilber, K. (2006). *Integral Spirituality: A startling new role for religion in the modern and postmodern world.* Boston: Integral Books, p. 69.

2. The Mercator projection is a cylindrical map projection developed by Flemish cartographer Gerardus Mercator in 1569 and used primarily for nautical purposes. The technique of creating the projection distorts the size and shape of large objects as the scale increases from the equator to the poles. Nineteenth-century mathemetician Carl Freiderich Gauss (who made contributions to the normal or Gaussian curve) proposed to correct the distortions using a geoid presentation, which led to the precise Geoid Solution in the 1990s.

3. For a popular summary of some of the problems of assessing intelligence see Murdoch, S. (2007). *Intelligence: A smart history of a failed idea.* New York: Wiley.

4. Sternberg, R., et al. (2004). Theory-based university admissions testing for a new millennium. *Educational Psychologist, 39,* 185–198. See also Sternberg, R. J., & Grigorenko, E. L. (2007). *Teaching for successful intelligence: To increase student learning and achievement.* Thousand Oaks, CA: Corwin.

5. For the clinician concerned with intelligence per se, there is evidence that brief measures can have the reliability and validity of more expensive, complex measures. See Walters, S. O., & Weaver, K. A. (2003). Relationships between the Kaufman Brief Intelligence Test and the Wechsler Adult Intelligence Scale–third edition. *Psychological Reports, 92,* 1111–1115.

6. Cook-Greuter, S. (1990). Maps for living: Ego development stages from symbiosis to conscious universal embeddedness. In M. L. Commons, C. Armon, L. Kohlberg, F. A. Richards, & T. A. Grotzer (Eds.), *Adult development, Vol. 2: Models and methods in the study of adolescent and adult thought* (pp. 79–104). New York: Praeger.

7. Lectical assessment claims to be a developmental assessment system that scores the developmental level of a sample of reasoning across multiple lines that occur throughout the life span. There is still debate as to what extent this assessment reflects the proximate self but the debate is important and worthwhile. See www.devtestservice. com for research in this area.

8. Jung got this term from Rudolf Otto in Otto, R. (1958). *The idea of the holy.* London: Oxford.

9. Jung, C. G. (1958). *The collected works of C.G. Jung: Vol. 11: Psychology and religion: East and West* (H. Read, M. Fordham, & G. Adler, Eds.). Princeton, NJ: Bollingen.

10. A reaction formation is a defensive process where anxiety-producing emotions are dealt with by expressing their exact opposite.

11. I refer to personality disorders as "so-called" because, as noted in Chapter 6, these are among the least valid and reliable of *DSM* diagnoses and will likely change substantially in *DSM-V*. That said, although there is no doubt some people have a personality style that causes them much pain and, if it can be made an object of awareness, it can be crafted to more ego-syntonic goals. See First, M. B., Cuthbert, B., Malison, R., Reiss, D., & Widiger, T. (2002). Personality disorders and relational disorders. In D. J. Kupfer, M. B. First, & D. A. Regier (Eds.), *A research agenda for DSM-* (pp. 123–199). Washington DC: American Psychiatric Association.

12. In substance abuse treatment, it is estimated that long-term users may require most of a year (about 9 months) before their bodies can return to the pre-drug neurochemical homeostasis.

13. In our popular culture, labels quickly become accessories as evidenced by the "emo" movement. See http://www.luv-emo.com/

14. See Whitman, B. Y. (2008). Human behavior genetics: Implications for neurodevelopmental disorders. In P. J. Accardo (Ed.), *Caputo and Accardo's neurodevelopmental disabilities in infancy and childhood: Vol. 1: Neurodevelopmental diagnosis and treatment* (3rd ed., pp. 175–197).

15. Hossein, F. S. et al. (2008). Maternal infection leads to abnormal gene regulation and brain atrophy in mouse offspring: Implications for genesis of neurodevelopmental disorders. *Schizophrenia Research, 99*, 56–70.

16. Stahl, S. (2000). *Essential psychopharmacology* (2nd Ed.). Cambridge, MA: Cambridge University Press, p. 106.

17. We have one of the first early childhood mental health programs at Cleveland State University and most of the courses focus on gene–environment interactions and epigenetics (those variables related to the processes of gene expression).

18. These are puzzles designed by architecture professor Erno Rubik. Each of the six faces of the cube is covered with a certain color sticker. A pivot mechanism allows each face to turn independently so the puzzle solver must bring the cube back to the original position where all six faces show the same color sticker. This nicely illustrates the interplay of variables associated with psychopathology.

19. Marquis, A. (2008). *The integral intake: A guide to comprehensive idiographic assessment in integral psychotherapy.* New York: Routledge.

20. The common factors associated with psychotherapy change are treated in Hubble, M. A., Duncan, B. L., & Miller, S. D. (1999). *The heart and soul of change: What works in therapy.* Washington, DC: American Psychological Association.

Notes to Chapter 8

1. Robinson, D. (1995). *An intellectual history of psychology* (3rd ed.). Madison, WI: University of Wisconsin Press, p. 331.

2. Engler, J. (1986). Therapeutic aims in psychotherapy and meditation: Developmental stages in the representation of self. In K. Wilber, J. Enger, & D. P. Brown(Eds.), *Transformations of consciousness: Conventional and contemplative perspectives on development.* Boston: Shambhala, p. 24.

3. Allport, G. W. (1950). *The individual and his religion: A psychological interpretation.* New York: Macmillan, p. 70.

4. The Boulder model is named after Boulder, Colorado where the conference to design the model was held. There are other models like the Vail model, which is more focused on clinical skills and was developed in a conference in Vail, Colorado for guiding the curricula of PsyD programs. I doubt we'll see an "Iron City model" or a "Youngstown model" anytime soon. See Overholser, J. C. (2007). The Boulder model in academia: Struggling to integrate the science and practice of psychology. *Journal of Contemporary Psychotherapy, 37,* 205–211.

5. Micenbaum, D. (2005). Can a matrix make a training model? No. Let's not throw out the Boulder model. *Journal of Clinical Psychology, 61,* 1151–1153.

6. Nathan, P. E. (2000). The Boulder model: A dream deferred–or lost? *American Psychologist, 55,* 250–252.

7. Wilber, K. (2000). *Integral psychology: Consciousness, spirit, psychology therapy.* Boston: Shambhala.

8. Wilber (2000), p. vii.

9. The Weber–Fechner Law was displaced by Stevens' Power Law. Stevens' Power Law developed by Stanley Stevens in the 1950s allowed for differentially plotted curves for different senses, something that the Weber–Fechner Law did not include. Despite increased accuracy, however, this law too is heavily criticized and the relationship between stimuli and the senses has yet to be outfitted with a generally agreed-upon law derived from generally agreed upon methods.

10. See Fechner, G. T. (2005). *The little book of life after death.* New York: Weiser. (Original work published 1903)

11. See Boring, E. G. (1929). *A history of experimental psychology* (2nd ed.). New York: Appleton-Century-Crofts.

12. Robinson, D. (1995). *An intellectual history of psychology* (3rd ed.). Madison: University of Wisconsin Press, p. 339.

13. See Wundt, W. (1916). *Elements of folk psychology: Outlines of a psychological history of the development of mankind.* London: Allen & Unwin. See also the discussion of Baldwin in Chapter 3.

14. For a concise summary of Wundt's contributions see Hilgard, E. R. (1987). *Psychology in America: A historical survey.* New York: Harcourt Brace Jovanovich.

15. See Robinson, D. (2008). *Consciousness and mental life.* New York: Columbia University Press. We've made this point several times in the book but it cannot be overstated. We simply do not know how something mental can "cause" something physical and how something physical can "cause" something mental.

16. For a list of these see Ingersoll, R. E. (2005). An introduction to integral psychology. *AQAL Journal of Integral Theory and Practice, 1,* 2–16.

17. This was the thesis of Wilber, K. (1995). *Sex, ecology, spirituality: The spirit of evolution.* Boston: Shambhala.

18. Robinson, D. (1979). *Systems of modern psychology: A critical sketch.* New York: Columbia University Press.

19. This point has been made by many psychologists. Baldwin, for example, took exception to the assumptions that scientific and philosophical thinking should keep exclusive of each other, that philosophical thought is not totally speculative. For more on this see Broughton, J. M., & Freeman-Moir, D. J. (Eds.), (1982). *The cognitive-developmental psychology of James Mark Baldwin.* New York: Ablex.

20. Russell, B. (1964). *The problems of philosophy.* London: Oxford University Press.

21. Wilber, K. (2003). *Kosmic consciousness* (audio CD). Boulder, CO: Sounds True.

22. Starbuck, E. D. (1899). *The psychology of religion.* New York: Scribner.

23. Ames, E. S. (1910). *The psychology of religious experience.* Boston: Houghton Mifflin.

24. Arnold, D. J. (1985). Psychology of religion: Placing paradigm in a historical and metatheoretical perspective. *American Psychologist, 9,* 1060–1062.

25. Taylor, E. (1999). *Shadow culture: Psychology and spirituality in America.* Washington, DC: Counterpoint.

26. Barlow, D. H. & Durand, V. M. (2002). *Abnormal psychology: An integrative approach* (3rd ed.). New York: Thomson.

27. For examples of this approach, see Miller, W. R. (Ed.). (1999). *Integrating spirituality into treatment: Resources for practitioners.* Washington, DC: American Psychological Association and Wiggins-Frame, M. (2003). *Integrating religion and spirituality into counseling: A comprehensive approach.* Pacific Grove, CA: Brooks/Cole.

28. Bollinger, T. E. (1969). *The spiritual needs of the aging: In need for a specific ministry.* New York: Knopf.

29. Magill, F. N., & McGral, I. P. (Eds.) (1988). *Christian spirituality: The essential guide to the most influential spiritual writings on the Christian tradition.* San Francisco: Harper.

30. Witmer, J. M. (1989). Reaching toward wholeness: An integrated approach to well-being over the life span. In T. J. Sweeney (Ed.), *Adlerian counseling: A practical approach for a new decade.* Muncie, IN: Accelerated Press.

31. May, G. (1988). *Addiction and grace: Love and spirituality in the healing of addictions.* San Francisco: Harper.

32. Clinebell, H. (1992). *Well-being: A personal plan for exploring and enriching the seven dimensions of life.* San Francisco: Harper.

33. James, W. (1902). *The varieties of religious experience: A study in human nature.* New York: Holt.

34. Allport, G. W. (1950). *The individual and his religion: A psychological interpretation.* Cambridge, MA: Harvard University Press.

35. Thoresen, C. E. (2007). Spirituality, religion, and health: What's the deal? In T. G. Plante & C. E. Thoresen (Eds.), *Spirit, science, and health: How the spiritual mind fuels physical wellness* (pp. 3–10). Westport, CT: Praeger.

36. Moberg, D. O. (1979). *Spiritual well-being: Sociological perspectives.* Washington, DC: University Press of American.

37. Ingersoll, R. E. (1994) Spirituality, religion, and counseling: Dimensions and relationships, *Counseling and Values, 38,* 98–112.

38. For examples of scales, see Ellison, C. W. (1983). Spiritual well-being: Conceptualization and measurement. *Journal of Psychology and Theology, 11,* 330–340. Also see Ingersoll, R. E. (1998). Refining dimensions of spiritual wellness: A cross-traditional approach. *Counseling & Values, 42,* 156–165. This latter inventory is available to the public at my Web site www.elliottingersoll.com

39. Wulff, D. M. (1996). The psychology of religion: An overview. In E. P. Shafranske (Ed.), *Religion and the clinical practice of psychology* (pp. 43–70). Washington, DC: American Psychological Association.

40. Richards, P. S., & Bergin, A. E. (1997). *A spiritual strategy for counseling and psychotherapy.* Washington, DC: American Psychological Association, p. 13.

41. Richards, P. S., & Bergin, A. E. (2000). Religious diversity and psychotherapy: Conclusions, recommendations, and future directions. In P. S. Richards & A. E. Bergin (Eds.), *Handbook of psychotherapy and religious diversity* (pp. 469–489). Washington, DC: American Psychological Association.

42. Scotton, H. W. (1996). Introduction and definition of transpersonal psychiatry. In B. W. Scotton, A. B. Chinen, & J. R. Battista (Eds.) *Textbook of transpersonal psychiatry and psychology* (pp. 4–8). New York: Basic Books.

43. See Aten, J. D., & Leach, M. M. (Eds.). (2009). *Spirituality and the therapeutic process: A comprehensive resource from intake to termination.* Washington, DC: American Psychiatric Association. And Sperry, L., & Shafranske, E. P. (Eds.). (2005). *Spiritually oriented psychotherapy.* Washington, DC: American Psychological Association.

44. See Zinnbauer, B. J., Pargament, K. I., & Scott, A. B. (1999). The emerging meanings of religiousness and spirituality: Problems and prospects. *Journal of Personality, 67,* 879–919 and Pargament, K. I. (1997). *The psychology of religion and coping.* New York: Guilford.

45. Sperry, L. (2001). *Spirituality in clinical practice: Incorporating the spiritual dimension in psychotherapy and counseling.* New York: Brunner Routledge.

46. Cook-Greuter, S. (2000). Mature ego development: A gateway to ego transcendence? *Journal of Adult Development, 7,* 227–240.

47. Scotton, B. W., Chinen, A. B., & Battista, J. R. (Eds.). (1996). *Textbook of transpersonal psychiatry and psychology.* New York: Basic Books.

48. Scotton, Chinen, & Battista (1996), p. 409

49. Bond, K., Ospina, M. B., Shannahoff-Khalsa, Dusek, J., & Carlson, L. E. (2009). Defining a complex intervention: The development of demarcation criteria for "meditation." *Psychology of Religion and Spirituality, 1,* 129–137

50. Scotton, Chinen, & Battista (1996), p. 410.

51. Combs, A. (2002). *The radiance of being: Understanding the grand integral vision; living the integral life.* St. Paul, MN: Paragon.

52. For the sake of clarity, what I am suggesting is that we add a z-axis to the Wilber–Combs matrix for practical purposes. In psychotherapy, then, that z-axis would be the spectrum of health and pathology, as expressed in self-system translations, relative to structural issues from both the x-axis and y-axis. Other fields can create similar tools by adding a z-axis of their own. The point is that the x-axis and y-axis map the stages of consciousness, whereas the z-axis maps the translations thereof, and

how those translations point back to fissures or disruptions. Life conditions (mapped on the quadrants) would also lie on the z-axis, because G.A.F. score can be easily integrated into the integral psychotherapist's analysis of spiritual or religious issues. In the Integral Psychotherapy cube the z-axis would shoot at an angle through the three dimensions of the cube.

53. That subset consists of people who are transforming from structure stages of consciousness described by Wilber as "orange" into structure stages described as "green" or "teal." We have purposely avoided entering the domain of theoretical structures of consciousness because whole volumes could be devoted to the topic and because, at present, there is very little mainstream research in psychology proper alluding to such structures. This will be the topic of future publications but here we want to stay as close to the mainstream as possible.

54. Scotton, Chinen, & Battista (1996), p. 236.

55. Turner, R. Lukoff, D., Barnhouse, R. T., & Lu, F. (1995). Religious or spiritual problem: A culturally sensitive diagnostic category in the DSM-IV. *The Journal of Nervous and Mental Disease, 183* 435–444.

56. Wilber, K. (2006). Integral spirituality: A startlingly new role for religion in the modern and postmodern world. Boston: Shambhala, p. 119.

57. And for anyone who thought that DNA evidence was "airtight," enter the complexity of people who actually are chimeras—two or more sets of DNA contained differentially across their cellular nuclei. This may pose problems for orange scientism, but for the integral scientist, morphogenetic fields shape and guide cellular differentiation.

58. Again, this bears repeating because so many people are convinced that mental and emotional disorders are physiological The DSM-V task force has stated that there are no pathophysiologic markers for any of the mental/emotional disorders. See S. J., & Zalcman, S. J. (2002). Neuroscience research agenda to guide development of a pathophysiologically based classification system. In D. J.Kupfer, M. B. First, & D. A. Regier (Eds.), A research agenda for DSM-V (pp.31–84). Washington, DC: American Psychiatric Association.

59. Duman, R., S., Heninger, G. R., & Nestler, E. J. (1997). A molecular and cellular theory of depression. Archives of General Psychiatry, 54, 597–608.

60. PDM Task Force. (2006). Psychodynamic diagnostic manual (PDM). Silver Springs, MD: Alliance of Psychoanalytic Organizations.

61. Coyne, J. C. (1999). Thinking interactionally about depression: A radical restatement. In T. Joiner & J. C. Coyne (Eds.), The interactional nature of depression (pp. 365–392. Washington, DC: American Psychological Association.

62. Anhedonia is described as a loss of joy and pleasure in those activities or things that used to bring joy or pleasure.

63. Kegan, R. (1982). The evolving self: Problem and process in human development Cambridge, MA: Harvard University Press, pp. 264–288.

64. This comes across in interviews with people who identify at the magician level. Many of them simply note the loneliness that comes with seeing the world in a way few can share. See Miller, M. E., & Cook-Greuter, S. R. (1994). Transcendence and mature thought in adulthood: The further reaches of adult development. Boston: Rowman & Litllefield.

65. This is why Aaron Beck's insight of suicide stemming from hopelessness is so important. Beck surely got to the bottom of the issue–and now it is time for us to get "to the top" of this issue as well. If the cognitive line leads development then it "leads" integration as well (just as the emotional line "leads" differentiation and embrace).

66. See Ingersoll, R. E., & Rak, C. F. (2006). Psychotropic medication for helping professionals: An integral approach. Pacific Grove, CA: Brooks/Cole.

Notes to Appendix

1. This was a hypnotic regression with the purpose of inquiring into the impact (if any) that the separation of Mark's parents had on him when he was 3 years old. Mark also created a new relationship to his parents that assisted him in his relationship with his parents. Some deeply seated "rules" were finally becoming "tools" because of the regression work.

2. Palmer, H. (1991). *The enneagram: Understanding yourself and others in your life.* New York: HarperOne.

3. The pluralist will often go through a lengthy process that is not guaranteed to reach any conclusion, and is likely conclude that torture is never valid. The achiever may consider the face validity of torture, if at all, and comes to decision much faster. To the untrained eye the strategist appears to be somewhere in between. Intrapsychically speaking, for the strategist the relativity of values is a "tool" for them to use, and the "rule" becomes simultaneously witnessing the systems-of-systems that grants the strategist a capacity to see the relative value of relativity itself. This leads to a capacity for hierarchically organizing where and when considerations of relativity take precedence, also known as a holarchy of values.

4. Ken Wilber, Bert Parlee, Jeff Soulen, Willow Pearson, and David M. Zeitler.

5. This combination is approved for, and appears to have good efficacy for treating, acute bipolar depression. Currently, these two drugs have been combined in one formulation called Symbyax. For an outstanding summary of bipolar disorder, including a comparison of both well-researched and "alternative" medical approaches, and an excellent summary of medications and their contraindications, see Brigham, P. (2000–2004). *The psychopharmacology of bipolar disorder.* Retrieved December 28, 2005 from http://home.comcast.net/~pmbrig/BP_pharm.html.

6. Consider the following quote from one session: "It's not the work itself that makes me stressed or tired–it's being aware that I am tired of always keeping the work in perfect order. It doesn't always help anyway, and it will definitely wear you out, having to keep it all working the right way. Even with my business . . . I mean, there are other ways of raising your kids, so maybe this way–my way, my business–isn't the only 'right-way' out there. But it works well, it works for me, and it's successful. . . . I guess I need help with emotional nourishment, I don't know. I thought I had handled the miscarriage, and by all accounts I had. But I still felt empty and alone, even surrounded by my family. Maybe it was the miscarriage, but I wanted to feel connected" (Paraphrase of dialogue from several therapy sessions). Note the two voices of the established "strive-drive" achiever self-identity and the budding "human-bonding" Pluralist self-identity.

7. Technically the combination of MDD and dysthymia (chronic, low-grade depression) is referred to as "double-depression." The prognosis is poorer in such cases than in clients suffering from either MDD or dysthymia alone.

8. Careful charting of mood is imperative with client's who exhibit symptoms of depression, and even more necessary because of the fact that if they are not reporting manic episodes, placing them on antidepressant drugs will often induce a manic episode. Hypomania is less clear clinically as the symptoms themselves, by definition do not cause distress or impairment.

9. Polypharmacy reflects the "art" of medicine and is when doctors combine medications in a "hit-or-miss" fashion to see if they help. More recently, co-therapies have been developed where multiple drugs are tested against single agents. A recent co-therapy for Bipolar I Disorder is a combination of lithium and divalproex.

10. Often, a mood-stabilizer like Zyprexa is used in conjunction with another drug for bipolar disorder, such as an SSRI like Prozac. As noted above these two agents are now combined in one formulation called Symbyax.

11. This same fluid-boundary system is likely one of the reasons that individuals who suffer from borderline personality disorder cycle through psychiatric wards in such a regular fashion. The fluid boundary may feel comfortable to them, in that it challenges them to "hold" a lower-right balance of boundaries, while also supporting door slamming and invitations to fuse with them. Individuals who suffer from borderline personality disorder and bipolar disorder also share a lability of mood, although the frequency and duration of the lability is quite different. However, it seems likely that the lwer-right-quadrant organization of the typical inpatient unit may facilitate the expression of symptoms in both of these disorders. For more on the complex relationship between bipolar mood disorders and borderline personality disorders, see Akiskal, H. S. et al. (1985). Borderline: an adjective in search of a noun. *Journal of Clinical Psychiatry, 46*(2), 41–48.

12. Through his family, Mark was influenced by Reform Judaism (stepfather), Mormonism and atheism (mother), Catholicism (father), secular materialism (stepmother), and agnosticism (older brother). Somewhat painfully, none of these people seemed interested in hearing about his intense spiritual experience when he was 14, despite the broad and eclectic worldviews they together represented.

13. This is a specific kind of reframing technique that uses the principles of stage transformation. More specifically, it follows Kegan's guidelines for bridge-building techniques with guiding metaphors.

14. As it later turned out, this was somewhat true. Cheryl and her husband were indeed "psych-savvy," and used their marriage to help them make sense of the event. But the miscarriage resonated with other issues, which was something neither Cheryl nor her husband had expected—because of this, for better or worse, they had not given the admitting nurses and doctors this information. They had agreed to "not discuss it" and to "get on with their lives."

15. In clinical work, it matters not whether disintegrating life conditions (quadrants) and meaning-making (translations) lead to a developmental shift (stage or level transcendence) or vice-versa. In terms of empirical research, this is one of those important questions as to how much learning and assimilation has on micro-accommodation (Piaget's term for mini-developments) and overall transformation.

16. Whenever post-achiever stage dialogues are warranted, Mark waits until group therapy is over to discuss these themes. He did this because he did not want to validate any erroneous hallucinations or delusional associations that someone suffering from psychosis may be having. Mark doubted the evaluation of Cheryl as psychotic—if anything, her genuine psychotic symptoms were originated in acute events, and fueled by developmental transformation.

17. Had this been a client he was seeing on a regular basis, Mark would eventually frame a dialogue concerning the differences between the two general types of "synchronicity" around the pre/trans fallacy.

18. Wilber has written on the many forms of unconsciousness that affect us in sickness and in health. Here, the traditional psychoanalytic notion of "unconscious" is represented by the "repressed-submergent-unconscious." This refers to existing translations that are troubling to the person, and are therefore actively "submerged." To this, Wilber adds a developmental unconscious, the "repressed-emergent-unconscious." This form of unconsciousness refers to a stage of identification that should be "emerging" as a self-identity, but for one reason or another is not. Up to and including the achiever stage, there are many sociocultural referents for these developmental arrests, and entire industries (like the "self-esteem" movement) dedicated to point people in the right direction. However, for any structures that have emerged beyond achiever (pluralist, strategist, magician, and possibly unitive), there are few cultures of embeddedness, as Kegan calls them, to grant one succor. For a detailed explanation of the many forms of unconsciousness, see

Wilber, K. (1996). *The atman project: A transpersonal view of human development.* Wheaton, IL: Quest Books, pp. 97–108.

19. In transpersonal terms, Cheryl might be incorrectly categorized as having "mystical episodes with psychotic features," David Lukoff's proposed diagnostic category for the *DSM*. Although some people have spiritual experiences during stage transformation, Cheryl did not seem to have such experiences. Integral Psychotherapy would differentiate between the state, the stage, and the pathology influences on a someone's thoughts and behaviors.

20. To "cathect" means to invest emotional energy into an object (third person), individual (second person), or idea (first person).

21. Mark reflected on the fact that he was standing in a doorway with Cheryl when this happened, a lower-right quadrant space of transition between rooms. The lower-right quadrant can be used in fascinating ways. For example, Dr. Jeff Soulen maintains his office with three chairs for his clients to choose from, which are situated to be inviting for either anxiety, depression, or narcissism. Usually, the choice of chair that they take in their first session ends up accurately reflecting their form of suffering. The classic example, of course, is Freud's office, set up so that clients could not see him, fostering transference.

22. Commons, M. L., & Richards, F. A. (2003). Four postformal stages. In J. Demick & C. Andreoletti (Eds.), *Handbook of adult development.* New York: Springer.

23. Fowler J. (1981). *Stages of faith: The psychology of human development and the quest for meaning.* San Francisco: Harper & Row.

24. In a psychiatric ward, clients receive regular physicals. Be sure that your client is fit enough to engage in any rigorous physical practice by having them check with their physician before you suggest it.

25. Barrett Brown pointed out that Mark's suggestion of yoga speaks to "both" sides of folks in this transformation—the competitive-achiever and human-bonding-pluralist.

26. Mark attempted to talk about exoteric versus esoteric religious perspectives with Cheryl, but this did not seem to "stick" with her. Perhaps it was her personality type, or perhaps it was the fact that she appeared to be in a repudiation subphase of development. Either way, she seemed disinterested in exploring esoteric Judaism, in the form of Kabbalah.

27. This was an area of counter-transference for me, a long-time music lover and self-proclaimed audiophile. Mark did not act on his urge to proselytize to Cheryl about the virtues of music. Cheryl's "musical intelligence" line is included, however, as an anomaly that Mark would have pursued if he were in a long term therapeutic relationship with Cheryl.

28. Palmer, H. (1991). *The Enneagram: Understanding yourself and others in your life*. New York: HarperOne.

29. See Kegan (1994), pp. 283–287, for a discussion of the average age of emergence of identification via the self-related streams of development with the achiever stage, which corresponds with Kegan's 4th Order of consciousness.

30. Wilber, K. (2000). *Integral psychology: Consciousness, spirit, psychology, therapy.* Boston & London: Shambhala. pp. 238–240.

31. Not to mention the contraindications that we know of, and the likely contraindications that we have yet to study (the most egregious being long-term drug interactions, which are almost never studied).

32. See Ingersoll, R. E. (2002). An integral approach for teaching and practicing diagnosis. *Journal of Transpersonal Psychology, 34*(2), 115–128.

33. It may mirror in some ways the transformation out of an opportunist self-identity into a diplomat self-identity. Anyone going through this transformation must give up their belief that people who take the feelings and needs of others into account before they act are suckers.

34. Cheryl was eventually "running" group therapy, with Mark's blessing. This also "spoke" to both sides of her—she was able to engage in open hearted dialogue and even learn about group consensus (pluralist stage meanings about the inherent value of human-bonding), all in the context of "running" therapy (achiever-stage mastery). This was a new developmental occasion for Mark as well, due to the flex-flow of the new group dynamic revolving around Cheryl's transformation. Ironically, although Mark was handing over half of the reigns, he was still in a sense "running" group therapy. It became another context for Cheryl to feel supported and challenged all at once.

35. For more on these themes, see Kegan, R. (1994). *In over our heads: The mental demands of modern life*. Cambridge, MA: Harvard University Press, pp. 309–313.

36. This was another risk because of the resonance with the miscarriage. Mark suspected that Cheryl would not decompose or regress in the face of objectively putting these things together. There was a serious probability that she would have dismissed Mark's value as a therapist had he failed to match her strength by challenging her old patterns of identity. In doing so, Mark was forced to go outside of his own comfort zone.

37. One of his only regrets about not having enough time with Cheryl was that Mark never had the opportunity to give her a practice of forgiveness. Cheryl needed to forgive herself, because her unconsciously held belief was that she was guilty of a double-

homicide—of her infant and her achiever self-identity. By helping her forgive herself, Mark feels that he could have further helped Cheryl with her reintegration process. Alas, we have only a limited time with any client, particularly in a short-term setting.

38. Kegan, R. (1982). *The evolving self: Problem and process in human development*. Cambridge, MA: Harvard University Press, p. 276.

39. These include at least one episode of any three manic symptoms: inflated self-esteem; decreased need for sleep; increased talkativeness; flight of ideas or racing thoughts; distractibility; increased goal-directed activity; increased participation in pleasurable activities with potentially painful consequences (i.e., risky behavior).

40. This tendency apparently dissolves with the transformation into the strategist stage, or in Kegan's model, the 5th Order of consciousness, and the lack of doing so is the basis for a term that this author has trouble with "second-tier levels."

Index